THE ETHICS OF INCLUSIVE EDUCATION

The Ethics of Inclusive Education clarifies the idea of inclusion and its normative content, and presents a coherent theoretical framework for inclusion and inclusive education. It serves as one of the first extended philosophical defenses in the field of inclusive education that goes beyond a simple assertion of educational value.

Integrating perspectives from the history, sociology and psychology of inclusive education, this book develops a holistic concept of inclusion, while clearly and systematically examining the ethical-normative content of inclusive education. It also offers:

- an interdisciplinary analysis of inclusion and inclusive schooling, ranging from historical to sociological analysis of their predecessors and preconditions, to the investigation of their philosophical and educational content,
- an in-depth analysis of the moral significance of exclusion, the value of inclusion and inclusive education from an analytical point of view, and
- practice-oriented investigations of the individual and social conditions for inclusion and inclusive education.

The Ethics of Inclusive Education serves researchers, practitioners and politicians, to make key educational decisions about how to understand, explore or realize inclusive educational aims, especially with respect to disability and special needs.

Franziska Felder is a Professor for Inclusive Education and Disability Research at the Department of Education at the University of Vienna, Austria.

THE ETHICS OF INCLUSIVE EDUCATION

Presenting a New
Theoretical Framework

Franziska Felder

LONDON AND NEW YORK

Cover image: Digital image, The Museum of Modern Art, New York/
Scala, Florence

First published 2022
by Routledge
2 Park Square, Milton Park, Abingdon, Oxon OX14 4RN

and by Routledge
605 Third Avenue, New York, NY 10158

Routledge is an imprint of the Taylor & Francis Group, an informa business

© 2022 Franziska Felder

The right of Franziska Felder to be identified as author of this work has been asserted in accordance with sections 77 and 78 of the Copyright, Designs and Patents Act 1988.

All rights reserved. No part of this book may be reprinted or reproduced or utilised in any form or by any electronic, mechanical, or other means, now known or hereafter invented, including photocopying and recording, or in any information storage or retrieval system, without permission in writing from the publishers.

Trademark notice: Product or corporate names may be trademarks or registered trademarks, and are used only for identification and explanation without intent to infringe.

British Library Cataloguing-in-Publication Data
A catalogue record for this book is available from the British Library

Library of Congress Cataloging-in-Publication Data
Names: Felder, Franziska, author.
Title: The ethics of inclusive education : presenting a new theoretical framework / Franziska Felder.
Description: Abingdon, Oxon ; New York, NY : Routledge, 2022. | Includes bibliographical references and index. | Identifiers: LCCN 2021037146 (print) | LCCN 2021037147 (ebook) | ISBN 9781032117478 (hardback) | ISBN 9781032117492 (paperback) | ISBN 9781003221326 (ebook)
Subjects: LCSH: Inclusive education—Moral and ethical aspects.
Classification: LCC LC1200 .F45 2022 (print) | LCC LC1200 (ebook) | DDC 371.9/046—dc23
LC record available at https://lccn.loc.gov/2021037146
LC ebook record available at https://lccn.loc.gov/2021037147

ISBN: 978-1-032-11747-8 (hbk)
ISBN: 978-1-032-11749-2 (pbk)
ISBN: 978-1-003-22132-6 (ebk)

DOI: 10.4324/9781003221326

Typeset in Bembo
by codeMantra

For Luis, Raoul and Robert who make life complete, and in memory of Ursula, who was the inspiration for so much.

CONTENTS

Preface   ix

1 Introduction   1
The Fenty story 1
The missing social dimension in the inclusion debate 3
The structure of this book 7

2 The approach, scope and method   10
Introduction 10
The comparison with slavery 13
The limits of rights-based approaches 16
The methodological approach: nonideal theorising 18
Conclusion 27

3 A brief review of the history of (inclusive) education   31
Introduction 31
The status of disabled people before the eighteenth century 32
The Age of Enlightenment 32
Shifting backgrounds and the importance of compulsory education 36
The rupture of the Second World War and the growing importance of human rights 38
The emergence of the concept of "inclusion" 40
The difficult role of special education today 43
Conclusion 44

4 The concept of inclusion — 50
A confusing plethora of definitions 50
The strong focus on schools and the lack of a debate on exclusion 52
Inclusion between description and evaluation 53
Inclusion as a "thick concept" 55
Two camps and the problems associated with them 57
Inclusion: the proposal 60
The sociological perspective 63
The elements of inclusion 76
The ontogenesis of inclusion in evolutionary biology and individual psychology 91
Conclusion 95

5 Disability — 105
Introduction 105
Change of emphasis within the inclusion literature 107
The "deconstruction" model 109
The "barrier" model 112
The difference made by disability 116
The social-relational model 119
Conclusion 123

6 Inclusive education — 128
The current inclusion discourse and its shortcomings 128
The school as an organisation and institution 130
School versus family 136
The functions of school 141
Conclusion 149

7 Values that matter — 155
Introduction 155
Step 1: exclusion 161
Step 2: the ethical-normative significance of inclusion 176
Step 3: inclusion and education 197
Conclusion 208

8 Conclusion: the transformation of education — 216
The shift towards inclusion 217
Closing remarks 220

References 223
Index 243

PREFACE

The title of this book – *The Ethics of Inclusive Education: Presenting a New Theoretical Framework* – might suggest two misconceptions: That there is only *one* ethics of inclusive education, and that there is exactly one form of inclusive education. Of course, neither is the case. The practical sphere of inclusive education is broad, and the conceptual and ethical-normative approaches involved are correspondingly heterogeneous. Nevertheless, I think it is fair to say that there have been only scarce attempts to explore the potential of the term 'inclusion', as well as the ethical-normative meaning of inclusion and – in particular – inclusive education, in any systematic way. The intention of this book, therefore, is by no means to stifle debate by presenting a definitive viewpoint. Quite the opposite: This work proposes a new framework within an ongoing discourse. The hope is that the discipline and profession of inclusive education will come to recognise how much content can be brought into a genuinely critical-constructive debate, not least when it comes to the ethical-normative relevance of goal orientations such as inclusion.

A theoretical proposal of this kind does not just develop in a dark, quiet room, of course. Rather, the theory of inclusive education presented here has grown over the course of many conversations, resulting in changes through the years. I would particularly like to thank Jörg Michael Kastl, Gary Thomas and Heikki Ikäheimo, the three people who have probably influenced me the most in terms of content in recent years. From Jörg Michael Kastl, I adopted – at least I hope – a clear and analytical view of inclusion. In practice, only two additions have been made to his theory. First, I do not limit inclusion to structural inclusion and, second, I add the aspect of psychologically perceived belonging to its systematisation. Gary Thomas from the University of Birmingham helped me to have faith in my theory. It meant a lot to me that this encouragement came from someone who had for decades been engaged in prominent theoretical and empirical research on inclusion in Great Britain. Finally, Heikki Ikäheimo, a renowned expert in theories of recognition, was my host at the University of New South Wales in Sydney. He greatly shaped my own analytical thinking – not least through thrilling discussions about the philosophical import of recognition and its application to education.

The list of those who have deeply influenced me and to whom I would like to express my gratitude is by no means exhaustive. I would also like to thank the following people – in no alphabetical order, or order of importance. In Australia: Karen Soldatic, Michaelis Michael, Rosemary Kayess, Laura Davy, Dinesh Wadiwel, Ros Madden, Karen Fisher, Kelley Johnson and Linda Barclay; at the School of Education at the University of Birmingham: Graeme Douglas, Julie Allan, Rachel Hewett, Liz Hodges, Lila Kossyvaki, Neil Hall, Emmanouela Terlektsi, Mike McLinden, Matthew Schuelka and Ben Kotzee, among others; at the University of Zurich and beyond: Kai Felkendorff, Christian Liesen, Rahel Huber, Corinna Badilatti, and Elisabeth Moser Opitz and her team at the Institute of Education at the University of Zurich. I would also like to thank my entire team at the University of Vienna, and especially my student assistant Elvira Seitinger, who helped in the preparation of the manuscript with a critical eye. I further wish to thank Alison Foyle, Akshara Dafre, and Kavya Shekar for their wonderful support with Routledge, and Marya Vrba, who translated the mainly German manuscript into English.

Many people, including friends and family, also contributed to the creation of this book even when our conversations about its contents lasted no more than five minutes. And others have inspired my thinking without intending to. My thanks go to all of them – in a general way and without mentioning individual names – not least because, with them, it is possible not only to talk about inclusion, but also to experience it.

1
INTRODUCTION

The Fenty story

In 2019, the American singer Rihanna and the French luxury brand LVHM founded a new fashion label under Rihanna's surname, Fenty. Rihanna, in the media's view, brought something very new to the fashion industry with the potential to turn it inside out: values of diversity and inclusion. "These two values", according to the German newspaper *Der Spiegel*, "represent core values for millennials and Generation Z: That every human being is unique. That everyone is fine the way they are. That everyone is beautiful. That everyone has the right to be just as they are" (Blümner, 2019, w. p.). Fenty has had its biggest success so far in the field of beauty products. The company is reported to have generated revenue of around 500 million euros in its first year of business. This success is not least attributed to the concept of offering makeup shades for 50 different skin tones. There is already talk of a "Fenty effect" within the fashion industry.

We can also observe a phenomenon comparable to the Fenty effect in education, which is increasingly viewed as a forum for the acceptance and even celebration of diversity and inclusion. This perspective has resulted in a search for approaches to education and learning that take full account of pupils' diversity and aim for their inclusion.

Inclusion, however, not only represents one of the main values and elements of an ambitious vision in current educational practice and policy; it also poses one of the biggest challenges ever faced by school systems around the world (Ainscow, 2007; Ainscow & Miles, 2008; Schuelka, Johnstone, Thomas, & Artiles, 2019a). In that respect, the United Nations Convention on the Rights of Persons with Disabilities (UNCRPD) – adopted by the United Nations General Assembly in December 2006, open for signature since March 2007 and in force since May 3, 2008 (after its 20th ratification) – is often seen as a tremendous achievement.

DOI: 10.4324/9781003221326-1

In reality, the UNCRPD only marks the latest step in the development of international policy that tackles issues of exclusion and inclusion. With respect to education, the Convention has had many predecessors, including the Universal Declaration of Human Rights (United Nations, 1948),[1] the United Nations Convention on the Rights of the Child (United Nations, 1989),[2] the World Declaration on Education for All (United Nations 1990) and the United Nations Standard Rules on Equalization of Opportunities for Persons with Disabilities (United Nations 1993), marking the right to education as one of the most important rights in international human rights law (De Beco, 2014). One text of special importance for the advancement (or – as some would say – replacement) of special needs education through inclusive education is the Salamanca Statement and Framework for Action on Special Needs Education, established in 1994. It can be considered the first widely circulated document that accepted the language of inclusion on an international policy level (Vislie, 2003).[3] It refers to the need for schools to develop an inclusive orientation and describes inclusive schools as "the most effective means of combating discriminatory attitudes, creating welcoming communities, building an inclusive society and achieving education for all" (UNESCO, 1994, ix).

But although inclusion is such a dominant issue in education globally – also appearing under the labels "inclusive schooling", "inclusive education" and (only occasionally) "progressive inclusion" – *and* despite the existence of prominent and powerful legislation supported by the UNCRPD and by UNESCO's Salamanca Statement (to name just two examples), "few issues have received the attention and generated the controversy and polarization of perspectives as has the movement to include all children with disabilities into general classrooms" (Winzer & Mazurek, 2010, p. 87). There is an ongoing debate about the meaning of inclusion, what it symbolises and the circumstances under which progress is being made (Artiles & Kozleski, 2016; Artiles, Kozleski, Dorn, & Christensen, 2006; Nilholm & Göransson, 2017).

This book aims to address some of the questions related to inclusion, inclusive education and disability from a philosophical perspective that is both theoretical and analytical. In *Reclaiming Philosophy for Educational Research*, Richard Pring (2007a) argues that it is crucial both to think philosophically and to engage in philosophical thinking if we want to go beyond a superficial understanding of the theories and practices of education. And that is precisely the motivation behind this book: To penetrate the surface of the phenomenon known as inclusion or inclusive education.

While inclusion is most commonly viewed as a means of addressing the needs of diverse student groups (Stentiford & Koutsouris, 2020), disability seems to be the most difficult and controversial category of all, which is why this book addresses it specifically. I do not mean to suggest in any way that the focus of inclusion as a concept is restricted to disability or special needs. Quite the contrary. As Ainscow, Booth and Dyson (2006, 25) argue, inclusion implies "the presence, participation and achievement of all students vulnerable to exclusionary pressures, not only those with impairments or those who are categorised as 'having special educational needs'". Thus, the very idea of inclusion entails the implicit consideration of how to reframe education so that even the descriptor "inclusive" is made redundant. Although special emphasis is placed here on disability as one of the most persistent challenges in the realisation of inclusion and inclusive education, I specifically rebuff two assumptions a reader might hold: First, that inclusion and exclusion are solely a "disability issue"; second, that we have no need to look beyond disability, and can dispense with a broader examination of the identity intersections found in race, gender, social class, immigration and language status, for example.

The basis of our moral reasons for implementing an inclusive school system constitutes the central theme of this book. In that context, the current *zeitgeist* will be examined critically. The questions addressed here include the following: Can we consider inclusion and inclusive education as the equivalent of offering 50 different shades of makeup, in the analogy suggested at the outset, or is something else required? Does inclusiveness mean that all individuals are considered "unique and good just as they are"? And generally speaking, how do these and other considerations translate into educational practice and policy with a mandate to develop and transform? If we are to understand the implications of the current trends in inclusive education, we need to thoroughly examine the value of inclusion itself. Precisely, this kind of examination lies at the heart of this book.

The missing social dimension in the inclusion debate

The most fundamental questions I address are the following: Does inclusive education relate to diversity as such or does disability – as suggested above – constitute a special case? In other words, is the linkage of inclusive education to disability a "retrograde step", as Slee (2001a, 120) assumes? And furthermore, is the challenge for schools' inclusivity mainly that of ensuring access to infrastructure, including technical resources and aids, as well as new methods of teaching – or is it primarily a matter of teachers and politicians having the right attitudes and values? If so, what are these "inclusive values and attitudes" and what is their relationship to formal and informal curricula? And is it only certain people – foremost teachers, headmasters and other school staff – who need to incorporate those values, or indeed all people within society, and even organisations and institutions with extra-individual characteristics? Generally, and related to this: Is inclusive education chiefly about the structure of society and about having access to societal goods, or is it also – even mainly – about having interpersonal relationships and a sense of belonging? If it is more, or something else, than access to goods and the structural foundations of society, how do those elements relate to interpersonal relationships and personal feelings of belonging? What kinds of educational, social and personal experiences do we want children to have, and in what ways does an inclusive school ensure or enable these (Cummings, Dyson, & Millward, 2003)? And finally, even if it seems obvious that we value inclusion and aspire to it, what exactly do we value when it comes to inclusion?

When I started thinking about inclusion and inclusive education, the questions that first emerged – regarding differences in teaching methods and ways of dealing with diversity in the classroom, for example – seemed to be precise, target-oriented and pragmatic, but it soon became clear that they are interwoven with deeper and more general, complex issues that are at stake in the pursuit of inclusion, such as the means and goals of education itself. While I reflected on my own ableism and the often medicalised assumptions I had about disability and the possibilities and limits of inclusive education, it also struck me that even the most serious and vocal proponents of inclusion and inclusive education often shared the same assumptions as their critics when it came to the nature of inclusion or the means, goals and functions of schooling, all areas that I found ripe for critique. I especially failed to be convinced by the assumption that there is no need for inclusive education to address disability in particular, but only diversity in general; nor was I persuaded by the view that inclusive education is only concerned with disability and can therefore be regarded as a special issue. It seemed to me, furthermore, that many of the theoretical difficulties involved in the conceptualisation of inclusion and inclusive education stem from a lack of engagement with the goals and functions of education and schooling in modern societies, as well as a failure to take account of more broad-based social theories on the nature of the relationship between communities and the larger society, for instance. While the opponents of inclusive education have tacitly taken for granted and considered as legitimate those aims and goals of education that are currently most prominently promoted, its proponents have also tended to ignore neglected functions of schools and goals of education that are nonetheless important for life in a late modern society. I therefore came to agree with Göransson and Nilholm's (2014) observation that differences in the way inclusion is defined often arise from divergent views on what schools can and should achieve.

Consider, for instance, the late John Wilson as a representative of the first group, the critical commentators. Wilson wrote (1999, 110):

> On the one hand, we have the feeling that it is wrong if people are left out of some community, are excluded, marginalised, unable to participate, not treated as equals or done justice to, in some ways are not full members of that community. On the other hand, we recognise that any community, social group or context of activity has its own aims or values. It exists *for* something, an orchestra to play music well, a cricket team to perform well on the field, a particular class to learn higher level mathematics etc. The clash between these two perspectives is that including everybody within some group seems inconsistent with fulfilling a particular group's purpose.

One page later (ibid., 111), he continues:

> The hard, inescapable fact is that learning, however broadly defined, is a particular kind of human activity, something which people do (not

something given to them), and which different people may be more or less good at. So even the very general idea of 'learning' contains the seeds of exclusion or marginalisation, just as the general idea of running or jumping, which almost anyone can do to some degree or other, leads to selectivity and exclusion as soon as it is put into a practical context, the moment we conceive it as doing *well*.

According to Wilson, it would of course be possible to design activities in such a way that everybody could join. But in the context of school education, this would, in his opinion, hardly represent a serious idea of schooling anymore. If we followed Wilson, we would have to live with the fact that school education is exclusive and that inclusion clashes with the idea of excellence at the core of successful learning in schools.

Advocates of inclusive education, meanwhile, do not share this idea of a dichotomy between learning and (social) inclusion; yet, they have often said remarkably little about what is learned in inclusive schools, what such schools look like and how they are organised (Dyson, 1999, 45), even if they acknowledge the role of schools as societal institutions. Take, for example, Len Barton's vision of inclusive education or "education for all" as he has called it: "Education for all", he argued in Barton (1997, 234):

> [...] involves a serious commitment to the task of identifying, challenging and contributing to the removal of injustices. Part of this task involves a self-critical analysis of the role schools play in the production and reproduction of injustices such as disabling barriers of various forms. Schools need therefore to be welcoming institutions. It is more than mere questions of access that are at stake here. It is a quest for the removal of policies and practices of exclusion and the realization of effective participatory democracy. It also involves a wider concern, that of clarifying the role of schools in combating institutional discrimination in relation to, for instance, the position of disabled people in society.

The task he attributes to inclusive education has obviously to do with the negative definition of inclusion – its flipside, so to speak. Barton defines inclusion largely as the *absence* of discrimination, exclusionary boundaries and injustices.

But what exactly is the gestalt of this institutional discrimination faced by disabled children and youth? And what would a positive definition of inclusive education look like if we were to follow Barton? Could we just flip the coin, as it were, to yield a self-evident, positive definition of inclusion? That seems difficult to imagine; at least, Barton's definition tells us surprisingly little about a positive ideal of this kind. While it is certainly true that we have a clearer idea about what inclusion is *not* – namely, some sort of serious exclusion, disadvantage, discrimination, oppression or similar phenomena – this does not at the same time yield an equally distinct idea of inclusion (we might add that it does not even give us a very clear-cut idea of exclusion). The modest constructive and positive insight we can derive from Barton's definition is that inclusion "realises effective participatory democracy". What this implies, however, is very much open to interpretation.

It turned out that Barton was not alone in providing answers that I found convincing on a very general level, but which left as many gaps and unidentified and unexamined aspects as the critical literature on inclusive education. This is reflected, for instance, in the observation that both the negative and the sympathetic literatures treat the term "social" as a kind of filler that makes no clear contribution to the idea of "plain inclusion". Even while authors like Wilson use the qualifier "social" to denounce the whole notion of inclusion as a naïve ideology of do-gooders blinded by romantic illusions, the proponents of inclusion have often deemed it unnecessary to explain why inclusion should be understood as a social phenomenon, or how it relates to education and other areas of life. Moreover, the term "social" either seems to indicate a sharp, yet implicit distinction from (academic) learning – as in Wilson's case – or it is used as a redundant and thus rather meaningless term, mostly by the proponents' camp. It does not clarify how inclusion and inclusive education are *distinctively* social, in contrast, for instance, to an understanding of inclusion as a matter of individual status, of rights (human or legal) or of technical and infrastructural access for individual people.

The problems with the term "social" are not superficial, I came to realise. Of course, we often use words and concepts without defining them precisely. This is not much different in academic work than in everyday language. Sometimes, we consider that a commonly shared understanding is broad and uncontroversial enough that we can employ terms and exchange ideas without having to provide lengthy explanations of their content and use. In academic books and articles, it is usually the case that only core concepts are defined, in the assumption that all the other terms circling around them are sufficiently simple or undisputed for regular use, or else carry little enough weight that differing interpretations do not jeopardise the understanding of the core concept.[4] In general, it seems like a necessary and unavoidable step to assume a shared understanding in some sense, to "get off the ground". Only a certain level of (presumed) common understanding allows for a smooth, ongoing exchange among interlocutors.

But I have grown ever more convinced that the term "social", often used to reinforce "inclusion", serves as an under-theorised background for other, seemingly more important terms that carry the bulk of the meaning. Not just filler, the term "social" points to something distinctive about inclusion that calls for closer examination.

The problem with the implicit use of "social" in the debate on inclusive education also does not fade when it is joined to negative concepts such as discrimination, oppression and exclusion. At first glance, it seems uncontroversial to assume that schools are an ideal place to reveal and combat barriers to inclusion, as schools generate discriminatory social attitudes and other more material forms of discrimination, including the denial of opportunities for accreditation, employment, social interaction and so on. This could lead to an assumption that the analysis and criticism of these barriers do not require a complex model of school-society relationships, nor indeed any sophisticated model of the "social" element at all (Cummings et al., 2003, 51). That would be a shortcut, however. As Wilson's work and other examples in the literature show, it is still far from clear what "counts" as inclusion in schools (Göransson & Nilholm, 2014; Nilholm & Göransson, 2017; Qvortrup & Qvortrup, 2018).

I agree specifically with Cummings et al. (2003, 52) that a vision of inclusion

> has to be concerned not just with 'barriers', but also with issues of curriculum, pedagogy, resourcing and achievement. Likewise, it requires a different – perhaps richer – analysis of the relationship between school and society, one which understands how social and economic disadvantage produces educational 'failure', how educational interventions support social and economic interventions to create a more equal society and what such a society might look like.

As the authors suggest, this does indeed call for a more substantial understanding of the term "social" in the context of social and societal inclusion, providing yet another argument for the importance of clarifying this concept. It also points to the need for analysis of the structural, political and organisational conditions of schooling and education in modern societies.

The structure of this book

Because of the multiple, complex issues associated with inclusive education, the arguments in this book take several "detours". The first of these concerns the methodology adopted here and the kinds of knowledge and the approaches needed to answer the questions at hand. In Chapter 2, I suggest a specific methodological approach that aims at developing a nonideal theory of inclusive education. The intention behind nonideal approaches, mostly adopted in political philosophy, is to integrate both philosophical and applied elements of inclusion. This is an aspect that plays an important role in many educational issues, but especially in inclusive education with its amalgamation of practical and moral concerns.

Chapter 3 comprises the second detour of the book, one which is informed by history and sociology. The idea behind this chapter is that, if we are to understand the political and socio-cultural structures that shape education at large and thus also affect the possibilities and constraints of inclusive education, we need to be aware of the historically determined institutional and structural barriers and conditions that restrict and enable access to educational opportunities and outcomes. In that respect, although the aim of this book is not to provide a detailed analysis of the development of inclusive education, a brief review of its historical evolution and the concepts underlying the various ancestors of inclusion is a necessary step if we are to better grasp the nature of what is currently at stake with inclusive education, and why it is unlikely that this movement will go away any time soon.

Chapter 4 focuses on the generic concept of inclusion. There, I suggest that we might view inclusion as an umbrella concept that incorporates four elements: Structural access, participation in goods, interpersonal relationships and personal belonging. This chapter discusses classic sociological works and shows how their insights can be used to build a coherent and integrated theory of inclusion. In addition, drawing on the work of the developmental and comparative psychologist Michael Tomasello, this chapter highlights the importance of inclusion and collaboration for human ontogeny as well as individual development.

Chapter 5 addresses disability as a specific issue with respect to inclusion, comprising the final detour of this book. It examines the question: Why, and in what respects, does disability pose a problem for inclusive education? This chapter interprets disability in a new way, in that it proposes a social-relational view of disability and rejects both the barrier model and the social-construction model of disability.

Chapter 6 focuses on school education in terms of its form, functions and structural and organisational conditions. The introduction and expansion of inclusive education cannot be comprehended, I believe, without a deeper understanding of how educational systems work in general and how they interact with different societal spheres, and also of the function education has for people's lives in the modern world. Conversely, we need to clarify the importance and the place of education within a broader concept of social inclusion. Given that schools in particular prepare people for democratic life on a larger scale and thus also for democratic inclusion, the relationship between democracy and inclusion calls for special attention. This chapter furthermore addresses the differences between schools and families, which are both organisational systems that educate children. It suggests that schools should concentrate on an additional function, namely an inclusive function, that addresses current and future challenges for societies. Lastly, this chapter shows that we can find a stimulating source of inspiration in John Dewey's philosophy.

The importance of the quest and struggle for inclusion and inclusive education becomes even clearer when we examine the value of inclusion itself, and the special potential of education to address this value. In Chapter 7, therefore, the descriptive concept of inclusion is finally imbued with normative meaning. Here, a central role is given to the question of why, and in what ways, inclusion is important for human well-being and justice. The value of inclusion is elaborated in three steps, starting with the value of exclusion, followed by that of inclusion, then inclusive education. The first step proposes a two-stage model in which exclusion is first understood as a violation of essential human needs and capabilities, then, second, in a more direct material and epistemological way. The second step then turns to inclusion and its moral value. There, I suggest that we might view the value of inclusion in three layers, namely through its intriguing connection to equality, freedom and recognition. In the last step, these values are interpreted specifically for the school setting. In this context, we see how the values in our discussion are shaped by the structures and tasks of education.

Finally, Chapter 8 examines the possibilities for transforming education to make it more inclusive than it presently is, and provides a brief summary of the book as a whole.

Notes

1 Article 26 of this text asserts that "everyone has the right to education".
2 The CRC includes detailed provisions on the right to education that have had a broad impact, as it remains the most widely ratified international human rights treaty to date. Worldwide, only the United States and Somalia have not ratified the CRC. Although the CRC does not provide for a right to inclusive education, its Article 2 does mention disability in the list of prohibited discrimination criteria. Moreover, Article 23 states that children with disabilities must have access to education "in a manner conducive to the child's achieving the fullest possible social integration and individual development".
3 Any assumption that the Salamanca Statement can be considered a founding document of inclusive education is exaggerated, to say the least. The report issued following the conference states, "The trend in social policy during the past two decades has been to promote integration and participation and to combat exclusion. Inclusion and participation are essential to human dignity and to the enjoyment and exercise of human rights. Within the field of education, this is reflected in the development of strategies that seek to bring about a genuine equalization of opportunity. Experience in many countries demonstrates that the integration of children and youth with special educational needs is best achieved within inclusive schools that serve all children within a community. It is within this context that those with special educational needs can achieve the fullest educational progress and social integration" (UNESCO, 1994, 11). It is noteworthy that this document mentions "inclusion" in a manner not intended to delineate it from other, similar terms (such as integration or participation), but as a complement to them. We can also observe that the last sentence presents inclusion as a precondition for integration. The assumption is that pupils need to be included in the first place so that integration can occur.
4 A good example of this is found in Iris Marion Young's *Inclusion and Democracy* (Young, 2000). Young's introduction provides an idea of what she means by inclusion. However, she never defines the term "inclusion" itself. Young (ibid., p. 5f.) writes: "This book highlights one norm often invoked by those seeking to widen and deepen democratic practices: inclusion. The normative legitimacy of a democratic decision depends on the degree to which those affected by it have been included in the decision-making processes and have had the opportunity to influence the outcomes. Calls for inclusion arise from experiences of exclusion – from basic political rights, from opportunities to participate, from the hegemonic terms of debate. Some of the most powerful and successful social movements of this century have mobilized around demands for oppressed and marginalized people to be included as full and equal citizens in their polities. Demands for voting rights have focused some of these movements; especially today, however, when most adults in most societies have nominal voting rights, voting equality is only a minimal condition of political equality. *Inclusion and Democracy* explores additional and deeper conditions of political inclusion and exclusion, such as those involving modes of communication, attending to social difference, representation, civic organizing, and the borders of political jurisdictions".

2
THE APPROACH, SCOPE AND METHOD

Introduction

In light of the main aim of this work, which is to reposition and sharpen the ideological focus of the debate on inclusion, it will also be necessary in the following to clarify the relationships between conceptual description, empirical research and normative justification. This is because we are dealing here with two contrasting and seemingly contradictory tendencies that are rarely debated in the scholarly literature, although they are easily noticeable at academic conferences, in practice and in education policy. This dichotomy of perspectives can also be observed in the separate forums established by the two camps, which at times display open hostility to representatives of the other side, with little attempt to relate constructively to one another in scientific or political contexts.

On the one side, there is the criticism levelled mainly by empirical researchers that inclusion is an ideologically overloaded and (to a large extent) empirically useless concept, or just an empty word that lends a quasi-scientific touch to good intentions. Members of this camp who employ the term "inclusion" usually do so for political reasons, choosing simply to accept or exploit the place of inclusion as a key value in contemporary pedagogy. And of course, they do not want their own empirical studies and practical efforts to be seen as lagging far behind the times. On the other side, theoretical and philosophical researchers have criticised quantitative empirical approaches, in particular, for failing to pay attention to the theoretical and philosophical justification and elaboration of the concept of inclusion. They argue that the United Nations Convention on the Rights of Persons with Disabilities (United Nations, 2006) and earlier education policy agreements such as the Salamanca Statement (UNESCO, 1994) have often been used as a substitute for much-needed theoretical clarification.

DOI: 10.4324/9781003221326-2

In light of the objections raised by the two sides, and the occasionally hostile atmosphere between them, is it possible, or indeed necessary, for a compromise to be found? For the research context, in particular, we need to ask how the relationship between empirical and theoretical or philosophical research is generally to be framed and conceptualised in this area of education studies. Should it be viewed in the narrow sense of an instrumental relationship, as described by Fazal Rizvi and Bob Lingard (1996), with empirical research (presumably) taking the lead, even as it strives to ensure that theoretical and normative considerations do not "contaminate" the empirical material? And if so, is that a problem?

For a number of reasons, it is certainly problematic that these two camps seem to stand in irreconcilable opposition to one another. As will become clearer later on, empirical research into inclusive education is in fact dependent on theories and ethical-normative reflections, or even aims to generate them, just as theoretical and philosophical analysis – to the extent that it does not seek to produce abstract, idealised versions of inclusive education – also relies on empiricism, or at least certain descriptions of lived experience. Therefore, if we wish to avoid an antagonistic or cynical standoff between empiricism and the theoretical and ethical-normative justification of inclusion, we have no choice but to develop proposals for a more compatible and mutually enriching relationship between theoretical, ethical and empirical research, also in terms of practical and political implementation.

One way of constructively addressing the tension between theoretical, ethical-normative and empirical research is through the use of "nonideal" theories. These have become increasingly popular in recent years, especially in political philosophy (Anderson, 2010; Jaggar & Tobin, 2013; Mills, 2005; Wolff, 2019).

However, before we take a closer look at these approaches and explore their significance for inclusion in schools and society, we need to focus on a different, but related question: Why are the answers to ethical-normative questions – for example, whether inclusion is a postulate of social justice, and if so, how – important in the first place? Why are references to the Salamanca Statement or the UN Convention on the Rights of Persons with Disabilities insufficient, and why can they not serve as a substitute for more extensive normative justifications? Certainly, the human rights that these texts call for and enshrine are founded on a normative basis. And with respect to empirical research, we might ask: Why is it that empirical studies alone cannot provide justifications in favour of inclusion or against it? After all, it is empirical studies that provide us with information about the conditions for the success of inclusive education and shed light on certain correlations – for example, between social integration and school performance – which, in turn, assist in justifying and reaching political and practical decisions.

Let us first turn to the latter assumption. Empirical findings cannot provide the necessary justifications for a simple reason: Normative principles for or against inclusion *precede* all else – including the findings of empirical research. All educational ideals ultimately express and encompass normative ideals. And that also applies when such ideals are reshaped by bureaucracy or – as in the case of curricula – when they represent an educational policy agenda or perhaps even a social consensus. Normative principles and values permeate all areas, including the practice and politics of education, although often in a way that is not obvious or deliberate. We cannot escape these principles and values, circumvent them or declare them to be secondary. Normative principles re-emerge at the latest in the implementation of recommendations, including those derived from empirical studies. On this basis, Gary Thomas (1997, 104) rightly notes:

> Principles are the key. Research can provide only a crude pointer to the success or appropriateness of inclusion. Ultimately, whether or not desegregation proceeds and mainstream schools become more inclusive will hinge on society's values and its attitudes. If inclusion succeeds in displacing special segregated education it will have done so because society considers that it is right to do so.

Of course, this does not mean that educational content needs to be reconstructed on an ethical-normative basis in all areas. That is not always possible, for reasons of efficiency, nor is it always advisable. And this is not to imply that ethical-normative questions and issues of practical utility, empirical research and political feasibility (for example) should not be considered in conjunction. On the contrary, a distinction must be made between empirical and moral arguments. It makes a difference whether we say, for instance, that deaf pupils should be taught in mainstream schools because they would receive a better education, because they would benefit in other ways, or because other pupils in the class would learn something in this way, *or* whether we say that it is morally desirable for deaf pupils to be included or to be educated with other children. The distinction becomes particularly clear if we examine the validity of the two statements. Although the first group of arguments put forward does include some value statements ("better education", "benefit in other ways") as well as some conceptual challenges (what might be considered a better education, for example?), this reasoning remains empirical at its core, because it proceeds from certain effects that can be verified empirically. That is not the case with the statement that it is morally desirable for deaf children to be educated in mainstream schools. The latter assertion is not influenced by empirical arguments, not because inclusion here represents a mechanical reason for a moral good, but because it is assumed that the adoption of inclusive policy is right for moral reasons, *irrespective* of its empirical and real-world consequences (Barrow, 2001, 238). To better understand the reasoning involved, we need to enquire into the moral grounds for such a decision, not into the empirical evidence supporting it.

Yet, the assertion that ethical-normative assumptions always precede empirical research is not particularly helpful here, especially with regard to the question of which values – apart from inclusion – should guide our thinking and actions. And therefore, this point does not deal a knockout blow to the value of empirical research on inclusion and inclusive education. In the above-cited passage by Gary Thomas, for example, he bases his remarks on *prevailing social* values and norms, and thus on established social conventions, which may or may not be adequate for purposes of justice or other normative considerations. It is important to stress that we should not mistake existing social value perceptions for ethical-normative justifications. First, while Thomas is concerned with the status quo of societal value judgements, an ethical-normative justification is also intended to make programmatic claims about values that we *should* have, but perhaps do not currently have. Values, in other words, that we have good reason to adopt, both on an individual and societal level, as framed within prescriptive statements.

Second, Thomas relates his comments only to the general and abstract primacy of ideological or normative aspects, which are always tied to values in the context of education and instruction due to their inherent goal orientation. Education and instruction are necessarily goal-oriented, and thus value-oriented, because they imply beliefs and assumptions about who can be considered an educated person and what the goals of an educational process are: Autonomy, human well-being and flourishing, economic prosperity and independence, to name but a few possible answers to this question. In a sense, then, applying the concept of inclusion to the topic or field of education doubles the challenge of normativity, as both elements are intrinsically normative by virtue of their goal orientation and the visions they encompass.[1] It is therefore not surprising that the justice discourse is highly fragmented in inclusive education (Artiles, Harris-Murri, & Rostenberg, 2006; Schuelka, Johnstone, Thomas, & Artiles, 2019b).

The mere repetition of seemingly clear moral postulates, however, does not solve the problem of the relationship between normativity and description, also with relation to the gestalt of inclusion and the wide range of normative, political and practical claims that might arise from this hybrid and multifaceted gestalt. In other words, it is not automatically apparent what is meant by inclusion, or whether a particular decision is fair and right in a specific case (Barrow, 2000).

The comparison with slavery

In very general terms, it is doubtful whether inclusion can substantively be considered a moral postulate as clear as the condemnation of slavery, as Biklen and Bogdan (1985) believe. The authors introduce the following analogy into the discussion, presenting the reader with the rhetorical question: Should Lincoln have consulted research experts such as economists, sociologists and political analysts to determine and weigh up the reasons for and against slavery? The answer, not surprisingly, is no. As in the case of support for inclusion, the reasons for opposing slavery are moral, not scientific or economic.

It seems generally evident that opposition to slavery no longer requires any specific justification nowadays. But the comparison of inclusion with slavery is flawed in several respects. First, slavery, unlike inclusion, is not (any longer) a highly controversial concept. It refers to the deprivation of individual freedom for purposes of exploitation and oppression by others. The instrumentalisation of the individual self at the core of slavery cuts deeply into physical and mental integrity, without providing any advantages to the enslaved. On the contrary, it is associated not only with oppression, humiliation and abuse, often lifelong, but in many cases also with hunger, disease and death. Second, it is clear that slavery is now morally condemned by the vast majority of people, not least on the basis of (modern) assumptions of the importance of individual freedom and human dignity. Although slavery is still effectively practised in certain parts of the world (for example, in the Gulf States, where thousands of migrant workers are building the stadiums for the 2022 World Cup in inhumane conditions), it is banned in liberal, democratic states and is not considered compatible with the values of modern societies. Slavery, like most forms of social exclusion (including those exercised on the basis of gender, skin colour or sexual orientation), is no longer deemed legitimate, and is also condemned in terms of (human) rights. Normative standards and real-world practice overlap here to a high degree, at least considered on a global scale.

But the same does not apply to inclusion and exclusion in the sense, for example, of the idea that there should no longer be special schools for children and young people with disabilities. This is an issue that appears to be far more controversial than slavery. There also seems to be much more complexity involved in determining the legitimacy of special education, at least from the perspective of the twenty-first century. Certainly, as will be discussed in more detail in the next chapter, our views of certain phenomena and institutions, including schools and their rules for admission and exclusion, have undergone historical shifts. Some countries now already have extensive systems of inclusive education in place, for example, in Canada, New Zealand and Scandinavia. Moreover, certain forms of exclusion in the context of disability are unimaginable today – for example, the confinement and neglect of people with cognitive impairments in huge institutions, far away from their families and benevolent caregivers, as in the case of professor and activist Burton Blatt and photographer Fred Kaplan in the United States of the 1960s (Blatt & Kaplan, 1966). It seems unrealistic, however, to expect that the educational segregation of current times might one day be subject to the same moral condemnation as slavery.

This is not least because of the uncertainty about what should be regarded as exclusion, both a priori and in general, and in particular what counts as *morally reprehensible* exclusion, especially in countries where schooling or instruction is compulsory for all children and young people without exception. First, we should note that both exclusion and inclusion are *conditional phenomena*. This means that people can only be included or excluded in relation *to something*. The moral evaluation of any given instance of exclusion or inclusion therefore takes place against the backdrop of various relational considerations. The context itself plays a crucial role, but so does the nature of the individual and the conditions that apply to that person and to their participation in a specific group. It makes a difference, for example, whether someone is excluded from school or is not admitted to a local shooting club. And it is important to note that inclusive education is usually not a matter of pursuing voluntary further education in adulthood, but of receiving a basic education in the context of (mainly public) schooling during the formative years of childhood and youth.[2] It is during this period that major foundations are laid, basic skills such as reading, writing and arithmetic are acquired, and social competencies relevant for (democratic) co-existence with others are learned and practised. In sum, this learning content is by no means a *quantité négligeable*, which points to the strong, although hardly self-explanatory importance of inclusive education (especially when it comes to inclusion in the specific context of mainstream schools, not education in general). At the same time, different individuals face very different challenges. For a child in a wheelchair, the main aim is to remove certain external barriers and thus ensure structural access, but other adjustments will be called for in the case of a child with Asperger syndrome, for instance, and these may be much more difficult to accommodate under the structural, spatial and staffing conditions of a mainstream school. This is partly because the barriers faced by such children are not solely external, and thus are not fully modifiable.

Conditional phenomena are dependent on context, and on the rules applicable in specific environments. The rules of admission may be clear and unambiguous in many settings, perhaps in the aforementioned shooting club. The requirements and expectations of modern societies, however, have increasingly become ambiguous, contradictory and ambivalent (Norwich, 2014a). This applies in particular to schools. As open and loosely bound systems, schools are influenced by and responsive to their environments. In particular, schools reflect in their internal structure the cultural perceptions and rules of their wider institutional settings (Crowson & Boyd, 1996). These include the political environment, the norms of the professions exercised, and the socio-cultural beliefs and attitudes within society (Mitchell, 1995). Considering this last element alone, we can observe major fragmentation in modern societies, which must also increasingly be viewed from a global perspective (in light of migration, global competition for talent, more diverse lifestyles, etc.), and this, in turn, has an impact on the conditions of inclusion.

Meanwhile, inclusion also depends in certain respects on contingent, socially allocated resources (and not only on individual attitudes, beliefs and values). Precisely where concrete resources (including equipment such as braille readers, glasses, wheelchairs and hearing aids, but also sign language interpreters, occupational therapists, psychomotor therapists and special needs teachers) are required to enable all persons to participate equally in a given context, for example, in school, these resources must be justified solely on grounds of justice, which must be differentiated from other claims (including other justice considerations, but also economic claims, for example). Individual needs and legitimacy need to be clarified internally – that is, vis-à-vis the potential beneficiaries of such offerings – but also externally. Inclusion must, in other words, be justified not only to the people it affects, and to their relatives and friends, but also to other social groups and decision-makers, such as educational policy-makers and societal stakeholders (for example, unemployed single mothers with small children) at whose expense the resources required for inclusion may (or will) be spent (Liesen, 2006).

Consideration of these factors in parallel does not have to mean that various socially marginalised groups are pitted cynically against one another. Rather, it means taking account of the fact that inclusion – or at least the inclusion of children and young people with disabilities – is in most cases not simply associated with changed attitudes and behaviour on the part of people with political power or gate-keepers such as teachers and school headmasters (i.e. it is not just a question of interpersonal recognition), but also, as noted earlier, with resources that are *not* infinitely available (in contrast, at least potentially, to resources like love and air). This is also a crucial difference to slavery, the abolishment of which was long opposed for the reason that slaves *themselves* were resources for their owners. Thus, the elimination of slavery was, if anything, costly only to those who wished to perpetuate the oppression. Notwithstanding the cynical but widespread belief among slave owners and a large proportion of privileged society that slaves were not even capable of freedom, the prohibition and condemnation of slavery was a boon to the enslaved, and in general meant the end of an oppressive power structure.

In the field of education studies, there are presumably some authors who believe that inclusive education for children and young people with disabilities has the same meaning as the end of slavery for former slaves. But on the whole, this analogy seems particularly convincing when applied to children and young people have (had) no access to education at all.[3] While many such cases still exist worldwide, they account for only a small fraction of the vast literature on inclusive education and the concrete cases that interest educators and policy-makers. Much of the literature as well as the practical scenarios examined in this area involve arguments in favour of the idea that children and young people who were previously educated and supported in special schools or other segregated institutions should now be taught in mainstream schools as a matter of course: This is an important objective, but one that requires justification (in contrast to the question of providing general access to education).

The limits of rights-based approaches

Another issue is pertinent at this stage: While enslaved persons and those generally excluded from any form of education are clearly denied the status of individuals with rights, this does not obviously apply for special education, or at least it must be demonstrated how, exactly, rights are violated in that context. Rights are obviously a crucial factor in the fight for inclusion and against exclusion, discrimination and slavery. They also highlight the ways in which groups and issues are represented in society overall. It is not surprising that conventions such as the recent UN Convention on the Rights of Persons with Disabilities (hereinafter the UNCRPD), which in its Article 24 calls for a right to inclusion in education, have acquired such importance. The significance granted to this Convention, and specifically the attention paid to Article 24, has been accompanied by greater social awareness in general, with respect to both the issue of disability and the meaning of school education for people's lives in modern societies. However, what exactly it means to have a right to inclusive education does not seem so clear, especially when access to schooling is guaranteed in principle, but not alongside peers in mainstream schools. It seems reasonable to suppose that there is a moral problem here that cannot be brushed aside with the argument that a general entitlement to education does, after all, exist. But the precise nature of this problem cannot be deduced simply by reasoning, inversely, that the elimination of exclusion or segregation would amount to inclusion. For inclusion is a complex and multifaceted concept, and its implementation in practice involves many hurdles and trade-offs, not merely the reversal of exclusion. If we are to understand which forms of different treatment or even exclusion are legitimate and which are not, we need a nuanced understanding of the form and content of inclusion and inclusive education.

It is not sufficient to make (often implicit) allusions to real-world matters that need to be tackled, for the following reason: While human feelings and international agreements may be a sound basis for the practical and political implementation of inclusion, they cannot satisfy the demands of justification and legitimation. To a certain extent, these demands are independent of felt experience and the current political agenda. But this is not to suggest that feelings as well as changed political conditions and power relations do not play a major role in realising these demands in practice – quite the contrary (Nussbaum, 2013). Good intentions are a fine *medium* and *prerequisite* for implementing inclusion, but they do not automatically resolve the question of what, exactly, the *goal* of inclusion encompasses.[4] The relationship between the justification of inclusion and its implementation is therefore not purely instrumental; it is complex, with certain elements that remain independent of instrumentality. Following Joseph Raz (1986, 198ff), we can furthermore conclude, at least with respect to inclusion in the educational context, that education is (among other things) a *public good*. A public good can be recognised, first, in that everyone benefits from having more of that good within society, but – in a related aspect that is important for our topic – the provision of a public good can only be influenced partially and imperfectly by individuals, because people's interests, dispositions and characters cannot be fully controlled or shaped. For this reason, although cooperation between people and institutions is essential, it cannot be fully achieved or managed in any technical manner. Education is furthermore – and this idea is perhaps unusual – at least partly a *social good*. In other words, it is not only better for all individuals if there is more of this good (characteristic of a public good), but it is also the case that certain aspects of education can only be provided and realised socially, that is, they can be experienced on an individual level, but they cannot be generated individually. Such aspects and functions of education – including the function of building and sustaining a democratic society – are of enormous importance for inclusive education.

Major challenges arise here for inclusive education, both for purposes of empirical research and for the implementation of rights. For empirical research, the first challenge is the *attributability of the effects* of inclusion and inclusive education. For, if the good of inclusion can only be realised on a collective basis, i.e. in cooperation between people and institutions, but at the same time it cannot be fully controlled by them, this means that attribution of the resulting effects is only possible to a limited extent, if at all. This also means, in turn, that empirical studies cannot make any definitive determination about the exact origins of inclusive or exclusive effects.

In the implementation of rights, therefore, the subjects and holders of rights are not the only aspects to be considered; the bearers of duties, the objects of rights and naturally the subject matter of the right in question (here, inclusion) are also important. For it is in the very nature of rights – including rights to inclusion and inclusive education – that a subject of rights is always set against an object of rights. To have a right implies being able to obligate another party (whether a person or an institution) to realise the subject matter of the right (Feinberg, 1970). The implementation of a right thus depends both on the subject matter itself and on the possibilities for influencing the relevant bearer(s) of duties.

If it is the case that education, and thus inclusive education, places certain parties under an obligation (of a political, practical or legal nature), then it should be possible actually to realise this right, namely through the powers of action and the abilities possessed by the objects of the right. However, this does not seem to be fully the case with inclusive education. For if inclusive education is a public good of a complex nature, one consequence is that it can only be partially influenced by individuals, as it involves dispositions, interests and characteristics – not just of individuals, but also of institutions (to the extent that such features can be ascribed to institutions at all) – that evade the full enforcement of a right. And if inclusive education is moreover partly a social good, this raises the question of whether and how its provision can and should be obligatory.[5]

As we will see later, in the fourth chapter, that which we commonly refer to as "inclusion" is really a multifaceted phenomenon consisting of several analytically distinct aspects. In the following, however, we will first address the challenge posed by the fact that inclusion is both a normative objective, which can be applied in a pedagogical or extra-pedagogical context, and at the same time a phenomenon that can be described and researched in practical and empirical terms.

The methodological approach: nonideal theorising

Theories generally describe, explain and interpret social phenomena and practices in an attempt to form some kind of coherent whole out of them. According to Harry Brighouse (2015, 215), normative theorising has three tasks. First, it must demonstrate descriptively which values matter, and how much they matter, particularly in terms of their relationships to one another. It accomplishes this task by means of intuition, reflection, logic and thought experiments, among other methods. Second, normative theorising has an evaluative function. We want to know how good or bad our world and our institutions are – including schools. Here, we need abstract theories to a certain extent.[6] Third, normative theorising should provide practical reasons for our actions. We want to know what we should and should not do, and even what we can be obligated to do. Ethical-normative theories are essential for investigating these issues.

But the question is whether ideal theories are necessary for this purpose, as Brighouse suggests, or whether nonideal theories should be brought into play directly (Mills, 2005; Robeyns, 2008; Sen, 2006; Valentini, 2017; Wolff, 1998). History argues for the ideal approach to theory generation. In the Platonic understanding, philosophy helps us to identify ideals which are not bound to any context, historical conditions or time periods, and which can be understood abstractly, that is, without *needing* to be applied. In his *Republic*, Plato compares this process to the creation of a statue, which can be polished to a state of ultimate perfection after it is built (Plato, 2000). Ideals represent, in a sense, the timeless standards against which our human aspirations for justice, truth and beauty should be measured. Of course, we humans, as imperfect beings, are not capable of fully achieving our ideals, but the reality of human imperfections does not lead us to alter ideals themselves. Rather, we are constantly in the process of working towards ideals, which we view as our source of inspiration.

A nonideal approach is quite different: It does not simply acknowledge that human limitations prevent the full attainment of ideals. Instead, it proceeds from the assumption that justice and inclusion, for example, are always incomplete and provisional as objectives, due to the various constraints they involve. Ideals such as inclusion can be viewed as heuristics that help us to operationalise goals in real circumstances. If they are regarded in that way, not as fixed, ultimately unattainable objectives, but as processes of considering possible courses of action and their conditions, then nonideal theories emerge from this mode of thinking (Burbules, 2018).

And it is precisely such a view of ideals like inclusion that will guide us through this book. But there are further reasons why I consider nonideal theorising in the field of education to be the most appropriate way to better understand the specific pedagogical and ethical-normative objectives involved, among them inclusion. A nonideal approach is superior to an ideal approach because, among other things, the idea of inclusive education has to take into account the institution of the school and its various organisational forms and entities, which have now been refined and consolidated over the course of more than two centuries. Only with a nonideal approach can this genesis and development be properly incorporated and understood. And in general, we might say that the themes and topics of education studies, with their highly practical and political implications and significance, serve to encourage the application and even the development of nonideal theories.

It is interesting to note, however, that apart from a few publications (Ahlberg & Brighouse, 2014; Brighouse, 2015; Jaggar, 2015; Levinson, 2012), nonideal approaches to pedagogical questions have not yet found much resonance in education studies in general, or in the philosophy of education in particular, especially outside the English-speaking world. The low profile of nonideal theories in education studies has specific reasons, stemming from the predominance of ideal theory in philosophy and the resulting effect on perceptions of nonideal theory, as concretely expressed in the philosophy of education:

> Nonideal theory is usually regarded as derivative of ideal theory. Don't we first need to know what an ideally just society would be, to identify the ways our current society falls short? Shouldn't the principles for an ideal society be settled first, so that we can work out how to get there from here?,

asks Elizabeth Anderson (2010, 30) rhetorically. No, she then argues: Nonideal theories follow a different methodological logic.

The difference between ideal and nonideal theories

Now we might ask what is the nature of nonideal theories, and what distinguishes them from ideal theories, which after all constitute the main focus of normative theorising in education studies.

The methodological approach of nonideal theorising essentially runs counter to two types of theories. The first type comprises ideal theories that establish or defend principles on the basis of purely conceptual considerations, and only then apply them to practical and political questions. Typical representatives of such an approach include deontologists and contract theorists, such as Immanuel Kant and John Rawls, respectively. Their philosophical theories work from top to bottom, so to speak, with praxis and education policy at the bottom and philosophical theory at the top. An ideal theory represents abstract ideas that can be regarded as context-independent or only applicable to practical or political aspects in retrospect (after all, the proponents of ideal approaches do not claim that their theories are irrelevant to practical or political questions, nor that people are in any way saintlike).

Normally, any approach that combines theory and practice or policy relies on some ideal of a just society as a support construct. This can then be used as an architectural model or blueprint, as it were, for practical or policy purposes. An ideal approach also implies the assumption that policy or practice is something entirely different from philosophical theory, both in terms of how practice, politics and empiricism are approached and with respect to the basic epistemological assumptions involved. In this view, empirical research, practice and policy in the field of education generate or depend on political arguments, practical knowledge and empirical findings, whereas the field of philosophy, by its nature, produces theoretical and philosophical knowledge on which it consequently relies (at the exclusion of all other knowledge). Furthermore, even if we cannot build our houses or education systems from scratch – to use the architectural metaphor again – we are still able to reshape and expand upon that which already exists. Applied to phenomena such as inclusive education, this means building around the imperfections and inadequacies of social institutions and human behaviour. In this process, we should also align our institutions and behaviour as closely as possible with the architectural model. Meanwhile, nonideal approaches to philosophical questions, in contrast to ideal approaches, not only dispute the idea that it makes sense to be guided by a kind of architectural model to improve social practice, but also raise doubts as to whether this is even possible. And they treat as problematic any strict delineation of practical, empirical and philosophical sources of knowledge.

The second type of theory opposed by nonideal approaches consists of hermeneutical, phenomenological or strictly "context-immanent" theories. At first glance, these approaches seem to resemble nonideal theorising. Michael Walzer, as a representative of a theory of justice of this kind, assumes that every assertion of justice is only valid in relation to certain contexts or spheres, i.e. that the theory itself is divided into several, context-related sub-theories (Walzer, 1983). In the preface to his book *Spheres of Justice*, Walzer (ibid., xiv) recommends such an approach to questions of justice as follows:

> One way to begin the philosophical enterprise – perhaps the original way – is to walk out of the cave, leave the city, climb the mountain, fashion for oneself (what can never be fashioned for ordinary men and women) an objective and universal standpoint. Then one describes the terrain of everyday life from far away, so that it loses its particular contours and takes on a general shape. But I mean to stand in the cave, in the city, on the ground.

Walzer thus chooses a nature metaphor, inspired by ancient thinkers who understood the philosophical enterprise as applied thought and discussion. He also presumes that justice reveals itself differently in different spheres of social life, i.e. that justice in the political context differs fundamentally from educational justice, for example.

Even if this approach is undoubtedly closer to the nonideal approach – which will be presented in more detail later – than to an ideal approach along the lines of those proposed by Kant or Rawls, this route is not without its problems, and is also subject to critique by the proponents of nonideal theories. A major problem lies precisely in the context-bound nature of Walzer's method. The assumption behind his approach is that a society's distributive norms are plural and cannot be put into a particular order. This means that there can be no uniform principle of distribution, but only separate measures of justice. The value of various goods is socially produced or assigned. As a consequence, the mode of distribution must also differ depending on the good, the culture and the life situation in question. Walzer's theory is thus not only context-sensitive, but it is also particularistic. And this is where we encounter the problem, for Walzer assumes that each of these spheres is autonomous in itself. This ultimately means that the status of a person in relation to a particular social good (e.g. education) cannot and should not be determined by that person's status in another sphere (e.g. politics). To take one example, power as a principle of distribution should not have any influence on questions of inclusive education, because according to Walzer power is the guiding principle of politics. In this way, however, Walzer not only assumes that power is not a principle for determining the distribution of inclusive education; he also derives the relevant principles from actual practice. In other words, he identifies values by analysing the existing practices of distribution.

However, a key criterion is missing for a critical examination of distribution practices, because Walzer's approach does not include any independent "external" criteria at all. But this is exactly what we need in order to critique and improve practices of inclusion as well as our theoretical reflections on inclusion. It is hardly reasonable to assume, moreover, that problems (such as the abuse of power, or a lack of influence and scope for action) are limited to one sphere only – for example, in Walzer's theory, to politics. Especially when it comes to questions of education and instruction, and specifically the call for inclusive education, it is apparent that one reason for the lack of acceptance of inclusive education in many countries is the low degree of public visibility and leverage that people with disabilities and their families often have, with the result that many of their concerns are unheeded, ignored or devalued. Besides the distribution of goods, the aspects of power and social representation also play an important role in inclusive education, and these should not be underestimated (Waitoller & Thorius, 2015). The definition of separate spheres, each with its own strictly delineated logic of justice, therefore does not seem to be a meaningful way of conceptualising justice in this area.

But any belief that norms of justice can only be obtained through abstract reflection, or behind the "veil of ignorance" as in Rawls, is also mistaken. To think that we should always know what cases should ideally be derived from a philosophical theory is to misunderstand how our thinking about normative facts works. This is the view proposed by Anderson (2010, 30), who favours a nonideal approach to the formulation of philosophical theories. Human beings, she argues, are hardly pure rational thinkers who go around developing ideal theories:

> Unreflective habits guide most of our activity. We are not jarred into critical thinking about our conduct until we confront a problem that stops us from carrying on unreflectively. We recognize the existence of a problem before we have any idea of what would be best or most just. Nor do we need to know what is ideal in order to improve. Knowledge of the better does not require knowledge of the best. Figuring out how to address a just claim on our conduct now does not require knowing what system of principles of conduct would settle all possible claims on our conduct in all possible worlds, or in the best of all possible worlds.

This is exactly where it could be argued, from the perspective of empirical research, that we encounter a reason to study inclusive education on a purely empirical basis and to dispense with more substantive assumptions, especially normative ones. I have already noted that this is not fully possible. Empirical research can help us to understand the conditions and prerequisites for the success of inclusive processes, and when and why they fail. But it cannot answer the question of what, exactly, is constituted by the goals of inclusion and inclusive education, and why they are important.

The appeal of empirical research, however, goes even further, or can be considered to illuminate a deeper problem. For some of the confusion surrounding ideal and nonideal theories can be traced back to the deep rift between empirical and philosophical research that emerged after the "realistic turn", that is, the shift away from purely humanities-based pedagogy towards empirically oriented research in education studies. This shift – which began in the 1960s in German-language education studies and somewhat earlier elsewhere – has led, among other things, to a situation in which empirical research often no longer draws on theoretical or philosophical research, and thus in a sense appears nonideal, although it is not, at least not in the manner discussed here. In this context, values often appear as part of background theories (and often in quotation marks) – especially the values contained in the UNCRPD, such as dignity, justice and equal opportunities. But these values are not explained or justified in depth. It seems that they are often just strung together, in a way that might be (somewhat polemically) described as "more is more". In substantive terms, at any rate, we rarely get more than a list of values (such as equality, justice and human dignity), which sometimes do not even align with one other.

Confusion about ideal and nonideal theories also has to do with the ambiguity attached to the words "ideal" and "theory". According to Valentini (2012, 654), "ideal" can be understood in at least three ways: As referring to full compliance, to a utopian or idealistic quality, or to the optimal or end state to be achieved. Analogously, nonideal theories may be variously interpreted as referring to the partial achievement of a state, a realistic goal, or a phase of transition towards an ideal state (as opposed to an optimal or end state per se). Meanwhile, a "theory" may be either a methodology in the broader sense (theoretical as opposed to empirical, for example) or the product thereof, that is, the term "theory" in the narrower sense. The ambiguity of these two words – which form a more comprehensive and stable concept in "nonideal theory" – means that it is not clear from the outset what is meant by nonideal theories, or how they differ from other theories.

For our purposes here, "nonideal" refers to a realistic and true-to-life view of social issues, with a focus on the possibilities for further development of theory, politics and practice. This is associated with a basic neo-institutionalist view, in which it is assumed that institutions go through various phases of development over time, and thus usually cannot be created from scratch like a blueprint or an architectural model. This is particularly true for education systems. Institutions do not exist in a vacuum, nor do they suddenly disappear. Rather, they "surface" in a specific historical situation, as a response to social and societal pressures, and within a complex framework of social, political and philosophical considerations (Foucault, 1972). The development of institutions and systems, including an education system, is therefore "path-dependent". This means that systems change gradually, building on previous forms of institutionalisation and organisation. Any reforms can (indeed must) draw on existing institutions and organisations, which are often difficult to change because of the investments already made in them (Powell, Edelstein, & Blanck, 2016). Their relative rigidity is often a source of disillusionment, but also a source of information about potential (i.e. realistic) changes.

Against this background, nonideal theorising, understood as a process, is intended to develop an ethical-normative theory of inclusive education that critiques existing institutions and organisational forms while also assuming a realistic (rather than utopian) potential for change. In this sense, a nonideal theory also tends to be politically moderate. Furthermore, there is no contradiction in holding inclusion to be an abstract, ideal state to be aspired to, in line with the ideal approach, while at the same time presuming, in a processual, nonideal manner, that this ideal can only ever be partly attained due to internal and external constraints.

This argument must be clarified, however. I do not mean simply to suggest that the kind of theorising proposed here is about formulating an ideal state that cannot be fully realised in social practice due to existing limitations. That, in essence, would amount to ideal theorising, in which it is certainly possible to acknowledge that ideals may not be attained due to human and other limitations. Instead, another implicit distinction is important here, one already hinted at, and also addressed by Onora O'Neill (1996), namely the difference between abstraction and idealisation. Abstraction is unavoidable, to an extent, in both theory and practice. We cannot describe each individual case in detail. Such an approach would overburden the work of theory formulation, in particular. Nor is it the purpose or meaning of theories to serve as a collection of recipes, so to speak. Rather, we have to make certain abstract assumptions when constructing theories (e.g. when thinking of people as social beings who are fundamentally reliant on interpersonal recognition, even without having detailed information, for instance, about the conditions faced by a particular man with autism named Max within his local beekeeping association).

Idealisation – as distinct from abstraction – is problematic for three reasons: First, it describes actors as having cognitive and volitional capabilities *not* possessed by normal people (or at least not in every case or all the time). Second, none of us can put our preferences in a strict hierarchical order or command a complete set of information in any given situation. Third, we are incapable of looking at ourselves with complete neutrality from the "outside", just as we lack thorough insight into the preferences, motivations and desires of others, not to mention full independence from the institutions and values with which we grow up. Idealisation is a problem not only because it creates unrealistic assumptions about what it means to be human, but because it elevates these assumptions to ideals themselves, by striving to make people become one way or another (O'Neill, 2018, 56). And this is often exactly what happens with ideal theorising.

From the above discussion, we can thus deduce three aspects in which nonideal theory development differs from ideal theorising. First, a dual perspective on theory and practice or empirical research implies a more modest view of objectivity, which, as espoused here, does not include transperspectivity or a theoretical metaperspective. Rather, it is embedded in, and reflective of, a lived social environment that is not least *interpersonal*. Second, nonideal theorising always operates on a scale of various practical perspectives that social actors with knowledge and powers of reflection are able to adopt and effectively integrate in their social activities. Thus, the very plurality of individual and social perspectives, rather than an idealised mono-perspective, plays an important role in the development of nonideal theories. Third, nonideal theorising encompasses naturalising epistemologies and methodologies (although not problematic naturalising ontologies, as discussed in the fifth chapter on disability), as researchers seek to tie their research results to empirical research and practical experience, but also to the boundaries imposed in principle by natural limitations (e.g. people cannot fly without aids). This also means that idealisations are refrained from, and that abstractions, while they raise empirical realities and practical experiences to a general level, must ultimately *always* be related back to the empirical realities, practical experiences and possibilities of human life, whether fundamental or contingent.

The work of one philosopher and educator, in particular, offers an example of the process described here, and provides us with methodological and conceptual resources that are specifically relevant. The American pragmatist John Dewey (1859–1952) left behind a huge oeuvre during his long life. His philosophy and its importance for this book will be further discussed later, in Chapter 6, where we examine the link between democratic inclusion and school education. At this point, however, the focus is on Dewey as representative of a pragmatic, nonideal approach to pedagogical theory development.

Dewey's nonideal theorising

Although Dewey never used the terms "nonideal theory" or "nonideal theorising" in his myriad writings, that is pretty much what lies at the heart of his methodological approach and epistemological assumptions.

First, Dewey suggests that philosophical enquiry always begins with lived experience. He considers that ideals are derived from experience and they can and should, in turn, be used as a basis for experience. In his view, ideals develop from the inside out, moving from the specific and concrete to the general and abstract, so that they can always be linked back to concrete experiences and specific contexts. Second, ideals are not external aims for Dewey. Rather, they are formed through scrutiny of existing societies and human practices. As such, they are close to what he calls "ends-in-view".[7] For Dewey, aims always arise from the realities of certain existing practices, "in view" of our current position. These ends-in-view act as a kind of signpost that should regulate our future behaviour, but at the same time they are strongly linked to our present behaviour and social practices (Wilson & Ryg, 2015, 137).

Dewey, however, does not believe that ideals simply depict existing realities or serve only to promote the societal status quo. Rather, he assumes that an ideal must be understood as a set of dynamic regulatory criteria for explaining and guiding human behaviour. Ideals must be considered within a social context, where they are necessarily oriented around the human problems that they are intended to solve. "In this sense, while ideals *emerge from* experience, they must be directed *back to it*, in ways that build richer and more meaningful experiences. Ideals are not fixed ends, static states, or even necessarily substantive nouns" (ibid., 138). Dewey instead emphasises the transformation of ideals into dynamic criteria, hypotheses and questions, thus bringing together the levels of theory, empirical investigation and practical application.

Third, Dewey's reflections offer new conceptual resources for understanding inclusion not only as a process shaped by educational and social policies and other institutional conditions, but also as a dynamic process structured by a combination of practices, experiences and habits. In this view, inclusion is not an abstract ideal, but a continuous process of negotiation about, and critical engagement with, the conditions of our social life and coexistence. Dewey is less interested in how individuals relate to one another in a democracy than in how society as a whole is organised, how institutions are formed and how they influence the capacity to encourage moral action. He is especially interested in the importance of schools and civil society. Both of these elements, he believes, must be restructured according to democratic principles. This calls not only for an expansion of the right to vote, but also for improved possibilities for communication within a society, so that public opinion is better informed about the experiences and problems of all members of that society. For Dewey, science and scientific discoveries in particular constitute another key tool in the development of democracy. He sees democracy as the social expression of experimental intelligence, informed by sympathy and respect for every citizen (Dewey 2004, 89ff). The consequences of norms and decisions should be seriously considered from the outset, even in the way they are conceptualised, compared with alternatives and endorsed.

In this view, democracy is a means or method of addressing and solving collective problems that increases the overall likelihood of finding intelligent solutions. In addition – and this can be seen as Dewey's second understanding of democracy (as most notably expressed in *Democracy and Education* (1916)) – democracy should be viewed as a way of life or an experiential space in which both passive and active elements are inscribed. Democracy, in this understanding, is an end in itself, not merely the means to an end. It is a form of societal cooperation that is not confined to the political sphere, as in political liberalism. The extent to which Dewey's understanding of democracy can be harnessed for the topic of inclusive education will, as I have noted, be addressed in greater depth later. In what follows, the first step is to clarify how a realistic, nonideal theory of inclusion and inclusive education, of the kind proposed here, might in fact be developed.

Conclusion

Tying these remarks on Dewey back to our initial discussion, we can see the task of philosophical theorising, in the context of inclusion, as that of developing realistic utopias (Jaggar, 2015, p. 119).[8] Utopias of this kind feature a naturalistic and realistic orientation around real-world social practices. They thus imply that institutions such as public schools can develop and change, but that such development must take place, or be achieved, in a path-dependent manner. At the same time – and here the idealistic and critical aspect is apparent – the intention is to formulate objectives that go beyond current practice, in an institutional and organisational future that is aspired to, i.e. to create objectives with a utopian horizon. This also points to a tension that should not be underestimated or ignored, as Erik Olin Wright notes:

> The idea of real utopias embraces this tension between dreams and practice. It is grounded in the belief that what is pragmatically possible is not fixed independently of our imaginations, but is itself shaped by our visions. Self-fulfilling prophecies are powerful forces in history, and while it may be naively optimistic to say 'where there is a will there is a way', it is certainly true that without 'will' many 'ways' become impossible. Nurturing clear-sighted understandings of what it would take to create social institutions free of oppression is part of creating a political will for radical social changes to reduce oppression. A vital belief in a utopian ideal may be necessary to motivate people to leave on the journey from the status quo in the first place, even though the likely actual destination may fall short of the utopian ideal. Yet, vague utopian fantasies may lead us astray, encouraging us to embark on trips that have no real destinations at all, or worse still, which lead us toward some unforeseen abyss. Along with 'where there is a will there is a way', the human struggle for emancipation confronts 'the road to hell is paved with good intentions'. What we need, then, is 'real utopias': utopian ideals that are grounded in the real potentials of humanity, utopian destinations that have accessible waystations, utopian designs of institutions that can inform our practical tasks of navigating a world of imperfect conditions for social change
>
> *(Wright, 2010, 4)*

The assumption is that the limits of what is possible are also, to some extent, limits of the mind, or of belief in the possibility of certain changes. This distinguishes them from equally real (as yet), insurmountable physical and biological limits, such as humans' inability to fly through space at the speed of light. The latter limits are distinct from the social limits that interest us in the context of inclusion (Wright, 2010, 16):

> Claims about social limits of possibility are different from these claims about physical and biological limits, for in the social case the beliefs people hold about limits systematically affect what is possible. Developing systematic, compelling accounts of viable alternatives to existing social structures and institutions of power and privilege, therefore, is one component of the social process through which the social limits on achievable alternatives can themselves be changed.

The limits of inclusion are thus also mental limits, to a considerable extent. To reflect on and critique these barriers of the mind must therefore be an integral part of the development of inclusive education.

Cognitive limitations and fantasies about what inclusive schools might become, beyond the existing organisational forms, are, in turn, tied not least to the historical genesis of modern education systems, although they have been subject to historical shifts concerning the phenomenon of disability and other forms of social inequality. As we will see in the next chapter, the very manner in which school education is organised is an invention of the industrial era. During industrialisation, not only did the acquisition of more complex skills and abilities such as reading, writing and arithmetic become increasingly essential, but the question also arose of how children might be cared for, instead of being left to their own devices, while their parents worked long days. Consequently, the school in its modern, organised form was always an institution both of learning and of custodial care, which was necessarily oriented around the needs of the adult world. Among the multiple functions that a modern school developed and exhibited, those of special education, followed later by integrative and inclusive education, were largely derivative or subsidiary. This aspect of pedagogical efforts to include disabled children and young people in school education has thus always been focused on the acceptance and integration of children for whom mainstream schools were considered not responsible or, for various reasons, not capable of providing an education.

While we now criticise this subsidiary function of special education, which has developed over more than a century, and can often be observed in practices that are described as inclusive as well as the way in which school education is organised in general, it is also the case that such practices can only be altered with a view to their origins (Archer, 1981, 280):

> The system in operation today was structured yesterday; the patterns of governance and accountability now observed were shaped by past struggles for control and shape future processes of change; the educational interests

which are currently defended were distributed earlier in time. In other words some of the causes of continuation are inscribed in the origins of educational systems, whose structure created and perpetuates vested interests in its maintenance.

Thus, if we wish to expand the cognitive boundaries of what we consider possible and appropriate in society today, we cannot avoid turning our attention to the historical development of a system that continues to undergo shifts in its orientation towards inclusion, namely the education system, and in this case the special education system in particular. In the following, I examine the core features of the main developments in this area, with a specific, extended focus on the treatment of people with disabilities. In this context, we can observe that the idea of inclusive education, as we understand it today, is historically very young, but also capable of absorbing older and extra-pedagogical impulses. Ideas inherited from the Enlightenment, while fostering inclusion, have both stimulated the development of an inclusive education system and have proved an obstacle to such development.

Notes

1 Education should also not be confused with learning here. The former is a teleological undertaking, the praxis of which is constituted and framed by goals. Learning, by contrast, is not necessarily teleological, and may also occur in an unintentional and purposeless manner (Biesta, 2012).
2 Although I consider the significance of inclusion outside of and beyond school to be underestimated, in the course of the book, it will also become clear why the inclusion of people in basic education is so crucial.
3 About 8% of children worldwide do not receive a basic, formal primary education, while 16% do not receive any basic secondary education (UNESCO, 2020).
4 This is already evident from the fact that various societal measures have social (re) inclusion as their goal, but without promoting good intentions as a means to achieve it. Examples include prisons and the quarantine of people with highly contagious diseases.
5 At the time of writing this book, this issue is relevant to another good that is also partly social, namely health. In the spring of 2020, when the highly contagious COVID-19 virus began to spread, the question arose as to which measures would have the most beneficial and lasting effects for the entire population of a given country. While countries such as Italy, France and Spain opted to impose sweeping restrictions on movement and contact, thus temporarily depriving their citizens of important civil liberties, others such as Sweden relied on persuasion and voluntary compliance with protective measures.
6 We do not need them in every case. For example, we do not rely on an ideal (meaning here: abstract) theory to calculate the size of a mountain, to use Amartya Sen's (2009) example. In other words, we do not need a conception of ideal height to measure the relative height of various mountains. However, if we wish to compare and evaluate differing states of inclusion, we need to have an idea of what ideal inclusion is before we undertake the comparison. As we shall see, this notion of ideal inclusion is based on abstract, yet realistic ideas about the phenomenon.
7 See Chapter 8 of Dewey's *Democracy and Education* (2004), entitled "Aims in education".

8 Ahlberg and Brighouse, for example, are critical of such an approach when they write:

> Schools are undoubtedly unique sites for society to have input on the shaping of students' attitudes and behaviors as future citizens. Further, schools appear to be possible locations for modeling aspects of ideal social arrangements (we could design them to be micro participatory democracies), or locations for directly mitigating important aspects of social injustice (lessening gaps in opportunity prospects between disadvantaged and advantaged children, for example). Given possibilities like these, it is appealing to think that educational interventions might, through modeling features of a fully just world, bring our unjust realities in line with that world. If they could do so, such interventions would be 'real utopian'
> (Ahlberg & Brighouse, 2014, 52)

But they are not, according to Ahlberg and Brighouse, who instead argue for the development of "real moderately bettertopias" (ibid.). I suspect that much of their criticism hinges on the understanding of "utopia". If one emphasises the term "realistic" in "realistic utopia", as I do, then the objectives comprising the utopia are measured against Dewey's pragmatic, realistic and naturalistic views of our lived social environment.

3
A BRIEF REVIEW OF THE HISTORY OF (INCLUSIVE) EDUCATION

Introduction

Inclusion, as a motive and value, does not exist independently of social discourses, as I have noted previously. Discourses describe how motives and values are established and communicated. They are therefore a product of socio-cultural evolution. Values like inclusion become so important because they are accepted as valid by society and thus exert a practical and political impact (Vanderstraeten, 2006). For this very reason, it is essential that we research and illuminate the historical background of ideas such as inclusion. And conversely, reviewing the history of the idea of inclusion is a way of contributing to its conceptual clarification (Florian, 2014), as this process reveals precisely the path dependency that provides a backdrop for the possibilities of further developing inclusion and inclusive education – at least based on nonideal assumptions.

However, in our attempt to elucidate the genesis of inclusive education, as well as its development with regard to disability, it is not enough to stress the oft-cited – and, in my opinion, over-burdened – modern human rights background and the discourse of calls for inclusion and inclusive education. It is far more important that we turn our attention to the disciplinary and conceptual tradition of a field that has both fuelled the idea of inclusion and unquestionably hindered its progress: special education (Danforth & Jones, 2015, 2). This discipline, concerned with the education of disabled children and young people as well as their support and care beyond and after school, has come under heavy fire in the context of inclusion.[1] The framework established with early special education, in particular the subsidiary function it assumed with respect to mainstream education, has increasingly been viewed as a problem for inclusion and inclusive education. Ideas associated with this framework are also falling out of favour, including the dual motive of protection, on the one hand, and support and development

DOI: 10.4324/9781003221326-3

on the other. A historical perspective allows us to chart these trends while also revealing contemporary paradoxes that can be traced back to the roots of special education efforts in the Enlightenment (Richardson & Powell, 2011).

Reaching back into the past of special education in this chapter, we will only be able to sketch the broad outlines. It is not possible to provide a detailed history of special education here because, strictly speaking, that would have to be a global history, and thus include developments in the Global South, for example. As far as I know, no such history has ever been attempted.[2] And moreover, the historical thread would quickly lead us astray from the issue we are actually interested in, namely the ethical significance of inclusion and inclusive education.

The status of disabled people before the eighteenth century

Even before setting out a fully developed concept of exclusion, it seems safe to observe that the situation of disabled people (as well as poor and marginalised people in general) was largely characterised by social exclusion before the eighteenth century. People with disabilities were met with incomprehension, indifference or even cruelty in their society. Children born with obvious disabilities were usually abandoned or killed. In antiquity and the Middle Ages, disabled people were grouped into the general category of "idiots".[3] Members of this category were born "idiots" and remained so, as a rule (Parker, 2005). The label "idiot" was associated with wide-scale exclusion from public and social life. Furthermore, in classical and medieval times, it was assumed that people with disabilities were unable to learn or to benefit from instruction or training, which also meant that they were not taught about practical life skills. As it was furthermore believed that a disability was conferred by God (or the gods), or even the devil, and therefore could only be healed through supernatural intervention, the accounts of those times are full of cures for disabilities, often shrouded in religiosity (Winzer, 2009). People with disabilities were thus also branded as different and deviant in spiritual terms, even if this marking-out implied a degree of integration. The far-reaching societal exclusion and judgement of disability only changed, albeit tentatively and slowly, with the Enlightenment.

The Age of Enlightenment

People with disabilities began to experience positive developments from around the middle of the eighteenth century, during the Age of Enlightenment. Philosophical reflections on ways to compensate for differences in sensory perception were the intellectual precursors to what we now call special education (Richardson & Powell, 2011, 63). Philosophers such as Jean-Jacques Rousseau, Denis Diderot and Voltaire rejected the prevailing philosophical metaphysics of previous centuries. Specifically, they turned away from explanations of the world that were fundamentally of a religious nature in favour of a more scientific and socially conscious approach (Winzer, 1986). The spirit of the reforms that emerged during this time, initially perceptible in the observations and theories of early Enlightenment philosophers, allowed for new perspectives on disability and disabled people as well as the pioneers who set out to instruct and educate them (Winzer, 2006).

The true interests of the Enlightenment philosophers were of a genuinely philosophical nature. Interest in people with disabilities, and positive outcomes for them, tended to be the side effects and real-world applications of philosophical concerns and questions. Implementation of these ideas was carried out by others.

The intellectual project of the Enlightenment was, at its core, to establish knowledge about the world, humankind and nature on a scientific (rather than religious) basis. The humanistic philosophy that emerged in this context introduced the philosophical ideas that still lie at the heart of our liberal, democratic thinking today, namely, a belief in the freedom and equality of all people and in the human responsibility to care for others, including those who do not belong directly to one's own personal and private sphere. Reform movements also arose that were concerned with improving the living conditions of various groups in society: The poor, slaves, prisoners – and those whom we subsume today under the category of disabled people.

People with disabilities as objects and subjects of the Enlightenment

Deaf people were the first group of people with disabilities to become the focus of Enlightenment enquiry. They appeared practically to be the "natural" objects for application of the main ideas of the Enlightenment (Davis, 1997). After all, Enlightenment thinkers were (among other things) interested in discovering the origin and seat of human language, and wondered specifically, for example, about the question (a disturbing one for today's readers) of whether people who could not hear could be led to participate in rational thought and education, or indeed were capable of such activities at all. The conjunction of philosophical interests and concrete pedagogical concerns that arose from the thinking of Enlightenment philosophers, in turn, paved the way for the emergence and development of special education as it appeared in many places around the world in the course of the nineteenth century, initially mainly in France and England. The approaches adopted in that context, despite national differences, were strikingly similar. Often, educators were inspired by Enlightenment ideas and at the same time motivated by a religious, evangelical sense of commitment.

It is therefore not surprising that the early pioneers in this area were mostly members of the clergy. One famous example is Charles Michel de l'Epée (1712–1789), a French priest. He is considered the first in the world to have applied Enlightenment ideas of equality and the development of language to the case of disabled people, more specifically the deaf, and in the process devised an early form of systematic sign language.[4] That was a revolutionary step for the period, considering that L'Epée conceived his ideas at the same time as the philosophical theories of Locke, Diderot and Rousseau, and furthermore believed that sign language was the most effective medium for the intellectual development of deaf people. De l'Epée entered into fruitful dialogue with the philosophers of his time. He rejected the previous goal of (one-sided) assimilation into the hearing world and paved the way for today's empowered deaf community, and thus, to some extent, for early forms of inclusion, understood as a process of assimilation *and* accommodation. De l'Epée, like Locke and certain French philosophers, embraced a sensual philosophy that was responsible for introducing new concepts of language development and human learning (Winzer, 2006).[5] His influence was so profound and lasting that it also facilitated progress for other groups of disabled people, most notably the blind, the deaf-blind and people with intellectual disabilities (Winzer, 1993). The world's first school for the blind, for example, opened its doors in Paris as early as 1784.

Interest in the education of children with intellectual disabilities grew rapidly from the late eighteenth to the early nineteenth century, when Jean-Marc Gaspard Itard (1774–1838), a young physician associated with the National Institute for the Deaf in Paris, published a report describing the early results of (ultimately unsuccessful) efforts to educate a "wild child" named Victor (the "wild boy from Aveyron") (Itard, 1994). However, it was primarily Itard's own student, Édouard Séguin, a French physician and teacher, who continued, developed and popularised Itard's work. Influenced by the intellectual currents of the Enlightenment, Séguin believed that education was a human right and that society had a duty to improve the lives of all citizens. In 1848, political pressure forced Séguin to emigrate to the United States, where his beliefs and educational approaches quickly spread throughout the North American continent. He settled first in Ohio and later in New York as a practising physician. And because the teaching and education of children with intellectual disabilities remained an unsolved problem, and the ideas circulating on the subject were based on European methods that were often Séguin's own, he was quickly invited to help establish institutions and professional organisations as well as develop curricula. Séguin's teaching methods were cutting-edge, and remain so in many respects. His highly structured approach focused on autonomy and daily life skills; it relied on an individual needs orientation and appealed to multiple senses, often through the use of games and songs; and it was based on the principle of positive reinforcement and motivation (Kauffman, 1976).[6]

The dual motive of special education

As a kind of applied social philosophy, early special education was reformist in orientation, but it was not radical, at least not in today's sense (Winzer, 2006). The reformers had multiple motives, including a desire to control disabled people as well as improve their lives. These two motives especially epitomised progressive ideas about the prevention of social problems, in which the aim was both to help disadvantaged people and to combat the spread of social ills at the societal level (Winzer, 2009, 18).

The intent and impact of early special educators was thus first to protect and educate vulnerable children, and to do so on an individual basis according to their needs and specific learning requirements. Institutional settings were created to shield those who needed help and support in the face of relentless assault by society, while also pursuing the (often Christian) vision of saving every soul, including those of disabled children. The supra- or extra-educational aim was to transform and mould objects and consumers of social welfare into subjects so that they would later be able to earn their own living (Winzer, 2006). Second, however, these efforts also had the goal, or at least the effect, of protecting privileged members of society from the social dangers of poverty and other perceived threats. Special institutions were established to provide housing and care, but at the same time they limited the opportunities and options of those they were supposed to serve, and created islands of exclusion.

The early institutions for special education thus served the purpose both of protecting children and youth from a cruel society and of protecting the world from disabled, ultimately unproductive and dependent people: "In this way, special schooling became a convenient place for inconvenient people and thus served the interests of advantaged members of society by maintaining and rationalizing the further marginalization of those it purported to help" (Winzer, 2009, 8). Furthermore, because the early reformers believed that life in the city was unhealthy and that people with disabilities needed a different form of organisation, whereas rural life was conducive to health, and a self-contained institution (or "total institution" (Goffman, 1968)) was most suited to the treatment of these people, many institutions were built in the countryside, far from civilisation, where they took care of all aspects and needs of daily life. In this way, they were like villages of their own, standing apart from nearby communities. Those that have survived the test of time are still located in these remote places today, and their geographical isolation often hinders inclusion in the sense of integration into rich and varied social and community life.

The late eighteenth century[7] thus marked the rise of special education ideas and principles that, in turn, led, from the mid-nineteenth century and especially the late nineteenth century, both to the establishment of institutions, at first primarily for the blind and deaf, and to the introduction of compulsory state education (beginning in Prussia in 1763 (Vanderstraeten, 2006, 130)). The latter development resulted in a dramatic increase in the diversity of pupils in public schools (Richardson & Powell, 2011, 64), creating a need for further differentiation and organisation. A rapidly growing number of educational entities (from secondary schools to nascent special education institutions) accommodated an ever more diverse school population.

The expansion of public education thus gave rise to a new reality. For the first time, school education might potentially include all individuals, regardless of their social background. Education in this context was divided into two structurally independent social subsystems: the family and the school (Vanderstraeten, 2006, 137). The emerging conditions represented a clear social gain, because a motive of equality was thus installed, at least in rudimentary form, and with it the idea that all children and young people – irrespective of their social opportunities and monetary resources – should receive elementary schooling (often organised by the state). At the same time, the structural conditions for schooling (and hence the various forms of special education) as we know them today were put in place through the establishment of these motives and their organisational implementation.

Shifting backgrounds and the importance of compulsory education

The large-scale expansion of state-planned and compulsory basic schooling for children paved the way for the inclusion of entire populations in education, not only within the family, but also (and most importantly) in school. The idea developed of a generalised and homogenised form of "public sphere" that was detached from the hierarchical distinctions of earlier societies, but also and not least from the specific family backgrounds of the individual pupils (at least in theory). But it was not just a stronger degree of abstraction that was thus made possible. The functional orientation of the school also meant that the treatment of pupils as "generalised others" became the formalised way of viewing individual children and young people. At the same time, attention was given to isolated, specific aspects of pupils, namely their learning abilities (Vanderstraeten, 2006, 130):

> As education differentiated 'out' of traditional family contexts, more attention could be devoted to the development and application of specific educational criteria. Notions such as talent, endowment, or genius, which surfaced in the late 18th century, express this concern with identifying each individual's own, innate abilities as a prerequisite to determining her/his life course and proper role in society. Education could develop its own distinctions to observe and 'treat' its public. It could create its own space for meaningful communication.

This orientation certainly did entail social progress. However – as will become clearer in the sixth and seventh chapters – it also introduced a systematic problem into schooling: The formalised view of children and young people and the motive of equality in the form of equal treatment, although meant to do away with certain disabilities conferred through social disadvantage (an aim that was never realised), in effect also created new "problem cases", namely pupils who, for various reasons, could not meet the egalitarian performance standards of the school.

The nation states that began to emerge in the eighteenth century depended for their existence on the participation of their citizens. And this very condition of participation, in turn, drew attention to the need for citizens to be educated.

The idea of national education (*Nationalerziehung, éducation nationale*), in turn, translated concerns about inclusion into specific, nationalistically conceived terms (Vanderstraeten, 2006).[8]

Thus, it was predominantly "reasons of state" that historically underpinned and justified the call to educate as many citizens as possible. Education was expected to contribute to the development of a homogeneous national culture and a collective identity. At the same time, the schooling that "everyone" now received was also supposed to benefit the nation state and thus, in turn, "everyone". Gradually, the idea of school education began to shift away from the political system (and its conditions). This entailed new possibilities for the self-organisation of the education system, which henceforth was able to transform diverging external tensions, triggered by the expectations of politics and emergent nation states, into internal degrees of freedom. This was also associated with the potential for internal self-determination and structuring, which, however, came at the price of school processes being partially withdrawn from (state) supervision, as they remain today.

For centuries, questions about the form, content, aims and means of educational activity, and about the relationship between the generations and the transmission of cultural heritage, did not arise at all in the context of societal mediation. Education and instruction as we essentially still know them today only became important when religion split into multiple denominations, the feudal order declined, industry began to call for appropriately trained and educated workers, the expansion of the state administrative apparatus required its own training pathways and the emerging natural sciences began to question the idea of the religious and providential determination of human lives and associated world views.

Although initially some types of education were reserved for the elite, over time, starting in the mid-nineteenth century, a principle calling for all children to learn certain academic skills was increasingly enshrined in national curricula, resulting in the phenomenon of mass schooling (Baker & LeTendre, 2005, 7):

> Since then mass schooling has become one of the most impressive cases of successful transmission of a cultural model in the history of human society, developing and spreading in relatively short time without limitations. Using mass schooling, most nations have achieved mass literacy within just the last hundred years, and currently there are no real alternatives to mass schooling anywhere. Full enrolment in elementary education was achieved before the middle of the twentieth century in wealthier nations and over the next forty years in poorer nations. (…) Mass schooling has developed and intensified over time as an institution, deepening its meaning for everyday life.

Mass schooling, and with it the development of modern education systems, involved a number of interrelated trends and changes. First, it was aimed at all children and young people as a matter of principle; second, teaching became more professionalised; and third, new didactic and methodological approaches were developed, along with new curricular content, which made it possible to address all pupils, at least potentially and in spatial terms (Vanderstraeten, 2004a, 262f.). The perceived limits to the possibility of educating all children and young people led to historical solutions of subsidiarity and thus to the creation of a profession, and later a discipline – special education – that assumed the task of schooling the children and young people deemed to lie outside those limits.

The rise of mass schooling, and later also institutionalised special education, was closely linked to two further developments: First, as already mentioned, the formation of nation states, which made it possible for the emerging special education sector to draw on state resources and no longer on charity and donations (a situation that had previously resulted in the founding of numerous special education institutions, but also their rapid failure); and second, the establishment of individual rights, which were tied to citizenship.[9] As we will see in the next chapter, the systematic expansion of rights in particular has been an important element leading to a present-day concept of inclusion that draws on an ethical-normative discourse, namely one that is specifically based on human rights.

The strong emphasis placed today on a human rights approach to inclusion and disability has its origins not only in the development of mass schooling and early special education, whereby education was increasingly regarded as an individual right, but also in the rupture of the Second World War and the resulting consequences for countries where the planned and systematic murder of disabled people and the elimination of all education for children and young people with disabilities (as well as appropriate professional training for teachers) are elements omitted from the national historical narrative. Indeed, the experiences of the Second World War paved the way for developments that culminated, among other things, in the protests and socio-political developments of the years around 1968, which also affected special education, albeit with a delay, and continue to exert an influence.

The rupture of the Second World War and the growing importance of human rights

Until the Great Depression at the end of the 1920s, most Western nations were in an optimistic mood, which, in turn, had an impact on the systematic development of special education as a profession and discipline. In many countries, an increasing number of special classes were formed, while the requisite teaching staff were trained in special programmes. The University of Zurich, for example, appointed Heinrich Hanselmann as the first holder of a chair for special education in Europe as early as 1931. He engaged in extensive travel and research activities and initiated international collaborations, as did other lecturers at European universities. However, these and many other efforts and developments were abruptly interrupted by the Second World War. The war years had devastating consequences – at least in Europe – and not only for the professionalisation of the field, which had been progressing steadily up to that point. During the war, training courses were discontinued, staff were drafted for military service and numerous institutions were closed or turned into death factories. For many people with disabilities, especially in Germany and Austria, the Second World War meant a life-or-death struggle, which they most often lost.

The devastating experiences of the Second World War

During the years from 1939 to 1945, approximately 300,000 people with disabilities (depending on estimates) fell victim to the various forms of euthanasia perpetrated under National Socialism, and thus to mass, organised murder, in Germany, Austria, Czechoslovakia, Poland and the Soviet Union, among other countries (Aly, 2013). From the passage of the first German sterilisation law (1933) – which was directly based on legislation in the United States on the sterilisation of "defectives" – until the end of 1945, the Nazi government oversaw the systematic murder of disabled German citizens (Proctor, 1988, 110).[10] The campaign to destroy "life unworthy of life" began early, at the same time as the construction of concentration and labour camps (Mitchell & Snyder, 2003, 857). Almost every hospital participated in the euthanasia programmes, which were mainly implemented through lethal injections and the withholding of food. Although the murder was carried out on a large scale and comprised various schemes, the "T4" programme (named after the department responsible for it at Tiergartenstrasse 4 in Berlin) has become particularly notorious. In that programme alone, approximately 70,000 people (around 60% of whom were diagnosed with schizophrenia) were murdered using carbon monoxide gas.[11]

Trauma recovery and burgeoning protests

The post-war world was shaped by reconstruction efforts and processing of the trauma suffered, not least in the field of education. The demographic shifts in the post-war period and the rebounding school enrolment rates led to challenges for the organisation of schools and the practice of special education.

The late 1940s saw the revival and reassessment of pre-war critiques of earlier approaches, concepts and practices (Winzer, 2009, 81), taking place in parallel to burgeoning movements that included feminism and the civil rights movement in the United States. From the 1950s to the 1970s, there were demands for better planning and teaching in special education programmes worldwide, championed not least by the parents of children and young people with disabilities[12] as well as disability rights organisations. Various laws, for example, the Rehabilitation Act of 1973 and the Education for All Handicapped Children Act of 1975 in the United States, "were undoubtedly related to disability rights organization, the merging independent living movement, right-to-education litigation, exposés of school exclusion policies and institutional abuse, as well as to the recent success of other rights movements, most notably civil rights and feminism" (Biklen, 1987, 515).

Criticism, however, also came from special schools, special education teachers and teachers' associations themselves. There was growing dissatisfaction, for example, with inadequately planned classes taught by untrained or poorly trained teachers. Objections were also raised about the complete separation of children in special and mainstream schools, respectively, which had far-reaching consequences not only for the segregated young people, but also for their teachers (Winzer, 2009, 84):

> Teachers involved in special education were isolated both pedagogically and physically. On the one side, they developed mind-sets different from those of regular teachers. On the other, classes were located in obscure places in schools – in basements, down dark hallways, in former closets, or in the back of the school building. Children were often totally segregated; although in the same building, they entered and left school at different times and were kept apart at recess.

Entirely separate spheres of responsibility also influenced the self-perception of education professionals (ibid., 197):

> Teachers of students with special needs assiduously developed their own sense of professionalism and authority. Increasingly, they developed a belief about their mission, how it should be carried out, and the credentials that qualified a person to enter the profession. In doing so, they generated new beliefs about educators' status and power in relation to the clients, to parents, to allied disciplines, and to the world at large. Professional affiliation was concretely manifested in new and more encompassing professional associations, journals, conventions, and meetings.

Critics further complained that the philosophy and practices of progressive education had been misinterpreted, that its curricula should be fundamentally child-centred and that its didactics and methodology should differ dramatically from traditional approaches. There was a steady increase in objections from professionals and parents (ibid. 80f.). In the longer term, however, this growing dissatisfaction and these critical voices coincided with social trends that accommodated and harmonised with their demands: The protests of the years around 1968, often identified with that specific year, and the subsequent socio-political developments thus set into motion.

The emergence of the concept of "inclusion"

While some scholars had already begun to question the alternative placement of disabled children before the 1960s, Lloyd M. Dunn's article "Special Education for the Mildly Retarded: Is Much of it Justifiable?" (1968) was certainly one of the first and most well-known publications to challenge the legitimacy of special education classes. Dunn argued that the practices in place for educating children with disabilities were misguided on both educational and moral grounds. From an institutional perspective, his criticism was directed both internally and externally. He accused mainstream education of simply surrendering to special education those children with whom it could not cope. Meanwhile, he criticised his own profession for subsisting largely on the charity of mainstream education, and for being inefficient and generally ill-prepared to teach children with disabilities.

The voices calling for the merger of special education and mainstream education as a consequence of this inefficiency became louder and more vehement over the years (see also Florian, 2014; Osgood, 2005; Stainback & Stainback, 1984). Critics of special education also shared a desire to present, design and ultimately implement alternative approaches and paradigms for educating pupils with disabilities. To realise these designs, they believed that a fundamental restructuring was required, not only of special education, but also of the entire public school system. A little later, in the early 1970s, many prominent educators within and outside the field of special education were already in open revolt against the entrenched and segregative system of special education. These debates set the tone for the 1970s and beyond and led to a period of intense introspection within the discipline (Osgood, 2005, 83f.).

The critiques emerging from, and within, special education were eventually channelled and resulted, in the late 1980s, in the concept of "inclusion" being used as an umbrella term for many associated demands. Researchers called for "the joining of demonstrably effective practices from special, compensatory, and general education to establish a general educational system that is more *inclusive*, and better serves all students, particularly those who require greater-than-usual educational support" (Reynolds, Wang, & Walberg, 1987, 394, italics inserted by the author).

The field of special education, which had come under such criticism, was also quick to take up the calls for the reform of general education. The demand for inclusive education for pupils with disabilities became the dominant ideology in special education. In essence, inclusion in the context of special education implied a fundamental conceptual shift relating to the status of people with disabilities in society as well as the granting of educational rights. The goal was "an educational model for all students – supple, variegated, and individualized – in an integrated setting" (Gartner & Lipsky, 1987, 368). In this sense, inclusion moved the field away from a redefinition of special education towards a demand for the reform of general education. Inclusive schooling in this context was equated with the restructuring of schools (Slee, 1997). Placement – the specific educational environment in which services were provided – became the central focus of the inclusion movement.

As a result, not only children and young people with disabilities gained attention, but also other social groups that had grown more prominent, in part due to changing demographics – especially in the United States and Canada – as these groups also clearly faced severe discrimination and disadvantages in existing school systems. They included, for example, black children and other young people of colour as well as those from families dependent on state welfare due to material poverty (Winzer 2009, 199):

> It was imperative in any effort to confront the new social demands on education that reforms should change the schools, not the students. This reform demanded reconstruction of the entire education system as the solution for preparing at-risk children, culturally and linguistically diverse students, and other young people for a global and technological society. If structural processes created inequality, then restructured schools would counter long-standing patterns of unequal access to the outcomes of educational programs and would pave a route to guarantee equity and equal opportunity.

Demands for inclusion thus had a socio-political *and* an ethical underpinning. The associated debates were based on considerations of social justice, non-discrimination, equal opportunities and related issues. The inclusion reform movement was explicitly *not* founded on research-based practices. The effectiveness of inclusion as a "treatment variable" remained unknown and was of no interest at all to most reformers. Some proponents of the reforms (Biklen, 1985; Gartner & Lipsky, 1987; Kerzner Lipsky & Gartner, 1996; Stainback & Stainback, 1988) even expressly opposed efforts to conduct empirical research on the success of inclusive education. They argued that it was a moral imperative to restructure the system and that ethical-normative arguments should be given more weight than empirical research. As the question of how to provide optimal education could, in their opinion, only be answered through moral enquiry, issues around the location of schooling and equal treatment of the concerns of pupils and relatives were prioritised over scientific authority. Research, writes Biklen (1985, 183f.), "cannot tell us that integration is right. We can answer it only by determining what we believe, what we consider important". This moral imperative also resulted in the rejection of epistemological arguments from traditional logical positivism, which had become increasingly prevalent in pedagogical research (Winzer, 2009, 200). It seemed that special education faced a choice: Either it moved towards a moral and political understanding of inclusive education, or it formed an alliance with a general-education approach that was increasingly scientific and positivistic in its arguments.

The downfall (or not) of special education

We in fact find a more complex situation than is suggested by the two seemingly clear outcomes mentioned above. Special education did not disappear, nor did it merge with general education or inclusive education. To be sure, it has never escaped criticism, and there are still many who see its existence as *the* main problem in the development of a genuinely inclusive general education system. In terms of *realpolitik*, however, special education has been a model of success in many countries around the world. Indeed, the number of pupils in special education is reported to increase every year.[13] The practical reality, from a global perspective, is that while most national and supranational education policies embrace, incorporate and promote the idea of inclusive education, they maintain a traditional orientation towards the special needs or disabilities of children and young people, even in systems or under labels claiming to be inclusive.

The reasons for the increasing number of pupils with special educational support needs are disputed: Are there really more and more children with disabilities, i.e. are diagnoses now more sensitive to individual learning difficulties, or does this suggest a destigmatisation of certain types of disability, which can now be openly displayed and embraced? Or do schools perpetually produce new forms of disability as a result of their behavioural expectations, i.e. do they individualise or transfer structural problems onto pupils? It is likely that both interpretations are correct to a certain extent.

In the context of this ongoing conflict, special education can be seen as a problem, but also as a solution to the challenge or goal of inclusion (Florian, 2007). This paradox is also emphatically reflected in the discourse. So far, very different approaches have existed largely unconnected to each other, with contrasting disciplinary positions on their axes. On one end of the continuum are those who explicitly identify as inclusive educators and reject the discipline and practice of special education; on the other are those who support the idea of inclusion but still see themselves as special educators.

It is worth noting that the positions here coincide with the respective stances taken towards the place of disability in this discourse. While traditional special educators focus on disability as a specific diversity trait (often exclusively and without considering other diversity traits), advocates of inclusion reject such a focus as too narrow or even misguided. Instead, they believe that inclusion should focus on (general) diversity and the differences of all people. The interesting question this raises is, of course, whether they succeed – or who succeeds – in sidestepping the problematic dual motives embedded in the history of special education and their consequences for inclusive education, or in finding appropriate ways of dealing with them.

The difficult role of special education today

Special education is now caught in a dilemma, to some extent. On the one hand, it has been criticised since its beginnings for not being available to enough children and young people, or for providing too few of them with specific, personalised support. From the 1960s onwards, there have been calls from some, especially from parents of children with disabilities, for more and better programmes and an expansion of special education for their children. On the other hand, there are many who fault special education for prematurely identifying children as disabled and placing them in separate classes (Lazerson, 1983, 16). Special education thus incorporates in a paradigmatic way what Martha Minow (1990) has called the "dilemma of difference". It occupies the space between the inclusion and exclusion of disabled people and functions in the service of a societal dual purpose of segregation and generalisation.

The work of special educators who attend to children with disabilities or "special needs" does indeed aim to include children who are excluded from the mainstream culture, curricula and school community (Booth & Ainscow, 2002). But special educators work in an education system that is built on complex and subtly deterministic assumptions about difference, deviance and ability, thus resulting from the outset in structural exclusion, at the very least (Florian, 2007). Both within and outside the education system, special education faces dwindling acceptance. In some cases, its continued existence is even seen as a sign of failed public responsibility.

The persistence of special education has also meant a continued focus on individualised approaches, such as the identification and assessment of individual needs, as well as the provision of specially trained staff. These measures do achieve a realisation of the right to education for those who, without them, would either be completely excluded from school education or would not be able to acquire it in a substantial way. However, this approach creates problems of inequality *within* education by enabling access to education, but at the same time (at least potentially) perpetuating discrimination, or even exacerbating it, as well as causing lifelong consequences for the people affected, both outside and after school (Florian, 2019, 701).

Conclusion

It might generally be argued that few issues in the field of education have historically attracted as much attention as inclusion. And only a handful of topics have exerted such a polarising effect, or generated so much (ongoing) controversy within the context of education studies.

Inclusion can look back on a long history, which has its roots (at least partly) in special education. Important ideas that can be broadly described as inclusive at this point – even without yet presenting a well-founded concept of inclusion – can be recognised as originating in and through special education. After all, special education was from the outset concerned with the fundamental equality and freedom of all human beings, and viewed education as a means of expressing and developing the essence of humanity. Even though people with disabilities were more the experimental objects than the subjects of Enlightenment ideas in the perspective of the eighteenth and nineteenth centuries, quite a few Enlightenment philosophers interested in education, as well as educators inspired by ideas of that time, succeeded in raising new and more widespread awareness in society for the concerns of people with disabilities, specifically in education. The

Enlightenment thus acted as a kind of "philosophy of liberation" for education in general, which, in turn, also benefited people with disabilities. Education was in this way liberated from traditional authorities, especially religious ones. Early French Enlightenment philosophers such as Diderot, Voltaire and Rousseau believed in progress achieved through science and reason, the perfectibility of man, individual freedom and the efficacy of empiricism (Winzer, 1986). Special education developed in parallel to these ideas and to general education in many respects, albeit with a slight delay.

If we compare the mass schooling that emerged in the wake of the Enlightenment in the eighteenth century, as well as the industrialisation and nation-building of the nineteenth century, with the way education was understood in pre-modern times and indeed throughout the major part of human history, we can see how revolutionary the idea of educating the masses really was. Education had previously always been a practical, situational and limited activity. Children and young people were expected to acquire a narrow set of skills, which usually did not include literacy or numeracy, that is, the schooling and skills acquisition that we are familiar with today. For the most part, they learned what they needed to know for life in their family, clan or tribe, and *only* that. They were brought up in the midst of everyday life, in an essentially non-reflective way, learning through direct participation in the life activities of adults. Only a relatively small proportion of society, an elite, had the opportunity to learn reading, writing and arithmetic. Therefore, most people, whether they had an impairment or not, were excluded from education in the sense we know it today.

We have seen that the historical development and expansion of special education had two different sources, one exogenous and the other endogenous. The first wave of development occurred after the introduction of universal compulsory education, which, in turn, was followed by a sharp increase in the heterogeneity of pupils in public schools. New organisational forms were created to cope with this heightened degree of diversity. Educational expansion and the simultaneous trend of diversification thus laid the groundwork for aspiring to the goal of educating all children. At the same time, however, growing diversity led to tensions between access and organisational constraints. Rules of admission and eligibility governed the exclusion of persons classified as "ineducable" or "disabled" (Richardson, 1999). In this way, education began – logically or fatally, depending on one's viewpoint – to "produce" its own disabilities.

The institutional dilemma of difference that emerged with the Enlightenment and the establishment of education systems has persisted for centuries. And in a way, it was education itself, with its strong orientation towards Enlightenment ideals, that produced its own "underclass" in the form of people with mental and severe multiple disabilities, that is, all disabled persons who experience severe limitations in cognition, autonomy and self-determination and thus are unable to fulfil Enlightenment ideals of ability due to their individual constraints.

In particular, the experiences of the Second World War and the euthanasia of disabled people demonstrated the fatal results of focusing on abilities (and the question of how they are to be used) or on the "otherness" of people in general, which ultimately led to the inhumane treatment of disabled people. The after-effects of those traumatic events can still be observed today, pointing to the profound consequences of the radical exclusion of people with disabilities. The experiences of the war had the result, on the one hand, that its lessons remained in collective memory, persistently reminding society of what can happen when an education system that regards itself as humanistic is misused for inhumane practices. The mission of special education today can therefore be regarded as the sustained and tenacious defence of the knowledge it has gained as well as its inherent humanistic potential. But, on the other hand, the trauma of the Second World War has also been used, especially in certain circles of German-language inclusive education, to describe special education *per se* as heinous and exclusionary: Partly with good reason, as some of its representatives once proved to be stooges of the Nazi regime of injustice, but partly also in a radical (*too* radical, in my opinion) and not very constructive sense. For example, it is common in these circles to supplement talks on inclusion with pictures of mass graves in concentration camps, the sign at the entrance of the Auschwitz concentration camp – "*Arbeit macht frei*" [Work sets you free] – or with the remark that the way disabled children and young people are educated today (in German schools, *nota bene*!) is identical to the way Jews were treated during the Second World War. Such comments are deeply disturbing for critical, historically informed listeners because they ultimately also lead to the denial or at least relativisation of the Holocaust in its historical dimensions. But these remarks also have another consequence that goes beyond historically dangerous comparisons, namely, they help to reinforce, albeit subtly, the now widely shared view in the field of inclusive education that inclusive schooling does not require any justification. The guillotine of historical change, some believe, has long since fallen.

For many educators, stakeholders and parents, inclusion was and remains a clarion call to reshape the field of education and discard many of the traditional categories for organising specific educational activities. The notion of special education as a parallel or separate education system to that available to the majority of children is also challenged by inclusive ideas. The debate is not so much about inclusion as a goal, but about the means to achieve it.

An interested observer of the two camps in this context might conclude that the main issue at stake is how to identify these means of achieving inclusion, as well as the degree and radicality of their implementation, so as then to promote them in various political arenas. But that would be a false impression, one that fails to take into account two aspects: First, it would mean simply assuming that no further clarification is needed about the exact nature of inclusion and inclusive education, beyond a general allusion to the right to education, without further explanations or elaborations. That, however, would be a major argumentative shortcut, as will become clear. And second, this assumption would also be problematic in that the issue of how to achieve inclusion would be detached, or at least distanced, from any discussion of the goals of inclusive measures.

There is also a further reason why we should not be too quick to discuss ways and means of achieving and implementing inclusive education at this point, but should focus on its aims. It can be assumed that the idea of inclusive education is itself historically contingent, and that its prospects of realisation are also measured by how it succeeds in meeting the needs of modern times. The historian Andreas Rödder (2017), in his widely acclaimed *Eine kurze Geschichte der Gegenwart* [A brief history of the present age], which situates the twenty-first century in its historical context, describes recent shifts in how the social order is conceived as creating a "culture of inclusion". Rödder also notes that the concept of inclusion was popularised through education, in particular through calls for children and young people with disabilities to be included in mainstream schools. The foundations of inclusion, however, are deeper and lie in modern developments that have resulted in the "valuing of people in the diversity of ways in which they live and appear, as well as the recognition of diversity as normality" (ibid., 116). Many modern societies are characterised by pluralism, which Hans Magnus Enzensberger (1988, 246) has celebrated for the German-speaking world in the following flowery description:

> Lower Bavarian market towns, villages in the Eifel and small towns in Holstein are inhabited by people no one would have dreamed of seeing there just thirty years ago. These include golf-playing butchers, wives imported from Thailand, undercover agents with allotment gardens, Turkish mullahs, female pharmacists on Nicaragua committees, Mercedes-driving vagrants, autonomists with organic gardens, gun-collecting tax officials, pigeon-breeding small farmers, militant lesbians, Tamil ice-cream sellers, classical philologists with commodities futures businesses, mercenaries on home leave, extremist animal rights activists, cocaine dealers with tanning studios, and dominatrixes with clients from higher management [...], carpenters supplying golden doors to Saudi Arabia, art forgers, Karl May researchers, bodyguards, jazz experts, assisted death specialists and porn producers.

Full inclusion, in other words.

In his analysis, Rödder draws a historical line of development from the emergence of human rights agreements (and human rights discourses), through questions of gender justice, to the growing encounter with diversity in a globalised world and the experience of social inequality. Against this background, he understands the "culture of inclusion" as the formation of a new normality, which is based not least on transformation of the concepts of equality, freedom, recognition and justice. In Rödder's view, a genuinely egalitarian ideal of justice has come to the fore, replacing the notions of justice formerly promoted by the liberal bourgeoisie. However, these new ideas about the social order are frequently in conflict with societal reality, which often proves to be anything but tolerant of heterogeneity, not to mention liberal, affirmative or egalitarian.

The resulting clashes naturally give rise to questions, both of how it might be possible to create an inclusive society given the conflict between reality and rhetorical aspirations, and of how we are to understand the construct of inclusion itself: How can a concept with such a socially formative dimension be discussed from a scientific or research perspective? And how might we even begin to analyse such a multidimensional idea that is valuable for both descriptive *and* ethical-normative enquiries (e.g. with respect to questions of justice)? These are the very two questions on which the next chapter focuses.

Notes

1 I also consider special education to encompass aspects of care and support provided to adults with disabilities.
2 Something close to a global perspective on disability, including with respect to education, might only be considered to exist in the form of the World Report on Disability issued by the WHO and the World Bank (2011) as well as the aggregated country reports and the monitoring of the UNCRPD. However, these are not intended to present a historical overview, but to portray the current situation of disabled people around the world as well as the status of human rights compliance.
3 "Idiot" of course referred to a much broader category than that of people with disabilities, and it was differently framed. Although the word is now used as a slur for people considered to be stupid, it derives from the Greek and originally meant something like "private person". In the ancient Greek *polis*, it referred to individuals who remained outside of public and political affairs and did not hold office, even if it was possible for them to do so. In ancient Greek democracy, which prioritised active, informed, male citizens *(politai)*, the *idiotai* enjoyed little recognition.
4 The early French pioneers in this area, it is worth noting, did not have much influence in Great Britain, perhaps due in part to British animosity towards all things French.
5 The first permanent institution for people with disabilities in North America – the Connecticut Asylum for the Education and Instruction of Deaf and Dumb Persons, founded in 1817 by Thomas Hopkins Gallaudet – became the model for many institutions that followed. The schools established at that time were run in a strikingly uniform way in terms of philosophy and practice. In their early days, around 40% of the teaching staff were deaf men. With the use of deaf teachers, sign language, special curricula and an isolated rural environment, these institutions became organisational hubs for deaf people. American institutions can therefore be described without exaggeration as the birthplaces of global deaf culture.
6 Many of these early ideas and instructional techniques live on today in the teaching methods developed by Maria Montessori and her successors.
7 Because the eighteenth century saw the emergence of the idea that human potential could be developed, it has often been called the "pedagogical century".
8 Communities such as the Jesuit order (and many Catholic orders in general), for example, came under suspicion of being more aligned with Rome than with the nations in which they were established. Debates on the religious orientation of education were integral to social and political changes, which included advances in secularisation and state-building. The need for a national education system, and thus a certain understanding of inclusion, was also used as a means to oppose other (often religious) interests.
9 Full citizenship for people with disabilities is a recent historical development that was accompanied and made possible by the expansion of (human) rights and the political struggle waged by disability associations (Carey, 2009).

10 Even if this killing represented the ultimate realisation of eugenic ideas, as it were, it must not be forgotten that eugenics reflected a social philosophy that was widespread at the time:

> Eugenics, primarily articulated as a benign practice to 'help' take care of disabled people who were by definition incapable of caring for themselves, provided a fertile field for multi-national cooperative engagement at the ideological level of biological aesthetics. By adopting a targeted catalogue of 'defective' conditions – epilepsy, feeblemindedness, deafness, blindness, congenital impairment, chronic depression, schizophrenia, alcoholism – European and North American eugenics resulted in a shared campaign of biological targeting that addressed deviance as a scourge to be banished from a trans-Atlantic hereditary pool.
> (Mitchell & Snyer, 2003, 845)

11 The programme, which was launched in October 1939 with the dispatch of notifications to sanatoriums and nursing homes, was officially suspended on August 24, 1941 after public protests by the Bishop of Münster, Clemens August Kardinal von Galen, but continued secretly until the end of the war through the murder of ill people in paediatric wards, homes for the poor and institutions specialising in medicated killings (Rotzoll et al., 2010; Seeman, 2006).

12 In Australia, for example, a small group of concerned parents and citizens met as early as the late 1940s to discuss the future of their mentally disabled children. Such meetings led to the establishment of schools, centres and homes for these children in Australia. By the 1960s, every Australian state had at least one such group. Altogether, these associations founded several hundred schools, workshops and homes, and they also engaged in successful political lobbying to obtain funding for their causes. But most importantly, widespread public campaigns led to a shift in the public discourse around mental disability (Earl, 2011).

13 In the US, for example, the number of pupils in special education rose from 6.4 to 7.1 million in the years from 2011–2012 to 2018–2019, while the proportion of pupils receiving special education services increased from 13% to 14% of the total school enrolment (National Center for Education Statistics, 2020).

4
THE CONCEPT OF INCLUSION

A confusing plethora of definitions

This chapter examines the use of "inclusion" as a term and concept. In aiming to determine the exact content and meaning of inclusion, we find a very fragmented field of discourse in education, where the term is defined in myriad ways. The orientations and focal points of these definitions vary greatly. First, they differ in terms of their systemic scope. At one extreme of the spectrum are definitions limited to the dimension of physical placement, which Göransson and Nilholm (2014) refer to as "placement definitions". At the other end, we find definitions that emphasise the transformation of education systems, sometimes even entire societies (Artiles, Kozleski, Dorn & Christensen, 2006; Florian, 2014).[1] Second, the definitions differ in terms of their social scope and the groups on which they focus. On the one hand, there are those that concentrate on pupils with disabilities or "special needs", while, on the other hand, some definitions regard inclusion as relating to *all* pupils (Göransson & Nilholm, 2014; Nilholm & Göransson, 2017).[2] Third, the definitions also diverge vertically in terms of the levels they address. Many are based on the level of individuals – as with the two sets of definitions mentioned above (specific needs of pupils with disabilities versus the needs of all pupils) – while others relate directly or indirectly to the community or society as the unit of consideration. The levels of application of most definitions range from the individual (mainly pupils or teachers) to the classroom and the school, which is understood both as a larger social organisational unit and as an institution within society (Florian, 2014), but they rarely shift to the societal level, and if they do, then at most in an affirmative way, i.e. as a call for society as a whole to change.

Len Barton, for example, favours a relatively vague, community-oriented definition of inclusion. This is evident, among other things, in the way he refrains from treating diversity in terms of the specific otherness of individuals, instead addressing it in a generic manner that is rather impersonal, objectified and abstract. Barton defines inclusion as follows:

> Inclusive education is about responding to diversity; it is about listening to unfamiliar voices, being open, empowering all members and about celebrating 'difference' in dignified ways. From this perspective, the goal is not to leave anyone out of school. Inclusive experience is about learning to live with one another.
>
> *(Barton, 1997, 233f.)*

And this community-oriented view is found even more directly in Allen and Schwartz (2001, 2), who also distance themselves from more restrained definitions of inclusion: "Inclusion is not a set of strategies or a placement issue. Inclusion is about belonging to a community – a group of friends, a school community, or a neighborhood".

In community-based understandings of inclusion, the relationship between individuals and the classroom community receives special attention. This is apparent, for example, in the definition proposed by Stainback and Stainback (1990, 3):

> Inclusion means providing all students with the mainstream appropriate educational programs that are challenging yet geared to their capabilities and needs as well as any support assistance they and/or their teachers may need to be successful in the mainstream. But an inclusive school also goes beyond this. An inclusive school is a place where everyone belongs, is accepted, supports, and is supported by her or her peers and other members of the school community in the course of having his or her educational needs met.

Here, the authors explicitly stress that inclusive education should not be limited to individualised teaching and learning methods, but should ultimately also have a social and normative value. School should function as a place of social acceptance and belonging.

At this point, it is necessary to qualify my above references to "definitions" of inclusion. Even a cursory glance at the literature on inclusive education suggests that it is an exaggeration to speak of definitions in the proper, technical sense. Many are not definitions at all, strictly speaking, but evocations or approximations of an idea of inclusion that often remains quite vague. Most attempts cannot be considered true definitions for two reasons: Either they are completely or nearly tautological (e.g. when inclusion is understood as "increasing participation and decreasing exclusion"), or they present substitute terms, leading us to wonder what is genuinely specific to "inclusion" in the first place, and what justifies the use of a certain term as delineated from other existing terms or concepts.[3]

The strong focus on schools and the lack of a debate on exclusion

In addition to the heavy emphasis on disability, two other points are noteworthy in the inclusion discourse. First, it is striking to observe how implicitly inclusion is associated with education and schools, without any additional thread of argumentation (Allan, 2012; Thomas, 1997). It requires a long search to find texts or approaches that do *not* deal with inclusion in the limited context of education and schools, which means that the prevailing approaches effectively equate inclusion with inclusive education or at least limit its application to that area. However, to use the concept of inclusion in this way without detours or further justifications is to ignore other, equally relevant spheres of life and contexts of participation (as well as their intersections), for example, housing, work, healthcare, democratic participation and access to the legal system. And moreover, with this narrow approach, it is assumed (at least implicitly) that inclusion in the education system, in schools and in the classroom has some kind of specific and paramount importance (compared to what applies in all other areas of life), but without clarifying exactly what this special significance is. Considering that most people spend only a small part of their lives in school, this direct application of the inclusion idea to schooling is astonishing, to say the least. However, the strong focus on education is not only problematic because other areas of life tend to get overlooked as a result. It also poses a difficulty for another reason. Following Hannah Arendt (1958, 8), we can observe that problems caused by adults and institutions are transferred onto schools and children, who, in turn, are expected to find solutions to the lack of social inclusiveness in other areas of life.

Second, it is remarkable that the debate focuses almost solely on inclusion itself, while only a few authors within education or education studies attempt any more exact definition of the dialectical negative term – "exclusion" (Kronauer, 2015). Instead, the authors who do discuss the latter term usually install a kind of automatism between inclusion and exclusion, which, in turn, requires justification. This can be observed, for example, in a definition of inclusion as "the processes of increasing the participation of students in, and *reducing their exclusion* from, the curricula, cultures and communities of local schools" (Ainscow, Booth, & Dyson, 2006, 25). It remains unclear, however, to what extent increasing participation means reducing exclusion, or what exactly the relationship between the two is supposed to be.[4]

In my view, the positive value orientation that accompanies the concept of inclusion – and especially the strong political and moral importance that is clearly attached to it – can only be recognised if we also understand what exactly is being combatted (and this, in turn, means that the relationship between inclusion and exclusion cannot be understood as a kind of complementary, automatic mechanism).

The assumption of a historically consistent line of development from segregation to integration to inclusion, as is often expressed at least in the German-language debate, cannot be defended either. This was already touched upon in the last chapter, where it was observed that even early Enlightenment ideas fundamentally aimed at achieving some kind of social involvement, and succeeded in rudimentary form, even while social exclusion was and remains a reality for people with disabilities. In this chapter, I show that it is not possible, even with the help of theoretical arguments, to maintain the assumption that exclusion has historically been overcome and that inclusion has thus been achieved. Specifically, I indicate that such an assumption lacks sufficient complexity in theoretical terms, for several reasons. Generally speaking, a meaningful concept of inclusion must not only succeed in describing phenomena accurately, but it must also be able to describe them in a way that is *different* from other concepts. If an existing concept were capable of representing all of the phenomena associated with "inclusion", then there would be no compelling reason to employ that term.

In our search for a definition of inclusion, we are confronted with a number of meta-theoretical questions, which I address below.

Inclusion between description and evaluation

To arrive at the core of a plausible definition of inclusion, it is not only necessary to answer questions such as "What is the significance of the category of disability, if indeed it has one?" and "What is the importance of education for inclusion?", but also to address very fundamental theoretical questions. One issue, the epistemological question of how different sources of knowledge are connected has already been discussed in the second chapter, leading to my proposal to reconstruct inclusion in a nonideal way. But a further question remains to be clarified, namely that of the relationship between description and ethical-normative evaluation in the idea of inclusion.

In conceptual terms, inclusion certainly combines both of these levels. As a term, "inclusion" can be used to *describe* states or processes as inclusive (or not), but it also clearly represents a pedagogical (and broader ethical-normative) objective. The concept of inclusion therefore has moral content; it *evaluates* something. We can distinctly see this link between description and evaluation in the proposed definitions of inclusion mentioned earlier. Consider, for instance, the definition set out by Stainback and Stainback (1990, 3):

> Inclusion means providing all students with the mainstream appropriate educational programs that are challenging yet geared to their capabilities and needs as well as any support assistance they and/or their teachers may need to be successful in the mainstream. But an inclusive school also goes beyond this. An inclusive school is a place where everyone belongs, is accepted, supports, and is supported by her or her peers and other members of the school community in the course of having his or her educational needs met.

Here, by way of example, first we see that the authors' aim is one of description, for example, when they state that "Inclusion means providing all students with the mainstream appropriate educational programs [...]" (ibid.). They are referring to learning material that should be accessible to all pupils in the same way (whereby the normative aspect is already apparent, even as the authors seek to describe or find other words for inclusion). By the time we reach the references to "belonging" and "acceptance", it is clear that a certain normative understanding of the two concepts is being applied. For there is no doubt that this usage implies not only a psychological or sociological interpretation of "belonging" and "acceptance", but also a prescriptive understanding built upon a normative one, in the sense of "this is how inclusive schools should be".

But how do these descriptive and normative elements manifest in the definitions of inclusion found in the literature? It is interesting to note that all of the definitions of inclusion, with the exception of some very restrained, placement-based examples,[5] exhibit strong normative features. Thus, for example, if inclusion is understood as something that enhances the degree or quality of participation that a person enjoys (i.e. quantitatively or qualitatively), the word "participation" certainly brings to mind various ways of describing what it means to take part. If, however, it is further assumed that inclusion reduces or even prevents discrimination, it becomes clear that strong moral evaluations are being made, because discrimination is obviously an ethical-normative concept. And within a genuinely positive perspective, also, for example, when inclusion is associated with "belonging to a community", or with "empowerment", the "celebration of difference" or "being open", as proposed by Barton (1997), a number of ethical-normative values and evaluative concepts are invoked that at least hint why inclusion might be considered morally valuable.

A definition of inclusion which, like one of those mentioned earlier, combines description ("participation") with evaluation ("discrimination") seems intuitively most appropriate for the phenomenon of inclusion. For we are really concerned here with certain conditions or processes in people's lived experience which are described as inclusive (or exclusive) for particular reasons and, moreover, are evaluated – for moral reasons – as good or bad. The latter aspect is then often expressed, as I have noted, through other positive values such as freedom, justice, recognition, equality or dignity, but also through negative values such as discrimination, marginalisation, stigmatisation or exclusion.

In many definitions of inclusion, however, this moral dimension is reflected not only in the ethical-normative values that accompany the concept of inclusion (and thus "pad it out"), but also in the action words used to describe it. When Barton, for example, argues that inclusion is about "being open, empowering all members and about celebrating 'difference' in dignified ways", this refers to attitudes and activities that people should have or do, which then result in inclusion as a positive outcome, or express inclusion itself.

The oft-encountered blend of descriptive and normative elements is not problematic at first glance. For it is clear that inclusion often has to do with physical presence, and with finding other ways of dealing with, or other attitudes towards, the difference and heterogeneity of children and young people. Nor is it very controversial to associate inclusion with anti-discrimination measures, or even specifically with the UNCRPD, which itself is clearly founded on an idea of inclusion.[6]

What is critical about the combination of descriptive and normative elements, however, is that the relationship between description and evaluation remains ambiguous. Little clarity is provided as to why, for example, physical presence should be considered an element of inclusion, i.e. why it is ethically valuable or a factor that contributes to full, positive inclusion. If we add to this the problem mentioned earlier, that authors often employ substitute terms for inclusion, or – like Barton – jump right in with evaluation and thus fail to clarify which *specific* states or processes are actually being described, then we can discern a larger problem that is also important from a theoretical and research perspective; it is a problem that can be resolved, however, if inclusion is understood as a "thick concept". We turn next to the meaning and benefits of this approach.

Inclusion as a "thick concept"

The idea of "thick concepts" can be traced back to the work of the British philosopher Bernard Williams. He introduced the approach in his book *Ethics and the limits of philosophy* (1985, 217f.) – not least as a way of addressing the separation of facts and values that had remained unchallenged since Hume – and thus became the first philosopher to use the term.[7] In Williams' view, thick concepts differ from genuinely and exclusively moral concepts, which might be called "thin concepts",[8] in that the former have descriptive *and* evaluative content, while the latter have evaluative content only. Thin concepts, then, following Williams, are represented by words like "good", "right" or "should",[9] whereas thick concepts are found in notions such as freedom, equality, justice, or – if we apply Williams' thinking – inclusion.[10]

Williams considers that "thin concepts" are only action-guiding, while "thick concepts" are both action-guiding and world-guiding. With "world-guiding", he is referring to something like explanations or categorisations (for social objects) in the world, not abstract categorisations as in the case of "thin objects". Thick concepts, for Williams, are therefore ultimately practical concepts. Even if they do not lead directly to action, they provide reasons for acting one way or another.[11] I proceed from the assumption that inclusion is precisely this kind of concept.

Interdependence theory versus two-component theory

A key question in the debate around thick concepts is whether their descriptive and evaluative components can at all be separated. "Separationists", or representatives of a two-component theory, such as Richard M. Hare (1952), assume that the elements of description and evaluation can and should be considered separately. In Hare's view, the statement "Nero was a cruel ruler" might thus be divided into a value-neutral description ("Nero caused deep suffering among his subjects".) and a normative evaluation (such as "It is bad that Nero as a ruler caused deep suffering among his subjects".). Critics of a two-component theory, such as Hilary Putnam (2002), object that this kind of separation does not take seriously the underlying link contained in statements such as "Nero was a cruel ruler". The descriptive component of "cruel" does not mean "causing deep suffering", as deep suffering can also be caused by acts that are not cruel. And the converse is also true: Behaviour can be cruel even if it does not cause deep suffering.[12]

Following the arguments of the critics of a two-component theory, this means that description and evaluation are somehow intertwined. This is the opinion expressed, for example, by the virtue ethicist Philippa Foot (1958), with the following justification: Evaluations always relate to things in the world. It is things in the world that prompt certain evaluations (for whatever reason) and not others. For example, it would be absurd to be proud of the number of planets in the universe or to consider a person crude just for breathing. But if, in a sense, the evaluation – or at least its focus – lies in the "thing in the world", then this means that the descriptive and evaluative components of a concept are combined in a way that calls for a specific kind of analysis.

The special link between description and evaluation expressed in thick concepts should not be understood in a metaphysical sense, but rather as serving a quite practical purpose, namely to improve our understanding of the world. In this regard, Kirchin (2013a, 18) writes:

> Thick concepts hold our interest in part because they seem to unite evaluation and description, in some way and, further, make us question what evaluation is. But, if that was all that they did, our interest in them would not be as high as it is. They are practical concepts and everyday concepts. They are concepts that pull us – and others – in certain directions and justify some actions and not others. We can use them to shape our world and colour it in special ways. Thick concepts are important to us and our world because they seem to be a necessary way of understanding what the world and its people are. If we understand what these concepts are and how they work, we might better understand ourselves and the world we find ourselves in.

It would be too much of a leap here to elaborate on the meta-theoretical disputes within the debate about the nature of thick concepts, as that would lead us into theoretical depths far removed from the topic at hand (Kirchin, 2013b; Putnam, 1992; Roberts, 2013). I believe that it is sufficient to focus on the basic idea of thick concepts that we can identify in the overlap between Putnam and Williams (as representatives of two different perspectives on thick concepts), even if they may disagree on the more nuanced question of how exactly the components of description and evaluation relate to one another. While Putnam (2002) namely assumes that these components are deeply intertwined and ultimately inseparable, Williams (1985) believes that it is possible to achieve a clear separation of the two. The common ground of their approaches lies in the referencing of descriptive and normative levels, as well as the view that thick concepts are able to provide an understanding of social facts and contexts, and thus an explanation of the world, while at the same time guiding our actions or at least their focus.

Two camps and the problems associated with them

We have seen that inclusion has been defined in widely varying ways, and with different emphases. From a theoretical perspective, many of the proposed definitions are problematic in that their descriptive and ethical-normative content remains unclear, or because they fall, generally speaking, into one of two problematic camps: Either they are too utopian and normative, or else they are too descriptive and restrained, and often excessively one-sided.

These camps thus pose two contrasting dangers. For the one set of definitions (which are comprehensive and strongly normative), there is the risk of ending up with a rather unrealistic definition of inclusion,[13] one overloaded with (partly contradictory) demands that hardly any person or institution in the world could satisfy, or that at least do not offer a remedy for all people or all institutions.[14] For the other set of definitions (which are highly restrained and descriptive), the opposite is true: They have almost no normative content and thus leave a substantial blank space, with the status of inclusion as a vision and educational objective remaining largely obscure. It is thus unclear what might be inferred from such a description of inclusion, or how it would actually be possible to gauge the success of inclusive measures or attempts to implement inclusion.

In the following, I go into more detail about the problems associated with the two camps. In this context, it will also be important to show when and why human-rights justifications of inclusion (by now very widespread) are problematic, and conversely, to identify the problem associated with very restrained definitions of inclusion that can particularly be found in quantitative empirical social research.

The problem of the first camp

The problem with the first group, as already mentioned, is the heavy normative weight attached to their definitions. But that in itself is characteristic of many debates in normative ethics. The specific problem here is the application of widely varying ethical-normative values as a matter of course, where the reader cannot help feeling that the authors or the representatives of such definitions regard them as self-explanatory. There is no other way to interpret the lack of in-depth analysis (and critical discussion) of the ethical-normative content of inclusion. While "theoretical terms are not sacred runes, they are tools to better understand reality. They can be changed. It's unfortunate when they lose their sharpness and cloud our view of reality", as Kastl (2014, 1, translation by the author) aptly puts it. Normative concepts may not aspire to the status of unchanging truths. As with descriptive theoretical concepts, they must propose intelligible categories that help us to better understand things and values in our world.

At this point, it is important to stress that references to "inclusion as a human right", or more specifically to the UNCRPD and the human right to inclusion ostensibly enshrined there, are not a way of sidestepping the desideratum of an ethical-normative justification of inclusion, for the following two reasons: First, the term "inclusion" is not defined or systematically elaborated in the UN-CRPD, but rather used in a pragmatic way, often in alternation with other terms such as "participation" or "sharing", from which it is not delineated. Second, the Convention also avoids using formulations that would imply individual legal rights clearly linked to inclusion (Kastl, 2016). Rather, the UNCRPD mentions inclusion in a relatively vague way in the "General principles" (Article 3) and occasionally makes specific reference to it, as in the clear example of Article 24, on education.[15]

This does not mean, of course, that there is no connection between (human) rights and inclusion (see also Kastl, 2015). The point here is only that references to human rights (whether established only in theory or granted and enforced through case law) cannot *replace* the justification of inclusion and its ethical-normative significance. Delegating the task of justification to the courts would surely have the unintended consequence of restricting the definition of inclusion to that which is legally enforceable. Such an outcome would be disastrous, not least because rights often cover a much narrower scope than one might assume, and certainly do not encompass the entire range of ethical-normative justifications. We can see this illustrated, for example, in Article 19 of the UNCRPD, which stipulates that people with disabilities should be allowed to decide for themselves where and how they want to live. They therefore cannot be obligated to live in special accommodation (for example, an institution for disabled persons). However, this right is negative or defensive in nature. It means that the state may not force anyone to live in a particular type of housing, for example, a care home, but it does *not* mean that the state must also actively promote and support the forms of housing that people with disabilities may prefer (for example, open, socially mixed accommodation with a range of services and assistance available on an outpatient basis). But that is exactly what would be necessary or at least desirable from a moral point of view. This example shows that ethical-normative justification usually ranges further than rights, which means that it encompasses more claims.

From a legal perspective, certainly, it makes sense not to understand rights in absolute terms, in the sense of striving to have them penetrate into every corner of our interpersonal lives. For it must not be forgotten that rights, in addition to imparting freedom, also have a freedom-restricting effect, in particular for the bearers of the resulting duties or from the perspective of the legal subjects affected. These may be states, institutions or individuals. For a broader understanding of inclusion that also makes sense in terms of education, a concept of inclusion that focuses exclusively on rights and obligations would be calamitous. Especially in educational practice, inclusion should not be reduced to a defensive right that is clearly limited in its scope, nor to (more extensive) positive rights of entitlement. Rather, we must recognise that inclusion and inclusive education also involve issues that cannot be dealt with or implemented through a rights-based approach, or only with difficulty, for example, in close interpersonal relationships and questions of psychologically perceived belonging.

But let us now turn to the issues that arise with the other camp, whose definitions are characterised by (an intention of) restraint in ethical-normative terms and the presentation of purely descriptive statements.

The problem of the second camp

Restrained definitions of inclusion are often encountered in empirical social research. Certainly, the most limited of all, including in terms of normative content, are known as "placement definitions" (Göransson & Nilholm, 2014). Although few authors explicitly employ them, such definitions do contain an idea of inclusion that reflects an implicit understanding at the core of quantitative empirical research in particular.[16] Often, inclusion is understood to be the structural placement and affiliation of pupils with certain diagnosed educational needs (e.g. "special needs") or special education support needs in mainstream classrooms.

For all approaches falling under this category of restrained definitions, including those that are more densely descriptive, problems arise that are to some extent the opposite of those in the first camp: First, these definitions are often too restricted in normative terms, and second, they are not complex enough from a theoretical standpoint.

Normative restraint becomes a problem whenever a definition utterly fails to clarify the nature of the normative content at hand, for example, the issue of physical placement. It is crucial for a normative substance or vision to be alluded to, or a potential orientation at least suggested, because even the most restrained definitions are ultimately based on the assumption that inclusion is a pedagogical objective and not a description of the *status quo*. In other words, while such definitions do treat inclusion implicitly as a thick concept, they at most only hint at the nature of its ethical-normative content.[17]

When we consult our own beliefs and perceptions, it becomes clear that a definition which treats inclusion mainly as a question of physical placement is too simplistic: Would we consider a pupil who sits in a classroom but otherwise cannot participate in any academic or social way to be included? The answer is clearly no.[18] We can conclude that such normatively restrained definitions are too simplistic from a theoretical perspective, *because and insofar as* they cover only a fraction of what inclusion means, and moreover because they cannot be tied to normative attributions of meaning, i.e. they cannot ultimately *also* serve as an educational objective.[19]

Now that we have identified the major shortcomings of both camps, it seems that a happy medium would lie in developing a concept of inclusion which contains distinct descriptive content, and in particular does not reduce inclusion to limited aspects such as physical placement, but which also (consequently) discloses a nuanced ethical-normative meaning. The latter element in particular must amount to more than a mere juxtaposition of values that are neither explained nor substantiated in terms of how they relate to each other.

Inclusion: the proposal

The celebrated German physicist and philosopher Hans Reichenbach once wrote that we should approach philosophical language like a zoologist observing a rare species of beetle, that is to say, as a neutral observer (Reichenbach, 1968). His analogy is appropriate for how philosophers analyse terms, critique them and propose new uses for "old" terms. In this context, the rare beetle is not the term "inclusion" itself, but all the existing definitions of inclusion, with their varying degrees of intuitive persuasiveness. I aim to counter these definitions, which generally fall into one of the two camps described – as being either too restrained or too normative – with a proposal of my own. With the exception of its final element, a form of this proposal can be found in *Einführung in die Soziologie der Behinderung* [Introduction to the sociology of disability] by Jörg Michael Kastl (2010, 2017), so far published only in German, unfortunately.[20] In this work, Kastl implicitly differentiates three elements of "inclusion" or "participation",[21] but only identifies the first, the structural involvement of individuals in societal contexts (i.e. systems, subsystems, organisations, groups or institutions) as inclusion in the proper sense.[22] However, I also wish to incorporate in my concept of inclusion two other modes of involvement that Kastl mentions but does not refer to as inclusion. These are, first, (social) participation, understood in a positive sense as taking part in social activity and having a share in resources, and, second, social integration. From an individual perspective, the latter aspect encompasses interpersonal engagement or the ties of individuals within their social environment. From a social perspective, integration can also be understood as group cohesion.

If Kastl (2010, 2017) only considers the first of these elements to constitute inclusion in the proper sense, that is due to his disciplinary focus on sociology. The terms and concepts "inclusion" and "exclusion" indeed boast a long and rich sociological tradition. As suggested by a reading of Kastl's book, it is therefore logical and worthwhile to explore the potential here for a concept of inclusion that can prove fruitful both in education studies and in education itself. As a sociologist, Kastl is interested in using the term "inclusion" correctly in the theoretical tradition of his own discipline, and is naturally less concerned with the ethical-normative aspects observed in education studies (aspects that I also find essential for the present context). However, as the project presented here does not claim to be an introduction to the sociology of disability (or of inclusion), we do not have to limit our examination to sociological literature or disability-related aspects that are mainly of sociological interest. In the next chapter, we will rather consider the justification of inclusive schools and inclusive education, a subject that is inherently normative. But beyond that, and more importantly at this point, the method I propose here requires us to comprehend and describe the *phenomenon* of inclusion in lived experience (and not primarily as a term discussed in a disciplinary context). So, it is also a question here of understanding what we (can and should) mean in everyday life when we refer to states or processes broadly as inclusive.[23] That is why we need to consider a wider range of sources. In addition to the sociological literature already mentioned, the psychological and biological literature (notably in the areas of developmental psychology and evolutionary biology) will also play an important role, allowing us subsequently to build a bridge to philosophical approaches, especially those that conceive of the individual as being embedded in social-relational contexts (Donati & Archer, 2015; Tomasello, 2009, 2019a, b). Theories and studies in developmental psychology and evolutionary biology are drawn upon in particular because they are able to substantiate the connection between interpersonal relationships and cognitive, social and emotional development and belonging in a way that also distinguishes us from our closest relatives, the great apes. By bringing together literature from sociology, evolutionary biology *and* developmental psychology, we can better understand and describe the broad meaning of inclusion, helping us, in turn, to explore the ethical-normative content of inclusion and inclusive education.

When I argue that the ethical-normative content of inclusion should be neither too ambitious nor too restrained, I am aiming for a medium-range theory that is able to guide our actions without claiming to present an overarching, grand and comprehensive theory. An approach of this scope can be soundly substantiated historically and theoretically, but above all it reflects a conscious understanding of inclusion in everyday life, one that can be derived from social practice, i.e. reconstructed from the application of the concept in our lived experience.

It might be objected that this commitment to a lived-experience understanding of inclusion is an attempt to pull oneself up by the bootstraps. In other words, it may seem that I am merely proposing what appears most convincing to me, the author, while in a sense falling into the very trap I was trying to escape. But is that really the case?

On closer reflection, it appears that an approach of the kind I am proposing is ultimately indispensable. Unlike the objects of study in the empirical (natural) sciences, the objects of ethical discourses on what is right in normative terms and what is good in evaluative terms (aspects that are always at issue in educational objectives) are *also* based on everyday moral discourses, even if they only represent socially embodied and realised versions of theoretical concepts (such as Kant's categorical imperative, for example) or else critically reflect the prevailing moral praxis. In this respect, theoretical and ethical-normative arguments do not differ from everyday moral arguments in structure or composition, but rather in degrees (in terms of content). They do, however, differ from arguments in the natural sciences, which at least aspire theoretically to the differentiation of true and false statements. Pedagogical-ethical objectives are not based on such claims to truth.

If we furthermore consider the path dependence that characterises the development of educational and other societal institutions mentioned in the last chapter, with the aim – as proposed in Chapter 2 – of building a nonideal theory of inclusion, it becomes clear that we *also* need to reconstruct inclusion precisely on the basis of everyday moral discourses. Only discourses and understandings of this kind are anchored in real lived experience, which, in turn, provides the starting point for critical analysis and scrutiny of their content.

The aim of reconstructing inclusion in terms of everyday understanding and making it explicit is, however, coupled with the challenge of not falling into conventionalism, i.e. of not simply reconstructing descriptively what "people think" and passing this off as a definition of inclusion. Applied to the context of schools, that would mean simply inserting the idea of inclusion into "school as it is". Any such attempt would fail to take seriously the critical potential inherent in calls for inclusion. In other words, the thorn in the demand for inclusion would be removed in advance. For there is no doubt about the importance, within the inclusion debate, of the strong tendency to criticise current conditions and express utopian aspirations. These aspects should not be smoothed over or excised.

However, if we are to develop a critique of existing conditions in the first place, we need to have an understanding of what we mean when we speak of "inclusion", and that is the focus of the rest of this chapter.

The definition

I begin with a very broad understanding of inclusion, in which it is conceived as *involvement in human, social modes of life*.[24]

Inclusion in a full, holistic sense thus refers to[25]:

1   The aspect of the *structural involvement* of individuals in social systems, in particular in the functional sub-sectors of society, for example, the economy or the education and training system (Luhmann, 1997, 2002; Parsons, 1967, 1971; Vanderstraeten, 2004a).[26]
2   The aspect of *participation*, which includes both having access to and sharing in social goods and resources such as education, political participation and other basic goods of society that serve to safeguard social justice (Rawls, 1971), as well as participation in social resources that are not subject to the logic of distribution (such as supportive communities).
3   The aspect of *integration*, i.e. the nature and extent of individuals' involvement in social relationships, as well as the degree of social solidarity or

cohesion of communities, groups and societies. Our level of observation shifts depending on whether we examine the situation of one or more individual subjects or social cohesion in a community, group or society, but in both cases, we are considering the aspect of social relations.

4   The aspect of a sense of *subjective involvement* and individual well-being in and related to social contexts. This aspect is crucial because it extends the question of social integration beyond the intersubjective and group levels to include the inner psychological sphere, and thus calls us to consider inclusion processes in terms of how individuals actually feel about their structural involvement in a given context, about being able to participate in that context (in whatever way) or about enjoying certain types of social integration. But the aspect of the subjective sense of involvement is also important for further two reasons: First, it can be used to better understand the particular challenges faced by certain groups – for example, people with mental illnesses such as depression or dissociative disorders – simply by making it possible to conceptualise and clarify their situation. And second, this aspect takes into account the fact that inclusion in various concrete modes of life depends (at least in part) on the value that the people concerned themselves attach to these modes of life.[27]

I have already noted that the definitions of inclusion presented in the pedagogical literature are unsatisfactory for a variety of reasons. Inspiration for the comprehensive and systematic definitions of inclusion proposed above can be found in sociology in particular, but also in evolutionary biology and developmental psychology. In the following, I will therefore set out the theoretical underpinnings for my proposal of how inclusion might be described and understood.

The sociological perspective

Our enquiry begins in the field of sociology. While in the field of education, the concepts of "inclusion" and "exclusion" as well as "integration" and "participation" cannot be regarded as indigenous, they are very much native to sociology (Bourdieu & Passeron, 1990; Castel, 1996, 2002; Luhmann, 1977b; Marshall, 1950; Parsons, 1970). The issue of societal cohesion and integration can even be described as one of the cardinal themes of sociology. This area was already of interest to early French and German sociologists such as Emile Durkheim, Ferdinand Tönnies, Georg Simmel and Max Weber.[28] Later sociologists who expressly studied inclusion and exclusion (as well as the terms and concepts employed in that context) were able to build on these early, fundamental ideas and theories. These thinkers came in particular from a background of systems theory[29] and French social theory,[30] with the latter adopting a normatively applicable perspective based on inequality theory that is especially relevant for the topic at hand.[31]

The study of societal cohesion in early sociology

For early sociologists, the backdrop to reflections on societal cohesion was their first-hand experience of the emergence of modern societies and nation states, whose transformation they sought to capture in their own theoretical work. They observed that the formation and development of modern, complex societies meant that cohesion could no longer be established through shared ancestry, religious belief or morality. Instead, they found that modern societies are characterised by functional differentiation and the division of labour. Autonomous subsystems emerge for different societal tasks, each fulfilling important social functions according to its own logic. People in modern times have also increasingly turned away from close religious and moral ties, especially to churches. These developments began in the course of the Enlightenment and intensified with the formation and consolidation of nation states in the nineteenth century.

The French sociologist Emile Durkheim used the concepts of the "social division of labour" and "organic solidarity" to describe these societal trends. In his first work, originally published in 1893, *De la division du travail social* (translated as *The division of labour in society*), he is particularly interested in societal "organic" solidarity as well as "social cohesion" and "integration" (Durkheim, 1984, 24) – or, as Luhmann (1977a, 22) later writes in his introduction to the German edition of Durkheim's first work – the "tear resistance" (*Zerreissfestigkeit*) of society.

Durkheim thinks of the division of labour – understood as cooperation and (positive) sociality – as being closely related to the formation of societal bonds. He sees the existence and social cohesion of a society as depending on the solidarity of its members in their actions. In this view, the evolution of a society is measured by the shift from "mechanical" to "organic" solidarity, or rather the displacement of the former by the latter. For Durkheim, this evolutionary change depends on, or is linked to, the size of a society. His hypothesis is that solidarity in small societies manifests itself "mechanically", namely through collective consciousness and a high degree of homogeneity among individuals. However, when a society reaches a certain size, not clearly specified by Durkheim, integration and social cohesion are only possible "organically", i.e. through solidarity based on the division of labour (Durkheim, 1984, 68ff). The association of like individuals is replaced by the cooperation of diverse individuals.[32]

The German sociologist Ferdinand Tönnies takes a somewhat different approach in his argumentation and epistemological interests. In his main work *Gemeinschaft und Gesellschaft*, first published in 1887 and translated into English not quite accurately as *Community and Civil Society*,[33] he hypothesises that true solidarity can only exist in small societies that feature a low degree of differentiation. Tönnies thus paints a rather glorified picture of the past and expresses scepticism about social differentiation in modern societies. With these premises, Tönnies not only develops his own theory of the historical development of society – which he views as originating archaically from the basis of communities – but also criticises the modernity that societies represent.

The basic elements of Tönnies' theory are easy to grasp, and indeed he makes his aims clear from the outset of his book (Tönnies, 2001, 17):

> My theory will concentrate on investigating only relationships that are based on positive mutual affirmation. Every relationship of this kind involves some kind of balance between unity and diversity. This consists of mutual encouragement and the sharing of burdens and achievements, which can be seen as expressions of people's energies and wills. The social group brought into existence by this positive relationship, envisaged as functioning both inwardly and outwardly as a unified living entity, is known by some collective term as a *union, fraternity* or *association*. The relationship itself, and the social bond that stems from it, may be conceived either as having real organic life, and that is the essence of *Community (Gemeinschaft)*; or else as a purely mechanical construction, existing in the mind, and that is what we think of as *Society (Gesellschaft)*.

He continues (ibid., 18):

> All kinds of social co-existence that are familiar, comfortable and exclusive are to be understood as belonging to *Gemeinschaft*. *Gesellschaft* means life in the public sphere, in the outside world. In *Gemeinschaft* we are united from the moment of our birth with our own folk for better or for worse. We go out into *Gesellschaft* as if into a foreign land.

Tönnies' work is distinguished not only by this quasi-ontogenetic perspective, and thus the assumption that we are first part of a community before we enter the foreign land of society; for Tönnies, society is also characterised by having only external goals, not internal ones as community does. In his view, although we may speak of a religious *community* or a religious *society*, these are two different things. A person is socialised in the former, but a religious society has specific qualities that include its system of codification and its relationship to the state. The functions and goals of the society and its institutions are imposed externally, i.e. from the outside.

In Tönnies' dialectic of community and society, a tendency to be deeply critical of modernity is apparent early in the book when he writes (ibid., 19): "Community means genuine, enduring life together, whereas Society is a transient and superficial thing. Thus *Gemeinschaft* must be understood as a living organism in its own right, while *Gesellschaft* is a mechanical aggregate and artefact". It is clear that Tönnies would like to see more community, and laments its loss due to modernity. Durkheim, however, is far less pessimistic about modernity and at the same time more critical of ideas of community, which he sees as susceptible to totalitarianism. He too assumes that "mechanical" solidarity can only flourish in small, clearly defined groups of people who perform similar activities. But he further posits that "organic" solidarity can develop among individual actors engaged in different roles and functions precisely *because* they are ultimately dependent on each other. Thus, while mechanical solidarity is based on similarity, organic solidarity arises from the contrasts among actors in their various activities.[34]

But how exactly is this theory to be understood? While, in Durkheim's view, mechanical solidarity is the social bond, the cement, that holds society together via the supra-individual "collective consciousness" (what Rousseau called the "general will" and Comte the "consensus"), the assumption is that this mechanism would recede with the transition to organic solidarity (for Durkheim) or society (for Tönnies) and then disappear altogether. But this raises the underlying question of what actually holds together societies, or indeed any groups larger than compact communities. Such cohesion must obviously involve factors other than similarity among members of the collectivity, as Parsons later conjectured (1968, 314).

The special twist in Durkheim's argument is his attempt to show that the very cause responsible for destroying the old form of solidarity – namely the increasing division of labour – could at the same time be considered the basis and origin of the new form of organic solidarity. The division of labour itself generates the morality needed by the society based upon it.

But how is this to be explained when similarity as a moral resource is less and less available in modern societies, where people interact mainly as abstract others due to the functional differentiation in place? Durkheim believes that emotional attachment does not only have to arise through similarity; on the contrary, very often we feel drawn to people precisely because they are *not* like us. From the observation that it is typical for a society based on the division of labour to combine dissimilar elements (i.e. people with differing characteristics, abilities and activities) in a durable association, Durkheim generalises as follows (1984, 16):

> We are therefore led to consider the division of labour in a new light. In this case, indeed, the economic services that it can render are insignificant compared with the moral effect that it produces, and its true function is to create between two or more people a sense of solidarity. However this result is accomplished, it is this that gives rise to the associations of friends and sets it mark upon them.

It would of course be too short-sighted to relate these observations only to friendships, as is implied in Durkheim's quotation. Another type of social relationship that results from the division of labour is the exchange of labour products. As we will see later, in a discussion of Michael Tomasello's empirical studies, this exchange cannot be reduced to purely economic or self-serving interests. Rather, there are many direct social relationships between individuals that are based on interdependence and, because of this, lead to an emotional bond between them, precisely *because* they rely on each other in the division of labour.[35]

Durkheim's work itself does not provide compelling evidence for these conclusions, for he restricts his remarks to the link between the division of labour and the emotional attachment found in friendships and other personal ties, thus leaving open the question of whether the same might apply for more extended groups. In essence, Durkheim, unlike Tönnies, paints a harmonious picture of the transition from community to society. Morality and solidarity are not rendered superfluous by the mechanisms of a modern society based on the division of labour, nor are they simply inherited from other societal forms. Rather, modern societies create genuinely new and distinct forms of solidarity and morality, the exact nature of which is left unclear in Durkheim's work.

We also do not get much help on this point from the early sociologist Tönnies. His work does, however, contain other ideas that are important for the present context, such as his dialectical analysis of community and society. If we put aside for a moment his view of society, which is so critical of modernisation, we find a crucial hidden element that sheds light on the motivational foundations of various aspects of inclusion.

But let us first take a closer look at what Tönnies actually means by community and society. In a community, which Tönnies views as originating on a small scale, in the "primal relationship" between mother and child and the family more generally, growing outwards towards "community of place" (the neighbourhood) and "community of spirit" (friendship or comradeship) (Tönnies, 2001, 27ff), he sees sources of mutual support, concord and harmony. He writes: "Mutual understanding and concord are one and the same thing: namely the will of the community in its most basic forms. Understanding operates in the relations between *individuals*, concord is the strength and character of the *whole*" (ibid., 34). According to Tönnies, this harmony cannot simply be manufactured or forced. Rather, he argues: "Understanding and concord grow and flourish when the conditions are right for them, from seeds which are already there" (ibid., 35). This is a crucial difference that will concern us later on.

Community is particular, and it is reciprocal. In this respect, Tönnies (ibid., 36) writes: "Community life means *mutual* possession and enjoyment, and possession and enjoyment of goods held in *common*. The motivating force behind possession and enjoyment is the desire to have and to hold". So, community is constituted by what is collective, shared and particular. And this spirit does not have to be restricted to close family ties, neighbourhood relations or friendships (ibid., 28):

> The spirit of kinship is certainly not limited by the walls of the house or by mere physical proximity. Wherever it is strong and lively in the most intimate relationships, it can find its own nourishment, feeding upon past memories and recalling close-knit communal activity, however far it may be from home. In such circumstances we cleave to physical closeness all the more, because only in this way can our longing for love find rest and harmony. The ordinary man, in the long term and for the most part, will

> feel at his best and happiest when he is surrounded by his family and his own circle. He is at home (*chez soi*).

Physical proximity is thus not the crux of community, even if – as Tönnies assumes – it is an aspect of what is most comfortable to people, a sense of their roots. The key aspects are rather shared feelings, unity and harmony. Society is contrasted to this as follows (ibid., 52):

> The theory of *Gesellschaft* takes as its starting point a group of people who, as in *Gemeinschaft*, live peacefully alongside one another, but in this case without being essentially united – indeed, on the contrary, they are here essentially detached. In *Gemeinschaft* they stay together in spite of everything that separates them; in *Gesellschaft* they remain separate in spite of everything that unites them. As a result, there are no activities taking place which are derived from an a priori and pre-determined unity and which therefore express the will and spirit of this unity through any individual who performs them. Nothing happens in *Gesellschaft* that is more important for the individual's wider group than it is for himself. On the contrary, everyone is out for himself alone and living in a state of tension against everyone else. The various spheres of power and activity are sharply demarcated, so that everyone resists contact with others and excludes them from his own spheres, regarding any such overtures as hostile. Such a negative attitude is the normal and basic way in which these power-conscious people relate to one another, and it is characteristic of *Gesellschaft* at any given moment in time. Nobody wants to do anything for anyone else, nobody wants to yield or give anything unless he gets something in return that he regards as at least an equal trade-off.

In society, people are essentially separate and so are goods, as Tönnies argues:

> All goods are assumed to be separate from each other, and so are their owners. Whatever anyone has and enjoys, he has and enjoys to the exclusion of all others – in fact, there is no such thing as a 'common good'.
>
> *(ibid., 52)*

People appear in society as universal others, no longer as particular beings. They are bearers of roles and thus of rights and duties that are ascribed universally, in the sense of "in relation to their role".[36]

If we transfer this understanding to the topic of inclusion, two objects of analysis emerge, with Tönnies in mind. These are, first, societal modes of involvement, which operate predominantly via structures, institutions and roles, are largely universal and which do not take into account particular demands and needs insofar as they are affectively neutral. In modern societies, such forms of inclusion are moreover strongly functionalist and specific, often framed in legal terms. Second, we have communal forms of involvement and the bonds between people in intersubjectively shaped relationships, which are described by Tönnies in such warm terms and by Durkheim in a much less glowing way, because he suspects them of latent totalitarianism.[37] In theory, communal forms of involvement are affective, i.e. emotionally engaged (whether they need to be described so effusively as "warm", as in Tönnies, is another matter) and, unlike forms of societal involvement, relate to people in their entirety, i.e. with their specific, particular needs, interests and desires. These forms of involvement obviously have great significance, especially of an ontogenetic nature, in that we inhabitants of the modern age also first grow up within these forms of interpersonal belonging *before* we are considered substantially, in biographical terms, to be (active) members of society (which of course does not mean that we are not already born into and grow up in a society with its pre-structured institutions as well as its codifications, rules, duties and rights).

The basic dialectical constructs of the founding fathers of sociology acquire even greater clarity if we further consider the ideas of the German sociologist Max Weber. Unlike Tönnies and Durkheim, with their interest in the question of how solidarity and social cohesion remain possible at all in modern societies, Weber's focus is on the *processes* of building society- and community-based bonds and their influence on the institutions of society (especially the degree to which they are open or closed). These processes are defined by Weber (1978, 40f.) as follows:

> A social relationship will be called 'communal' (*Vergemeinschaftung*) if and so far as the orientation of social action – whether in the individual case, on the average, or in the pure type – is based on a subjective feeling of the parties, whether affectual or traditional, that they belong together. A social relationship will be called 'associative' (*Vergesellschaftung*) if and insofar as the orientation of social action within it rests on a rationally motivated adjustment of interests or a similarly motivated agreement, whether the basis of rational judgment be absolute values or reasons of expediency. It is especially common, though by no means inevitable, for the associative type of relationship to rest on a rational agreement by mutual consent. In that case the corresponding action is, at the pole of rationality, oriented either to a value-rational belief in one's own obligation, or to a rational (*zweckrationale*) expectation that the other party will live up to it.

Interestingly, Weber assumes that any association in which people act together over a longer period of time (i.e. thus also draw close to each other through the pursuit of common goals) will result in a tendency to create communal bonds (*Vergemeinschaftung*) (ibid., 41).

For Weber, relationships are open when affiliation and participation are possible for all, and closed when participation and affiliation are conditional. He writes:

> A social relationship, regardless of whether it is communal or associative in character, will be spoken of as 'open' to outsiders if and insofar as its system

of order does not deny participation to anyone who wishes to join and is actually in a position to do so. A relationship will, on the other hand, bes (sic!) called 'closed' against outsiders so far as, according to its subjective meaning and its binding rules, participation of certain persons is excluded, limited, or subjected to conditions.

(ibid., 43)

The degree to which relationships are open or closed results, according to Weber, from reasons of tradition, affect, values or rational purpose.

With this definition, Weber already outlines in an ideal-typical way what we now call inclusion and exclusion in sociology. It becomes clear that inclusion and exclusion should first be viewed independently of whether the formation of communal or associative (society-based) bonds is being considered – i.e. whether we are looking at the open or closed nature of bonds in larger, more abstract, non-particular and institutionalised contexts or in smaller, particular and socially intimate ones. And second, it becomes apparent that Weber is referring and assigning meaning to reciprocal social action.

Weber's theory of closed relationships, unlike the theories of Tönnies and Durkheim, allows for the analysis of *processes* in which social actors seek to monopolise resources, privileges or power and thus exclude other actors (Mackert, 2004). In this context, theories of social exclusion can be underpinned on the one hand by inequality theory and illuminated on the other by theories of power. This means that we can assume, with Weber, that inclusion and exclusion affect important life opportunities and that we should pay attention to the asymmetrical power relations prevailing among social actors. These two aspects will also be of interest to us later, not least because of their relevance for French inequality theory.[38] Finally, a fourth classic sociological approach should be mentioned, one that is not very useful for the concept of inclusion, but gives us insights into its dialectical counterpart: exclusion. These are the ideas proposed by Georg Simmel.

The work of the German sociologist Georg Simmel is relevant to the present context because he was the first early sociologist to interpret inclusion and exclusion (although he did not call them as such) as a *relationship of simultaneity*.[39] He illustrates this view using the social position of the poor and welfare recipients as an example, regarding their life situation and status in society (1908) via a theoretical frame of reference where "inside" and "outside" play a simultaneous role, and thus not in terms of a binary "either/or" distinction (which is a perspective often adopted today). Simmel understands this dual relationship as follows: As mere objects of societal care, without rights in themselves, the poor appear in the role of the excluded vis-à-vis society. However, the fact that society provides them with welfare services is a demonstration that the poor are also part of society after all. Simmel further emphasises that it is not spatial, physical or territorial boundaries that are decisive for enabling or preventing participation, but social boundaries, which concern the negotiations and conditions involved in the prevailing societal regime.

Interim conclusion

If we briefly revisit the work of the founding fathers of sociology and their contributions to a theory of inclusion in modern societies, we see new outlines emerge. We will not adopt Tönnies' critical attitude towards modernisation, nor, in particular, his scepticism towards society-based bonds and his (naïve) glorification of community. But we can benefit from the analytical distinction he draws between communal and societal inclusion, where the latter produces and requires organic solidarity rather than mechanical solidarity, just as we can make use of Durkheim's reflections on the relationship between cooperation and sociality. And we will incorporate Tönnies' seemingly unremarkable observation that we are born into communities, grow up in them and are shaped by them before we enter society as if arriving in a foreign land. This idea, i.e. the quasi-ontogenetic view of human life and social cohesion, highlights the importance of the individual and social development of cooperation and sociality in the context of inclusion. This perspective is crucial not only because of its major ontogenetic significance for the upbringing of children, but also because it helps us to identify difficult but important transitions (e.g. between family and school or between school and the world of work) that still receive comparatively little attention in the inclusion debate.

Although the rough analytical distinction made between communal and societal inclusion is at least a provisionally useful construct (which Parsons later explored more dynamically and flexibly with his "pattern variables"), this does not mean that society is something that happens apart from or outside of communities. We must not make the mistake here of regarding community and society as two spheres that are distinct in social reality, and thus assume that people fall into one or the other or progress from one (a community, typically the family) into the other (a society), thus burning the community bridges behind them, as it were. On the contrary, community and society are plural, relational and conceptually complex. But the basic analytical construct reveals the key differences between communal and societal forms of inclusion, which are also of practical and political interest to us. While the former contexts are affectively charged and appear to be particular, often small-scale and exclusive, the latter are affectively neutral, tend to be objective, de-spatialised (even if only partially, as in the case of nation states) and inclusive in the sense that more and more people are included in society and its structures and systems – not least through political, civil and social rights. As we will see later, the broad analytical construct of community and society that Tönnies developed is laid like a net over the four elements of inclusion. For even if processes of building communal bonds primarily involve the aspects of social integration and psychologically perceived belonging, it has become apparent, for example, in the current pandemic crisis, that some forms of community-building also relate to questions of structural involvement and participation in goods. And the reverse is also true: The ways in which the bonds of society are formed should not be understood as completely divorced from close interpersonal relationships. This point applies in particular to inclusive education, which must be experienced through community, but whose conditions are often predetermined or shaped by society and are also intended to achieve societal results (for example, in the form of inclusion in the labour market).

At this point, we can add to our analysis the work of Durkheim, who allows us to conceive of societal inclusion as cooperation in the context of a societal division of labour. Durkheim, like Tönnies, is interested in identifying what makes society function, namely the cooperation of a diverse range of people. The structures that shape society, as Simmel also shows, have an effect on people independently of their individual feelings. It remains unclear whether these structures are thus more than the sum of individual attitudes and the subjective behaviours of actors (Simmel) or whether they are the results of the processes of building associative bonds that first produce rationality (and thus rational action by individuals) and, in turn, also shape it (an interpretation suggested by Weber).

Finally, from Weber, we can take the idea of inclusion in society not as a static state, but as a process. We can find further relevance in Weber's theory of closed social relationships, the broad potential of which was not recognised for a long time because the theory was applied in a limited way to the sphere of economics, more specifically to the analysis of how economic opportunities are maximised (Mackert, 2004).

Following Weber and Simmel, we can also identify three structural features that we can initially regard as purely analytical in nature. First, inclusion and exclusion, and open and closed relationships, occur in all contexts, whether on a large or small scale. Inclusion and exclusion thus have an impact not only on the education system or school classes, but also on a wide range of dimensions in interpersonal and social life, such as friendships, participation in sports clubs and so on. The extent to which certain instances of inclusion lead to or determine other instances of inclusion or exclusion is an empirical question. There are certainly contexts that could be described in general as rather marginal – or better yet, as specific and individual – while others have a wider social significance, not least because of their gate-keeping character. Second, it is the social – not physical – boundaries that determine whether participation is enabled or prevented. So, it is not (at least not primarily) a question of whether a child is physically present in a classroom, but of the opportunities for social participation that this physical presence makes possible. Third, we are dealing with relationships of simultaneity, not either/or relationships. Therefore, it does not have to be a contradiction to say that a child is effectively included in one respect (for example, because he or she has structural access to inclusive education), but poorly included in another respect (for example, because he or she has no friends, and thus is poorly integrated socially). And fourth, participation is always a matter of negotiating and dealing with the conditions of the existing order. Criticism of circumstances is measured against the prevailing regimes, not least of an epistemic nature, which are often hidden or unquestioned, and which must be exposed and subjected to critical reflection. To interpret inclusion and exclusion as relations of simultaneity, as

Simmel suggests, is fruitful in several respects, not least because it opens our eyes to other ideas that are important in the context of inclusive education, reminding us that school education in general and inclusive education in particular are subject to a number of tensions and dilemmas (Berlak & Berlak, 1981; Norwich, 2008, 2013; Tomlinson, 1996).

However, Tönnies' assessment that society only possesses external goals, unlike communities, which in his view are formed and maintained via internal, i.e. self-imposed goals, deserves critical scrutiny. While his perspective makes some sense in the case of communities, it is questionable whether it applies to societies with such clarity. After all, we can witness – as indeed we are currently experiencing in the context of the COVID-19 pandemic and the debate on structural racism that has erupted in the United States – how societal values are renegotiated, the goals of life within society are re-examined, and seeming certainties or conditions taken for granted (such as streets named after the representatives of unjust regimes) are undermined and increasingly criticised by large segments of society. Of course, the forums for these processes are diverse, sometimes fragile, prone to (new forms of) demonstrations of power (think here, for example, of the power of "big tech" companies like Twitter, YouTube and Facebook, as well as various forms of deliberate, sometimes state-controlled, misinformation) and more difficult to build and maintain. But they certainly exist and are one of the reasons why we can no longer say today that societal forms of cohesion do not produce internal goals, i.e. goals that society sets for itself. Indeed, that is precisely the outcome that civil-society debates – in addition to the division of labour – can produce, or at least hybrid forms of solidarity, cohesion and discussions of societal values.

In general, apart from the fact that we should not allow ourselves to be guided too much by the tendencies of early sociologists (especially Tönnies) to be critical of modernisation, we can observe the following with respect to each of the four early sociologists mentioned: With lifespans ranging from around 1850/1860 to the end of the First World War and the interwar period in Europe, they could not have anticipated the enormity of the developments stemming from globalisation and the resulting dynamics, nor the extreme degree and speed of social differentiation that has continued to shape the world at least since the end of the Second World War. Accordingly, the ideas that we can take from Durkheim, Tönnies, Weber and Simmel for the context of inclusion in our present-day societies are only general in nature, and to some extent untenable in their sweeping character, for all their analytical merit. We can render the content of their ideas more specific by considering the potential relevance of work produced by their successors, as discussed in the following.

More recent developments: systems theory and (French) social theory

While the first generation of sociologists, including Tönnies, Durkheim, Weber and Simmel, clearly laid the foundations for exploring questions of cohesion and the existence of society in general in the modern era, the second generation – among them in particular Thomas H. Marshall and later Talcott Parsons in the United States, Niklas Luhmann in Germany and representatives of French social theory, especially Robert Castel and Pierre Bourdieu – can be regarded as the founders of *explicit* sociological concepts of inclusion. They were all certainly inspired by the ideas of the original pioneers of sociology and went on to further refine that thinking. But they did not share Tönnies' critical view of modernisation or rely on Durkheim's rather vague construct of "organic" solidarity. Instead, they generated new analytical approaches that are still influential today and are helpful for the understanding of inclusion that is presented here.

In particular, the article "Citizenship and Social Class" by the British sociologist Thomas H. Marshall (1950) was seminal in the development of a sociological concept of inclusion, even though Marshall does not use the term "inclusion" in that text. He understands the involvement of more and more social groups in society – and thus their inclusion – as the successive expansion of civic rights. More precisely, he defines this expansion in terms of historically successive phases: Civil rights in a narrow sense, which are mostly negative, i.e. defensive (taking the form, for example, of freedom of speech, freedom of expression, the right to property, freedom of contract, etc.), followed by political rights (the right of co-determination, the right to vote) and finally social rights (such as rights to education, social benefits or a minimum standard of economic well-being). Marshall thus sees the inclusion of ever more groups in society as a progression of three stages (of rights). In his view, these are the elements that determine exactly which processes, resources and systems a person has access to, and when and how. In concrete terms, this might be access to voting, education, marriage or socio-economic support, for example.[40]

The first sociologist to use the terms "inclusion" and "exclusion" explicitly was not Marshall, but the American Talcott Parsons, in his article "Full Citizenship for the Negro American?" (Parsons, 1969). If there is such a thing as the genesis of (the explicit sociology of) inclusion and exclusion, it is that article by Parsons. Specifically, he there sets out the analytical perspective for understanding the inclusion of ever larger segments of the population as a key process in the differentiation of functional systems in the modern era. For Parsons, as for Marshall, inclusion is linked to the acquisition and expansion of civil rights. In that respect, he too makes the connection between inclusion and societal development processes.

Parsons' insights clearly contribute a great deal to our basic sociological knowledge. In particular, he elaborates on Durkheim's observation that growing societal differentiation is related to and dependent on demographic changes in the size and density of societies. He argues that we should look not so much at the size of an association, but at the specific social mechanisms that regulate participation in societal systems.[41] Unlike Tönnies in particular, who speaks rather crudely of communal and societal associations (or forms of inclusion), Parsons proposes the more nuanced concept of "pattern variables" (Parsons, 1960). This term generally refers to dichotomous decision alternatives that each individual can and must choose between, whether consciously or unconsciously.[42] According to Parsons, there are five pattern variables: Affectivity versus affective neutrality, universalism versus particularism, ascription versus performance, diffuseness versus specificity and self-orientation versus collectivity orientation.

A key assumption in the ideas of both Marshall and Parsons is that modern societies are structured in multiple subsystems, which means that differentiation must be seen as a feature inherent to them. Differentiation is also what distinguishes modern societies from pre-modern societies, because the latter (to follow Luhmann (2013)) initially form in segments, i.e. they are divided into small, spatially delimited associations such as tribes and villages, in which all members essentially occupy the same social role. Later, societies become stratified, that is, divided into hierarchically structured social levels. In descending order of societal power, these strata are the nobility, the bourgeoisie, the peasants and the destitute. Beginning in the early modern period, autonomous societal (sub-)systems then emerge which define themselves primarily through functions.

This trend, which intensified over the course of the modern era, meant that people no longer belonged to one system or class, but to many subsystems. This is a decisive and formative fact of modern societies, of which Luhmann (1980, 31) writes the following:

> Everyone must have legal capacity, be able to found a family, be able to exercise or control political power, be educated in schools, receive medical care if necessary, and be able to participate in economic transactions. The principle of inclusion replaces the solidarity that was based on belonging to one and only one group.[43]

Two assumptions are expressed in this quotation: First, in modern societies, people are involved in societal contexts in a variety of ways (and no longer just in relation to *one* role). This also means that individuals are treated in relation to various roles, which in a way protects them from being encroached upon in their entirety as persons, as indeed they were in earlier societies and communities, where they were addressed in their whole personhood, including their preferences, character traits, interests and needs. And second, in the final sentence of this quote, Luhmann refers to the phenomenon that in modern societies the bonds of solidarity (and thus the communal bonds between people) are loosened or at least take on a new form.

If that diagnosis is correct, then in a sense we might also conclude that disintegration – the detachment of people from close social ties – is the prerequisite for structural inclusion and functional differentiation (Kastl, 2017, 216f.). This is an extremely important point, because if it is true, then disintegration, taking the form of treatment as an abstract other, for example, as a pupil, is a *precondition* for structural inclusion, e.g. in the context of school education in modern societies. Disintegration would thus not be (*per se* at least) an expression of social indifference, marginalisation or stigmatisation, but a prerequisite for and an expression of structural involvement. This is a conclusion that admittedly takes some getting used to at first, because in a way it implies that a certain social distancing (in the form of abstraction from the purely individual and personal) is necessary for modern forms of inclusion (namely in the guise of organic solidarity, which refers, among other things, to a division of labour that is societal and no longer communal).[44]

Luhmann, as an important representative of a systems-theoretical view, further concludes that modern societies are characterised by full inclusion. This means that everyone is structurally involved in society in some way. Such involvement can be in a "performance role", for example, as a doctor, or in an "audience role", for example, as a patient (Luhmann & Schorr, 1988, 31).[45] Audience roles (such as that of a spectator at a football match, or a pupil or patient) are open to everyone at all times, at least in principle and formally (at a football match, for example, one first has to get there, and if the stadium is not accessible for a wheelchair user, this remains only a formal possibility). Performance roles (e.g. as footballer, teacher, doctor) are different, because they are tied to individual prerequisites, which may relate to education, career, skills, position or choice, among other factors. Such inclusion is structural insofar as it is granted and safeguarded through reliable and reciprocally predictable arrangements and features of institutions, i.e. it is in principle already attuned or oriented towards certain persons or categories of persons (Kastl, 2017, 228).[46] But of course, pure audience roles do represent a problem of non-inclusion, or of a kind of inclusion that is often problematic and not necessarily morally valuable, which disabled people commonly experience. Time and again, people with disabilities report how others speak *about* them instead of *with* them.[47] That is one way of demonstrating exclusion and – perhaps even prompted by good motives – expressing a lack of respect by not recognising the other as a self-determined, independent person.

This for now concludes our review of some of the major classics of early and more recent sociology in the context of inclusion and exclusion. As is certainly evident, these ideas will shape the concept of inclusion developed in the following.

The elements of inclusion

Structural involvement

Among the ideas that we can take from the early sociologists is that, as society entered modernity and began to exhibit functional differentiation, it also "invented" ideals of inclusion, as it were, in the form of structural involvement, which is achieved through three societal mechanisms: rights, roles and resources. Resources in particular prove to be crucial for the second aspect of inclusion, namely participation.

Rights

Rights are of special significance for structural inclusion. As Marshall (1950) has shown, in modern societies, these are especially human, basic and civil rights as well as positive legal norms that are linked to them (anchored, for example, in social law, educational law, civil law, procedural law and voting legislation). These rights and norms govern access to societal structures and social contexts (often including those with a communal orientation, such as registered associations).

Rights are of enormous importance in developed, functionally differentiated societies, among other things because the loosening of social community ties and the heightened individuality and freedom resulting from various forms of inclusion in more and more areas of society have led to a tremendous expansion of life opportunities for many people. In this context, individuals have become the authors of their own lives and are able to achieve, through a variety of affiliations, (at least partial) social advancement and recognised status. They are thus the self-determined shapers of their own lives and the beneficiaries of social esteem. However, the decline of relationships of mechanical solidarity, i.e. close communal ties, as well as the increase in functional differentiation and diverse societal relationships, often anonymous in nature, also mean that people are largely unprotected from the effects of these very forms of inclusion. They are thus also increasingly victims of larger societal trends and upheaval. Rights offer a kind of protection against such uncertainty. Both the Universal Declaration of Human Rights and the UNCRPD therefore place a very high value on the defence of human dignity. At least in democratic, liberal countries, it is also true that all rights apply without restriction to people with disabilities, who are, in other words, full members of society and the rights-based community like everyone else.[48]

Roles

Let us now turn our attention to the second aspect, that of societal roles, which, in addition to rights, are crucial for inclusion in modern societies.[49] Societal roles reveal that social status – in contrast to that of pre-modern societies – is no longer predetermined by hierarchy, but is instead based on function and sector. It also becomes clear that exclusion in modern societies should not be described or understood as "falling out" of societal relationships. Persons excluded from modern systems are not excluded in such a way that no expectations are placed on them, so that they "disappear" socially in some sense; on the contrary, in many cases, the excluded – among them, for example, the poor, the disenfranchised and the disabled – are faced with rather clear, strict and far-reaching expectations of various kinds. For example, unemployed people are expected to keep appointments at the employment office and there to provide detailed information about their expenses. Low-wage workers are expected to lovingly read children's world literature to their kids at bedtime, even in times of dire hardship or after ten hours of work at the supermarket till, thus independently preventing the onset or progression of "educational poverty". And chronically ill and disabled people are expected to cooperate gladly and actively in both diagnostic and therapeutic activities, no matter how embarrassing or invasive they may be.

The "exclusion" of certain groups of people described as marginalised must therefore be understood not as complete exclusion, but as a form of inclusion that is vulnerable and precarious (Castel, 1999). We can only recognise the difficulties such people face when we consider the range of expectations placed on them and compare their situation to an idea of "full inclusion". Simultaneous inclusion and exclusion, already described by Simmel, is thus the reality in modern societies, rather than any complete societal exclusion from all systems. Unlike in hierarchical societies, in which the excluded – for example, vagrants or other people without rights or status – actually no longer belong to society, whether conceptually or physically, and are therefore no longer taken into consideration, in modern societies all people are recognised in some way, be it as recipients of social welfare or as disturbers of the peace in the case of people begging for money. The inclusion of vulnerable people is often ambivalent, as it is also linked to the motive of controlling their social and living situation (Stichweh, 2016). This dual motive, as already shown in the third chapter, also permeates the history of special education and, to a great extent, the treatment of children and young people with disabilities as subjects (and objects) of educational efforts. Whether the tensions thus generated can be avoided at all with the help, or in the form, of inclusive education, and if so, how, is a question that will concern us in chapter eight.

As the exercise of a role can be restricted or made more difficult in the case of disability, modern societies – not least in the wake of the UNCRPD – have developed assistance models and legalised claims to aid. This, in turn, means that they have created new roles. The purpose of assistance models is to enable disabled individuals to perform roles as instructed and in line with their own interests. Self-determination is thus given a legal form and the disabled persons assume the role of employers, no longer recipients of welfare benefits (although of course they still are). This also generates – via the means of assistance – societal inclusion in the form of structural involvement, which, in turn, is driven by the hope of achieving social integration and psychological well-being (or psychological belonging).

Another way to increase inclusion in terms of structural involvement is to modify societal roles themselves, for example, by creating what are effectively special roles. This might be target-differentiated teaching in a mainstream school (to give one example in the field of inclusive education), a change to the status of people with severe disabilities under employment law, or the establishment of a second, protected labour market with appropriate roles for working people with specific entitlements (for example, upon the partial receipt of state support). However, this goal of inclusion via the creation of special roles or conditions may also mean stronger protection against dismissal, entitlement to extra rest periods or longer holidays, or even special workplace equipment for adults with disabilities. Inevitably, special roles also involve the acceptance of needs specific to groups or individuals. After all, these measures only make sense if it is assumed or anticipated that people with disabilities would suffer considerable disadvantages without them.

Resources

The third aspect we must consider is that functional and structural involvement in modern societies relies not only on rights and roles, but on the availability of formats for social action that can be used with or without assistance. This, in turn, requires personal resources (knowledge, skills, abilities, technical aids, etc.) that enable the effective performance of societal roles and the enjoyment of associated rights. If the appropriate resources are not present, both rights and roles turn out to be hollow, because they cannot be substantially realised or lived out even if they do exist formally. This phenomenon was already touched upon in the above discussion through the example of eroded rights and the restriction of entitlements, and the same applies for resources. As Kastl (2017, 232) rightly notes, "only when there are rules governing the conditions under which resources can be provided, and the authorities responsible for doing so, can people with disabilities be enabled in practice to take on concrete social roles".

Resources can be related to individuals or to the environment, and they can have an internal or an external origin. Personal resources are directly linked to the individual concerned, or can be managed by that person. These include the skills and abilities necessary to perform a particular role (such as physical abilities, language skills or educational qualifications), but also the possession of financial resources, goods or support (for example, from family or friends). The latter resources make it possible to assume roles in the first place, but unlike skills and abilities, they are of external origin. Environmental resources, meanwhile, relate to the social, physical and cultural environments in which people live. Such resources also crucially include attitude-related aspects, whether these are expressed directly or embodied by institutions. Environmental resources are important because it is not possible to determine on the basis of personal resources alone exactly what opportunities an individual will have to live the life of their choice. To do that, people also need to have a certain environment. This can be illustrated through a simple example. In a largely agrarian society, not being able to read (i.e. suffering in a sense from a lack of personal, individual resources) is not associated with any significant disadvantages, but in our highly literate society, it is. In a technologically advanced society, by contrast, physical strength confers only a marginal advantage in life, unlike in the aforementioned agrarian society. We could find many other examples demonstrating how personal, individual resources are to a large extent linked to environmental conditions. These, in turn, are influenced by changes and historical developments that cannot be reversed without major repercussions.[50]

It is the combination of personal and environmental resources that determine the set of opportunities available to a person. For this reason, it is also clear that compensation for disadvantages suffered (a path suggested by a free-market approach or an insurance model) is appropriate only to a limited extent when it comes to including people with disabilities in a structural sense. For, if the person concerned simply receives monetary resources (in accordance with the motive of freedom), but without consideration of what kind of participation this compensation actually enables, this means that the goal of inclusion itself is abandoned or at least is not addressed. That is precisely why many state resources are only available in the form of targeted resources (Wolff, 2009a). The state thus aims to pursue the goal of inclusion (or the idea that the state has of it) directly and to prevent the possibility of replacing this goal with others. In so doing, it also sends a signal regarding the societal importance of this goal and the societal possibilities for supporting and promoting it. Wheelchairs, for example, are not a private good to which a disabled person has unrestricted access (at least not where wheelchairs are provided as part of state benefits). A wheelchair provided by the health authority may therefore not be sold by physically disabled persons (even if they do decide to turn it into a go-kart for their children). The wheelchair is provided in order to fulfil a very specific purpose, namely to ensure the mobility of the recipient (as one of the prerequisites for their inclusion). The resource of the wheelchair is made available for this reason only. The same applies to personal assistants, who also constitute a targeted resource for people with disabilities. Assistants may not be called on without restriction, i.e. they are not slaves; rather, they are there to support the disabled person's capacity for action. A disabled person would not be able to employ a carer as a banker who could then make profits on the stock market, which, in turn, would allow another carer to be employed and thus save money in total. At the same time, a conflictual relationship becomes particularly clear in the case of this human resource, as persons providing care are of course not instruments without will, plans or interests of their own, as would be the case with robots. They are also concerned with their own social and societal inclusion (which means they may have personal preferences, interests and needs that conflict with those of the people they should be caring for). "Targeted resource enhancement" and "personal enhancement" – encompassing measures to improve people's personal, internal capabilities – are often generally the focus of more conservative inclusion literature. Both aspects help people to cope adequately, or better, in the real world around them, and in this way are also instruments of assimilation.

I deliberately use the word "conservative" in the preceding paragraph because the focus on personal resources, to the exclusion of environmental resources, is precisely what is criticised by more progressive or radical advocates of inclusion. The latter believe that it is predominantly (or only) environmental resources that impede the inclusion of people with disabilities in education and other areas of life. Those advocates of inclusion who subscribe to a social model of disability, and who therefore see disability mainly in terms of social structures, thus prefer a different way of distributing resources, namely "status enhancement" (Wolff, 2009a). They focus on the cultural, social and political changes that they consider necessary within society to achieve structural involvement. Among these essential changes, they suggest shifts in attitudes and the dismantling of basic barriers to access. Resources do come into play in "status enhancement", but the direct focus is on changing the very societal structures for which access – albeit indirectly and subsequently – may also require other types of resources.

The message sent in this debate is not that disabled people should be assimilated into existing conditions, but that the world should be adapted to accommodate the needs of disabled people:

> Changing the world rather than the person is a way of accepting individuals in their differences, rather than making them adapt to the world. Hence it respects individuals and communicates a message of acceptance and inclusion. It is also, typically, non-stigmatising, in that no one need to be identified as disabled in order to benefit from social policies of status enhancement. For example, once hotel rooms and other buildings are made fully accessible, no wheelchair user will need to ask for special treatment.
> *(Wolff, 2009a, 406)*

Here, it also becomes clear why status enhancement, to the extent that it is genuinely inclusive, is often a better response to disability, as "it sends a message of acceptance of people as they are, rather than how we need them to be for the sake of convenience" (Wolff, 2009b, 56).

Participation

The issue of resources has already focused our attention on the second element of inclusion: participation. In the sense proposed here, participation always refers to *positively* valued forms of involvement in social affairs. To have resources is to enjoy the access to, acquisition of and/or participation in goods, values and rewards; however, these are defined. They may include money and financial security (economic capital), participation in decision-making processes (political co-determination), positively valued social relationships (friendship, love, relationships of solidarity), education and culture (cultural capital) as well as prestige and social recognition (symbolic capital).

At this point, some readers will already have recognised the theory of capital proposed by the French sociologist Pierre Bourdieu.[51] And with Bourdieu, a theoretical tradition strongly influenced by French sociologists also enters the picture, one that can be linked to a normative understanding of inclusion, even if it has not fully taken that step itself. This potential exists, among other reasons, because the debate about inclusion and exclusion in this theoretical perspective is invariably tied to questions of social inequality and does not simply relate to diversity in a descriptive, neutral sense. Rather, social inequality is understood as vertical inequality and thus as a form of societal disadvantage that can and should be subject to social critique.

To understand the significance of Bourdieu's idea of capital, it is crucial to consider two other terms coined by him: habitus and field. Bourdieu views habitus as a mediating instance between structure and subject, i.e. as the embodied characteristics of the social sphere that arise through socialisation and generate certain patterns of action and perception. Meanwhile, in Bourdieu's work, the idea of social space is differentiated into various "fields" that replace the concept of society with all its dubious connotations (for example, as with Tönnies, the idea that society only has external goals) and unclear contours.

What unites Bourdieu's various forms of capital is that they involve accumulation strategies, i.e. the creation of profit in a broad sense (Jurt, 2012, 23). Bourdieu distinguishes between four types of capital: First, economic capital, which can be directly converted into money, such as material goods, inheritances or means of production; second, cultural capital, i.e. intellectual abilities, which are then institutionalised through academic titles, among other things; third, social capital, i.e. the capital of social obligations and relationships; and last, symbolic capital and thus esteem, which is acquired partly in conjunction with the other types of capital and is linked to them. According to Bourdieu (1984), it is not only economic capital (property) and the resulting social capital (networks of relationships) that lead to specific opportunities for participation as well as risks of exclusion.

Cultural capital in its various forms is also particularly important, especially in relation to education, as it allows us to better understand a large range of social inequalities and disparities of opportunity within society. Cultural capital appears in three forms: First, as an internalised state in the form of lasting dispositions; second, in an objectified state, in the form of cultural goods such as books, reference works or films; and third, in an institutionalised state, such as in the form of titles and jobs that confirm the possession of cultural capital (Bourdieu, 1986).

At this point, we can already identify empirical reasons why exclusion from mainstream schools is associated with wider and problematic exclusion or marginalisation. First, studies have suggested that the acquisition of cultural capital as a disposition (what is consequently called *Bildung* in the German-speaking world) suffers under conditions of special education (Peetsma, Vergeer, Roeleveld, & Karsten, 2001).[52] And second, it has been clearly shown empirically that children and young people who attend a special school are significantly less likely to acquire an educational qualification and thus an official certificate, which – following Bourdieu – represents an institutionalised form of cultural capital (Brzinsky-Fay & Solga, 2016; Solga, 2015).

According to Bourdieu, every field, including education, is characterised by its own values and rules. Capital exists only in relation to a field, more precisely through the associated means of production and reproduction, through the rules that determine the normal functioning of the field, and thus also through the profit that can be generated. Bourdieu also considers that what we call "society" ultimately consists of numerous distinct fields that cannot be subsumed under a single societal logic (for example, that of capitalism) (Bourdieu & Wacquant, 1992). The people who are "players" in these fields bring very different resources to them. But there are resources that can be considered trump cards because they can be used successfully in a variety of "games":

> In other words, there are cards that are valid, efficacious in all fields – there are the fundamental species of capital – but their relative value as trump cards is determined by each field and even by the successive states of the same field.
>
> *(ibid., 98)*

Formal education in modern societies represents just such a trump card. The growing importance of formal education (and associated credentials) is – as we will later see in more detail – one of the main reasons for the urgency and the political pressure to make education inclusive and to offer all children fair opportunities to acquire educational qualifications. And this represents a further argument for considering the issue of exclusion from mainstream schools as particularly pressing, in that it promotes inequalities among people.

The analytical difference, but also the close connection, between the aspect of structural involvement and that of participation in social goods, should by now have become clear. In particular, resources as part of structural involvement have proven to be a link between rights and roles, on the one hand, and opportunities for participation in modern societies, on the other. Only the possession of resources makes it possible for formally granted rights and roles to be substantially realised. Participation in societal goods is therefore key to inclusion, because only in this way is structural involvement enabled in a substantive sense. This aspect is also illustrated through Bourdieu's theory of capital, as discussed above.

The capability approach developed by Martha Nussbaum (2000) and Amartya Sen (1999) also highlights the reality that people can only participate substantially in goods if they actually have choices, and thus freedoms. If they are forced to lead a certain life, or have no choices at all, then they may be considered to participate formally in goods, but not in any manner that can be described as substantial. Understood in this way, structural involvement is a prerequisite for participation, but it does not ensure or merge with participation itself. Rather, as we have seen, it represents an independent element of full inclusion.

We also have to be careful here not to relate participation aspects to material resources and goods only, but also to consider the epistemic resources of a society. How exactly these are to be conceptualised, and what it means to be able to participate in the "knowledge" and creation thereof within a society, will be clarified later on. For now, it is enough to recognise that goods exist not only in the form of material capital of various types, but also in the guise of participation and the power to help shape and be part of social patterns of interpretation and societal knowledge.

A third, additional element of inclusion, understood in a holistic way, is that of social integration. But how does this element differ from structural involvement, and for that matter from participation?

Social integration

To understand social integration substantively, we first need to appreciate how the term "integration" relates to that of "inclusion" in education debates. A widespread view, at least in the German-speaking world, is that inclusion has replaced integration as the goal of educational efforts (Feuser, 2002; Hinz, 2002). This vision of change and displacement is linked to two ideas: One, already mentioned above, is the idea that inclusion concerns *all* people, while integration focuses on people with disabilities. The second idea is that inclusion is a matter of changing society as a whole, not about assimilating individuals or social groups. Of course, it is possible to agree with both ideas to a certain extent, i.e. with calls to move away from a pure and exclusive focus on disability and people with disabilities, as well as the shift away from assimilation as the only possible response to a lack of inclusion.

It is also possible, however, to pursue these two ideas (the idea of a broader understanding of inclusion that is not only related to disability, and the idea of accommodation *and* assimilation) without abandoning the concept of integration, or considering its use to be regressive or inappropriate. Indeed, the idea of integration serves to capture an important intuition, with an analytical emphasis on one aspect of inclusion that we have not yet addressed: To say that a person is well-integrated into their environment is, at least colloquially, to comment on the success of that person's social involvement, *not* structural involvement. In everyday language usage, integration is thus primarily a matter of dense and stable relationships within a social context (in a group of friends or a family, school class, sports club, etc.). And second, we do not mean that an integrated person necessarily has a lot of resources, goods or capital. Although social capital is part of our everyday understanding of social integration, it is not limited to that aspect. Social integration is only partly something that a person *has*. It is also not least something that a person *is* – namely a part of a social relationship.

However, the search for suitable theoretical approaches in sociology proves to be difficult here. The sociological literature often defines social integration in a way that is much more formalistic and much less dense and substantial than is necessary to account for the genuine content of this element of inclusion. Indeed, in the mainstream sociological literature, social integration is often narrowly and crudely understood as a person's involvement in, or attachment to, their social environment (Lockwood, 1964), or, as in Bourdieu, as a form of capital. Social integration is thus described in sociological literature as something that would be visible, so to speak, in the threads between persons, which, in turn, when viewed as a whole, form a spider's web.

But that is precisely what social integration is *not* in our everyday understanding, or at least not fully. When we think of social integration, we have in mind phenomena that are often not found at the junctions but in the dense and frequently complex "interstices" of individual interconnections, networks, units, subunits and nodes, which are difficult to translate into a purely analytical language.

Friendships are a good example of this. Focusing solely on how many linear, reciprocal relationships someone has in their life does not say much about the quality of their network of friends or their friendships in general. Rather, what seems to be crucial for friendship (at least that of adults) is the degree of (dense) trust and intimacy in such relationships. For this very reason, hardly anyone would actually consider all of the "friends" they have on Facebook to be friends in the true sense of the word.[53] The same applies to a certain extent at the societal level. Again, we would not consider social integration in society to be limited to the fact that someone is a member of a particularly large number of associative relationships, networks and systems. Rather, we would also take into account the opportunities and possibilities that arise through these diverse forms of societal integration. Inevitably, our focus must then turn to the tensions between formal structural involvement, participation and social integration in the broader sense.

Systems-theory approaches in particular, with their formalistic approach, do not (adequately) succeed in making clear the tensions between structural involvement, the actual opportunities for participation in society and social integration. French social-theory approaches, such as that of Bourdieu, are more successful here. But even they are ultimately unable to illuminate the element of social integration in detail and to explore its interplay with structural issues and resource aspects. And there are deeper reasons for that. For the category of social integration is recognised in social theory only in a superficial way, conceived of either as a question of connectivity in networks or as a "transaction" between people. Neither of these views, however, focuses on social ties as *relations*. The two relational theorists Pierpaolo Donati and Margaret Archer sharply criticise this restricted approach (2015, 20f.):

> Anyone can be 'connected' to some source (for instance, a journal, a retail outlet, or a charity) simply by being placed on a distribution list, which are frequently sold between enterprises and therefore indicate no wish to belong on the part of recipients or interest in the contents received [...] Similarly, 'transactions' is also a polysemic term which does not *necessarily* invoke or depend upon social relations. Its first dictionary referent (from the Latin *transactio, transactor* being a broker) is to 'a piece of commercial business done; a deal'. Here, again, someone can buy and sell stocks and shares online, transacting without any contact with another at all. Similarly, if a public speaker convinces us that his/her argument is good, in

what sense is this a transaction when even our acceptance remains unknown? At the other extreme, when a couple confesses their love for one another, this is relational, but what has been transacted? Equally, when people join a voluntary association (for a variety of motives), what is the deal? Ontologically, we need to give more attention to the relationship itself rather than subsuming all relations under an abstract noun such as 'transactions'.

Not only is the description of social relations in sociology a thin one, the ontological level is practically non-existent. For, with few exceptions (Sayer, 2011; Smith, 2010; Taylor, 1985), the real social capabilities inherent to human beings vanish into sociological insignificance. But this leaves a major gap, because the experience of a lack of social integration is indeed one that affects people frequently in this day and age (Donati & Archer, 2015, 14):

> Late modern society is systematically based on immunization *against* social relations and leads to the repression of social relations. The inability of individuals to acknowledge social relations has become the illness of the century (the endemic disease of self-referentiality). This absence of social relations 'retaliates' by causing distress and disorientation for the self, which increasingly experiences isolation, poverty (in a vital sense), and a lack of support in everyday life. To emerge out of loneliness becomes an enormous enterprise – and often a hopeless one.

So, how can this sociological blind spot be remedied and how can social integration be fleshed out in a meaningful way as an aspect of inclusion? Interestingly, we succeed in this by looking beyond sociology to social philosophy, as well as social psychology, even though we encounter some of the same problems there. The idea of humans as social beings has been around since Aristotle. However, the social character of human individuality has been all but lost over the history of philosophy (Horkheimer & Adorno, 1973; Chapter 3) or it has taken a direction in which people function only as atomistic units, identified by their functions and roles and detached from their social relations. Any attempt to understand individuals socially in a dense sense is, in this view, subject to the danger of collectivism (Donati & Archer, 2015). This danger is undoubtedly real, but so is the opposite risk, that of losing the deeper meaning of community and social belonging that goes beyond purely utilitarian alliances.

To comprehend social integration in its entirety, therefore, we need a more nuanced understanding of social relations. Of course, not all relationships are social in nature. For example, a relationship between a customer who repeatedly buys electronic accessories online and the retailer who provides them can hardly be described as social (at least in the narrow sense). So, the underlying question is: What do we mean by the word "social" when we use it in the expression "social relationship", without employing it as empty filler?

The term "social" is by no means straightforward. On the contrary, it is ambiguous and thus open to a whole range of misunderstandings. In general, "social" is used as a synonym for "collective" in the sense of referring to a body of individuals. However, as already noted, this usage is not only associated with the danger of falling into a supra-individual collectivism, which the Nazis also had in mind with their references to the *Volkskörper* (body of the people) and the *Volksgemeinschaft* (people's community); it also leaves no room for people's individuality. So, if these two dangers are to be avoided, "social" must be interpreted as "relational" instead of "collective".

To say that something is social is, in my understanding, to say that it is relational in the sense of having a social existence (with respect to the social order and not to other orders of reality, for example, the position of the stars in the solar system). But what is characteristic of such a social relationship in a way that is constitutive for our understanding of social integration? First, it is important to recognise that relationships between people have both an objective and a subjective side (Donati & Archer, 2015).

The early sociologists with their analytical conceptual categories return to the fore at this point. The subjective side of human relationships was already described by Max Weber, in what has remained the classic definition to this day. Weber (1978, 26f.) writes:

> The term 'social relationships' will be used to denote the behavior of a plurality of actors insofar as, in its meaningful content, the action of each takes account of that of the others and is oriented in these terms. The social relationship thus consists entirely and exclusively in the existence of a probability that there will be a meaningful course of social action – irrespective, for the time being, of the basis of this probability.

The subjective side of a relationship thus refers to an understanding of the actions of others (as well as their meaningfulness) that can be used to guide our own actions. And from an objective point of view, a social relationship can be seen as a network, a bond or a reciprocal connection between subjects. In this objective view, such a relationship is the result of the efforts of individual actors.

Relationships and affiliations often do not arise naturally or for objective reasons. They are mostly the result of social interactions and thus represent categories that are negotiated among actors. On the one hand, actors seek relationships and affiliations on their own initiative, for example, by making friends or joining political groups. On the other hand, relationships and affiliations also come about through classifications made by others, and often also through prejudices, which then result in (ascriptions of) affiliation that can be detrimental to those affected. These possibilities of influencing the way in which relationships and affiliations are shaped will be dealt with in greater depth in the context of disability, particularly in the next chapter. There, it will be shown that people with disabilities often experience affiliations as a matter of fate (especially interpreted in a negative way) due to socially exclusionary interactions as well as derogatory and marginalising master narratives. But it is already clear that social integration is a difficult aspect of full inclusion for people with disabilities. This is particularly because it is closely related to a healthy psychological relationship to the self and a successful development of identity, and also because it shapes, or is strongly linked to, the aspect of structural involvement, especially with regard to the resources that individuals have at their disposal and the roles that they can assume.

If we understand social relationships in the relational way proposed here, we can appreciate their special link to resources (especially the personal, individual resources of others). Social relationships are in a sense nothing other than "second-order resources" (Boissevain, 1975). After all, relationships create access to the resources of others. This shows once again why social integration is of such vital importance for full inclusion and its various elements. Social integration constantly reproduces itself and thus generates not only selective social integration, but ultimately a whole network of social relationships and embedded aspects. It is itself a precondition for the acquisition of resources, and also an effect of their acquisition. Bourdieu (1984) captured this understanding with his concept of capital and showed how different forms of capital complement and reinforce each other. Especially in the educational context, it is not only cultural capital but also social capital that is acquired at school (including through crucial school friendships), and this, in turn, enters into reciprocal interactions with other forms of capital. Relational inequality thus manifests itself on the one hand in the *actions* of individuals in a Weberian sense, as "social closure", and thus in the practice of keeping social relations exclusive and monopolising their benefits. And, on the other hand, it is revealed in the *interpretation* of social communities in the form of classifications, which are made not only via official designations, medical or educational categorisations (e.g. "pupil with special needs") or media reports, but also in fleeting encounters, private conversations and symbolic signs.

Often such classifications do not have the status of overt designations or official diagnoses, yet they subtly exert a lasting impact on both the external perception and the self-perception of the persons concerned. It is precisely because of their subtle, often hidden but omnipresent character that classifications are highly formative yet difficult to criticise openly. On the one hand, this is because they are often based on, or expressed through, personal feelings and not obvious structural conditions (e.g. lack of access to buildings) and are therefore less susceptible to critique. On the other hand, classifications also affect and even shape the self-perception of individuals, and consequently the social relationships that they can and will enter into.

The aspect of social integration contrasts with the patterns that come into play in structural involvement, which is conceived and designed from the outset to be rather juridical, universalistic, structural, functionally specific and affectively neutral. Social integration is often the opposite of this, which is one reason why it is poorly understood when its scope is considered solely in terms of formal networks or processes of exchange between groups. Social integration is often affectively binding, particular, not easily framed in law[54] and thus functionally rather unspecific. The idea of disintegration as the prerequisite for structural inclusion therefore only applies for certain forms of social integration, namely those that go hand in hand with a functional role ascription. Disintegration, understood in this way, implies the transcendence of pre-modern social relations in which people were always considered in their entirety, but not as the bearers of certain roles and functions that are interrelated in a societal division of labour. However, social integration also has other facets that are related to structural involvement, even if not in this direct way. If we assume – as already noted – that relationships are something like "second-order resources", then it also becomes clear how relationships (not least dense and non-formalised ones), or parts thereof, influence personal social capital.

The final element that we need to address in this context is the subjective and psychologically experienced sense of belonging. This is also the aspect of full inclusion that is most rarely understood as being part of inclusion.

Subjective belonging

Unlike the other elements of holistic inclusion, the aspect of belonging cannot be formally and abstractly reconstructed or isolated from subjective, ultimately individual, psychological experiences, as can be achieved in principle with social integration, for example. In contrast to the other aspects of inclusion, belonging is always tied to specific individuals and their subjective view of life, as well as their needs, interests and plans. This does not however mean that belonging should be considered in a haphazard way or detached from structures, participation or social integration; on the contrary, rather, it is precisely these other aspects of inclusion that set the stage, so to speak, or create the environment in which subjective experience is embedded.

This also has a negative side. The subjective sense of exclusion is also significant because certain individual experiences of exclusion can compound into an exclusion syndrome that encompasses the whole person and becomes reinforced and entrenched. For example, those who, due to their perception and evaluation of their precarious living conditions, no longer see any opportunities or possibilities for positioning and involving themselves in society are excluded in a substantial sense. This is also why it is so important analytically to differentiate and scrutinise the linkages between a lack of structural involvement and a subjective sense of exclusion (Bude & Lantermann, 2006, 234). Even cumulative disadvantage need not lead to social exclusion and hopelessness. A person's subjective perception of their own opportunities proves to be crucial. Individuals who, despite obvious disadvantages, feel that they can master their lives and that they have a place in the world may indeed be marginalised, but they are not excluded in a comprehensive sense.

By turning our attention to the subjective component of inclusion, we can also better understand circumstances in which people or groups of people (for example, persons with disabilities in institutions for the disabled) are systematically recognised, enabled and provided with comprehensive care, but nevertheless feel disconnected and excluded. This is not so much a matter of the lack of structural belonging, specifically related to resources, rights or roles, but a question of the subtle dynamics of the institutionalisation of "secondary participation" through welfare state arrangements in which, on the one hand, entitlements to care are acquired through restrictions on societal participation and, on the other hand, spaces of social integration and thus, in effect, subjectively experienced belonging are almost inevitably closed off.[55] Bourdieu and Wacquant (1999, 58), for example, described the precarious situation of many French children born to immigrants in France as follows:

> It is because they feel integrated that they take their objective nonintegration so hard. They experience as unjust the unemployment that hits them more severely than other French people: underqualified because, for cultural reasons, they have failed at school, they denounce the employers who – to say the least – are far from being disposed these days to give preference to hiring young people of foreign origin. Meanwhile, by reacting like this, these young people unintentionally feed the vicious circle that marginalizes them. Feeling excluded, they are led to adopt behavior that excludes them even more, simultaneously discouraging the rare gestures of good will made toward them: the communal spaces made available to them are often wrecked, the employers who take them on must sometimes confront specific problems (thefts, violence, etc.).

So, perhaps this form of exclusion may find expression in violence and destruction. However, the causes of the lack of subjective belonging are of a structural nature.[56]

We can observe that the lack of (structural, participatory, integrative aspects of) inclusion does not only directly affect subjective feelings of belonging or exclusion, but also the development of individual moral capacities. The philosopher Adam Cureton, who is himself legally blind, has summed up this problem faced by disabled children and young people in school as follows, in a paper that has not yet been published:

> Many students with disabilities [...] face special obstacles to their moral development from the ways they are often regarded and treated in school settings. When their peers ignore, exclude, or snicker at them on account of their disabilities, when their teachers are evidently reluctant to rearrange lessons or irritated by requests for accommodations, and when administrators pity but mostly ignore them, these expressed attitudes and forms of treatment tend to impair the development of self-respect in disabled students by leading them to regard themselves as defective, deformed, helpless, burdensome, or stupid. When disabled students have difficulties with

learning material or know that their prospects for employment or higher education are bleak, when their peers tease them about their mistakes or largely avoid them, and when their teachers have low academic expectations for them and focus mainly on keeping them comfortable and compliant, disabled students tend to develop defeatist attitudes that interfere with developing a love of learning and an effective commitment to otherwise cultivate their own abilities as much as they can for their own sake. And when their peers exclude them from games or group activities, do not befriend them, regard them as burdensome, or begrudge them for receiving special benefits, disabled students are less likely to develop the kinds of reciprocal fellowship, trust, and loyalty that may be needed to motivate them to accept and act from moral principles of any kind.

The fact that moral feelings such as trust and loyalty as well as social cooperation among people in general – which for Durkheim is the basis of organic solidarity – require reciprocal social relations for their development and success clearly shows how severely people can be affected if they are denied such social foundations, which have an impact not only on feelings of individual belonging, but also on the formation of moral capacities and thus the subjective underpinnings of social integration.

So far, our discussion has focused on the structure of inclusion and the analytical framework connecting the various elements of a holistic understanding of inclusion. The more in-depth reflections below are an attempt to reinterpret these ideas, particularly with regard to the elements of social integration and personal belonging, in terms of evolutionary biology and individual psychology. If we refer to recent research in these two fields, we see that the psychological foundations of the interpersonal and personal aspects of inclusion are not only shaped early in individual development, but also form the core of what it means to be human. This ontogenetic view of inclusion was already introduced in the remarks on Tönnies (although it remained implicit in his work). The form and content of human cooperation and sociality, as explicitly addressed by both Tönnies and Durkheim, is made even clearer in more recent research in evolutionary biology and psychology, especially in the work of Michael Tomasello.

The ontogenesis of inclusion in evolutionary biology and individual psychology

There are close links between the social relations that observably make up the fabric of our society and social relations understood as a (potential) part of our human nature, and thus as prerequisites for individual psychological belonging that develop in both a biophysical and a social environment (Donati & Archer, 2015, 19).

Philosophers of action such as Michael Bratman (2014), John Searle (2010), Margaret Gilbert (2014) and Hans Bernhard Schmid (2005) describe the cognitive and motivational structuring of such collaborative activities as human capabilities and motivations of shared intentionality. One of the world's best-known researchers, who has devoted a great deal of attention specifically to the ontogeny of the personal and interpersonal foundations of such capabilities, is the American evolutionary biologist and primatologist Michael Tomasello. His work is addressed in the following because of the great interest it holds for the context of human inclusion.

Tomasello's main thesis, briefly summarised, is that humans differ from their closest relatives, other primates, in that they have the capacity for cultural learning.[57] This refers, in Tomasello's view, to the ability to recognise other people as peers, to empathise with their intentions and to exchange roles with them. First, Tomasello thus presents a highly social, relational vision of learning and human life, rather than a merely material one. And second, he assumes that our form of life possesses, at a very fundamental level, a sense of justice and equality that derives from our evolutionary interdependence and life in communities.

In the process of early development, according to Tomasello, children begin to understand themselves and others as intentional beings. The realisation that others are like oneself serves as a stimulus for individual cognitive development. In Tomasello's view, the basis of the specificity of human cognition becomes apparent from around the age of nine months, when a human individual can empathise with other actors and thus learn not only *from* them, but *through* them (Tomasello, 2004). The child at this age becomes an intentional actor. Tomasello understands intentionality as the ability to make insightful and considered judgements and to act in a deliberate and thoughtful way. Intentionality requires logical reasoning and rational self-control. For beings dealing with other actors, this also implies the ability to understand these others as being guided by their own perceptions and goals, and to interact with them accordingly. This, in turn, necessitates social cognition and social action.

When it comes to these abilities, humans are fundamentally different from other animals, including their closest relatives, the non-human primates. It is interesting to observe that at the beginning of their lives they do not differ much from the latter, at least in terms of cognition. Two-year-old humans do about as well as adult chimpanzees and orangutans on IQ tests in particular when it comes to demonstrating their understanding of space, quantity and causality (Tomasello, 2008). But striking differences become apparent in social coexistence. Humans, unlike apes, structure their common activities through shared goals and mutual agreement. For example, in Tomasello's studies, when children wished to interrupt or quit a shared activity, they asked for permission to leave the group. Another key difference can be seen in communication. While apes in Tomasello's studies communicated primarily with the aim of getting others to do what they wanted, human children also communicated to share information and be helpful to others. They also wanted to share their beliefs and feelings with others, for example, by pointing at a bird, looking at their mother and crying out joyfully.

These capacities for intentionality can also be seen as a prerequisite for human upbringing and education, in the process of adults passing on information that children receive and use in a trusting manner. Tomasello's studies showed that only human children, not apes, played games in which they might use a pencil, for example, as if it were a hammer. This kind of play with objects represents a preliminary stage in learning about specifically human social institutions. And such institutions can only be formed through joint action over the course of generations:

> Human beings have evolved to coordinate complex activities, to gossip and to playact together. It is because they are adapted for such cultural activities – and not because of their cleverness as individuals – that human beings are able to do so many exceptionally complex and impressive things.
>
> *(Tomasello, 2008, w.p.)*

Thus, humans are the only animals that succeed in perpetuating themselves, in a way, even across generations that are not directly related to one another, in what amounts to cultural attainment on a broad scale.

But why has the human species been able to develop cognitive capabilities that go beyond those of other species (including those of our closest relatives, the great apes)? What is specific to the human mode of life, Tomasello argues, is that, as we have already seen, humans, unlike non-human primates, are intentional social beings.[58]

People are prepared from birth to become functional adults because they have (with few exceptions) the necessary genes and live in a pre-structured cultural world that usually provides active support for their development as well as active instruction in certain skills. Unlike many animals, however, they are not yet fully developed beings when they are born. The attainment of human maturity is a major developmental challenge that must also be accomplished by and through other, adult human beings. When it comes to facing developmental hurdles, the cultural environment of a human individual is vitally important for a variety of reasons. The particular kind of social environment that we call "culture" is a species-specific and unique ontogenetic niche for human development. We can here identify two ways in which the human cultural environment provides the context for children's normal development: As a cognitive habitus and as a source of active teaching by people who are already adults. The ways of life inherent to a group (such as methods of food preparation, home furnishing and so on) are already passed on to children because they naturally have to participate in these life activities due to their dependence on the ways in which adults live. This habitus, which also manifests itself in certain modes of social interaction, has a direct impact on cognitive development. It provides the raw material, as it were, with which children must learn to live. But human adults furthermore assume a strong, interventionist role in the development of their offspring. In all cultures and societies, there are things that adults actively teach children, even if only by offering them assistance. Thus, one of the most important dimensions of the transmission of human culture is that of adults actively teaching children. Teaching (whether in or out of school) is thus a type of social learning in which humans engage. Learning by imitation and through cooperation are also forms of social learning. And all forms of social learning are made possible by intentionality and the ability of individuals to understand their conspecifics as beings similar to them, with feelings and a mental life of their own.[59]

Communal activity – that of celebrating festivities, raising a child or building a house, for example – is thus the source of human communication abilities and a range of other skills. This point should be understood quite substantively. In contrast to nativist theories such as those proposed by Noam Chomsky, this does *not* mean that people are born with language abilities, but that these only develop in and through community:

> Like all social animals, humans interact with others of their kind, even forming relationships with them. But, in addition, humans – and perhaps only humans – can enter into various kinds of larger social groups and structures by knowingly playing a role in them. Taking up a role in some larger social enterprise is qualitatively different from interacting with other individuals directly.
>
> *(Tomasello, 2019b, 1)*

Aptitudes, abilities and normative expectations make up the basic infrastructure of relational, human sociality.

According to Tomasello, there are two types of relational thinking (and subsequent action). The first type concerns the concrete physical world of space and quantity, in which we can compare aspects such as larger-smaller, lighter-darker, more-less, higher-lower, same-different, etc. This kind of thinking is also partly exhibited by non-human animals. But animals do not understand or have functional categories for elements that are defined by their role in some larger activity. Humans are thus exceptional in their creation of categories such as wife, pedestrian, customer, guest, student, etc., that is, what Arthur Markman and S. Hunt Stilwell (2001) call "role-governed categories". This second type of relational thinking, which concerns social roles, seems to be typically human. And these connections are formed early in individual ontogenesis:

> Even before young children understand societal roles – of the type focused on by most sociologists and social psychologists – they have to come to grasp the notion of a more local social role in a more local collaborative activity. And this notion of social role in an interdependent collaborative activity is crucial to children's coming to have a sense of equality with others, a responsibility to others, and an expectation that others display the same attitudes toward them. The normative standards of moral behavior originate in collaborative activities in which we both have legitimate

expectations about our partner's behavior if we are to fulfill our joint goal and/or joint commitment.

(Tomasello, 2019b, 13)

So, as soon as children begin to evaluate themselves from the perspective of the "we" in the community, they can be said to have a sense of self. And, in turn, when these evaluations become moral, we can infer that they have a moral self or moral identity (ibid., 14).

As we have seen from the example of Adam Cureton's experiences, people need not only individual psychological foundations in the form of cognitive abilities to think relationally, but above all – and to a certain extent as a prerequisite for this – the social opportunities and circumstances that allow them to learn and apply these abilities freely. This brings us all the way back to our discussion of the analytical content of full inclusion. It has been shown that there are major developmental-psychological foundations for social integration and psychologically perceived belonging that can only be fully understood against the backdrop of the presence of structural involvement and substantial participation.

Conclusion

In this chapter, a four-part model was set out consisting of structural involvement, participation in goods, social integration and psychologically perceived belonging. Inspiration for a concrete understanding of this model and its theoretical underpinnings is found in sociology, on the one hand, and in developmental psychology and biology on the other.

At this point, we can reiterate the following ideas drawn from classic works: Social cohesion in modern times is no longer generated only in small social groups, but in an organic form through a society based on the division of labour. In this type of society, people do not (necessarily) cooperate because they are similar to each other (rather, they are very often dissimilar), nor do they need to have a sense of close connection to one another. Rather, they are structurally involved via diverse processes. It is also not the case that people are either included *or* excluded; instead, they are included in a wide range of life spheres, but often with a precarious status or in an audience role instead of a performance role. Early sociologists like Durkheim and Tönnies already made these observations in rudimentary form.

The fundamental structural conditions of inclusion, as I have shown, first concern rights: Basic human rights, civil rights, political rights and social rights, as well as positive legal norms linked to these rights, such as educational or social legislation. In modern societies, these rights and norms ensure access to institutions such as schools (Marshall, 1950). People are no longer structurally involved in societal subsystems via their family or class, i.e. through stratification, as in pre-modern societies, but rather through functional relationships and differentiation. Rights play such an important part in this context because detachment from class structures also means a loosening of ties and a role-based perception of people who are now no longer viewed in terms of their whole person, from a societal perspective, but "only" in relation to certain sub-aspects, i.e. their role and social function. In modern societies, rights thus also provide a kind of protective sphere for individuals viewed from this somewhat abstract perspective. So, what appears at first glance to be a cold-hearted and distant social arrangement turns out, upon closer inspection, to be a step forward in civilisation and a major advance in societal status for individuals.

Compared to the beginning of the last century, when Simmel set out his sociological analyses, today's society is characterised by a much higher degree of "inside" relations. In concrete terms, this means that, especially due to the existence of the welfare state and improvements in the general standard of living, many more people are included in society. However, the tension between *simultaneous* inside and outside relations is perceived all the more acutely, namely as a drifting apart of the social (i.e. both external and internalised) demands on one's own way of life and the actual possibilities for its realisation; as a tension between bureaucratic care by welfare state institutions and stigmatising paternalism and dependence; and as an experience of inclusion *and* exclusion (Kronauer, 2010, 24).

For the purposes of full or holistic inclusion, it is thus not sufficient to be formally involved in structures. Indeed, it is not even enough to say that institutional inclusion is a precondition of full inclusion, for it is also a matter of participation in goods that are developed or acquired in specific contexts. Thus, two aspects are important when we speak of institutional inclusion: Involvement in structures (formal membership) and participation in goods or resources.

Resources are needed if a structural position, for example, a role, is to be assumed and maintained. In other words, goods are required in order for someone to be a pupil, a voter, a plaintiff in court, a shopper in a supermarket or a wife. These goods are first of all personal resources such as abilities, skills and knowledge. But they also include financial, infrastructure and other types of physical resources. While roles place us in a certain deontic position and thus confer authority, resources enable us to experience ourselves as agents. Put differently, it is our resources that allow us to do and be whatever we wish based on our own good reasons. This, in turn, makes it clear that the use and enjoyment of resources is also tied to the power and influence of being able to have a say in their existence and form within society in the first place.

Third, holistic inclusion also involves being intersubjectively integrated in some respect, namely in multiple and above all gradational ways[60]: as someone whose existence is meaningful to others; as someone who is perceived as a contributor in various roles (and beyond); as someone who is regarded as an equal who "counts" or as someone who is cared about. We could easily add to this list. The point is that – in contrast to institutional inclusion achieved via structures and resources that are allocated to individuals, but do not actually *relate* directly to them as individuals – these aspects are particular and affectively not always neutral; on the contrary, they are often emotionally charged and without functional specificity.

We have also seen the importance of a fourth element of inclusion, the psychological sense of belonging. Most approaches to inclusion do not take this element into account. However, I consider it essential, for several reasons, to pay attention to this inner psychological dimension within a concept of inclusion, and not to treat it like a distant cousin of inclusion. For it is only through this element that the relational relevance of social integration as a subjective, individually experienced phenomenon *between* people can really be recognised and comprehended. Furthermore, this element helps us to understand why differing forms of inclusion and exclusion can have different effects on people. Ultimately, this is often not due to the objective structure of inclusion or exclusion alone, for example, the lack of ramps for wheelchair users, but to the reality that people process their experiences psychologically in various ways, that they have differing interests and plans, and that their biographical backgrounds may diverge quite a lot from others' experiences (for example, if they grew up in a care home and/or were beaten as children). Only by addressing this dimension of inclusion can we assess holistically whether or not someone is included, and in what way.

Michael Tomasello's research has shown that the core of what it means to be human is the capacity for social intentionality. This ability influences how we navigate social structures, participate in social goods such as friendships and cooperate with others. It is responsible, among other things, for the relationships we can form and how they make us feel. Social intentionality is the ontogenetic precondition for more complex forms of human inclusion.

The world has changed dramatically from that of the early sociologists' analyses. I would like to highlight four of these trends and their critical importance for inclusion.

First of all, social differentiation today is more diverse and complex, more accelerated and changeable. Durkheim's original question – How is social cohesion possible in the context of differentiation? – is now more acute than ever. Traditional concepts of socialisation, however, usually have no answer to these new forms of differentiation. And even theories of inclusion and inclusive education often fail to make clear the significance of such societal challenges.

Second, the contextual conditions for the formation of a generalised "other" that appeared especially crucial for societal cohesion in early sociological approaches have long since ceased to apply. We are now without clear and lasting role expectations, normative consistency or extensive societal consensus on important issues that affect us all (for example, environmental destruction or war-related threats). Key moral safeguards or institutions that could provide such certainties (e.g. churches, political associations) have been under pressure for years and no longer attract majorities within society. What all of this means for inclusion will be illustrated by the example of inclusive education in Chapter 6.

Third, in the face of increasing social change, socialisation can no longer be credibly conceptualised as a largely passive process of "internalisation", partly because there is less and less to normalise, that is, to present as normal and normatively binding. Accordingly, the traditional agents of socialisation – the community (for Mead), the family (for Parsons) or social class (for Bourdieu) – can no longer be seen as almost solely responsible for the process. One of the main aspects that becomes clear in this context is the strong pressure on individuals to be the masters of their own lives.

Fourth, in recent years, we have seen the pace of globalisation (not least in education policies) and digitalisation accelerate enormously. Our lives are shifting into the digital sphere to a large extent, and this trend presents both risks and opportunities for inclusion for people with disabilities. The winners, on the one hand, are those for whom innovative technologies (for example, reading and hearing aids, translation and dictation tools, wheelchairs, robots or exoskeletons) are crucial because they help them achieve greater inclusion and quality of life. The losers, on the other hand, are those who either do not have access to these technical innovations or cannot make use of their potential for either internal or external reasons.

All of these changes have implications for schools, and what they can and should do with respect to inclusion in particular. Before we get to that discussion, however, the next chapter will focus on the importance of disability in the inclusion debate.

Notes

1 Empirical research in the field of inclusive education in particular gravitates towards "placement definitions".
2 The debate on inclusion focuses almost exclusively on the inclusion of people with disabilities (Miles & Singal, 2010; Schuelka, Johnstone, Thomas, & Artiles, 2019a). In concrete terms, this means that even if the rhetorical aim of many texts on inclusion is to open up the debate with regard to the general acceptance of heterogeneity, in practice, there is usually a clear emphasis on the issue of disability. As we will see, this narrow view is justified in one sense, because this context highlights a difficulty of specific importance for children and young people with disabilities, namely the expectations of ability that are institutionalised through school, and can then manifest as disability. But the focus on disability is also problematic, on the one hand, because the inclusion debate should undoubtedly and rightfully deal with the acceptance of diversity and heterogeneity as such, and, on the other hand, because the context of the school, which often generates disability in the first place, remains untouched by critiques of its functioning.
3 A substitute term for inclusion is used, for example, when an "inclusive" school is equated with a "good" school. Authors who define inclusion in this way leave open whether there is any difference between the two. And this, in turn, raises the question of whether we should simply speak of a "good" school instead of an "inclusive" school (although we would then have to define what would constitute a "good" school). In this example, we can see how the dog chases its own tail: Either a "good" school is the same thing as an "inclusive school", leading us to wonder why the term "inclusion" is needed in the first place, or else each term pushes the necessity of providing a justification onto the other term, thus ultimately clarifying nothing at all.
4 A slightly different way of referring to exclusion in the inclusion discourse can be observed in the German-speaking world, where exclusion is viewed as a phase to be

overcome historically, or – ideally – as one that has already been overcome. In this view, the understanding is that exclusion is succeeded by separation, then by integration and finally by inclusion, the "north star", as described by Andreas Hinz (2006), a leading figure in the German-language debate.

5 These definitions at least aspire to remain purely descriptive, so that they can be used in quantitative empirical studies, for example.
6 A thorough look at the UNCRPD reveals, however, that the term "inclusion" is used only six times, and is not defined at all. In four of these usages, it appears in the set phrase "inclusion and participation". I am grateful to Jörg Michael Kastl for this observation.
7 The debate around "thin" and "thick" concepts arose in response to controversy over the perceived demarcation between normative and descriptive statements, or between facts and values, as defended above all by logical empiricism (which remained very dominant until the 1950s) and other positivist approaches.
8 Williams himself did not use the term "thin concept", but referred instead to "the most abstract concepts".
9 The actual idea, however, goes back to a seminar held in the 1950s at the University of Oxford, initiated and led by Philippa Foot and Iris Murdoch.
10 Although thick concepts mainly play a role in relation to ethics, they are also pertinent to debates on aesthetic and epistemic values.
11 Whether the distinction between "thin" and "thick" concepts is one of kinds or degrees is a question that remains hotly debated in philosophy today (Kirchin, 2013a, 2013b).
12 Examples might include the following: Deep suffering can also be caused by an operation, so it does not have to be the result of cruelty. And for the opposite case, we can consider an example drawn from recent events in Germany. A mother pretended that her children were paralysed or otherwise severely disabled in order to defraud various care services, as well as the school, of social benefits. Such behaviour would have to be described as cruel even if her children – as seems to be the case here – do not themselves exhibit suffering (Langer, 2019).
13 By "unrealistic", I mean that such definitions do not take seriously enough the complexity and challenges of modern societies and their institutions. A concept that reflects these conditions too simplistically, if at all, has little realistic chance of being put into practice in the real world.
14 The point here is not that approaches of this kind are entirely unrealistic. Experience shows, however, that such visionary concepts of inclusion are effectively limited to pilot projects and rarely translate into comprehensive, general applications (e.g. becoming compulsory for all schools in a country). This, I suspect, is largely because their proponents and participants have already internalised these visions. While this is no doubt a positive thing for the pilot projects concerned, it also means overlooking a problem that would arise if they were implemented throughout society, namely how the sceptics and opponents of such visions of inclusion might be won over.
15 The same remarks apply to the UNESCO Salamanca Statement (1994), which, like the UNCRPD, neither formulates binding legal rights nor defines inclusion.
16 It only makes sense, for example, to discuss the social or academic outcomes of pupils with disabilities in mainstream classrooms if a "placement definition" of inclusion is ultimately applied.
17 A recognition of normative content paired with normative restraint is often apparent when references are made to the UNCRPD, which in a sense has to serve as a normative "substitute theory".
18 It seems likely that such definitions of inclusion are not chosen for reasons of plausibility, but because the understandings on which they are based are particularly amenable to empirical research.
19 This also means that it may be highly useful in some cases, especially in quantitative empirical studies, to adopt a quite narrow understanding of inclusion and inclusive

education, conceived, for example, in terms of physical placement or academic parity with peers. However, this narrow perspective must then be made explicit, i.e. it should not be claimed that the effects of inclusive education as a whole (for instance) are being investigated.

20 The eighth chapter of this work, which is relevant here because of its focus on inclusion, integration and participation, is only found in the second, revised and expanded edition.

21 In other, generally shorter publications by the author (Kastl, 2018), this differentiation is made explicit.

22 In this respect, it would be more accurate to say that Kastl distinguishes three types of participation, rather than facets of inclusion.

23 It should also be noted at this point that not much depends on the actual term "inclusion". We could very well call the phenomenon something else, indeed perhaps we ought to, as inclusion is a very static term (from Latin "inclusio" = to include) that has only a limited capacity to express the processual dynamics of what we mean by it. Historically, however, there is a clear tendency in the discourse to conceive of inclusion as a comprehensive term (displacing other terms such as "mainstreaming" or "integration"). I take this tendency as an opportunity to propose a fresh understanding of inclusion, but without choosing a different, new term for it.

24 I assume that inclusion in the form that interests us here is a social phenomenon occurring in a human life context, representing a human mode of life. This seems rather uncontroversial, as no one would call a person "included" who only spends time with a pack of wolves, for example. Rather, people are included when they can participate in human ways of life. Real and fictional accounts of "wolf children" and other "savages" living outside civilisation testify to major efforts to include them in shared human experience (Itard, 1994).

25 Aspects one through three draw on the work of Jörg Michael Kastl (2017, 2018), as already mentioned, while the fourth and final aspect is based on my own reflections. I also depart from Kastl's approach in another respect, in that I understand inclusion as an overarching concept and not purely as a mode of structural involvement.

26 Particularly in sociological work oriented around systems theory, this type of involvement is referred to as "inclusion". To avoid confusion with sociological approaches that limit the concept of inclusion to this aspect, I consistently refer to it using the term "structural involvement".

27 To give an example: A young man I know with Down syndrome is an avid musician. His dearest wish since childhood has been to play his instrument in the local community band. Such membership has so far been denied to him, with vague justifications that certainly have a lot to do with the fears, phobias and prejudices of the other members. To understand the meaning of this instance of exclusion, it is not enough to think abstractly about belonging and marginalisation. Rather, we need to be aware of the individual needs of the specific person affected, in addition to the general human needs and group-specific needs involved. Only in this way are we able to assess concretely the quality and value of forms of inclusion for individuals and their personal preferences.

28 Max Weber can be described as the father of political sociology (Prager, 1981). His commentaries, for example, on the state as the only institution with a monopoly on violence over state territory, and his explanations of the relationship between bureaucracy and power, remain sociological classics.

29 Two names in particular stand out here: Talcott Parsons and Niklas Luhmann.

30 These thinkers include, for example, Robert Castel, Pierre Bourdieu and to a certain extent Michel Foucault. For the German-speaking world, this debate is particularly associated with Martin Kronauer.

31 Normative applicability, we might say, is one of the aspects that distinguishes French social theory from systems theory.

32 The two forms of society differ, however, not only in terms of their size and relative homogeneity (in the case of mechanical solidarity) or heterogeneity (in the case of organic solidarity), but also in that the former is established through cultural integration, while the latter involves integration in morphological-structural terms, i.e. solidarity based on interdependence achieved through the division of labour.

33 An earlier translation of *Gemeinschaft und Gesellschaft* was *Community and Association* (see trans. C. P. Loomis, London, Routledge and Kegan Paul, 1955).

34 Durkheim underpinned this assumption with a moral-psychological twist on Darwin's biological arguments, claiming that evolutionary development is both facilitated and improved as the division of labour becomes more complex, allowing resources to be exploited more efficiently and ultimately ensuring the survival of a greater number of people (and thus society) (Durkheim, 1984, 144ff).

35 This point perhaps becomes particularly clear in crises. As I write these words, the COVID-19 pandemic is in full force around the world. Numerous countries have imposed "lockdowns", meaning that, except for businesses that cater to people's basic needs, production and distribution are at a standstill until further notice, and sweeping curfews have been implemented in many places. Such decisions and the general crisis triggered by the pandemic have clearly brought to light the interdependence of people. And it is interesting to observe that this situation fosters new manifestations of solidarity that are closely linked to experiences of interdependence. Entire cities, for example, have repeatedly shown their solidarity and gratitude towards health workers by applauding collectively on their balconies at agreed times communicated via social media. It remains to be seen, of course, whether and how such spontaneous demonstrations of solidarity will prove lasting beyond this crisis.

36 Later on, we will deal with the question of whether there really are no "common goods" in society. I will disagree with Tönnies' assessment and argue that a relational view of society highlights social "common goods" that require at least partial inclusion if they are to be produced and enjoyed.

37 For a more recent take on the same critique, see Young (1990a).

38 It can easily be concluded that the welfare state, through its provision of social services, plays a major role in social "closure", and that certain professionals in the school context, such as school psychologists, are key actors in that regard. School psychologists can be seen as gate-keepers of sorts, in the sense that their diagnoses are crucial for granting or denying access to mainstream education for children with disabilities.

39 The approach of understanding the relationship between inclusion and exclusion as one of simultaneity is not widespread in education; on the contrary, in education circles, inclusion is usually viewed as a goal to strive for, and exclusion as a challenge to overcome (or continue to suppress) (Barton, 1999). Inclusion and exclusion are thus fundamentally considered binarily distinct states.

40 Following Marshall, a right to inclusive education would thus belong to the last generation of rights, that of social rights. Unlike the civil rights of the first generation, social rights are not defensive in nature, but are instead positive rights of entitlement. This means that they do not prohibit or discourage certain actions, but require the proactive efforts and appropriate resources that make the exercise of these rights possible at all. However, these are the very rights that have proved notoriously controversial, especially with regard to their concrete implementation, and that is indeed the case for the right to inclusive education.

41 Unfortunately, Parsons himself does not give any concrete examples of these points, so that readers are left without a more precise idea of what he means. In his posthumously published monograph *American Society* (Parsons, 2007), he lists a number of societal inclusion mechanisms that have undergone historical expansion: The introduction of the "poor laws", the establishment of formal education and compulsory schooling, and the possibility for immigrants to acquire citizenship status, to name just a few examples, which are to some extent also specific to British and American contexts.

42 Although Parsons' pattern variables correspond in a certain way to Tönnies' distinction between communal and societal contexts, or can be reconstructed along the same lines, they represent a more refined and far more dynamic approach to questions of societal differentiation. In contrast to the binary distinction between society and community, they allow us to comprehend and describe processes and conditions that are contradictory and conflictual, and by no means always unambiguous.

43 It goes without saying that Luhmann has a completely different understanding of solidarity than do Durkheim and Tönnies, for example, for whom solidarity did not stand in contrast to society. And even today, especially in the context of the COVID-19 pandemic, we can observe that the principle of inclusion has by no means displaced that of solidarity. As the situation in the spring of 2020, at least, demonstrated in many European countries (in particular Spain and Italy), the opposite may even be the case.

44 For many who see inclusive education as the realisation of a humane idea of communal cohesion that is ultimately based on personal contact, lived solidarity and mutual goodwill, acceptance and interests, this must seem like a repudiation. We will particularly see how this point can be considered and evaluated in the sixth chapter, which deals with the form of inclusive schools, as well as the seventh chapter, which is concerned with the ethical-normative meaning of inclusion and inclusive education.

45 Luhmann was of the opinion that exclusion could no longer be considered to exist in modern societies, as all people were involved or included in the functional subsystems of society, at least in an audience role if not always in a performance role (Luhmann & Schorr, 1988, 31). It was not until he visited Brazilian favelas that he partially revised his assessment of full inclusion in modern societies (Luhmann, 1995).

46 The education system offers an interesting practical example. Here, inclusion in terms of systems theory can be understood as a form of professional care. The performance role falls to the professionals – typically teachers – while the audience role falls to the clients, the pupils. What is specific to the education system, however, is that pupils are not simply recipients of professional assessments – like customers who visit a retail shop to find out about the latest washing machines – but are, as it were, performers themselves. This means that interactions as well as negotiations of expected activity and participation are of immense importance (Stichweh, 2016, 24). Observations and analyses in the context of school education thus take on a complexity absent from the case of client-vendor relationships.

47 The fact that a major BBC programme on disability used to be called *Does he take sugar?* speaks volumes in this context, even if the title was of course meant ironically or even cynically.

48 This assertion must however be qualified. In recent years, we have seen two substantial – and not only formal – tendencies towards the effective dismantling of rights in many countries around the world. First, many rights are being eroded in their substance, so that while they are formally available to people with disabilities, the benefits that should be safeguarded by these rights no longer allow such persons to live in security and relative prosperity. This is the case, for example, when insurance pensions are inadequate to cover the living expenses of individuals, including extra costs related to their disability, which means that they are forced to live in material poverty. Second, it can be observed that rights may lose their substantial meaning insofar as they are made effectively less capable of covering the needs of ever fewer people. In Switzerland, for example, a change in the eligibility requirements for a disability-related pension came into force a few years ago, with the result that people suffering from chronic pain (for example, due to whiplash) were no longer entitled to such pensions. This meant that they were significantly worse off materially and legally compared to others, considering that they were often unable to work due to their pain, but at the same time could not claim any legal entitlement to aid. Although this decision has since been rescinded, it shows how tenuous the substance of rights can become when their content is eroded or entitlements are reallocated.

49 The social psychologist George Herbert Mead (1934), for example, used the concept of the "role" not only to describe structural aspects of human society, but moreover to show how individuals interact with others in society and how they construct an understanding of themselves in the process. Modern theories that follow Mead in this respect, especially symbolic interactionism, emphasise the importance of social roles, both at the level of macro-relationships within society and at the level of face-to-face interactions.

50 Anyone who believes, for example, that the inclusion of people with cognitive impairments who cannot read or write might be achieved by reducing the importance of written language underestimate the consequences for modern societies of such levelling-down for the purpose of ensuring the fullest possible inclusion of all members of society. And those who think that the poor structural involvement of deaf, signing people could be ameliorated by requiring all people to learn sign language in school fail to consider what this would mean for people who have difficulty learning foreign languages (of any kind). For them, this additional requirement would increase, not decrease, the risk of structural strain and exclusion.

51 Bourdieu uses the concept of capital differently from Marx, for example, because he does not define it economically or restrict it to such terms. This also implies a rejection of the view, widely held in communist circles, that all elements in a capitalist system can be converted into commodities or monetary values.

52 It has to be noted, however, that the empirical research findings here are not as clear-cut as advocates of inclusion might wish, and probably cannot be applied across the board for all groups of people with disabilities (Waddington & Reed, 2017).

53 Certainly, different relationships vary in the degree to which close trust and intimacy are constitutive for them. This is undoubtedly the case to a greater extent for personal ties such as love relationships or close friendships than it is for relationships between co-workers in the office. The degree to which close trust and intimacy (understood psychologically) are specifically constitutive for school classes, and are important, even indispensable, for the development of children and young people, is not least an empirical question that cannot be answered with abstract generalities.

54 In this context, a threat to an important personal good, namely psychological and physical integrity, is only deemed to exist in certain circumstances, for example, in the case of domestic violence. When the state intervenes here, however, and the threatened individual invokes their rights, the exercise of such rights is not intended to enable the social integration of this person, but above all, much less broadly, to protect the legal subject and thus preserve their structural integrity.

55 In many cases, this limitation or impoverishment of social integration is not directly planned or intended. Nevertheless, it is clear that certain structural and social arrangements at least increase the likelihood of experiencing a lack of social integration and psychologically perceived belonging.

56 Waves of violence as a reaction to a lack of belonging, due to structural oppression, are particularly striking in the United States today.

57 Frans de Waal, another famous primatologist, locates the basis of moral behaviour in our closest relatives, the other primates (de Waal, 2009), whereas Tomasello argues that these capabilities are uniquely human.

58 Non-human primates may well be intentional and causal beings, but they do not understand the world in intentional or causal terms. For instance, in their natural environment, non-human primates do not point to external objects, hold up objects to present them to others, try to lead others somewhere to see a particular object, actively engage in showing or demonstrating to others, or intentionally teach others new behaviours. As an example, when non-human primates see another of their kind go to a watering hole, they can deduce what will happen next (e.g. that the other will begin to drink) and they can even devise strategies to influence events they foresee, but they lack intentional understanding when it comes to social action. Humans, however, understand that another human heading towards the watering hole has a

goal in mind (to quench their thirst), and, in turn, they can seek to influence the mental and intentional states of others, not only their behaviour. According to Tomasello, the cooperative behaviour of animals is always competitive and individualistic. That is, animals possess an individualistic intentionality, unlike humans who exhibit social intentionality. This has far-reaching philosophical consequences, not least of an epistemological nature. A chimpanzee, for example, never wonders if it is perceiving an illusion or pretence, as it also does not wonder what the other chimpanzee next to it is experiencing. The chimpanzee is only ever aware of its own perceptions, in its own world. The human capacity for joint, shared attention is what makes human social perception so unique, and thus also the relationship of humans to the world. For Tomasello, four differences between humans and other primates highlight the specific aspects of human communication: Humans are motivated to provide information unconditionally (i.e. without necessarily receiving anything in return); they communicate with the motive of sharing beliefs and feelings; they have communicative intentions and they are capable of recursively understanding the intentional attitudes of others.

59 In this context, the vast majority of empirical findings suggest that only humans are capable of perceiving their conspecifics as intentional actors like themselves, and therefore only humans are capable of cultural learning processes. Indeed, the crucial difference between humans and other primates is that humans can identify more strongly with their conspecifics.

60 Perhaps the binary view of inclusion and exclusion also stems partly from the fact that the many deontic powers that render a person's institutional status visible are not gradational, whereas interpersonal inclusion (and recognition) is achieved in a gradational manner.

5
DISABILITY

Introduction

The conceptual shift from integration to inclusion that took place from the mid-1980s to the early 1990s, encompassing the merger of general and special education into a single inclusive system, was accompanied by a significant change of emphasis (Gartner & Lipsky, 1987). The concept of inclusion was established to replace integration, which had come to be seen as too limiting because it was overly complex yet restricted to the physical placement of children with special needs in mainstream schools (Florian, 1998). For most advocates of inclusive education, the idea of focusing on disability as a label was even a no-go, or was viewed as posing a serious threat to the very idea of inclusion. According to these authors, the embattled "restricted" approach reflected only children's syndromes, disorders and "defects" and thus reduced the whole effort of inclusion "to a default vocabulary for a Gray's Anatomy conception of educational inclusion" (Slee, 2001b, 168). Consequently, approaches that linked inclusion to the notion of "special needs" or disability had to be challenged (Barton, 1997, 233), not least because they presupposed a distinction between "normal learners" and "less than normal learners", which, in turn, implied exclusion, in the view of such authors (Booth, 1995).[1]

The question of whether inclusion is actually about disability at all is not only of practical relevance, e.g. in terms of eligibility for additional resources, special accommodations in the classroom and so on. It also relates to the epistemological level, where we can consider disability research and theory as a (distinct) field of knowledge. The epistemological basis of disability is not only interesting in its own right, as it involves asking whether disability is defined and located in individuals, in relationships and/or in structures; it also influences the direction we take in laying the epistemological foundations of special or inclusive education,

DOI: 10.4324/9781003221326-5

for instance, in terms of the relationship between theoretical knowledge and empirical data (Crockett, 2001; Danforth, 2006; Kavale & Mostert, 2003; Skrtic, 1995).

If we want to avoid the potential danger of ignoring the reality of impairment and ill health as well as the struggle against exclusion that people with disabilities face, we need to reflect on the proper place of disability within a concept of inclusion. The view defended here rests on an important distinction, namely between inclusion as a theoretical concept and inclusion as a practical, applied concept. In general, the idea is that inclusion, viewed on a theoretical, conceptual level, should not be conceived of as restricted to a specific group in society. In other words, the lack of inclusion, which can manifest itself in various forms of exclusion, marginalisation and social disadvantage, is not limited to a life situation that we describe as "disability". We might also say that inclusion is not a "disability issue". Exclusion, marginalisation and social disadvantage are, after all, problems that many groups in society are exposed to. But when we think about the practical and political consequences of the lack of inclusion, we find that problems arise in different ways for different societal groups, and the issues involved become more complex. For instance, it can be shown that people with disabilities are exposed to certain risks (e.g. risks to their health) more often and more systematically, and these risks may overlap with those of war refugees or LGTBQI people – to name just two groups whose members also experience exclusion, marginalisation and other forms of disadvantage in mainstream society – but frequently they do not.

The devil is in the details, however. Indeed, our understanding of specific factors for exclusion, marginalisation and social disadvantage when it comes to disability is strongly linked to our conceptualisation of the phenomenon of disability itself. We therefore need to examine the models of disability that are defended within the inclusion literature. It is important to have a clear understanding of these models even if their proponents believe that inclusion is not about disability at all. For, in a strict sense, even viewpoints that associate inclusion with diversity *per se* (and not with disability in particular) adopt a very specific view of disability.[2]

Therefore, to substantiate the point that disability deserves a special place in the inclusive education literature, I will first introduce three approaches or routes that are used in the "disability-critical" narrative, before proceeding to discuss the arguments as to why disability should not be a focus of the inclusion debate, or should at least be interpreted differently. As I discuss these claims, it will become evident that the various assertions put forward are open to a number of interpretations. Some of these within the "disability-critical" narrative I find more convincing than others. The more persuasive elements will be adopted as part of a social-relational model of disability, whose significance I will explain through the example of inclusive education. My conception of disability addresses its social nature, simply put, but it also does not overlook the biological basis of disability: Bodily dysfunction, disease and impairment, to name just a few aspects. Moreover, the approach proposed and defended here is a contextualised and situational one that looks beyond ideas of recognising or celebrating diversity in education that can be considered overly abstract and ultimately hollow. My approach furthermore takes into account the dynamic developmental processes of childhood, in which it is not only individuals' physical, social and cognitive development that is of great importance, but also their shifting environment and their evolving and growing abilities. As childhood progresses, children move from the close-knit ties of the family to the more abstract and detached environment of school, which encompasses "thin" relationships in place of the "thick" social network experienced in the family and other close relationships. As they age, children's abilities continue to develop with respect to both their social integration and their capacity to perceive and deal sensitively with diversity. This reality influences the possibilities for inclusion that are open to them, but also the expectations placed on them, for instance, in terms of roles, responsibilities and duties. The way in which inclusion is shaped in practice is therefore dependent on the age-appropriate development of children's abilities and skills, and not only on their environment.

Change of emphasis within the inclusion literature

We begin by examining three main features of the inclusion debate that are important for addressing disability:

First, unlike integration, the concept of inclusion has served to emphasise a turn towards a broader understanding of diversity and the acceptance and teaching of *all* children together. Thomas, Walker and Webb (1998, 15) summarise this newly established view as follows:

> The notion of inclusion [...] does not set parameters (as the notion of integration did) around particular kinds of putative disability. Rather, it is about a philosophy of acceptance; it is about providing a framework within which all children – regardless of ability, gender, language, ethnic or cultural origin – can be valued equally, treated with respect and provided with equal opportunities at school.[3]

Second, it has been argued that the focus in inclusive education should be on accommodation within an inclusive context, not on the assimilation of a child considered as not being "normal" or as disabled. The assumption is that "exclusive arrangements create disability as sickness, personal tragedy and object of charity [...] within a context that privileges some human characteristics over others" (Slee, 2001b, 168).

Third, instead of concentrating on individual learning difficulties as characteristic of special education, the idea of inclusion was intended to mark a move towards the language of rights and – we might add – identity politics (ibid., 174). Authors such as Ballard (2019) assume that a perspective which maintains the use of the terms "special needs" or "disability" would hinder the development of genuinely inclusive education as a human rights agenda.

The change of emphasis therefore appears to be threefold. It implies (a) a broader understanding of diversity, (b) consideration of context rather than individual children in isolation and (c) a focus on rights or identity politics rather than on individual difficulties that call for special support.

Various disability models can be identified depending on how this focal shift is interpreted. We can roughly distinguish three approaches to disability, one more moderate and the other two more radical. The latter two often endorse the view that inclusion is about human heterogeneity as such. And it should be noted that divergent orientations are often defended by the same people, even where the implications are not necessarily compatible.

The first, more moderate, approach identifies the core problem in the strong focus on individual health issues, mainly because inclusion is then regarded as a form of individual adaptation to environmental circumstances. This approach is critical of the one-sided focus on individual factors of disability, such as disorders and syndromes. And it regards as especially problematic the related failure to take a critical view of the environmental factors that shape inclusion.

The second approach assumes that disability is a socially constructed label. From this point of view, the establishment of inclusion thus implies the deconstruction of disability. Unlike the materialistic view of the third approach discussed below, this route is constructivist, as it assumes that labels often carry unintended stigma that mark pupils or service beneficiaries as defective.

The third view assumes that a disability consists of barriers to participation. The task of inclusion in this approach is first and foremost that of removing barriers, which are often physical in nature. If they are removed, it is assumed, the disability will disappear. This line of argumentation – like the second approach presented – directs the focus away from the individual and towards the environmental challenges to inclusion. Unlike the second view, however, it largely adheres to the British version of the social model of disability, sometimes referred to as the "strong social model" (Shakespeare, 2014, 11). This model clearly links disability and inclusion/exclusion.[4] Its underlying material ontology anchors the problem of a lack of inclusion within material social forces and physical environments, not only in ideas, cultures and discourses. It thus echoes the feminist redefinition of female experience: Sex as the biological difference between men and women corresponds to impairment, while gender as the socio-cultural difference between men and women parallels disability.

The first of these approaches is not contentious within the inclusion literature, and, more importantly, it is shared and embraced by the other two. But what distinguishes the second and third approaches from the first is not only that they lean towards a stronger interpretation of the social model of disability, but also that they incorporate specific assumptions about the measures that should be taken, namely the removal of barriers or the linguistic (and later also material) deconstruction of disability. Not least because the first, moderate approach to inclusion and disability seems relatively uncontroversial and not as vulnerable to critique as the others, the focus in the following will be on the second and third approaches, which I call the "deconstruction" model and the "barrier" model, respectively.

The "deconstruction" model

It is important to acknowledge from the outset that authors who claim that inclusion should be about diversity do not have to deny the reality of impairments. However, they argue that disability is a social construct. And it is indisputably the case that the degree of physical or cognitive limitation that counts as an impairment is often a matter of social judgement. Many impairments lie on a continuum, and most of them – except perhaps for obvious and undisputed examples, such as missing limbs – are constructs that encompass observable and thus interpretable behaviour. This is true even for apparently simple impairments such as ataxia or spasticity. They also occur in people with no underlying pathologies, as in the case of "functional weakness" (Wade, 2006).

All of these examples are consistent with the core assumptions of the first approach, which ultimately contends that the social, cultural and historical factors that give rise to disabilities should be taken seriously and that the problem should not be framed unilaterally in terms of the individual child. But what distinguishes the second approach from the first is that it further contains an implicit idea of what needs to be done to realise the inclusion of children and adolescents in education and schooling. Because it is assumed in this approach that disability is a social construct, the theory is also that pedagogical deconstruction is the appropriate course of action.

The issue, however, is that to speak of disability as a social construct is not quite as straightforward as may be believed by the interpreters and proponents of such a model of inclusion and disability.

According to Thomas Schramme (2003, 58ff), a conception of disability as a social construct can have at least four different meanings: The first and probably least controversial is the assumption that society evaluates impairment. The status of disability is thus only constructed through the negative meaning assigned by societal judgement. Certain historical examples demonstrate the appropriateness of this understanding of social construction, as we have already seen. These include well-documented cases, for instance, the almost complete and unproblematic inclusion of deaf people on Martha's Vineyard in the eighteenth and nineteenth centuries (Groce, 1985). We also know that in some traditional societies, people with cognitive disabilities have the status of saints, and as such are given special respect and care (Kastl, 2017, 260). These are two demonstrations that societal evaluation can indeed add to or even create a disability, but also diminish or eliminate it. We could cite many more examples that make this understanding of social construction very plausible. The assumption that certain aspects of disability are susceptible to societal evaluation is therefore quite uncontroversial.

Closely related to this interpretation, however, are two others that are not as unambiguous or uncontested as the first. A second interpretation is epistemological. In this view, the norms that are responsible for the attribution of disability are socially and culturally determined. This interpretation concerns the way our knowledge and judgements evolve. The third, more controversial thesis is causal. In this interpretation, disability is causally generated by society and societal institutions. The third interpretation differs from the first two in that it makes much stronger assumptions. Society and societal institutions are not seen as mediating factors in creating disability (as in the first two interpretations), but as being directly and causally responsible for producing it. This model excludes more nuanced explanations of disability as a phenomenon that results from the complex interaction of various factors, including (but not limited to) the fabric of society.

A fourth and final interpretation is even more forceful than the others. It proceeds from the assumption that disability is ontologically subjective, which means that there would be no disability without norms and values relating to disability. In other words, the view is advanced that disabilities and impairments owe their existence to the fact of social construction. The object – the disability – would not arise if there were no such constructions. In light of its ontological assumptions, the latter position might also be called "ontological" or "radical" constructivism (Kastl, 2017, 262). Although it is hard to imagine this model of disability applying in practice, there are a very small number of historical cases that lend some credence to this strong interpretation. For instance, the case of *drapetomania* – the supposed mental illness that makes slaves run away from their masters – can be seen as a disability that is entirely a social construct (Wakefield, 1992).

The first three interpretations draw our attention to two important aspects. First, they highlight the material, social, historical and cultural factors involved in creating disability, and second, they bring the epistemological level into focus. The latter in particular is an underestimated element in the generation and perpetuation of disabling life situations that result in stigmatisation, exclusion and marginalisation. The history of disability is full of alarming stories of people being stigmatised through the labels or names given to them.[5] In particular, labelling and categorisation are not trivial matters because of their potential to mark pupils and service recipients with unintended stigma.

The view that is frequently adopted in the inclusion literature is the fourth one. This is unfortunate for two reasons. First, it is dangerous because it misjudges the importance and usefulness of labels by generally considering any form of categorisation as an ultimately subjective ontological construct. But it is also perilous because it then makes existing social inequalities invisible by calling for a blanket recognition of difference. It thus does not offer a language for the different forms of disadvantage that disabled people experience in their daily lives.

We also need to recognise that labels have varying functions. First, they are not simply and always a means of oppression, marginalisation and exclusion. Categorisations or classifications of disability also serve as tools for important and inclusion-promoting socio-medical and legal practices, and sometimes also for educational practices (as in the case of dyslexia or dyscalculia, which affect academic learning in a very direct way). Clearly, we would not want to dispense with all categorisations in these vast areas of human life. Second, labels represent processes through which ideas and objects are recognised, differentiated and understood. Socio-medical and legal processes (as well as scientific endeavours) include and even presuppose certain criteria by which all objects can be categorised. In that process, the limits of classes are defined, and a coherent, unifying frame of reference is created. The frames of reference in socio-medical and legal practice, unlike those in scientific contexts, for instance, do not necessarily have a coherent theoretical basis. And that is not necessarily problematic, because they serve another purpose: They function as eligibility tools. Labels like "autism" or "attention deficit disorder" represent unifying concepts that trigger the provision of certain resources. As such, they have a "protective function" (Frederickson, 2010a). And although their role is ambiguous, such labels may even increase the likelihood of benevolent behaviour, as they provide an explanation for the difficulties a person faces.[6]

At this point, it must be emphasised that resource allocation which focuses on schools rather than on individual children does not avoid categorisation or the potential for unfair distribution: It does not simply replace one category (child) with another (school). It also leaves open the important question of whether such a "systems approach" ensures fair allocation better than approaches that focus on individual children. We know from population data that socio-economic status is not equally distributed within regions and cities. Socially disadvantaged life situations often cluster, including in terms of physical location. Social housing, for instance, is often concentrated in certain districts or regions. And the proportion of children with a migrant status as well as those from lower-income households is often higher in certain school districts, especially in urban clusters. It is therefore unlikely that allocation with a watering-can approach will lead to fair and equitable results, at least not any more than in the case of individual categorisation.

These objections are in no way meant to sidestep the problematic aspects of labelling, especially the connotations of incapacity, deficiency and dependency that colour the way we think and talk about disability, affecting not only disabled people, but also those close to them and the rest of society (Kittay, 1999). However, one of the dangers of abandoning labelling is that the terminology will change, but not necessarily the accompanying prejudices and attitudes. Indeed,

> changes in vocabulary will solve the problem only if contempt, hate, fear, and so on are solely generated through people's choice of words, rather than the words' also being a reflection of underlying attitudes. This is what lies behind the well-recognized effect of 'creeping stigmatization', where persistent and unacknowledged prejudices manage to contaminate novel, supposedly value-neutral terminology.
>
> *(Scully, 2008, 33)*

And the dilemmas that are frequently triggered by labelling are not easy to resolve in a harmonious way. It is, for instance, intrinsic to labels and categories – at least with respect to human beings – that they presuppose a "type" of population, which then causes the environment to treat individuals accordingly – with the potentially stigmatising effects mentioned above – but also causes the categorised individuals to develop or adapt their identities in response (Snyder & Mitchell, 2006, 11). All of this is problematic, but often unavoidable.

A second model, the "barrier" model, is also often defended in the inclusion literature. Although language and categorisation can be considered barriers, this model focuses on those that are more material and external in nature.

The "barrier" model

Many authors consider the "overcoming (of) barriers to learning and development for all children" (Booth & Ainscow, 2002) to be the main goal of inclusion. Consequently, much of the rhetoric of inclusive education is about removing or overcoming the barriers identified. In effect, the term "barrier" has largely come to replace the language of special needs. Proponents of a barrier model of disability also often imply that disabilities are neutral conditions, once the barriers are removed.

As with the "deconstruction" model of disability, however, references to barriers are not self-evident. Clarification is needed because barriers have two dimensions (Norwich, 2014a): One concerns the stability or alterability of causal factors, while the other relates to their internal or external locus. Thus, the latter dimension is concerned with the *origin* of a barrier. It raises the question: Is the barrier intrinsic, that is, does it originate within people, or is it extrinsic to them? The former dimension relates to the *alterability* of a barrier. Specifically, it asks: Is the barrier stable or is it dynamic? Is it perhaps only linked to certain social settings, and easy to modify or remove, or not?

This leaves us with at least four different practical manifestations of barriers. First, there are barriers that are intrinsic to people and yet are easily changed (at least in principle and in relative terms). We can take the simple example of a short-sighted person who goes to the ophthalmologist to get glasses. Individuals with eyeglasses are still short-sighted, but they are not necessarily disabled because the barriers that restrict them in the real world can often be removed entirely. Our world is full of barriers of this kind, whose existence thus adds to the disabilities experienced in many people's daily life. These barriers also differ vastly between societies. In societies with a high state of technical and digital development, solutions are found for many impediments in life, so that impairments and disabilities often do not negatively affect inclusion and participation, whereas in other societies even the fact of having a slight vision problem might pose a severe threat to inclusion when eyeglasses are not available. Of course, the question of which barriers can be removed, and when, also depends on historical and local conditions. While short-sightedness does not pose a problem for (most) people living in the Global North, it is problematic for many people living in the Global South. Equally, while poor eyesight was a serious, irremovable barrier for many people living in the Middle Ages, it is not so for most modern people.

There are, second, barriers that are intrinsic to people, but (relatively or completely) stable. Consider the example of vision problems again. This time, the person is not merely short-sighted, but congenitally blind. Again, this problem is clearly a personal characteristic. However, unlike in the case of short-sightedness (*and* assuming that there will not be any huge medical advances in the near future with regard to treatment of all the causes of congenital blindness), the blindness of this person will likely remain stable. Consequently, the barriers faced in this instance cannot be removed altogether. Note that this does not affect all of the barriers this person might face (especially not social barriers like stigmatisation or discrimination), nor does it imply that nothing needs to be done to remove barriers that this person encounters because of their blindness. It only means that some options will not be available to this person, or only to a limited extent, such as going to the movies or watching fireworks (however, the value of these possibilities is judged).

The third kind of barrier we must consider are those that are external to people and – at least relatively speaking – stable. Take, for instance, our natural environment. In certain areas, it poses stable barriers to most, if not all, people. Climbing Mount Everest, for instance, poses a barrier to all humans, except for a few very experienced and courageous mountaineers. Of course, this does not mean that there are no variations in these stable and external barriers, that they have no underlying historical relativity, or that not much can be done to overcome even very stable barriers such as mountains (consider, for instance, the example of blind mountaineers like Erik Weihenmayer and Andy Holzer, both of whom climbed Mount Everest). It is also the case that the differing natural conditions of various locations around the world pose divergent barriers for people: Being dependent on a wheelchair, for example, creates different barriers depending on whether you are in a sparsely populated mountain village at 3,500 metres above sea level or in flat, densely populated and well-developed Manhattan. Thus, stable external barriers exist for everyone, but affect people differently.

A fourth type of barrier can be distinguished from the third. This encompasses barriers that are external, but alterable or removable. In much inclusive thinking, this kind of barrier serves as the model. Perhaps the most conspicuous and prominent example is that of stairs, which hinder wheelchair access but can be replaced by ramps. If stairs are removed or ramps are added, the disability either vanishes or is at least diminished to a certain extent. Of course, this does not mean that the individuals affected are no longer dependent on their wheelchair. But the disabling effect, which does not necessarily result causally from the impairment, is made to disappear. External barriers that are in principle easy to change include not only many barriers resulting from architecture and design, but also social attitudes and opinions that people adopt, often implicitly. The challenge of how to change stubborn attitudes is one that has occupied many researchers and professionals in the field for decades.

Which of these four understandings of barriers is the most compelling? The straight answer is that all of them are important. Children and youth with disabilities face a great many barriers, some of which originate inside their minds and bodies. Part of the reality of educating children with disabilities, then, is addressing their intrinsic barriers resulting from impairments and underlying ill health. Take, for instance, the case of chronic illness, such as cancer, asthma or cystic fibrosis. Although these illnesses vary in severity and by individual case, what they have in common is that (a) daily activities are affected in harmful ways, (b) the children in these cases need to rely on assistive devices, special diets and/ or medication, and (c) they require health services that go beyond routine medical care (Thies, 1999). Thus, Sally French, who herself has a visual impairment, concedes: "Some of the most profound problems experienced by people with certain impairments are difficult, if not impossible, to solve by social manipulation" (French, 1993, 17). In other words, some aspects of their disabilities are intrinsic and pose stable barriers.

However, it is often not obvious whether barriers are intrinsic or extrinsic, and certainly the inclusion of children and young people is not only shaped by the internal and sometimes stable barriers that their impairments represent. Take the example of Down syndrome again. Someone with Down syndrome may face intrinsic barriers due to various impairments that are part of this syndrome. For instance, children with Down syndrome who stutter or exhibit some other form of irregular speech suffer problems of communication. It is difficult for those outside the family to understand them in this case. Stuttering and other forms of irregular speech present intrinsic barriers that are – in some cases and to some degree – stable for a person with Down syndrome. Yet, the social reactions towards people with Down syndrome are by no means explained by the syndrome and the related problems in communication; on the contrary, they are largely a matter of social attitudes and associated stigma, and thus are external to the person with Down syndrome, not internal, and also changeable, not stable. Therefore, although the syndrome as such represents a barrier that is intrinsic and stable, that is clearly not the case for the additional barriers that a person with Down syndrome has to face.

We can also note that some barriers are related to certain social situations or to the specifics of how the environment is constructed, such as barriers that arise from a person in a wheelchair having little or limited access to buildings because of the presence of stairs. These barriers are thus situational, but can create a recurring and stable experience of being rejected, disconnected, alienated and marginalised. Consequently, it is not a single barrier that restricts participation and inclusion, as we all experience certain barriers in our lives and restrictions at various times. It is the repetition and high frequency of experiences of external but alterable barriers that people with disabilities face, leading to the perception that the disability is constituted by these barriers, and not by the impairment itself.

This is not to assume, however, that inclusion is solely about the removal of barriers. Such an approach would oversimplify what is meant both by "removal" and by "barriers". But, as already noted, it is assumed unilaterally in much inclusive thinking that barriers to participation and learning are external and alterable. We can again take the example of stairs (external barrier) that impede wheelchair access being replaced by ramps or lifts (alterable barrier). As we have seen, though, impairments and health pathologies are very often a stable condition. It is possible that some internal factors might be altered or even compensated for to a certain extent. Returning to an easy example, visual impairment can be compensated for by wearing glasses, with no major effects on learning or daily life in general. In such cases, the measures implemented are capable of reducing the effects that the relevant impairments have on activity and participation in schools and elsewhere. However, it is also true that some external factors may not be easily alterable in these contexts, or if so, then only at considerable social costs. Take, for instance, the case of conventional written-language literacy standards. Removing these standards would impose social and personal costs for the majority of society who can achieve them, even while barriers are removed for illiterate people (Wolff, 2009a). This example again shows that we have to consider the side effects of certain propositions rather than simply making maximum statements.

We can therefore observe various problems in a barrier-free utopia of the sort often advanced most prominently in materialist versions of the social model of disability (Shakespeare, 2014, 36ff). First, nature is a major cause of the inaccessible environment that a lot of people with disabilities suffer from. But mountains, lakes and the sea – to name a few natural barriers – cannot be blamed for being inaccessible to people with physical impairments. Second, the idea of a barrier-free utopia sends the erroneous message that we can devise principles capable of liberating *all* people with disabilities in equal measure, and in combination. In practice, such principles often create conflict when combined. For example, wheelchair users need level access to get from the pavement to the street. Yet for blind people, the issue lies precisely in making a smooth transition between these two. They often find that ramps make it difficult for them to differentiate the pavement from the street, and leave them vulnerable to walking into the path of a car or other vehicle. Wheelchair users (especially those with back pain), meanwhile, may have problems with tactile paving that serves as an important indicator for visually impaired people. Moreover, different people with the same impairment require different forms of accommodation, because everyone experiences their own impairment differently and each impairment comes in unique forms and shapes, *and* because people have varying preferences for solving impairment problems. Third, fully accessible and barrier-free facilities are an important goal, but they must be balanced against other legitimate needs, even within the same institutions or for the same need. For example, providing books in multiple formats (in conventional written, audible and braille formats) may reduce a library's overall budget for buying new books or for pursuing other plans.

Fourth, once again, the removal of barriers in many cases necessitates societal reconstruction. What this means and implies is clear in the case of most sensory impairments and physical disabilities: For example, the provision of ramps for wheelchair users, verbal announcements in public transport for the blind and written announcements for the deaf and hard of hearing. However, it is not clear from the outset what the removal of barriers means in the case of cognitive disabilities, for example. It certainly means providing information in easy-to-read language. But it would be undesirable, or at least only achievable at considerable social cost, to create a world in which literacy and numeracy are not important capabilities for people, whether instrumentally or intrinsically. Fifth, to focus solely on barrier removal as the *sole* solution to the inclusion problem is to close our imagination off to other social responses that address the lack of inclusion. This can be well illustrated by the example of autism. Of course, we can and should conceive of education in a way that leads to more acceptance and support for people with autism. More recognition and assistance would certainly remove a significant source of distress for them. But we should not forget the practical limits to such efforts: There are those with autism for whom even the most well-meaning and respectful groups of people still are disturbing and confusing. If we use some imagination, perhaps facilities like shops could have special time slots reserved for these autistic people, where they could buy goods without feeling crowded or disturbed by the presence of other people. In schools, spaces might be created or redesigned in ways that reduce the stress levels caused by various stimuli. But the downside of such solutions is that they are segregative, and the provision of a special approach for people with autism partly contradicts the goal of inclusion for all.

One further important point should not be forgotten: The removal of barriers is not an end in itself. It is intended to facilitate the participation and improve the well-being of people with disabilities. In many cases, the removal of barriers and the provision of inclusive offerings represent the most appropriate and cost-effective way to achieve these aims, with the added benefit of minimising the segregation of disabled people from non-disabled people. But sometimes separate or alternative arrangements for people with disabilities may be a more effective way of enabling them to achieve well-founded and legitimate goals. This all paints a mixed picture, and often it is not immediately clear which barriers should be removed or reduced, and for whom, and in what way. Again, in many cases, it is not a matter of whether or not barriers should be generally and completely removed, but of recognising that barriers exist in the first place, and then of discussing how they might be removed or at least reduced, and what side effects might be associated with those decisions.

The difference made by disability

There are many striking similarities among social movements, including the women's liberation movement, gay rights movement and disability rights movement, among others. They all involve identity politics, they all challenge the medicalisation and biologisation of difference, and they all embrace academia and activism. There are also parallels between the theorisation of disability and that of race, gender and sexuality.

Yet, the oppression that disabled people face is different, and in many ways more complex, than that caused by sexism, racism or homophobia, and it therefore calls for different or additional theoretical reflection. We have seen that there can be no single response to disability, for various reasons. Neither the deconstruction of labels nor the removal of barriers can provide clear, or in any case adequate, answers to the lack of inclusion.

But in what ways does disability exactly differ from other forms of human heterogeneity, such as gender, race or sexual orientation? First, there is an ontological difference. At least within the gender debate, it can be argued that men and women are physiologically different, maybe also psychologically, but it is no longer considered accurate or accepted to argue that women are less capable because of their biology.[7] Similarly, only racists would see the biological differences among ethnic communities or differences in skin colour as the explanation for social differences. The case of disability is different in that, even in the absence of discrimination, social barriers or oppression, the presence of an impairment is still problematic, simply because many impairments are limiting or difficult in themselves (Shakespeare, 2014, 29). Disabled people experience various forms of biological disadvantage that go beyond social and environmental factors. Many people with physical impairments, for instance, frequently experience severe fatigue or muscle pain when moving. Moreover, an impairment and the sensory experiences associated with it often have an explanatory relevance that a person's skin colour, gender or sexual orientation does not.

Indeed, relatively few restrictions experienced by people with disabilities are completely social in origin. If disabled people were discriminated against only due to their impairment, and exclusions were imposed on them on that basis alone, with no relation to their abilities, then this would be a purely social restriction and would constitute discrimination in the fullest sense. Nightclubs that exclude disabled persons because they only cater to attractive young people, or the notorious "ugly laws" in early twentieth-century Chicago and elsewhere, banning disfigured people from public spaces, are clear examples of disadvantages and disabilities that are purely social in origin. This is where disability discrimination *precisely* parallels racism and other forms of discrimination or social exclusion. However, in most cases, disabled people experience both the intrinsic limitation of their impairment *and* externally imposed social discrimination. Thus, the dichotomy between impairment and disability is methodological and not ontological (Anastasiou & Kauffman, 2013). It allows us to introduce an analytical distinction between the level of physical trauma and the various social and cultural responses to people with disabilities.

This is not meant to imply that the phenomenon of disability can be broken down into two parts on the ontological level. Yet, that is exactly what the proponents of a radical social model assume: They differentiate impairment and disability ontologically. Having introduced a vertical line between the biological and social dimensions of disability, they make arguments only about the social dimensions, and on sociological grounds. In so doing, they split apart the biological and mental factors affecting the disabled subject. In effect, the subject is viewed not as an individual with a full set of (biological, social and psychological) assets, but, at best, as a "half-person" possessing only social properties, existing in a biologically naked state and helplessly exposed to the prevailing social values and roles. The problem with this approach is that the methodological differentiation of impairment and disability gradually slides into a false distinction that takes on an ontological quality.

This is especially problematic in the educational context, as schools by definition serve to develop children's internal skills and are therefore often concerned with their intrinsic barriers (which of course does not mean that there is no interplay between social circumstances and these intrinsic barriers). Part of teachers' role is to overcome internal barriers, so a problem arises for schools and teachers when these internal barriers seem to be very stable and learning progress is slow.

Of course, this by no means implies that these children should be cast aside or that they cannot attend their neighbourhood school. And it does not mean that we should discriminate against them or categorise them as abnormal. But it *does* mean that certain children are likely to need a lot of support and encouragement to make any progress in learning, and the progress they do make may be much slower and more modest than that of other children. It is also one aspect of human heterogeneity that there are children who can only learn very slowly because of damage to their bodily structures and functions.

Of course, there are many who would not object to the assertion that children generally learn at different speeds. And yet they would argue that this simply emphasises the need for different methodologies and didactics in teaching and learning. Usually, these proponents think that the main or even the whole problem of inclusive education is that such methodologies and didactics are not more widely known and available. Still others are of the opinion that the general problem of school education lies in its relatively narrow view of school-based learning, and thus of the various forms of learning overall. Accordingly, the expectations and attitudes of teachers or debt administrators, for example, are often flawed or one-sided.

It is indeed a problem of current school education that it has a closed and narrow understanding of its own functions and of learning in general. But we must also take into account that attitudes as well as teaching and learning styles are always embedded in a wider cultural and social environment. It is not the case, for instance, that teachers may simply decide, autonomously and on their own authority, to completely change their teaching style, didactics, methods or curricula. Therefore, it is also too simplistic to think that inclusive schooling is mainly or solely a question of methodology and didactics.

We also need to bear in mind that many of the arguments and statements frequently put forth in the inclusion debate are in effect empty phrases, or do not deliver as much as their defenders believe. What does it mean, for example, to say that all children learn at different paces? Or to demand that schools give up their expectations for learning? Of course, the first statement refers to a truth, but what does it mean in practice for teachers? Do they have to align their teaching style to (say) 25 individual students? We know that this is not possible. But more importantly, we need to remember that individualisation is not the only goal here. The same applies for the second statement: It is neither feasible nor morally justified to abandon all expectations within education. We can only replace certain expectations – perhaps problematic ones – with more just and diversity-friendly expectations.

A "split" approach to disability and inclusion moreover gives rise to epistemological and conceptual fallacies, with serious political consequences. Although inclusion can be used in the wider "for all" sense, ignoring disability as a special case carries the risk of not recognising that different educational approaches and considerations may apply in these areas of difference, with an overlapping, reinforcing or weakening effect. Not only is there a danger that the interests of persons with disabilities may be eclipsed or overlooked in the pursuit of other, less minority interests, such as gender and socio-economic class interests (Miles & Singal, 2010); if disabled people are considered only to share a common experience of oppression, i.e. regardless of their impairment, then it indeed becomes superfluous to engage in organising or analysis on the basis of impairment. In that case, both impairment-specific organisations – whether traditional charities or more modern self-help groups – and impairment-specific responses become problematic. Even if a disability model simply ignores the existence of impairment, the epistemological power nexus that defines and interprets impairment is still intact. The spheres of power and knowledge that are ostensibly subject to criticism therefore remain largely untouched, leaving under-theorised some major sources of the oppression of people with disabilities (Hughes & Paterson, 1997). All this is not to deny that it is indeed very difficult to determine where an impairment ends and a disability starts, "but such vagueness need not be debilitating. Disability is a complex dialectic of biological, psychological, cultural and socio-political factors, which cannot be extricated except with imprecision" (Shakespeare & Watson, 2001, 22).[8]

In this context, the next section presents a complex, social-relational model of disability that allows for the integration of bodily impairment and subjective experiences of ill health in conjunction with environmental factors.

The social-relational model

The social-relational model of disability, which was first proposed by Solveig M. Reindal (2008) and is based on a conception of disability in terms of capability theory, does not deny the reality of an oft-medicalised view of disability that still prevails in many predominantly therapeutic approaches towards the education of disabled children. On the contrary, it assumes that the sharp ontological distinction drawn between disability and ability is indeed problematic and detrimental to the development of genuinely inclusive education. The model thus clearly rejects individualistic understandings of disability and instead situates disabled persons in a broader context. According to Reindal (2008), her model is also more compatible with the morality of inclusion because it does not undercut the core theme of the social model, that of oppression. So, how is disability conceived of in this model?

The social-relational model of disability considers the existence of an impairment as a necessary precondition precisely *because* people with impairments and chronic illnesses do experience disablement in certain circumstances. An impairment, however, is not a sufficient condition and does not equal disability. That is to say, whether impairment results in disability is contingent upon many factors, including historical, cultural and social factors. Whether the reduced function or impairment and its effects become a disability is thus dependent on constraints imposed at various levels and in various societal spheres, in addition to the social impact that the impaired function has on the individual (Reindal, 2008, 144).

The social-relational model furthermore assumes that the needs of people with disabilities are not only medical but should be understood more broadly, in a way that encompasses social, educational and functional needs. Also, it is important "to recognize that medical treatments may be iatrogenic, creating dependency and thereby creating further disability and secondary conditions" (Simeonsson et al., 2003, 607). This, in turn, shows how dangerous it is to consider medical diagnoses (and certain medical needs) as all-encompassing, and thus in effect assume that a child has no other social, functional or educational needs, or has only needs that differ from those of other children and thus make the child "special".

Within this model, differences and inequalities are thus conceived of as relationships, not as internal properties. There is no fixed standard of normality from which someone deviates, for example, a deaf child from a hearing child. Everything is a matter of perspective and context. Furthermore, none of the elements is static; each involves feedback loops. For instance, new treatments may change the conditions involved or the impairment itself. Consider the developments in the treatment of children born with congenital impairments such as heart conditions. Many can benefit from such effective and early surgery (sometimes even prenatally) that their condition no longer results in a significant disability. In contrast, metabolic diseases are increasing at an alarming rate in certain parts of the world, and schools are confronted with new impairments and diseases, such as diabetes, in a way they did not experience in the past. It is also the case that changes at the structural level of society, for instance, via the introduction of new laws and legal frameworks both nationally and internationally, can and will alter the conditions for the emergence of disability.

A relational understanding of disability raises the question of how people can transform goods into opportunities in order to lead a good life (Terzi, 2007). This is precisely the focus of the capability approach, on which the relational model of disability is based on theoretical terms. This view implies that a person in a wheelchair cannot easily be compared in terms of income to a person who is not in a wheelchair. Both may have the same income. But the person who is not in a wheelchair has far more resources available for their life. Sen (1990) in particular emphasises that the evaluation of human well-being cannot be about goods themselves, but about what they allow people to do and be, and how they can be transformed into the elements of a good life. These factors are referred to as "conversion factors".

Material issues: disability and conversion factors

According to Ingrid Robeyns (2005, 99), three groups of conversion factors can be distinguished: personal (e.g. intelligence or physical strength), social (e.g. social norms, attitudes) and environmental (e.g. climate, structural environment). In all three areas, people with disabilities are at greater risk, compared with non-disabled people. At the individual level, they are exposed to the risk of a disadvantageous starting position, for example, due to damage to bodily functions and structures and the resulting impairment of activity and participation. Second, social and environmental factors also increase their structural risks. People with disabilities continually face problems in their efforts to lead a good life due to social norms and ideas, which are also linked to the power to shape social perceptions, as well as structural obstacles such as a lack of assistive devices or accessibility. And third, environmental problems, including environmental disasters, war and hunger, pose specific and additional risks for the lives of disabled people.

Epistemic issues: disability narratives and perceptions

It is not, however, only material questions – e.g. how to transform goods into a good life – that gain resonance in a relational model of disability; epistemic issues are also raised, and with them questions about how knowledge and narratives relating to disability emerge, and what forms they take. It becomes evident that discourses of success, happiness and joy are largely absent in narratives about disability (Sunderland, Catalano & Kendall, 2009). Instead, disability is usually understood as a story of personal suffering, as an inward-looking individual experience. Such conceptualisation does not challenge the structural or cultural context, nor does it provide alternative narratives to the dominant biomedical paradigm (Shakespeare, 1996).

The moral significance of narratives about disabilities lies in their direct and indirect impacts on people's moral ability to act, and thus in the way that narratives influence and shape the nature and extent of social inclusion. Master narratives describe what is socially accepted and what is rejected in the world. They describe types of people (e.g. teachers, criminals, pupils, mothers) as well as social or ontological groups (e.g. Muslims, middle-class people, white people). Master narratives are both explanatory and descriptive (Lindemann Nelson, 2001). As they represent a moral consensus, they develop enormous epistemological power, as Jackie Leach Scully (2008, 112) rightly remarks:

> Once past what I call first order recognition, when we quickly categorize other people by gender, skin color, age, or body size and shape, we start to fit people into the broad narrative categories that go with those characteristics, usually well before we have the kind of data that would enable us to do this with real accuracy. Identifying a person as female immediately allocates her to a set of possible narratives (daughter, mother, dentist, Catholic) while making others a bit less likely (colonel, archbishop) and some impossible (sperm donor, pope). And because master narratives are generated within existing structures of domination and status, they have staying power as well, locked in place by the persistence of those structures.

Particularly malicious are those narratives that deepen cultural prejudices and deny the people affected numerous (quantitative) and valuable (qualitative) life opportunities. Such narratives damage the identity and self-esteem of the persons targeted, and may even delay or hinder their development as individuals. This means that deficient or toxic master narratives can have a directly damaging effect by inhibiting and experiencing the formation of an adequate self-image, and an indirectly damaging effect by shutting down life opportunities that would otherwise be open.

However, for the same reasons, an over-idealised narrative can be harmful too; again, Scully (2008, 129) states:

> Over time, as the discrepancy between the idealized version and empirical reality is noticed, the idealized versions will lose credibility among non-disabled people and they will fail to mesh with the experienced reality of impairment. Disabled people whose lives do not match the ideal script – who are not supercrips or perpetually feisty disabled activists – will be damaged by this failure too. The idealized counterstory will rapidly become as harmful as any of the 'bad' narratives it was designed to replace.

Thus, in effect, stories that present people with disabilities as superheroes are potentially just as damaging as those that describe them as victims or sufferers.

Here, we come full circle. The recurrent problem with labelling lies in the impact it has on people's ability to act and their influence on their own inclusion. What is particularly troublesome is not only that master narratives hinder individual development and thus the opportunities for a person's inclusion (which, in the case of children and young people, naturally also affects their families). Rather, master narratives are also deeply embedded in our cultural and social self-perception and thus, in turn, shape ideas about which barriers to inclusion are stable and which are alterable. It is therefore not surprising that changes to master narratives (about disabilities, but also, for instance, about gender or race) influence our understanding of what barriers exist for the people concerned, and how they can be removed.

The social-relational model of disability takes these aspects into account. However, it does not restrict itself to conceptualising disability merely as a form of barrier or as a label that needs to be deconstructed. It instead assumes that disability consists of both individual, intrinsic factors and social and other environmental factors. Efforts to reduce exclusion, marginalisation and stigmatisation call for engagement with various aspects of disability, at multiple levels, with a focus that is relational.

Conclusion

In the inclusion literature, the idea of abandoning all notions of disability, or at least strongly reconceptualising it, goes roughly as follows: When inclusive education was understood as a matter of human diversity in general, disability seemed to be less distinctive. It was made both more ordinary and, to some extent, less significant. Seen in this light, disability appeared as part of the nearly infinite variety of human life. It was considered as being only one characteristic among many others, such as gender, ethnic and social origin, religious affiliation and sexual orientation. Therefore, the problems that surfaced within the context of school education were not seen as being exceptional either:

> The dilemmas generated by diversity do not arise simply in respect to students with 'disabilities' or 'special educational needs'. Rather, they point to fundamental issues of values, purposes and practices in mass education systems. From this perspective, the 'ghettoization' of inclusion as a disability or special education issue is a missed opportunity to address these issues.
> (Vlachou, 2004, 9)

One consequence of a view that applies inclusion issues to a vague notion of "diversity" is that there is nothing to distinguish people with disabilities from people who are otherwise socially handicapped, for instance, because they have children or pets to care for. A whole range of people could in fact be labelled as disabled due to the barriers or prejudices they face, e.g. women, people of colour or people migrating to escape war. In other words, there are no conceptual tools available that allow for the analysis of differing social situations. It thus becomes increasingly difficult to achieve an adequate intersectional perspective, which is, however, necessary to understanding the range of ways in which a lack of inclusion affects various people and social groups.

Among the main problems in discussing disability, or people with disabilities as a social group, is certainly the heterogeneity of the phenomenon as well as disagreement about what truly counts as a disability (e.g. is ADHD a disability?). But the impoverishment and one-sidedness of the debate on disability is also problematic. And we can furthermore perceive a dearth of empirical and phenomenological knowledge about the subjective and personal experiences of disabled people, including a lack of first-hand language for talking about disability. Finally, terms that have become discriminatory and thus are rejected by most people – such as "mental defect", "cripple" or "mongoloid" – often change to a terminology that is outwardly more positive, such as "cognitive disability", "physically impaired" or "trisomy 21". But this is not necessarily accompanied by a shift in the associated perceptions and attitudes, as Scully (2008, 33) remarks:

> Changes in vocabulary will solve the problem only if contempt, hate, fear, and so on are solely generated through people's choice of words, rather than the words' also being a reflection of underlying attitudes. This is what lies behind the well-recognized effect of 'creeping stigmatization', where persistent and unacknowledged prejudices manage to contaminate novel, supposedly value-neutral terminology.

The inclusion literature, by proposing that disability should no longer be regarded as a specific criterion, has taken a stand against the essentialist and medicalised view that it perceived in the special education literature. In so doing, however, it has often exchanged one form of essentialism for another. That found in the inclusion literature consists in the assumption that "each person has their unique sets of essential qualities, goals and potentialities, and these should be neither changed nor exchanged" (Wolff, 2002, 213).

The problem here is not the essentialism *per se*, but once again that it poses an empty assumption. Education *is* an undertaking that is intended to transform people. So, what does it mean to accept each person's unique set of potentialities, qualities and goals? Of course, it means that we should not discriminate against people or devalue their potential or distinctiveness. But it is also not a question of celebrating their particularities when in fact the point is to change people through education, by aiming to develop potential in pupils, awaken new interests in them and help them set new goals in life. And those are all aspects of good educational practice.

The real crux here lies not so much in the deconstruction of disability as a linguistic endeavour, but rather in the fact that disability itself is created and reinforced through expectations at school. For example, the behavioural disorders that have become so widespread are often only made visible through the existence of school behavioural expectations, as it emerges that most children with behavioural disorders experience their disabilities almost exclusively in a school context. If we were to regard such school expectations as a kind of barrier, then one possible solution could be considered the removal of this barrier, i.e. the abolition of school expectations. But as we have seen, various barriers exist in the lives of people with disabilities (and in the lives of all human beings): Barriers can be intrinsic to an individual, or extrinsic. And they can be stable in terms of expected changes over time and across settings, or else dynamic, perhaps contingent on specific social situations or conditions, and thus alterable or removable, at least in principle.

One possibility is certainly to reduce disability by changing external barriers and creating opportunities for inclusion. An option often implied in the inclusion literature is that of radically lowering educational expectations with the goal of status enhancement, and thus status equality. However, status enhancement as evoked by the inclusion movement is not always the right answer. Take the example of illiteracy. The idea of trying to tackle illiteracy purely by lowering expectations and changing society itself seems absurd, as Jonathan Wolff (2002, 213) reminds us:

> How could we change our world so that reading and writing gave one no advantage? Rather than adjusting the world so that illiteracy isn't a disadvantage, presumably we should help people overcome it. In the world as it is, it really is a defect, albeit socially dependent, and personal enhancement seems the natural response. But this is always going to be a sensitive and difficult matter.

We should thus not always prefer status enhancement, even though it surely has importance. Where medical help, as in the case of eyeglasses, is fast, safe and effective, and in most countries low-cost, the right approach seems to be to avoid disability simply by treating it individually and medically. Status enhancement can also be extremely expensive and have unexpected and negative side effects. If, for example, a minor improvement in mobility would result in fewer people receiving help or resources, because a measure such as retrofitting vehicles would cost so much that no resources would be left for other projects or people, then that would be a side effect worth considering.

But how can changes be implemented and the necessary status enhancement achieved while avoiding one-sided perspectives on health issues and uncritical stances towards environmental factors? Although we have to put off examining the transformation of systems and individual role bearers until Chapter 8, we can already draw the following conclusions from the disability model proposed here:

First, the social-relational model prompts us to break down traditional categories of disability to understand the information they represent. Disability categories encompass a range of information, some reflecting the social situation (e.g. service provision, expectations, classroom characteristics), some the personal situation of an individual (e.g. age, gender, ethnicity) and some a combination of both (e.g. socio-economic background). If we are to understand the problems involved, we must view them in relation to a child's personal situation, and not some abstract concept of a disorder. A child with Down syndrome, for instance, may have problems with language and communication, but probably not with mobility, whereas a child with spina bifida faces the opposite challenges. One effect of a social-relational view is thus that it leads us to adopt a specific, individualised view of disability.

Second, and somewhat related to the first point, this model makes it necessary for us to take a complex view of disability. This means, among other things, that we can no longer start from the assumption that certain factors only constitute causes, while others only constitute consequences. Instead, we have to assume that factors influence each other in a mutually reinforcing or weakening manner.

Third, due to its relational orientation, the model also clarifies the importance of status enhancement and thus of the structural position of disabled people in our society. This is not in conflict with the first point, because it does not mean that we should adopt a purely individual perspective on disability. Rather, it means that in practice we do have to pay attention to individual children and young people and in that way avoid generalisation, and consequently the stigmatisation of these individuals and discrimination against them. However, because the social-relational model considers disability to be dynamic, the environmental factors involved, and especially the social environmental factors, are also particularly pertinent. If we think of institutional structures as being ultimately formed and maintained by human beings (and not as lifeless entities), then the importance of these structural and institutional factors of disability and inclusion becomes clear.

Fourth, we gain a better understanding of the significance of certain role bearers for the emergence and avoidance of disability. The role of the teacher should be emphasised here. Of course, we do not assume – in most cases at least – that teachers are the cause of disabilities or impairments. But teachers do have great power to reinforce them or, at the other end of the spectrum, to make them more "normal" and "accepted". One way of doing this is through teacher feedback. Several studies show the influence of teacher behaviour and feedback on the values of pupils (Chang, 2003, 2004; Hughes, Cavell & Wilson, 2001; Mikami, Swaim Griggs, Reuland & Gregory, 2012; Wentzel, 1998; White & Jones, 2000; White, Sherman & Jones, 1996). Negative teacher feedback, in particular, had a major impact on the social acceptance of pupils (McAuliffe, Hubbard & Romano, 2009).[9] This finding also points, on the brighter side, to the significance of positive feedback and – more generally – to the importance of teachers as role models.

In the next chapter, the focus will be on the nature and design of inclusive education. We are now approaching the heart of our examination.

Notes

1 At this point, it is worth emphasising that the history of inclusion unfolded somewhat differently than its early proponents expected and hoped. Although the majority of authors in this area suggest otherwise, the language of inclusion still predominantly revolves around disability or special needs. An analysis of English-language education research databases conducted by Brahm Norwich, for instance, found that there are between 3 and 15 times more entries on inclusion or inclusive education with respect to special needs or disabilities than in relation to gender, ethnicity or other forms of heterogeneity (Norwich, 2013). It is unlikely that this has changed since the publication of Norwich's study.

2 In contrast to conventional, often individualised and medicalised models, these perspectives take a "minority" view of disability. Elizabeth Barnes, probably the most well-known defender of such a view, defines it at follows: "Being disabled is simply something that makes you a minority – it is a way of having a minority body" (Barnes, 2016, 78).
3 The view of disability as forming part of human diversity has also frequently led to the idea that diversity *per se* should be celebrated. Len Barton (1997, 233), for instance, expresses such a perspective on inclusive education as follows: "Inclusive education is about responding to diversity; it is about listening to unfamiliar voices, being open, empowering all members and about celebrating 'difference' in dignified ways".
4 The proponents of this model need not deny that impairments exist – they may even call non-socially imposed restrictions "impairment effects" (Thomas, 1999) – but they believe that the social phenomena labelled as disability should not be viewed as something distinct or as the direct result of the impairment of bodily structures and functions. They thus assume that disability is the disadvantage imposed upon people with impairments. However, in building a bridge between impairment and disability, they ignore the possibility that impairment itself can actually lead to disadvantage, for example, through the experience of severe physical pain that limits participation and activity.
5 An especially prominent example is that of Down syndrome. In 1866, the English physician John Langdon Down published an essay describing a phenotype of children whose shared characteristics differed from those of other children with cognitive disabilities. He was the first to make the distinction between children described as "cretins" (later found to have hypothyroidism) and children he labelled as "mongoloids". Down based the latter name on his impression that these children looked like people from Mongolia, whom he thought were of lower intelligence (Down, 1995 (1866)).
6 One study, for instance, showed that it was possible to get 13-year-olds to interact willingly with a child labelled as having a certain kind of impairment. And children aged 10–11 displayed more willingness to interact when the explanatory information was provided by the teacher and not by the parents of the child (Campbell, 2006). Another study (Ochs, Kremer-Sadlik, Solomon & Sirota, 2001) of children with high-functioning autism showed that those who provided a full explanation of their condition were more successful in obtaining social support and participating in playground activities.
7 Note that the first two arguments are also controversial within the feminist movement, but still find some support within mainstream society, whereas the last argument is only adopted in misogynistic circles.
8 Indeed, the attainment of knowledge about how personal and environmental factors interact, and how they limit or enhance the inclusion of people with disabilities, can be considered "the holy grail" of disability research (Dijkers, 2006, 93).
9 Interestingly, views of disability also correlate strongly with teachers' sense of responsibility for the children concerned (Jordan, Kircaali-Iftar & Diamond, 1993; Jordan, Lindsay & Stanovich, 1997; Jordan, Schwartz & McGhie-Richmond, 2009; Jordan & Stanovich, 2001). Jordan and her team (2009, 541) therefore deduce from this:

> Beliefs in the locus of responsibility as belonging to the classroom teacher may be a prerequisite to teachers' development of effective instructional techniques for all their students. What may be needed in both teacher education and in-service preparation is to challenge teachers' beliefs about ability and disability as immune to learning, and their resulting beliefs about their roles and responsibilities, as well as their epistemological beliefs about the nature of knowing, knowledge and the process of acquiring knowledge.

6
INCLUSIVE EDUCATION

The current inclusion discourse and its shortcomings

In our examination of the discourse surrounding inclusive education, a number of problematic tendencies have become apparent. First, a large proportion of authors do not explore the justification of inclusion, but instead focus solely on its implementation. The European Agency for Special Needs and Inclusive Education, for example, states the following: "The current debate is no longer about what inclusion is and why it is needed; the key question is how it is to be achieved" (European Agency for Special Needs and Inclusive Education, 2014, 5). Linked to this is the assumption that inclusive education represents a single well-defined set of goals that can be clearly and unambiguously understood as the finish line of a race, so to speak (Artiles & Dyson, 2005, 57). The inadequacy of this perspective is evident not least on the basis of epistemological considerations. Any implementation of inclusion points to a specific idea of what inclusion *is*. And conversely, particular notions of inclusion necessarily imply at least vague ideas about how it should be implemented, or which orientation and approach should be adopted, i.e. ideas of what inclusion *should be*. Implementation and justification are thus closely interlinked and reciprocal. As modes of implementation are always concrete and tied to specific circumstances, it is reasonable to assume that the image of a clear finish line is also flawed at the level of justification. Instead, we need always to think of inclusion in the plural, as *inclusions*.

Second, it is remarkable how often inclusion is discussed in a limited way in terms of accessibility or is viewed as a technical problem (Slee & Weiner, 2001) despite the vast scope of how inclusion is understood in the field of education (Artiles & Kozleski, 2016). Such conceptions of inclusion primarily relate to structural involvement and, as an expression of this, to physical placement, while neglecting the other elements of inclusion: participation in resources, social integration and psychologically perceived belonging. In addition, as discussed in the last chapter, problematic assumptions are made about the modifiability of barriers and the possibilities for removing them, while insufficient attention is paid to the side effects of certain measures.

Third, many implementation strategies in the field of education focus narrowly on regulatory measures, such as changes or adjustments to curricula, teacher attitudes or teaching systems, especially with regard to didactics and teaching methodology (Thomas, 1997). However, the linear and causal thinking that often goes along with this (e.g. "teaching method X leads to improved inclusion") artificially isolates individual cognition from a wide range of complex environmental factors that people to some extent face as pre-existing conditions affecting their actions, and are able to influence only to a limited extent (Artiles & Dyson, 2005, 47).

Fourth, between the literature that is sceptical of inclusion and that which is more enthusiastic, there tends to be quite a difference in how the function and status of schools are regarded. Both perspectives are problematic, however. Views that are more critical of inclusion, for example, assume that the primary function of schools is to provide pupils with the core academic skills necessary for modern societies. Some authors even draw an explicit distinction between school-based learning and inclusion. They believe that schools should focus on teaching and skills and not (at least primarily) on inclusion (Hegarty, 2001; Kauffman & Badar, 2014; Wilson, 1999, 2000). By contrast, the pro-inclusion literature often creates the impression that inclusive education is solely a values project in which individual motivations and beliefs take centre stage. In the implementation of this moral vision of inclusion, the school is given a place of great significance, but one that relies mostly on intuitive assumptions, in the end. However, no clarification is given as to why the school, in particular (and not, for example, the family), should be regarded as particularly important in the implementation of inclusion (of a broader nature, extending beyond the school sector), why attitudes should be considered especially crucial or what the relationship is between the task of inclusion and other tasks entrusted to the education system.

These points inevitably raise some questions that go beyond the realisation of inclusion. These include: What idea of learning is implied in inclusive education? That is, what is learned in school, and how? And how is school different from other spheres of life, especially the family? These questions will be the focus in the following.

Insights from classic works of sociology

In answering these school-related questions, we again find many pertinent approaches in the field of sociology. When it comes to exploration of the differences between family and school, one classic work is still unrivalled: Robert Dreeben's book *On What Is Learned in School* (Dreeben, 2002), originally published in 1968. In that work, Dreeben not only addresses in meticulous detail the question of what distinguishes the institution of school from the family, but also, quite fundamentally, the question of what is actually learned at school. As Dreeben demonstrates, there is a whole range of norms important for life in modern society that cannot be instilled by the family or family-like forms of community. Indeed, certain norms can be generated by the school precisely *because* it is functionally different from the family. These norms, as I will discuss in more detail, simultaneously enable and limit what can be done institutionally and organisationally in terms of inclusion in school.

A second theory that is particularly helpful in this chapter for the question of what functions the school performs is the scholastic theory of the Austrian sociologist of education, Helmut Fend. Fend's approach deals with a subject area that has been largely neglected in the English-speaking world. In his book *Neue Theorie der Schule* [New theory of school] (Fend, 2006),[1] he not only develops a theory of schooling based on the sociology of education, but also a comprehensive functional approach to modern education. Specifically, Fend's theory offers a macro-sociological perspective on the concept of school that allows us to critically examine various functions as well as the structure of modern education, while at the same time consistently applying the established sociological foundations of inclusion to the school sector. Like Dreeben, Fend draws both on systems theory[2] and on relevant sociology in the legacy of Max Weber, as well as constructivist theoretical traditions (Berger & Luckmann, 1971).

The school as an organisation and institution

Schools are situated between the macro- and micro-levels of society, in an ecological niche at the intermediate or meso-level. They are public-sector, state-established institutions[3] that engage in a variety of exchange relationships with numerous systems, such as the economic and political systems. Institutions such as the school are established, thanks to support mechanisms that include not only laws and regulations, but also routines, artefacts and symbolic and relational systems. But the school, meanwhile, also brings pupils' meso- and micro-systems together under the umbrella of a single institution. In school, the micro-systems (pupils) are no longer part of a different meso-system, namely the parental home. Instead, they are subject to a collective structure that includes a uniform set of expectations, rules and values specific to the school. Furthermore, because individuals maintain institutions by means of their social actions, they also serve as supportive agents for institutions.

The institutionalisation of teaching activity means that it is subject to the principles of formal organisation. For the modern school, this means that its organisational form is predetermined through legal regulations, curricula, state teacher training and the design of school types and school-leaving qualifications. The formal structuring of the school ensures that schooling can be generalised and standardised, in a way that detaches it from personal specificities and local, real-world distinctions. Learning is situated at a spatio-temporal distance from the real life of children (which of course does not mean that it is not relevant to actual life within a particular society, at a particular time). What children learn at school, they learn mainly for their lives as adults, i.e. for use later on. This also means that learning at school is often not directly related to current life practices and is conveyed mainly in symbolic terms (as is particularly evident in the case of mathematics). Learning takes place through representations of life: Beetles are studied on worksheets, and chemical processes are illustrated on charts. Learning content is pre-selected via curricula and is standardised in terms of schedules, timing, didactics and methodology. The activities of teachers are also pre-structured by means of organisational, role-based behavioural orientations. Teachers are embedded in hierarchical, organisational structures, with a role that requires them to treat pupils in a uniform way. However, organisational structures create both order and coercion. Neither the pupils nor the teachers can completely escape this coercion (Jackson, 1990). Thus, anyone who hopes to survive in school – and this applies equally to pupils and their teachers – must be guided by both the written and the unwritten curricula, the "hidden curriculum" (Jackson, 1986).[4]

The school, and especially the classroom, is a crowded and extremely lively experiential space that is shaped by numerous, high-paced activities, placing heavy demands on the social skills of those present. And this is not just the case temporarily, but on a recurring basis and over a long period of time. This situation results in the formation of a shared history, which is a major factor in the subjective experience of belonging (Doyle, 1986; Herzog, 2009). School is not only a socialising experience but also a social experience for pupils. It is where children and young people make the most important friendships of their childhood and adolescence (Ahlberg & Brighouse, 2014, 60f.).

The experiential space of school therefore presents both opportunities and risks. As a result of diversity in schools, people are brought into long-lasting contact with others who might have been prevented from such contact in other circumstances due to social or cultural barriers or physical distances. The informal structures in schools thus offer many chances to establish and maintain contacts. The radical plurality described by Enzensberger, which also pertains to schools, can result in esteem for people in the diversity of ways in which they live and appear, as well as the recognition of diversity as a new normality, in the emergence of what Rödder (2017) describes as a "culture of inclusion". School is both a source of this potential and a setting in which it can be applied.

However, both the coercive nature of school as an organisation and the plurality of classrooms can lead to negative chains of relationships or patterns of exclusion, which can be expressed, for example, through bullying or stigmatisation. Moreover, the broader the social environment and the more heterogeneous the group of pupils involved, the greater the likelihood that social contacts will be fragmented and that people will not interact in their full personal individuality or feel a sense of security about their status, but will instead remain largely free-floating and regard each other as different. The dangers of exclusion are inherent in the system of schooling, for the structures of norms that are formed in schools inevitably lead to the establishment of criteria of esteem and rejection.

These structures, which are manifested in particular through performance standards and expectations as well as acceptance or rejection by teachers, shape not only teachers' relationships with their pupils, but also pupils' interactions with each other. Due to this systematic orientation towards norms, role bearers inevitably transform equality into inequality. They thus motivate *and* discourage at the same time (Vanderstraeten, 2004b, 65) and create new inequalities in place of previous states of equality.

Features of schools in democratic societies

At least in democratic societies, school is ideally characterised by the following features (Dreeben, 2002):

First, it does not subject pupils to demands or obligations that encompass them in their whole personhood. The school treats children and young people in their role as pupils, rather than holistically. While this is often regarded as an impersonal or even inhumane approach, such views ignore the fact that universalisation is closely linked to ideas of fairness and equality. The universal treatment of pupils is intended to prevent nepotism, favouritism and arbitrariness, or at least to limit these factors organisationally and render them visible, thus making them open to critique.

Second, the school does not demand total emotional identification from pupils, but allows for objective distancing, which is not (or at least not immediately) regarded as a betrayal of the common cause.

Third, the protection of young people's personhood and the restriction of access to them as individuals can also be seen in the time limitations placed on schooling. School begins in the morning and ends sometime during the day, and with the exception of extracurricular offerings, it has no control, during non-teaching hours, over the children and young people entrusted to it, and especially not to their wishes, interests and mental states.

Fourth, rationality and argumentation are at the core of debates at school. These values are used to lead discussions and problematise lived realities. And education itself is also geared towards these values.

Fifth, and finally, independent thinking is valued and encouraged at school. The idea is that this will help children and young people to feel confident that their own opinions matter. This too, and not only the limitation of access to pupils and the fact that their whole personhood is not engaged, shows that in school – despite all the obligations of belonging to the institution and complying with organisational rules – certain spaces of autonomy are indeed supported.[5]

The vagueness, indeterminacy and ambiguity of school

The fact that school is formally organised in structural terms does not mean that structures and formal organisation constitute the core of schooling. Instead, many aspects of school are vague, indeterminate and uncertain.

Per Dalin (1998, 66) explains this as follows[6]: First of all, schools pursue many ambiguous objectives. The goals of curricula, for instance, often turn out to be general, vague and contradictory, or at least are open to interpretation and negotiation. Not all goals of schooling can be realised simultaneously and in full measure, and it may even be that one goal has to be abandoned or displaced in favour of another.

Second, the school is susceptible to societal trends and political influence. Indeed, the education system is controlled by various groups and systems within society (Fend, 2006, 55f.), first and foremost by the state and its administrative bodies, which, in turn, are guided by legal requirements.[7] The education system is also influenced by trade associations, political parties, parents, pupils and teachers. Many of these arenas are organised with a view to articulating and pooling interests, for example, in associations, political parties and (especially in the case of teachers) unions.[8] For this reason, schools are heavily dependent on financial and ideological support from societal and political actors. They generally have little opportunity for self-determination and they possess limited political power in the game of winning recognition and support.

Third, social integration within schools is weak. Teachers work with their classes in closed and self-contained classrooms. This spatial infrastructure automatically means that teachers are alone in their efforts, in effect, or at most act as part of a team of specialists, while cooperation across the boundaries of classes, levels and schools is made very difficult, to say the least. But this situation is also especially unfavourable for certain children and young people with disabilities, because of the paucity of accessible spatial structures or areas for retreat and recuperation in schools. If such spaces exist at all – in particular for children with autism, difficulty concentrating, special medical needs or a justified need for social withdrawal and physical or psychological recuperation – they are often small, dark and unattractive areas, for example, storage rooms where equipment or technical material is stored.

Fourth, the school operates on a weak knowledge base. Unlike other organisations, the school has hardly any technology at its disposal that might allow it to achieve the desired results in a systematic way. As already mentioned, the school seeks to bring stability into the uncertain, vague territory of education through various levers and mechanisms, such as curricula, courses, regulations and examinations. However, it does not succeed completely; indeed, it is somewhat constrained in this respect. This weak knowledge base is caused by the technology deficit of pedagogical activity already described by Luhmann and Schorr (1982), and it has direct implications for the possibilities of how inclusive education can be implemented in schools in practice, and also for empirical research in that field.

Education cannot simply be churned out like a machine-made product, namely for three reasons: (a) Teachers are not able to implement their intentions via clearly controlled actions in a way that allows them to achieve only *one* specific effect on young people. Even if teachers adopt a certain norm of inclusion (understood, for example, as recognition of the diversity of people) and convey this norm, they cannot ensure that it will be understood in exactly the same way by all pupils, or that it will therefore have an effect precisely as intended, especially in a unilaterally positive manner. For empirical research, this also means that certain effects of inclusion essentially cannot be attributed to the teacher at all. (b) The more extensive the intended effect and the broader the time frame involved for a given action, the more indeterminate and less clearly attributable that action becomes. This is true for many educational visions, especially that of inclusion. Therefore, it can also be argued that a ready-made pedagogical product called "inclusion" never actually exists. Rather, the process of achieving inclusion is always unfinished and ongoing. This reality applies in a special way to the process of inclusive education (here understood as education in a mainstream school) and the possibilities for connecting it to the goal of broader societal inclusion. The question of which factors specifically contribute to this goal, or have an effect that furthers it, is highly controversial, difficult to verify and made even more complex because the time frame of the goal extends far beyond schooling itself and thus also raises the question of what exactly, in retrospect, the contribution of the school to full societal inclusion actually has been. And finally, (c) the self-referentiality of each participant in the process of education also means, as already mentioned, that every intentional action taken by a teacher can ultimately only appear as an interpretative effort and the result of pupils' processing strategies, and cannot be viewed as an objectively identifiable product or piece of knowledge independent of its reception by sensing and perceiving subjects. Against the background of the concept of inclusion advocated here, this also means that the full success of inclusive education cannot be understood without a positive social and individual relationship to inclusion (or its collective processing in terms of social integration as well as personal processing through a sense of personal belonging).

Pedagogy as a profession, for these reasons, does not correspond to a hard technology, but to a "fragmented" or "soft" one. The reality that education is a soft, fractured technology and not one that can be directly defined, measured or produced has implications not only for teaching. Rather, it also influences the possibilities and structures of interaction inside and outside schools and school classes. As the foundations for interaction in school classes are in part laid outside the classroom and school, the structural preconditions for interaction also elude control. Consider, for example, the asymmetrical social structure within a school class: An adult teacher instructs numerous pupils who are all of approximately the same (young) age; consider, also, the hierarchical relationship between teachers and pupils, the timetable with its rhythm and the material to be taught or learned. The usual spatial and architectural arrangements – rectangular classrooms; parallel seating layouts; pupils who (have to) look at the teacher but cannot look at each other, etc. – complete these fragmented and partly contradictory preconditions for interaction (this is of course also the case when not all the above arrangements are in place).

The consensual areas of communication, understood as the coordination of experiential spaces, are often unclear in this context. In schools, it is not possible simply to issue information or to formulate and enforce expectations. Rather, it is necessary to provide orientation continuously and in an ongoing process. This is achieved, on the one hand, by means of values (such as that of inclusion) that are both enshrined in guidelines and put into practice, and, on the other hand, by means of ritualised patterns of interaction that promote the normative integration of the school, such as entrance exams, assessments, study and break schedules, regulations, school events and graduation ceremonies.

The social system of the school

The social density of the classroom and its semi-public character are responsible for the occurrence of numerous, rapidly shifting events that are visible to all, and which are, to a considerable extent, both unplanned and unpredictable, but which call for a quick response to avoid the risk of them having a socially destabilising effect. As responsibility for the design and orderly flow of lessons lies in the hands of teachers, they are particularly affected by the complexity of the teaching situation. However, as complexity is by definition not analytically controllable, teachers are encouraged to simplify what they teach. To do this, they usually rely on didactics, which provide them with models to help make lessons manageable.[9] And they also use their position of power in other ways, namely to enforce norms and expectations. They penalise, praise and reprimand; they designate the margins of success but also those of failure. It is therefore not surprising that empirical research finds a clear correlation between feedback (especially of a negative nature) given by teachers and the degree of popularity pupils enjoy with their peers (Cappella, Hughes & McCormick, 2017; Hendrickx et al., 2017).

As a social system, however, teaching is of course not something accomplished by the teacher alone. Rather, it is a collective achievement in which pupils participate as much as teachers. According to Goffman (1983), we can therefore speak of teaching as an interaction order, which is generated situationally and is characterised by a number of special features: presence, belonging, mutual awareness, communication and connection. The aspect of presence does not apply in an absolute sense, as temporary absences – for example, due to therapy sessions outside of school – are also possible.[10]

In a school class, all protagonists – especially the teachers and the pupils – engage in relationships with one another that cannot be reduced to role templates. Rather, these relationships – even if they are characterised by role-based distance – are of a personal nature. For example, everyone is addressed by name. Idiosyncrasies, habits and specific interests of individuals are known to others. Persons thus appear both in their individual nature (in their identity) and in their (social) function.

School versus family

In sociological terms, the family cannot be described as a subsystem of society like other societal systems (such as the political, economic, legal and science systems). As a private sphere of life, the family instead forms a kind of structural counterpart to society. The school's task is to mediate between the two, i.e. between the non-society of the family and society itself with its various systems. In other words, school serves to introduce a new generation to life in society.

But how do the institutional structures of the school and the interaction between family and school serve as contexts of experience? Dreeben (2002) compares the school with the family and finds similarities, but above all crucial structural differences. These differences in particular point to the possibilities (but also the limits) of inclusion in schools in comparison to families and other family-like or particular structures such as friendships.

Key differences

The school differs from the family in several ways. These differences have an impact not least on the behavioural expectations placed on pupils and their opportunities for action. First, all pupils must perform the same tasks, albeit with variations, or at least tasks assigned by the same person. Second, age classes establish a condition of homogeneity, as it were, that allows the teacher to engage pupils collectively with a single task. Third, as children progress from class to class, many of these transitions are also associated with new categories or conditions: New learning material is added, curriculum changes occur, teachers come and go.

> Most important, the experiences of membership in a group of age-equals and repeated boundary crossings make it possible for pupils to acquire a relativity of perspective, a capacity to view their own circumstances from other vantage points that they themselves have occupied.
> *(Dreeben, 2002, 76f.)*

But how does the family differ from the school in concrete terms?[11] First, school is different from the family in terms of the scope of its social setting. Families today – at least in Western societies – are predominantly small systems with fewer than ten, and often even fewer than five members (including the adults). School classes, however, frequently have between 20 and 30 (or even more) members. A school as a whole might be attended by several hundred people. Thus, unlike in families, a relative degree of anonymity prevails among the participants at school.

Second, school differs from the family in terms of the duration of the social relationship. It is true that children spend significantly more of their waking hours at school than at home during their school years. However, family relationships outlast the affiliation with the school and relationships with the actors participating there, such as teachers. While a person's relationship with their family lasts their entire life, they leave school after several years, by which time they have probably switched school classes or teachers on various occasions, leading to new group configurations.

Third, the relative proportions of adults and children are also an important difference between the school and the family. In school classes, a whole group of children is usually addressed by one adult (or a few adults). The numerical superiority and thus the relative power of the children are broken or curbed by the specific role of the teacher, who has authority and control over penalties, opportunities for action and key (learning) resources. The structure within the school class group, consisting of few adults and many pupils, also functions in a cyclical way, unlike in the family. Each week (with rare exceptions) follows the same plan and schedule set out in the timetable. This makes it possible to have a rhythm and organisational consistency, but it also shows how difficult it is, compared to the familial system, to react spontaneously (yet in a coordinated way) in schools, and to respond to specific, unplanned occurrences or to interrupt cyclical processes in general, or arrange them in a different, freer way.

Fourth, the makeup of the school is much more heterogeneous than that of the family.[12] The major exception to the heterogeneity of pupils is their age. Homogeneity is established in school through the formation of grades, or at least cross-grade clusters. It is very rare that more than three grades are grouped together. The main difference between school classes and families in terms of age composition is that in families, biological circumstances automatically lead to a heterogeneous age structure, whereas in schools, homogenisation already stems from the relevant legal requirements. In most cases, state laws stipulate that children must start attending school from the age of six.[13]

Fifth, the visibility of actions within the two systems is different. In the family, all members see each other in a variety of everyday, highly private situations over the course of many years. The situation is very different in school, where there is much less scope for action and less space for privacy (ibid., 19):

> A classroom has certain characteristics of a public place, more so than does a family. Many activities are carried on out loud and in front of everybody: Reports, recitations, replies to questions, discussions, praise, chastisement, instruction, laughter. Activities are frequently initiated by the teacher, and pupils are required to engage in public performance, often judged openly by the teacher and by other members of the class.

The (albeit limited) public nature of actions in schools makes it possible, on the one hand, for such actions to be discussed on a quasi-public level and thus made transparent in front of a group. On the other hand, this also means that a retreat into the private sphere is hindered or made impossible. As a result, the dangers and risks of public exposure, humiliation and marginalisation in schools are different – and sometimes more severe – than in the family.

Sixth, school presents to children a crucial distinction that is not necessarily introduced within the family – namely that made between a person and their position. School contributes in many ways to this distinction being accepted, as it forms an integral part of the institutional functioning of education. Through the establishment of shared positions (for example, that of "pupil") cutting across a range of differences (such as those relating to gender, race, religion or ethnicity), school also simultaneously creates an experience in which common interests and circumstances are given a priority that can transcend personal dissimilarities (ibid., 78).

Seventh, children's performance is systematically evaluated in school, but not in the family (at least ideally). This means that pupils are judged according to their achievements and not, for example, on the basis of affinities (Parsons, 1959). Here, we see that the values of universalism and specificity are closely linked (Fend, 2006, 79). Both represent the values of equal treatment and the limitation of institutions' access to specific aspects of the individual, at the same time preserving the integrity of their "core". The school has an institutional duty to refrain from using criteria other than performance in its policies on advancement and penalisation. Origin, affinity and skin colour, for instance, are not officially recognised as characteristics relevant for assessment. Furthermore, assessment of individuals should not be based on their entire character; rather, it must be limited to performance characteristics.

Eighth, pupils at school are prepared for very different situations than they are in family life. They learn things that will be useful in other contexts and at other times, for example, in professional life. It is true that there is overlap with the content taught in families. For example, there is a set of behavioural norms learned in families and in school that is important for both systems. However, much of what is taught and practised in families is mainly for the sake of family life itself (for example, setting and clearing the table, not getting up immediately after a meal and telling parents where one is going). This also means that such content is not standardised and cannot be automatically transferred to other associative contexts (e.g. other families) and systems.

Ninth, decisions on what and how pupils need to learn in schools are usually made without consulting pupils' families, that is, at the political level. This aspect also distinguishes the school from the family in terms of its role-based powers and duties, as well as its specific ties to the political sphere.

Tenth, it is evident that in many respects the school aligns its values with the requirements of a modern society and not with those of the family or particular communities. As a result, values that are lived or expressed in both systems also acquire different qualities and orientations in each case. While school, for example, should be comparatively neutral in affective terms, the family is characterised by a high degree of affectivity. This also means that values such as recognition are experienced differently. In the family, for instance, recognition is expressed in the form of love, while at school recognition mainly takes the form of social esteem for performance as well as respect in general.

School and the learning of norms

The school's contribution to the acceptance and formation of norms that permeate many areas of public life is crucial, not least because, ideally, children's experience in the family prior to school is strongly characterised by special treatment and parental regard for the whole child. Attention and affection within the family are undoubtedly very important to ensure a healthy upbringing and the successful development of identity. However, it is also important to emphasise the decisive contribution of schools to the learning of norms, which are important in many societal systems (e.g. in the economy, but also to some extent in the political system). Children learn through and in school that when they are societal actors, they are treated as members of a category, and thus not only – as is the case in the family – as specific others, as special cases, so to speak (Dreeben, 2002, 76). This, in turn, as I have noted, is not an expression of social callousness *per se*, but represents an important motive of equal, democratic participation in a society in which all adults – regardless of their specific interests and characteristics – are considered citizens.

School contributes to the learning of norms in four concrete ways (cf. ibid.):

> First, in terms of independence, pupils learn to accept that there are tasks they have to do on their own, in a very specific way, as instructed by the teacher. Parents also expect their children to act autonomously in many situations. But teachers systematically expect pupils to meet standards of independence when completing academic tasks. With this self-imposed obligation comes the idea that others have a legitimate right to expect such independent behaviour in certain circumstances. Independence, however, does not only refer to autonomy in the performance of work. At school, children are generally made independent of people with whom they have built up strong relationships of dependency, namely their own family of origin. Independence is also an organisational necessity, as the sheer size of a class setting limits each pupil's entitlement to personal contact with the teacher. Pupils are thus also condemned to independence, in a way, and this can be a major problem for younger and weaker children especially.

The second and third norms expressed in school, as described by Dreeben, are universalism and specificity. Children and young people are universally addressed in their role as pupils and are confronted with the specific requirements of task performance that result from this role or are linked to it.[14] For example, all pupils have to deal specifically with the demands of the curriculum and the fulfilment of its designated learning objectives.

Fourth, according to the norm of performance, pupils are called on to accept the requirements that they should perform their tasks as well as possible and behave appropriately. Classrooms are organised around a set of core activities, in which a teacher assigns tasks to pupils and evaluates and compares the quality of their work. The direct relevance of teaching to performance assessment is obvious. Lessons and the individual and group work that takes place in them are organised as an experiential space in the assignment-performance-assessment sequence. Teachers have an essential but difficult role to play in putting this norm across, especially as they have to communicate it in the classroom as the smallest organisational unit of the education system (Vanderstraeten, 2004b).

The normative standards of performance expectations always imply – regardless of where they are applied – that there will be some persons who do not achieve them, and who in the worst case may even receive consistently negative evaluations. On the one hand, this has an impact on teachers, who eventually no longer expect any achievements at all from certain children and young people who fail frequently, and who downgrade their own teaching efforts accordingly. The systematic non-expectation of performance is a major problem, especially for disabled children and young people (Hehir, 2002). On the other hand, this expectation or lack thereof naturally also (and above all) has an impact on the pupils who fail to perform, in particular on their self-esteem. They have to adapt their behaviour in certain ways in order to cope with such negative feedback. But these pupils may also reach a point where they no longer accept social norms as legitimate indicators of their own performance, or they may come to reject achievement in general as an undesirable goal, leading them to be considered "behaviourally challenged". This affective re-evaluation can then provoke a refusal of support for the norms and values deemed essential in school, or indeed to a refusal of school as a whole. In extreme cases, this situation can lead to a phenomenon of individually perceived alienation, and to revolt and anarchy at the social level (Jaeggi, 2005).

All the performance-oriented and -driven activities in school thus force pupils to contend with various degrees of success and failure. Pupils whose work is consistently poor not only have to participate in performance activities that lead to their failure, but must also learn to live with that failure. Consistently successful achievement, by contrast, requires pupils to contextualise the consequences of their own excellence in relation to their peers in a way that includes non-academic domains. They face the dilemma, for example, of having surpassed their peers in some respects while depending on their friendship and support in others, especially in extracurricular social activities. The classroom is thus not only the space where the experience of achievement itself takes place, but is also a by-product of it, in the form of such dilemmas. Moreover, unlike in group sports, academic failure is of an individual, not a collective nature. But due to the social situation in the classroom with its associated semi-public character, such failure also becomes visible and assessable for others.

The psychological consequences of failure are therefore more severe at school than at home, while positive experiences of achievement are more visible and varied. The school also offers less opportunity than the family to strengthen pupils' self-confidence and self-esteem in the face of failure and exclusion, not least because its core focus is on the qualification and training of pupils and not primarily on their psychological well-being. Furthermore, the performance demands placed on pupils increase as the years go by, at least for those who go on to further academic qualifications (for example, in a secondary school that prepares young people for higher education), and this, in turn, limits the possibilities for teachers to influence values other than performance. The number and variety of activities governed by performance principles also increase at higher levels (Dreeben, 2002, 73):

> As preparation for adult public life in which the application of these principles is widespread, schooling contributes to personal development in assuring that the majority of pupils not only will have performed tasks according to the achievement standard, but that they will have had experience in an expanding number of situations in which activities are organised according to it.

This all increases the danger of damage to the psyche as well as to social relationships.[15]

One reason for these various challenges is that school education is provided within a "people-changing organisation", as is also the case for religious, medical, legal and therapeutic support systems. However, education differs from these other systems in crucial ways. It is true that even in schools the purposes of the organisation cannot be achieved without the "commitment" of clients (Lortie, 1975). At the same time, school is a coercive institution. Unlike the clients of therapists, lawyers or doctors, for example, pupils in compulsory basic education do not attend school of their own free will.[16] School and teaching are therefore not based on a voluntary working alliance between teachers and pupils, as is the case with therapists or doctors and their clients. Therefore, unlike in these professions, acceptance of a need for help *cannot* be relied upon as a source of motivation for learning.[17] This has far-reaching consequences, especially for the goal of promoting social integration as an aspect of holistic inclusion. For here, too, a basic dilemmatic structure becomes apparent: On the one hand, social integration cannot be fostered or practised without the commitment of individuals (teachers as well as pupils). But on the other hand, the motivation necessary for this cannot be expected, at least from the pupils, in a compulsory context. For the care, interest and concern for fellow pupils implied in social integration must at its core be of a voluntary and self-chosen nature. Only in this way can it also serve as a source of psychologically perceived belonging that is experienced authentically.

The functions of school

In a modern, diverse and interconnected society, it is clear that the education system performs extremely important tasks. It provides the qualifications that are crucial for individual and societal life and survival. Especially in modern, highly industrialised societies, the education system has such a strong social allocation function that the school can be described as the "sieve" in the process of distributing job opportunities and positions (Fend, 2006, 44). On a social level, the education system thus serves the function of allocation, while on an individual level, education is one of the most important means of planning one's own life. Education furthermore promotes societal integration by imparting the values and norms that underpin the democratic and constitutional order. Finally, opportunities for integrating into the education system (and beyond), and thus into the social structure of society, are guided by universally applied achievement criteria that are reflected in curricula and other mechanisms (ibid., 34).

The four areas of responsibility or functions of the school can therefore be reconstructed as follows (ibid., 49f.)[18]: First, school performs the function of cultural reproduction, i.e. an enculturation function. This ranges from the mastery of basic symbol systems like language and writing to the internalisation of fundamental value orientations such as socially responsible action and altruism. Cultural participation and identity are thus achieved through socialisation and cultural initiation. This process promotes both the autonomy of persons on an individual level and their cultural affiliation.[19]

Second, school has a qualification function. Professionally relevant abilities are acquired through education, specifically through training and instruction. For individuals, this is where the opportunity arises to lead an independent working life. At the societal level, the aim is to improve economic competitiveness. This aspect is therefore relevant to the importance and contribution of inclusive education for post-school inclusion in the labour market.

Third, the school exhibits an allocation function, i.e. it has a bearing on the social structure and distribution of positions within a society. A legitimised position in the scholastic performance hierarchy is achieved through examinations and qualifications. This function thus aligns with the normative requirement of equal performance assessment. In this context, individuals get the opportunity to take fate into their own hands through subjective achievements and learning efforts. At the societal level, the aim is to ensure that all school leavers can in the future find a job that matches their abilities.[20] The considerable importance of schooling for the labour market is thus also evident in this function.

Fourth, according to Fend, the school has an integration and legitimation function, which, in a broader understanding, he views as one of peacekeeping. This function promotes the internal cohesion of a society. The idea, here, is that education can encourage participation and strengthen affiliation as part of the democratising processes of a modern society. This function creates a social bond at the individual level and lays the foundation for social responsibility, both by means of political education and through institutional regulatory systems and modes of governance.[21]

The inclusion function of school

Societal developments suggest that the functions of school described by Fend need to be complemented by a new function, which can be described as its inclusion function. But why is it necessary to attribute this function to the school, and what does it constitute in societal and individual terms?

The trends of increasing globalisation and digitalisation, which are turning the world into a village, as it were, and which lead to growing dynamism and interconnectedness, have the consequence, first of all, that there is ever less clarity and certainty about what should be learned at all, and to what extent, or how, in order to be able to succeed in today's world. Second, it has become apparent in recent years that the world is again increasingly subject to conflicts with an international, not just a regional, dynamic. Third, intensified migration and the formation of ever more multicultural societies mean that people today can and must learn to live and deal with societal diversity to a much greater extent. This is not only true in a negative sense, due to conflicts and wars that force people to flee and live in cultures and societies that are foreign to them, but also in a positive sense, thanks to the diversity of positive and enriching lifestyles adopted. The degree of societal pluralisation – in terms of sexual orientation, ideological perspective, religion, cultural interests and so on – has steadily increased in recent years. In this context, diversity and inclusion are keywords which highlight the importance of the greater acceptance (and not mere tolerance!) of heterogeneous modes of life.

Fourth, the extent of societal interconnectedness and reciprocal dependence on cooperation is growing in modern societies. Only very few societies or people can still live and survive in a way that is largely free of external influences. People in industrialised, urban areas of the world, at least, cannot help but understand their subsistence as linked to that of many other people. For school education, this means that children and young people must also increasingly be prepared for a globally networked, uncertain world in which they bear responsibility and in which they are expected to cooperate with others (Florian, 2019).

In view of these trends, it seems reasonable to attribute an inclusion function to the school. At the societal level, the inclusion function serves to structurally involve as many people as possible in cooperative processes to solve the complex problems at hand, while also promoting participation in the corresponding resources needed to find such solutions. On an individual level, this function serves to shore up the foundations of social integration and psychologically perceived belonging. This function of the school is, at its core, a democratic function that goes much further than that of integration, where the aim implies peacekeeping and maintaining the cohesion of a stable, relatively straightforward society. By contrast, the inclusion function, building on this, highlights the need for cooperation within society, collective participation in addressing new problems where a solution has yet to be found, and consideration of the perspectives of all those affected in a society. So, it is not only the formative and educational significance of democracy that is the emphasis here (including school as a place where democratic virtues such as respect and empathy are instilled), nor only its instrumental significance, i.e. the practice of democratic principles of participation and involvement. Rather, the inclusion function of school reaches further, to reflect the intrinsic significance of democracy as the participation of all citizens, in the understanding of inclusion as inherently valuable and important for the human well-being of all (Sen, 1999, 153).

Rediscovering Dewey

When it comes to the question of what a school oriented around inclusion might look like, it is no surprise that we can find new impulses in a democratically oriented pedagogy that is committed to the collective resolution of societal problems. The major formative figure in this respect is once again John Dewey. At various places in his vast oeuvre, most notably in one of his major works, *Democracy and Education* (Dewey, 2004), we find crucial ideas that support the increased societal importance of inclusion and therefore also suggest that schools should be seen as having an inclusion function (Danforth, 2015; Višňovský & Zolcer, 2016; Wahlström & Sundberg, 2018; Waks & English, 2017). In this approach, Dewey follows a long tradition of philosophers (including Kant, Rousseau, Schopenhauer and Arendt, to mention but four) who have dealt intensively with the relationship between democratic involvement and school education.[22]

For several reasons, Dewey's ideas are of crucial importance, or serve as an inspiration, for the questions we are dealing with here. First, for Dewey, social diversity is functionally beneficial, both for society as a whole and for individuals. Dewey sees social diversity as a fact of modern societal life that is also constitutive. He assumes that pluralisation and heterogeneity in the form of diverse perspectives contribute to a society's ability to solve problems, and he further posits that individuals are supported in their personal development by belonging to a variety of reference groups. If the number and diversity of social memberships increase, people are in a sense also forced to form plural, integrated identities that are not only oriented around one-sided conventions, and they must become assimilated in a way that allows a range of potentially conflicting role expectations to be consistently structured.

In a world characterised by pluralisation and heterogeneity, Dewey views the role of the school in two ways: First, the school acts to strengthen the community within its own boundaries, or even create it from the ground up. Second, the school community should prepare pupils to take the idea of community beyond the school into the neighbourhood and the wider world. For Dewey, there is a strong logical link between education, communication, community and personal growth (Pring, 2007b, 117):

Hence, a greater variety of peoples within the community (or different ethnicities, political values, religious convictions) should enrich the process of communication, thereby enhancing personal growth – that is, the openness to further ideas, the critical questioning of received assumptions, the readiness to enrich one's own understandings through their being tested in experience and in the critical engagement with others. Schools should be communities par excellence, but in fact too often their hierarchical and autocratic nature inhibits that sharing of aims and experiences. The learner is expected to receive what the teacher transmits without the opportunity to question or to internalise that which is transmitted.

Just as Dewey sees the goal of education as facilitating growth through appropriate experiences, the institutional organisation of education through schools must serve to create the conditions for such growth. And a democratic community is one of the main preconditions in this context. Only a community of this kind respects and enables the pursuit of individual goods that are compatible with the goods of all its members (ibid., 133).

To this end, Dewey outlines the perspective of a reflexive-experimental democracy. His ideal of democracy as a form of reflexive cooperation highlights the reasons why we need a rich, diverse and vibrant society as the motivational and educational foundation of a legitimate and effective political democracy. Dewey's work is also interesting, however, for other reasons having to do with the present-day societal challenges that are reflected in schools and questions related to inclusive education. First, Dewey advocates an approach that systematically links education and democratic participation, and thus can guide the meaning and function of school education beyond a narrow focus on curricular learning goals towards a more holistic picture of the contribution of schooling to the broader social inclusion of people. This approach does not, therefore, separate school-based learning from social inclusion, as is often the case for authors critical of inclusion today (Wilson, 2000, 1999). Second, Dewey's political and moral philosophy is closely tied to questions of education, which, in his understanding, are pragmatic and applied, and also directly connected to philosophical, moral and political issues. Such questions do not, as in much of the contemporary philosophical literature, appear only as an afterthought or context of application, as it were. Dewey also does not dissociate the application of (inclusive) education from its justification, as is the case with many advocates of inclusion. Third, the aspect of what might be called "the social" is at the heart of Dewey's philosophy. This approach can help to shed light on an important area that is either lost or is only vaguely addressed in the current educational discourse on inclusion. Fourth, Dewey's theory of education as growth offers an alternative view to much of the current education literature, which is largely oriented around measurable effects and accountability.

For Dewey, growth is the most important goal of education. He writes (2004, 57): "Since growth is the characteristic of life, education is all one with growing; it has no end beyond itself". Dewey's understanding of growth is far-reaching. It encompasses development in a biological, psychological, sociological and cultural sense, and it results from interaction with the environment. In *The Child and the Curriculum* (1966, 4), he writes:

> The fundamental factors in the educative process are an immature, undeveloped being; and certain social aims, meanings, values incarnate in the matured experience of the adult. The educative process is the due interaction of these forces. Such a conception of each in relation to the other as facilitates completest and freest interaction is the essence of educational theory.

This growth, which stems from the interaction between immature individuals and their natural and social environment, involves a transformation of past experiences into new and different experiences. Growth occurs when a person feels and thinks differently, when experience itself is transformed. For growth to take place, people need the capacity or potential to change, "the *ability* to develop", as Dewey (2004, 45) puts it. Growth and the potential to grow initiate the critical idea of reconstruction in Dewey's theory of experience. While growth is the goal of education, the reconstruction of experience is its mission. Dewey's technical definition of education is therefore as follows: "It is that reconstruction or reorganization of experience which adds to the meaning of experience, and which increases ability to direct the course of subsequent experience" (ibid., 83). Experience is the starting point of all philosophical reflection and is fundamental to Dewey's philosophical pluralism. His appreciation of diversity is not limited to his political theory of democracy, but is based on his understanding of human experience as rich and fertile with meaning. Because of the diversity of experience, people can and must share the meaning of their experiences, to the extent that they (like all people) live in social communities.

The fundamental criteria of experience for Dewey are communication and interaction. People interact with their natural and social environments. Their experiences are only full when they are involved in an activity that includes both active phases of doing and passive phases of experiencing. When both aspects are combined, this is when a meaningful experience takes place. But when these aspects are separated, as is often the case in schools today, learning is only academic in nature and does not have sufficient relevance to real-life problems. Such experiences are not educational; indeed, they are often the opposite, because they do not lead to further experiences, or may even interfere with them, for example, by resulting in boredom, fear or indoctrination. Second, the pedagogical aspect or value of these experiences lies in the development of human discriminatory capacity, namely people's ability to experience the world, not only in physical reaction to it, but in being able to engage with the world and participate in its further development and improvement as an outcome of education. Dewey's understanding of the value of education is not individualistic but social; that is, he sees the endeavour of education as a fundamentally social one. Both the formation and transformation of experience are namely social in three ways (Pring, 2007b, 29): First, if children were not born into a social group, they would not have the opportunity to gain further experiences that can be internalised and enable them to survive and grow in a particular society. Second, each person interacts with others who see things differently. To survive and thrive, we each have to adjust to the perspectives of others. We must constantly adapt and react to the perceptions and interpretations of other people and anticipate their actions on the basis of our own experience. This process is continuous and perpetually reciprocated. Third, when learning the language of a social group, people will likely adapt to some features of the environment more than to others, for language is a map of experience, a way of looking at things, a means of distinguishing between different kinds of experiences.

Dewey sees the link between democracy and education not only in the fact that schools must prepare pupils for a democratic life after school. In his view, democracy is paramount, and we need to ask ourselves what kind of education is necessary for the sake of democracy. Once again, the link between the two is communication. Genuine communication requires reciprocity and mutual respect. Each person in the communication process is of equal value, as each has an opinion or point of view worthy of serious consideration. Every individual brings a different set of experiences to our understanding of a situation. Persons are able to reorganise their perspectives through the process of sharing experiences and attending to others' critiques and accounts of experience, which, in turn, fosters their own ability to further contribute to shared experience and understanding.

In the connection between democracy and education, it is important to recognise that Dewey holds a specific view of democracy. He considers it to be the kind of community that enables maximum participation in deliberations on all matters that affect the lives of those within the community, and in the decisions that result from those deliberations. And such maximum participation is desirable not because it is likely to be more efficient, but because it is a precondition for human flourishing and well-being. It is thus this intrinsic meaning of democracy that is key for Dewey.

Dewey's theory expresses two understandings of democracy, which he views both as a specific experiential space and as a specific mechanism for resolving conflicts. Democracy, understood as an experiential space, encompasses active and passive components. Dewey's conception of democracy is characterised by the ideal of social cooperation, which is not – as in political liberalism – limited to the political sphere in the narrow sense. Rather, the cooperative forms of interaction relate to society as a whole and thus also to an area that is, in a sense, sub-political, namely the school. Dewey assumes that the democratic public sphere can only be animated when the various spheres of societal activity are regulated fairly and equitably, so that all members of society can see themselves as active participants. For, without a sense of shared responsibility and cooperation, individuals cannot possibly come to regard political decision-making processes as a means of collective problem solving (Honneth, 1998).

In his later works, especially in his book *The Public and its Problems* (1927), Dewey conceives of democracy as a specific conflict resolution mechanism. That is, he views democracy as a mode of dealing with collective problems, a process, which, in his view, makes intelligent solutions more likely. This second understanding encompasses political action in the narrower sense, referring to the means of actualising a large community: "The political and governmental phase of democracy is a means, the best means so far found, for realizing ends that lie in the wide domain of human relationships and the development of human personality" (Boydston, 2008, 217).

These two conceptions of democracy must be regarded as an interplay between means and ends, not as fundamentally different, contradictory understandings (Jörke, 2003, 207).

According to Dewey, in a society that is largely democratically constituted, conflict resolution mechanisms will also produce more intelligent outcomes, and the more democratically the political process is structured, the greater the likelihood of corresponding feedback effects on the other spheres of society. Insofar as Dewey's political theory aims at the democratisation of society, this interplay can be understood as a spiral, and namely one that, according to the basic pragmatist understanding, must not float in a vacuum, but must be anchored in existing practice and the beliefs reflected therein.

Democratic forms of association enable the growth of experience in a special way. Dewey sees socio-philosophical and epistemic reasons for this. On the socio-philosophical level, Dewey argues that the "purpose" of human nature is the growth of experience, that is, individual self-realisation, and that this goal can only be realised through communal action. This approach is based on the view that human beings are primarily social creatures, and that their character and desires only develop and evolve when they live with other people. And the more democratic the respective social spheres, the greater the chance for each individual to grow through engagement with the experiences of their fellow human beings. For Dewey, then, the plurality of human modes of life is not simply a necessary evil of modern and liberal societies, but is, on the contrary, the very lifeblood of a living, creative democracy. From an epistemic standpoint, the rational superiority of cooperation is apparent in Dewey's view. Knowledge can only evolve in the open discourse of a community that embraces the pursuit of knowledge. Epistemic democracy is subordinate to ethical-social democracy to the extent that it represents a means for improving it; however, this is not a simple dualism of ends and means. Rather, according to Dewey, both dimensions intertwine in a multi-layered way. Two insights can be gleaned here: First, that democracy and difference need not be mutually exclusive, but are rather constitutively related to each other. Second, it follows from this that the idea of democracy must not be limited to political decision-making, but is first and foremost a form of experience, a way of life. This leads us to the question of what moral and institutional preconditions are needed for such a substantive concept of democracy.

For Dewey, schools play a special role in developing and sustaining democracies. Schools can be the spaces where the experiences of all learners are respected and made the subject of communication processes. Richard Pring (2007b, 119) formulates this understanding as follows:

Democracy is deep and active communication between individuals. It welcomes and sustains diversity of experience and background. It reflects the constant attempt to break down the barriers that inhibit communication – those of social class, racial stereotyping or selective schooling. Any such separateness impoverishes the experience of all. It blocks off the experiences of others from which one's own experience would be enriched.

The mission of democracy never ends; it is a constant struggle against the marginalisation and discrimination faced by certain voices, experiences and people. Thus, the task of democracy, if we follow Dewey, is to create and maintain a freer and more humane world in which everyone can participate and contribute.

The school community, according to Dewey, is essentially a moral community in which children and young people grow as moral persons through active participation, in which they learn how to interact fruitfully with others, cooperate with them and form a shared world of experience. The importance of this moral aspect of schooling is still hugely relevant today, a hundred years after Dewey's most productive phase of exploring that topic. In Dewey's view, the school should be a source of inclusion – not for purposes of generating uniformity and eliminating diversity, but in the sense of enabling future citizens to understand and learn from each other, to respect life perspectives that differ from their own, and to solve societal problems together. This aim lies at the heart of the school's inclusion function.

Conclusion

Schooling occupies a major part of the long transition from childhood to adulthood. In order to understand how school education contributes to the development and, above all, to the inclusion of people, we must not only be aware of its diverse, often conflicting and by no means uncontroversial functions, but also situate it in the network of other important institutions, in particular the family, the economy and the political sphere.

We have seen that the school differs from the family in crucial ways and is geared to the requirements and conditions prevailing in modern societies. Two aspects deserve further mention: First, schools do not expect total identification of an emotional nature, and this extends to moral expectations of interpersonal accountability for inclusion. And second, schools cannot impose any sort of total obligation on their pupils. This also applies to the motivational and moral foundations for inclusion, especially social integration, as we will see later. These specific characteristics of modern schooling are not necessarily indicative of injustice, but rather reflect the requirements of modern life, and are even an expression of fairness and equality.

It has also become apparent that many aspects of school education are vague and contradictory, and thus call for interpretation and negotiation. Not all goals can be fully realised simultaneously or in conjunction with each other; one goal might even have to be abandoned or displaced by another. This reality also applies to the goal of inclusion, which often creates tension with other goals of the school, and is sometimes regarded as an aspect of lesser importance, or one that clashes with functions such as qualification or allocation. Nevertheless, with reference to relatively brief and schematic explanations of the challenges in modern societies, it has also become quite clear that such challenges result in the functions of schools expanding or shifting. In the broadest sense, the social and collaborative aspects of learning are becoming increasingly important in today's societies. We must learn to respond more quickly, flexibly, adaptively and positively to heterogeneity and new societal challenges. Heavy demands are placed on the school system in this context.

These demands directly have to do, on the one hand, with the increasing heterogeneity and diversity in societies, not simply on a factual level, triggered, for example, by conflict-related migration or the free movement of persons in European nations, but also due to perceptions of diversity and the growing individualisation of lifestyles and practices. These changes are shaping learning in schools. We all want to be addressed in our individuality, that is, not only in terms of our general requirements, but also on the level of our specific and individual needs. Pupils and parents expect to be treated not simply as one or a few among many, but as specific and distinct individuals.

On the other hand, the importance of school as a preparation for societal diversity (and the associated need to cope with uncertainty) is also increasing. Society has an interest not only in enabling future citizens to earn their own living, but also, directly, in ensuring that no one is excluded in such a way that their participation in goods is endangered, to the extent that they enter into long-term and irremediable dependency on the state. The state furthermore has an interest, albeit a more indirect one, in helping people to feel a sense of personal belonging and social integration (which, in turn, must be guided by what they can actually do and be within a given context, for example, in school education).

All these factors have led me to argue for an expansion of the school's functions, that is, to support the idea that the school also has an inclusion function (or should have one in the future). We must not forget, however, that the school has only a limited capacity to shape the current and future inclusion of pupils. This reality is rooted in the structure and function of the school.

A few points deserve mention here again. First, the school is not only a pedagogical institution. It also has other, non-pedagogical functions – as is currently evident in the era of COVID-19. In modern societies, the school also has a custodial function, for example. Schools thus have to solve societal problems that have arisen for reasons completely unrelated to education. And conversely, schools cannot solve all problems, not even those of a pedagogical nature. The problem, for instance, that certain children with severe cognitive impairments are unable to learn very much is simply a fact, which cannot be overcome even with the best didactics and methodology.

The narrow scope of the pedagogical management of difficult life situations points to the reality that educational institutions are intertwined in interdependent societal relationships. Educational activity gains its status through the provision of services for other subsystems: i.e. qualifications for the economic system, selection and normalisation of individuals for the social system by means of training, and participatory skills and legitimacy for the political system (Luhmann, 2002). This creates tension between an orientation towards full development of the subject's capacity for learning versus the social requirements in place (and the associated danger of the political, economic or social functionalisation of children as well as the risk of damaging their identity and self-confidence).

Second, much of schooling is public or at least semi-public in nature, which hugely increases the psychological costs of underachievement. Pupils must participate in activities in which they repeatedly fail, but at the same time they must uphold the values that define these activities, and find the motivation to do so. Meanwhile, their failure is regarded as something individual rather than structural or organisational (which, of course, it partly is). Thus all that which is expressed in inclusion – i.e. not only physical presence in class, but also social integration among peers, social attention from the teacher and, to some extent, psychological belonging – is semi-public and visible to everyone in the class, while a lack of inclusion is often blamed on the individual. But this leads to individual behaviour and cognition being abstracted from their social and structural contexts and atomistically individualised.

Third, social integration in schools has only a weak effect. Teachers work predominantly with their own classes in self-contained classrooms. In most schools, there is also little space for pupils who need to withdraw, for example, children with autism and perceptual disorders. The norms structure of the school, including its spatial structure, is geared towards pupils who are able to cope well with this tightly organised group structure and the spatial and didactic organisation of teaching. This is a problem for children who struggle with such structures, for example, because they cannot concentrate for long periods of time, get stressed in large groups or have medical needs that should not be addressed in public (for instance, because they need their bladder catheter changed).

The extent to which schools can actually succeed in becoming more inclusive will concern us in the final chapter. The next chapter focuses on the ethical-normative meaning of inclusion and inclusive education and thus brings us to the core of this book.

Notes

1 This work is based on an older, revised book and theory (Fend, 1980), which is why it is entitled *Neue Theorie der Schule* [New Theory of School].
2 Systems-theory considerations are important for both Fend and Dreeben, but for different reasons (Fend, 2006, 134f.): First, one crucial assumption of systems theory is that systems act in relation to environments, in particular social and psychological environments as well as cultural symbol systems. Systems are thus not isolated cosmoses set apart from societal settings. Second, another key assumption is that education systems operate according to a specific logic of their own that distinguishes them from other systems. Their primary environment is that of children and young people, whose behaviour can be differentiated into knowing and not-knowing. A third important assumption is that the education system is self-referential, i.e. that knowledge is formed within the system and that this knowledge and the system as a whole refer back to themselves. It must be possible to relate knowledge about the system to knowledge within the system. And fourth, there is the crucial systems-theory assumption that all socialisation is ultimately self-socialisation, i.e. that while it can be stimulated from the outside, it ultimately has to be achieved by individuals themselves.
3 But this does not apply to education, which is not itself an institution. Instead, according to Searle (2005), education can be understood as a form of human activity. This also means that education cannot simply be reduced to the institution of the school and thus to the responsibility of the state at the macro-level. At the same

time, education is not simply a micro-process that takes place at the level of teaching, interpersonal relationships and so on. Rather, intricate processes that shift back and forth between macro- and micro-levels are at work in the provision of education in schools. The complex interconnection of the various levels can be observed directly in curricula, which are negotiated, adopted and implemented at the level of the state and the political system, but which ultimately have to be applied at the micro-level of teaching. Education is a good (and ultimately, to follow Bourdieu, also a form of capital), and one that, in the case under consideration here, is acquired in school (which of course implies that a considerable share of education is not acquired in or through school). Second, education is a process in which individuals develop from a (somehow) unfinished state to a finished one. This process, which is characterised by the acquisition of a range of skills and attitudes, is shaped by institutions to a large extent.

4 This concept was explicitly introduced by Philip W. Jackson (1986). John Goodlad (1984) refers to the "implicit curriculum" in the same sense. By this, he means (ibid., 197)

> all those teachings that are conveyed by the ways the explicit curriculum is presented – emphasis on acquiring facts or solving problems, stress on individual performance or collaborative activities, the kinds of rules to be followed, the variety of learning styles encouraged, and so on.

Because the hidden or implicit curriculum encompasses goals that are generally considered to fall under the category of socialisation, school also performs functions that are normally attributed to the family. Given that socialisation is inherently present and expressed in social interactions at school, it is therefore unavoidable. "Any attempt to restrict it would in turn have a socialising effect", as Luhmann (2002, 53) rightly notes.

5 This aspect should be stressed here insofar as it already demonstrates that emotional and cognitive access to inclusion is also subject to certain limitations. Children and young people cannot be *obligated* to like other children, for instance, without violation of core features of the school, such as freedom of opinion and the associated importance of individual thought, along with the crucial limitation of control over children and their emotional attitudes and inner worlds.

6 Another aspect mentioned by Dalin has changed fundamentally in recent years, or has even been reversed. Dalin argues that schools, especially in comparison to other systems in society, are characterised by a lack of competition. They are subject to very little competitive pressure, according to Dalin, and their existence is not justified by the quality of their "output". Today, however, few would describe a lack of competition as a characteristic of schools; on the contrary, it seems evident that schools are nowadays considered much more from an economic point of view and are thus also increasingly subject to the logic of the economic system and its demands (for example, for an educated workforce). This point also highlights one of the problems that many young people with disabilities have to face at the end of their school education. For, even if they manage to obtain a school-leaving certificate that puts them in possession of institutionalised cultural capital, in highly capitalist societies, this does not guarantee them economic capital or the possibility of attaining capitalist self-sufficiency via a normal occupation. On the contrary, even then their societal inclusion is often precarious, not least because of structural hurdles and prejudices within society.

7 These requirements may be laid down in national law, but they may also be based on international legislation, as in the example of the UNCRPD.

8 Especially in countries where the development of an inclusive education system has been accompanied by a major change in the special education profession, associations and interest groups have expressed their reservations about what they see as rushed and poorly planned reforms. It is precisely through the bundling of interests that they sometimes gain considerable power in public and political discourse.

Inclusive education **153**

9 In many didactic models, however, it is precisely the sociality of teaching that is ignored. In the perspective of such models, teaching appears as a triangle between teachers, pupils and the material taught. This creates the impression that pupils' learning can be controlled by the teacher's actions: "What is thus left unexplored is the crucial aspect of teaching from a sociological perspective, namely its social character and the social dynamics of the school class" (Herzog, 2009, 167).

10 It seems clear, however, that a certain amount of physical presence is necessary if pupils are to be socially integrated and also able to participate in teaching as an interaction order. The motive of (social) belonging is particularly expressed in its absence, for example, in the form of psychological bullying.

11 Dreeben (2002) mentions a further difference which I do not elaborate on here, namely the aspect of heterogeneity among adults. In his view, gender heterogeneity in the (heterosexual) family contrasts with the surplus of female teachers that is often found in school education, empirically speaking. While the latter reality would still seem to apply, the heterosexuality of parental couples can no longer automatically be assumed, given the diversity of lifestyles that are now chosen. I do not explore this point in greater depth, as it is not of major importance for the topic at hand.

12 Adoptions and other family relationships involving children whose guardians are not their biological parents are of course an exceptional case here.

13 It is important to recognise that this does not allow us to escape a fundamental dilemma. For, on the one hand, an attempt can be made to bring together children with similar abilities and comparable levels of learning and knowledge, but this results in school classes with variable age structures (which, in turn, leads to organisational problems, including for the length of compulsory schooling); on the other hand, as already mentioned, classes containing children of approximately the same age naturally result in a grouping of greatly differing abilities (Dreeben, 2002, 15).

14 The values addressed here – especially the requirement of equal treatment of pupils associated with universality – are also reflected in expectations of the ideal teacher. Pupils want a teacher who is friendly, understanding and patient; the teacher should be able to master the material, explain it well and convey it in an interesting way, but also keep order in class, have no favourite pupils and impose reasonable penalties; the teacher should respect pupils and judge their performance fairly. These aspects play either no role or a different role in the family.

15 Empirical studies show disturbing results in the area of learning disabilities and cognitive impairment in particular. Compared to their peers, pupils with disabilities are less well-accepted (Frederickson, 2010a; Frederickson, Simmonds, Evans & Soulsby, 2007; Koster, Pijl, Nakken & Van Houten, 2010; Nowicki, 2003; Nowicki & Sandieson, 2002; Siperstein, Norins & Mohler, 2006). Approximately one in three pupils with disabilities is rejected by their peers (Pijl, Frostad & Flem, 2008). In a study conducted in the United States, only 10% of pupils without disabilities reported friendship with a child or young person who had a cognitive impairment (Siperstein, Parker, Bardon Norins & Widaman, 2007). In addition, most were not willing to interact with a child or young person with a cognitive impairment in friendly activities (e.g. inviting a child with a cognitive impairment to hang out with their own friends). In contrast to friendships between children without disabilities, friendships between children with and without learning difficulties were characterised by limited cooperation and shared decision-making, low levels of cooperative play and shared laughter, and an asymmetrical, hierarchical distribution of roles (Siperstein, Leffert & Wenz-Gross, 1997). The same was found in terms of interaction. Children without disabilities enjoyed significantly higher levels of interaction than children with disabilities (Guralnick et al., 1995).

16 This is not merely a matter of children not being asked whether they generally wish to be included in school education or not. There is also little or no room for manoeuvre in many other areas of schooling. In schools, we are always confronted with a range of institutional and societal requirements that have an impact on the freedom of action enjoyed by pupils.

17 This reality puts the school in a difficult situation, not only in terms of the relationship between the teacher and the pupils, but also regarding the form (and transparency) of behavioural expectations placed on the pupils. While in the narrower sense, scholastic expectations are clearly defined in the form of learning goals and curricula, the overarching behavioural expectations that underpin the smooth flow of learning are less clear and transparent, but nevertheless visible, powerful and real to all participants.

18 The functions mentioned so far are clearly not the only societal functions that can be attributed to schools. One aspect of schooling that is not always considered important is its absorption or safekeeping function (also referred to as a custodial function) (Dalin, 1998). Especially in the age of COVID-19, when the closure of schools has caused children and adolescents to be schooled at home – while their parents also work from home in many cases – the importance of this function for the smooth functioning of society has become very clear.

19 The fact that schools do not simply transmit culture but are themselves cultural products (Baker & LeTendre, 2005, 11) means, moreover, that they must be open to societal critique and thus to their own transformation and adaptation.

20 According to Fend (2006), this is not a matter of selection, i.e. the exclusion of people, but of assigning them to tasks with suitable requirements. For this reason, he chose to replace the term "selection", which he used earlier, with that of "allocation".

21 In a critical turn, the legitimation function might also be called an ideological function. Given that success at school is demonstrably not only determined by individual performance, but also substantially by social background, school appears to be an instrument of domination that reproduces social inequality. By imparting values and ideals that present socially and culturally conditioned inequalities as apparently natural, it conceals the failure of society in a key area of its political self-perception (Herzog, 2009, 158).

22 According to Axel Honneth (2016), the rupture of the connection between these aspects in recent years is due to two developments. First, there is the conviction in modern societies that democratic political systems require the cultural support of ethical mores and customs, which these systems themselves cannot produce or foster. This thesis that schools are dependent on value perspectives that they cannot generate themselves goes back to the German constitutional lawyer Ernst-Wolfgang Böckenförde (1976) and is sometimes referred to as the "Böckenförde dilemma". It represents the view that democracy survives because of the existence of moral attitudes that thrive only in tradition-oriented communities rooted in certain ethical or even religious understandings. As modern societies are increasingly detached from these foundations, and a common basis of values has largely disappeared, the assumption is that schools can no longer fulfil this role, or can only do so to a very limited extent, because they simply lack the necessary basis of legitimacy. Second, there is the normative tendency, especially in liberal theory, to interpret the idea of state neutrality so ambitiously and broadly that even the principles of democratically organised collective decision-making can no longer inform state schooling. The view in this case is that the school should be fully neutral and should not advocate any idea of the good life or specific desired communal goals. This is the position taken by Rawls (1971, 1996), for example. He also argues that future citizens must first have access to the key good of self-respect before they are able to participate in republican decision-making, in which they act as equals among equals.

7
VALUES THAT MATTER

Introduction

Discussion of the significance of the concept of inclusion, or of inclusive education, is naturally also linked to a broader question: Why should we want to pursue and implement the idea of inclusive education in the first place (Reindal, 2016)? This is a question that sheds light on the diverse justifications given for inclusion and inclusive education.

These justifications largely reflect ethical-normative values: Inclusion and inclusive education are viewed as better solutions than the alternatives, such as education in a special school or placement in an institution, for reasons that are primarily moral, not empirical. But we still need to ask: What ethical goals and normative aspirations underlie inclusion and inclusive education? And what structures, forms of participation, resources and attitudes are needed to achieve these goals and realise these aspirations?

This chapter brings together various strands that have been introduced in the course of this work, but have not yet been consistently applied to the questions of what specific values are encompassed in inclusion and inclusive education, and why it is important, not least for moral reasons, to make education inclusive.

In the second chapter, I proposed a methodological reconstruction of inclusion from a nonideal perspective. This approach implies, among other things, that inclusion as an objective can never be fully achieved, with the result that it will always remain an open-ended, context-bound and contingent state or process. This, in turn, means that we need to understand inclusion as something that is embedded in existing social, cultural and historical contexts. A nonideal approach first succeeds in bringing the "ends-in-view", as Dewey calls them, into focus. And second – as we saw in Chapter 3 – the potential for change in educational institutions such as schools can be grasped more realistically through

DOI: 10.4324/9781003221326-7

this approach. This is not least the case because it can be implied that pedagogical institutions (like other institutions) develop in a path-dependent manner, i.e. they consist of and emerge from real-world social and cultural practices that have evolved historically. In Chapter 4, I argued for understanding the concept of inclusion as a "thick" moral concept in epistemological terms. While the descriptive aspects in this context have already been highlighted, both generally in relation to the concept of inclusion and specifically with regard to inclusive education, this chapter will focus on the ethical-normative content of inclusion.

In Chapter 5, we addressed the question of whether disability should play a role at all in this kind of perspective on inclusion, or whether a focus on disability might even be an obstacle to the development of a genuinely inclusive understanding of education. At the level of theoretical conceptualisation, this focus is indeed problematic, not least because it reinforces the assumption of the difference of disabled children and young people compared to others, and thus already contributes to their stigmatisation, marginalisation or exclusion at the level of theory. However, the situation is different at the level of practical application. What is specific about disability, as opposed to other forms of social disadvantage, is that the disadvantage results from a dynamic and contingent combination of intrinsic, bodily factors *and* extrinsic, environmental factors. And these individual factors cannot simply be faded out or superimposed. Finally, in Chapter 6, we saw that the school is a societal institution that differs from the family in important ways, and also has key functions within society, such as the granting of qualifications. At the same time, it has become clear that school, with its functional orientation, fails to take sufficient account of pertinent developments within society. School furthermore has an inclusive function for a variety of reasons.

In all of the explanations and the assumptions presented in this context, it is of course possible to identify normative views and concrete moral dimensions implicitly at various points. For example, when disability is understood as a specific form of disadvantage, it is implied that disability is also a morally relevant form of inequality and not simply – or only – a morally neutral form of otherness.[1] In this chapter, we undertake a systematic and analytical exploration of the ethical-normative content of inclusion and inclusive education, which we have only touched upon so far.

This kind of approach has to date received relatively little attention in the inclusion debate. Even in the limited in-depth literature (referring to books and major anthologies) that is explicitly devoted to the ethical-normative content of inclusion (Goodin, 1996; Minow, 1990; Young, 2000), a rather implicit understanding is usually presented. This is well illustrated, for example, by Iris Marion Young's classic work, *Inclusion and Democracy* (2000). In this, one of her most important and best-known publications, Young (ibid., 5f.) summarises the philosophical thrust of her project as follows:

This book highlights one norm often invoked by those seeking to widen and deepen democratic practices: Inclusion. The normative legitimacy of a democratic decision depends on the degree to which those affected by it have been included in the decision-making processes and have had the opportunity to influence the outcomes. Calls for inclusion arise from experiences of exclusion – from basic political rights, from opportunities to participate, from the hegemonic terms of debate.

This passage shows that Young's understanding of inclusion – unlike that of democracy, as becomes clear in the course of her book – is couched in everyday language, and that the ethical-normative dimension of inclusion is not explored in detail or theoretical depth. Instead, Young assumes that inclusion can be understood as a form of participation in deliberative, democratic processes. The idea of her book is to show that deeper and more intensive participation in democratic processes calls for openness to diversity in the modes of communicative participation, and for social differences to be taken into account in a way that leads to the wisest and fairest political decisions.

This view is certainly not wrong, nor indeed problematic in the present context. We have already seen the strong relevance and influence of inclusion in the learning and practice of democratic processes, with reference to Dewey (2004). School provides children and young people with knowledge that will later be crucial for their deliberations as adults participating in democracy, such as information about what forms of democratic participation are possible (e.g. the preparation of referendums and initiatives in the Swiss political system) and how a democratic system is structured (e.g. the separation of executive, legislative and judicial branches of power). School also imparts, and provides practice in, the relevant abilities that citizens need to build and sustain a good democracy, in which the major concerns of all groups in society are taken seriously, and democratic decisions are widely accepted. These abilities include a range of cognitive skills, but also moral capacities such as empathy, mutual respect, critical faculties, tolerance and so on.

However, this approach to, or understanding of, inclusion ends up reducing its value to the contribution it can make to democratic life within society, in at least two ways: First, such a narrow focus fails to consider the situation in the nearly 10% of societies that are not organised as democracies. Is inclusion not practised in these societies, or does it have no value in or for them? Second, it is also problematic for inclusion to be restricted to involvement in societal decision-making because a holistic concept of inclusion – as I have already suggested in Chapter 4 – goes much further. It should also include aspects of participation, social integration and psychological belonging.

But what does a holistic approach of this kind entail for the ethical-normative significance of inclusion in general, and of inclusive education in particular? In other words: What values are expressed in a full understanding of inclusion? These are the questions that will occupy us in the following.

There is no doubt that inclusion and inclusive education do have ethical-normative content. Socio-political demands and related ethical-normative concepts such as social justice, equality, (human) rights and non-discrimination have been at the heart of the inclusion debate from the very beginning (Gajewski,

2017; Winzer & Mazurek, 2010). The problem in the literature, however, is that the questions of why these values are significant and, more importantly, how they relate to each other are often addressed only in an implicit or unclear way. For example, does the evocation of equality or social justice serve to reinforce inclusion as a value in itself, i.e. draw more attention to inclusion and thus clarify the core of what inclusion and inclusive education stand for? Or can inclusion be seen as a substitute and thus as a surrogate term for the notion of social justice or equality, for example? These are just two of the pertinent questions that are usually left open in debates about inclusion and inclusive education.

My enquiry into the ethical-normative value of inclusion in general, and inclusive education in particular, proceeds in three steps: In the first step – starting from the assumption that calls for inclusion and inclusive education ultimately arise from negative experiences of exclusion, discrimination, marginalisation and social inequality – I ask what constitutes the ethical-normative content of such negative experiences and phenomena.[2] In the second step, I turn to the topic of inclusion, specifically in order to examine the moral meaning of inclusion and the values in which it is manifested. Finally, the third step explores an applied aspect, even as it also serves to bring the first two steps together. At this point, I ask – based on the insights gained so far – what constitutes the ethical – normative significance of inclusive education, or inclusive schools, *and* how exclusion from or within school can be considered problematic.

Background assumptions: human well-being and justice

My remarks are underpinned by two basic assumptions relating to human well-being and justice. Both of these assumptions cover vast fields of discourse in their own right and can only be examined in part here. While I aim to make them transparent, there are two reasons why I can only suggest these assumptions rather than providing a detailed substantiation: First, I assume implicitly – and a bit controversially, I believe – that the content of morally valuable inclusion must ultimately be measured in terms of whether and how it can contribute to human well-being. Second, I assume that the special moral content of calls for inclusion and inclusive education arises from their connection to justice debates.

Grounds of justice are invoked for claims or demands that are deemed to have a particular urgency and importance in society. If ethical-normative content is discussed in a philosophical context with the assumption that this content concerns the truly substantial goods of human life, i.e. goods that everyone has an interest in possessing (Rawls, 1971), then we apply reasoning based on justice theory.

There is a virtually endless literature on the nature of justice and of the goods to be distributed in a just manner (including the discussion of whether distribution is the real issue at stake).[3] And of course, the various approaches lead to a range of different conclusions concerning the question of what we owe each other on grounds of justice. We cannot examine all of the conditions underpinning these in-depth debates, which go beyond our scope here. We will instead proceed from the relatively uncontroversial assumption that the ethical-normative justification of inclusion is of most interest for contexts with such great moral significance that we must also attach bold societal demands to them, at least in moral terms.

The link to human well-being is also not very controversial, at least on an abstract level.[4] In the debate on inclusion and inclusive education, concrete demands (for example, access to the mainstream school system for all children and young people, including those with disabilities) can only be understood if we relate them to notions of human well-being (which are often presented in a vague and implicit way). By invoking human well-being, we furthermore assume that there are forms and modes of inclusion that either make no significant contribution to human well-being – and for this reason are to some extent neutral from an ethical-normative perspective – or are even detrimental to it, for example, because they deprive people of fundamental freedoms (including the freedom to withdraw deliberately from certain contexts), or because they result in people being demeaned, marginalised or discriminated against.

The background framework of human well-being that is employed here falls somewhere in the mid-range, when measured against the philosophical debate on human well-being: It is vague, but also definite in some areas. It can thus be situated – to cite two prominent theories of justice with connections to human well-being – between the reserved and vague conceptions proposed by John Rawls (1971) and the substantial and strong conception of human well-being, tracing back to Aristotle, that is defended by Martha Nussbaum (2006). I share with Nussbaum the hope that it is possible to reach a political consensus on certain basic assumptions concerning the substance of human well-being, that such a consensus can be plausibly defended and that it need not have problematic consequences in liberal societies or for liberal thought.[5] However, unlike Nussbaum and more in line with Rawls, I do not think that we need a detailed, hierarchically structured list of human functions that a (good) human life must completely fulfil. This aspect has problematic theoretical and practical consequences, especially for people suffering from severe cognitive impairment, because their abilities are often not sufficient, strictly speaking, for purposes of leading a human life – let alone a *good* human life – in accordance with Nussbaum's list.

For this reason, a list of this kind is also problematic in the context of inclusive education. What we need are comprehensible, empirically proven and uncontroversial basic assumptions about the contours of human life, as well as somewhat more detailed assumptions at a relatively abstract level, which must then be made more concrete in relation to applied questions.

Human well-being clearly refers to the specifics of the human way of life, in three different respects: First, human behaviour is not only instinct-driven, but is also very much organised through shared norms. Whether these norms are inclusive or exclusionary depends largely on how they are understood and how they shape our institutions and behaviour. Second, people do not live solely for the present, nor do they seek only immediate satisfaction of their wants and needs. Rather, they are also concerned about their overall and future well-being. This includes the possibility, and the aim, of being able to anticipate future conditions and chains of events. Third, people also care about the welfare of others. This is due in part to intrinsic motives because, for example, the friendship or love of other people is considered highly meaningful. But people also care about others for instrumental reasons. Humans depend on cooperation, or at least on the actions of multiple people contributing to common goals and thus enabling individual survival and the collective reproduction of life. This also gives people reasons to care for others' well-being in addition to their own.

The conception of human well-being advocated here is also oriented towards subjective well-being, which plays an important role in the fourth element of inclusion, that of personal belonging. Nevertheless, well-being must not be restricted to its subjective component. Especially in educational contexts, such reductionism would be badly misguided. Education and training cannot be reduced to momentary, subjective happiness, or rather, that is not where they derive their value (at least not exclusively or primarily). Indeed, in institutionalised educational activities, we are particularly ready to accept limits on subjective happiness, at least temporarily (think here, for example, of the struggle involved in learning how to read or apply the rules of mathematics). Much of what needs to be learned from a societal perspective involves effort, perhaps even sacrifice, and is not ultimately a source of happiness for everyone, or at least not immediately. Moreover, children and adolescents often do not realise the later subjective happiness that can accompany the acquisition of skills (such as the pleasure that reading books can offer) while they are still young. Parents and educators take on the role of envisioning the future well-being of these young people.

All this does not mean that subjective happiness is unimportant; on the contrary, subjective well-being is necessary for the success of learning processes (especially in psychological terms), and it is both part of human well-being and an aspect of psychological belonging. Educational processes that are thus broadly and persistently detrimental to subjective well-being are also problematic because they have a negative impact on people's experiences of inclusion.

As a large number of the conditions for inclusion are social in nature, human beings depend on cooperation with other people and on social participation not only for their survival but also for their individual well-being. The forms of cooperation and participation that are crucial for survival and for a good life are, in turn, contingent on the existence of appropriate and supportive social structures, as well as participation in social goods, integration in interpersonal social associations and the feeling, or possibility of feeling, a sense of well-being through these forms of cooperation and participation.

But it is not only that well-being is important for inclusion, in that it determines the quality of individual experiences of inclusion; we can also say, conversely, that inclusion is important for human well-being. This is first of all for constitutive reasons: Inclusion is an inherent value and element of human well-being. This assertion ties back into the discussion of the social nature of human beings, and is plausible in that we can assume that social interaction and cooperation with other people are important for their well-being. The fact that humans are social beings means not only that they are dependent on others for their survival in certain phases of life (especially in the early years); they are also dependent on other people, and their care and help, in order to lead a *good* life. Inclusion is also valuable, second, for instrumental reasons because it makes an important contribution to human well-being. In this way, inclusion is also a *means* to leading a good life.

The school, as the institution and organisation specifically considered here, contributes to human well-being in three ways (Brighouse, 2008)[6]: Through the formal curriculum, through the informal curriculum and third, through the "hidden" curriculum that is the ethos of the school. First of all, at school we learn not only skills that will support future economic opportunities, i.e. training and jobs, but also a lot of things that will often be enjoyable later on – such as the appreciation of literature – which we only encounter through and in school. Second, the informal curriculum also makes a contribution, for instance, through music or physical education classes that are offered at school but are not part of the official curriculum. And the third contribution comes from the "hidden curriculum", the ethos of the school, which plays a particularly crucial role (ibid., 70):

Important as the academic offerings and the extra-curricular activities are, the ethos of the school lies at the centre of school life. The ethos is not a matter of the mission statement, but of the shared understandings among the responsible adults in the school of the values and purposes of their institution. What may seem like fairly trivial and "administrative" decisions about the life of the school do contribute to the ethos of the school which, in turn, affects its ability to live up to its values and fulfil its purposes – the central purpose being to promote the long-term prospects for the flourishing of the children in its charge.

We will see, especially in the next chapter, how much this school ethos can be a decisive factor in the institutional transformation of schools into inclusive educational spaces.

First, however, with these two basic considerations in the background, I will proceed to clarify the ethical-normative content of inclusion, and later also inclusive education in particular, in three steps. The first step brings us to the dialectical counterpart of inclusion, namely exclusion. Like inclusion, this is a broad phenomenon, which encompasses experiences and conditions as diverse as discrimination, stigmatisation, disadvantage and marginalisation.

Step 1: exclusion

In Chapter 4, we already noted Martin Kronauer's criticism (2015) that the pedagogical discourse of inclusion is largely devoid of any deeper understanding of exclusion. It is not that the literature in this area ignores exclusion (or related phenomena such as marginalisation, discrimination and stigmatisation); on the contrary, relatively few texts with a theoretical or ethical-normative focus can fail to address these elements. The difficulty, rather, is that this literature tends to view exclusion either as a denial or breakdown of justice, or as something that has been historically overcome, or still needs to be overcome.

Both views are problematic, for reasons that are separate but interrelated. The first view poses a problem because it establishes inclusion as a value in itself (which also implies, or is a reason for, the widespread view that there is nothing more to be said about this value), while exclusion is seen as something inherently bad.

But exclusion, just like inclusion, is initially a neutral term that only acquires its ethical-normative meaning through further assumptions that are specifically normative. Therefore, we can certainly agree with Robin Barrow (2000, 306) when he argues that "none of us sincerely believes that inclusion is good in itself: we believe it morally important and educationally advantageous to exclude (or select or differentiate) only for good (moral and/or educational) reasons". Applied to the context of inclusive education, Barrow's statement implies that discrimination *per se* (in the sense of differentiation) is not the issue here; we make differentiations all the time, both in school and vis-à-vis the outside world, for example, with respect to age and geographical catchment area. Discrimination in this sense is underpinned by assumptions, for instance, that it is good and important for the promotion of development and well-being when children and young people who have a similar progress level are able to attend school in the place where they live (partly because this enables extra-curricular forms of social integration). Such forms of discrimination thus cannot be the issue at stake here. We are more interested in the forms of discrimination that are objectionable on ethical-normative grounds, of which there are certainly many.

It is also problematic, second, to understand exclusion as something that has been historically overcome, or remains to be overcome. It is true, as we will see below, that there are certain forms of radical exclusion that are rightly deprecated and penalised in liberal, democratic societies which respect the fundamental rights of every human being. However, this does not mean that the concepts of exclusion and inclusion are mutually exclusive; on the contrary, Georg Simmel already recognised that inclusion and exclusion are better understood as concepts operating in a dialectical relationship of simultaneity. This relationship itself becomes more complex as the internal complexity of the groups in which inclusion takes place increases. And Simmel gives an explanation for why this is so, remarking: "This is not only because the whole thereby gives individuals an overwhelming independence, but above all because the more particular differentiations among the individuals dispose them to a whole range of nuances of that double relationship" (Simmel, 2009, 435).

To assume a binary separation of exclusion and inclusion is also erroneous purely on objective grounds (Wolff, 2017, 165f.): First, individuals can typically participate in or become a member of several groups, and may also be included in a group in one respect (for example, by being structurally integrated) even while they are excluded in another respect (for example, by not being able to participate despite their structural involvement). Second, the notion of exclusion often implies that there is some kind of "privileged mainstream". This can exist, and the mainstream school is certainly a place where it may occur. However, it is equally likely that there are multiple, competing mainstreams, especially when we turn our attention away from school to other life contexts (such as work, politics, or personal interests and hobbies). Ergo, an individual or group, may be included in one mainstream but not in another. Third, groups or individuals who are excluded may themselves exclude others in response, for example, by forming a kind of monopoly and using it to ensure that there is no encroachment from the outside. Exclusion can therefore take place in continuous, reinforcing and looped processes of other-exclusion and self-exclusion. And fourth, exclusion is a question of degrees, not least in moral terms. It can range from subtle modes of exclusion, such as gossip or spatial placement on the side lines at a social gathering (such as a birthday or wedding party), to overt exclusion, sometimes even in the form of organised violence. Here, we are not so much interested in relatively minor forms of exclusion, such as gossip, but in those that can be suspected of constituting problematic forms of exclusion from a justice perspective. This need not be overt violence. Marginalisation and powerlessness, i.e. the helplessness of not being able to author one's own life or contribute to shared life within society, are also morally problematic forms of exclusion (Young, 1990b).

We can also recall, with reference to Simmel (2009), that inclusion and exclusion do not preclude each other; rather, every idea of inclusion contains an idea of exclusion, even if it is often implicit. Descriptively, this simultaneity can be observed, for instance, in the fact the severance of close interpersonal ties (i.e. certain forms of social integration) is a prerequisite for structural forms of inclusion as we know them in modern societies, such as inclusion in the role of citizen or employee. Inclusion and the dissolution of close ties thus stand in a dynamic relationship that is not problematic *per se*. But such disengagement should certainly not go so far as to dissolve, inhibit or dismantle important communal forms of inclusion, i.e. in the sense of one aspect of inclusion destroying or impeding another.

For this reason, it is also crucial to enquire specifically into the ethical-normative significance of exclusion when clarifying the question of its ethical-normative content. For inclusion is also, in a sense, always a response to a set of real-life experiences of social disadvantage. In other words, the true call to action for the acquisition of new knowledge and the transformation of societal conditions lies in the aspiration of combating these negative circumstances and processes. But what is exclusion, exactly, and why or when is it problematic?

In addressing these questions, we can distinguish two approaches or systems. The first of these highlights the consequences of encroachment on the basic status of humanness, while the second deals with contexts in which exclusion is problematic in many respects, even if it does not involve the negation of fundamental aspects of humanness.

The first system of exclusion: humanness

People can be excluded and marginalised for a variety of reasons.[7] Not all possible forms of exclusion are morally reprehensible, and in some cases it can even be argued that they are necessary to safeguard human well-being.[8] Moreover, for temporal and spatial reasons alone, it is not feasible to be included in all conceivable life contexts. Certain options effectively rule each other out because they cannot be realised simultaneously or in combination. We can also assume that there are contexts that do not have the same level of importance for everyone. This has to do with the fact that not every form of inclusion relates to universal human needs (such as food, clothing or shelter) or to contexts that are significant from a societal perspective (such as school education); inclusion often also relates to people's individual and thus very specific needs and interests.

The subjectively perceived effects of such types of exclusion thus also differ accordingly. Most of the instances of exclusion that happen to us we do not perceive as such, either because they mean nothing to us or because they generally have no special relevance for our lives. For example, it is no problem for me if I am not included in the club of canary breeders in my city, and it is equally irrelevant for my life whether I am a member of the allotment garden association in my neighbourhood or not. These contexts are relatively meaningless for me and probably for many other people who are not interested in the activities pursued in bird breeding or gardening clubs.

However, exclusion can be bad, first of all, for someone who does not gain access to these clubs for hollow or spurious reasons that are not presented or applied to others, despite this person attaching a high subjective importance to the group's activities and goals. And second, such exclusion is significant if and when it results in a structure or life pattern of comprehensive non-belonging, not least when instances of exclusion coalesce into an overall feeling towards life.[9]

There are thus instances of exclusion that are bad only for *certain* people, for example, because they entail the loss or abandonment of these persons' individual life plans and related goals. These are not forms of exclusion that concern the quality of human life *per se*, but the (phenomenological) quality of the subjective life experiences of *specific* individuals. It seems uncontroversial to assume that the former kinds of exclusion are more pernicious, morally, because inclusion in the former is a prerequisite for the latter. Someone can, after all, be excluded in the sense that their specific, individual needs and interests are not taken into account, for example, when they are not recognised as a concrete other, even while their general needs and interests regarding inclusion – i.e. those that all people have – *are* considered. But the converse is not possible.

It is also important to stress that there are needs and interests that people can only freely determine to a limited extent. On the one hand, there are areas where no voluntary choice is made, because they are determined – at least in part – by human nature or by social circumstances. And on the other hand, closely related to this, some areas are important for people even if they do not desire them; thus, while they are not independent of desires, they also are not constituted by them.

This is true for important contexts and goods in human life, such as friendships or the learning and practice of social activities such as going for a walk or having an interesting conversation. Exclusions from these areas or activities are bad, and associated with suffering for all people, at least to the extent that they happen continually and affect numerous spheres of life. Of course, the point here is not to claim that every exclusion from a walk or rejection by a person who does not want to be friends is bad *per se*. Nor should we conclude from this that there must be a right, for example, to be able to go on walks with others, or that people should be obligated to enter into a friendship with any individual person. Otherwise, we would quickly encroach on important aspects of human freedom, and there are good reasons not to shape such social spheres through duties and rights, not even in the area of school education.

Level 1: the status of human being

These initial broad outlines allow us to establish a hierarchy in terms of exclusion. The worst form of exclusion is thus to be excluded from the human community or "family". For Margalit (1996, 108), this is characterised by "treating humans as nonhuman, or relating to humans as if they were not human. Treating persons as if they were not human is treating them as if they were objects or animals".[10]

The "as if" is important here: To humiliate people as slaves, for example, is still to presuppose that they are human beings. The prerequisite for a degrading act that impugns a person's humanness is therefore that the victim of the degradation is perceived *a priori* as a being with human value, even if only implicitly. According to Margalit, the core element of shaming and humiliation expressed through this form of exclusion is the "as if" of treating someone as if they *were* an object, instrument or animal. Slavery thus relies precisely on a view of slaves as human beings, even if not as full human beings, rather than as objects or animals. They are regarded as beings who are in some way subhuman, childlike, inherently immature and non-maturing. Margalit argues that this is basically the attitude that many people today have towards individuals with cognitive impairments.[11]

This form of exclusion is captured in a particularly poignant and shocking way in the photographic book *Christmas in Purgatory* (Blatt & Kaplan, 1966). This work documented the conditions at certain institutional facilities in the United States, where physically and cognitively impaired patients were kept like animals. They were crammed into common rooms without clothing, in very low temperatures, were offered no human stimulation in the form of education or games and were otherwise deprived of all interpersonal affection.

Of course, accounts of such forms of exclusion are mainly familiar to us from earlier times, most clearly and appallingly in the Nazi era. But even today, stories demonstrating that such conditions of exclusion are not a thing of the past often come to public attention.[12]

Level 2: the status of a being with rights

A second form of exclusion, differentiated from the first, is manifested in the (often indirect) denial of a person's status as a being with rights. Because rights serve to protect interests, including fundamental interests such as basic needs, this form of exclusion ultimately means either that the persons affected are considered not to have needs or interests as such (which would be analytically consistent with the first form of exclusion) or that their needs and interests are not accorded the same importance as those of other people. The latter aspect is what separates the first form of exclusion from the second. In this respect, the second form is certainly less bad than the first, because the persons concerned are at least assumed to be people with human needs. But it nevertheless has a detrimental effect on inclusion and human well-being, among other things because it hinders excluded individuals from enjoying entitlements on a par with other people.

This kind of exclusion may take many concrete forms. Two precedents in the Swiss legal system can serve as examples here. In one case, a young woman with cerebral palsy was prevented from continuing her schooling until the age of 20 by the local education authority, despite her official legal right to such education, on the grounds that her learning progress was too slow and she had no prospects of finding employment later on. In another case, a group of children with cognitive and motor impairments and their carers were refused entry to a bathing facility on the grounds that the children would not be well-accepted by the other bathers. The facility thus argued that it could not admit them on economic grounds.[13]

These cases obviously involve major discrimination, because they are directed at, or at least result in, a worse position or disadvantage for the persons affected, and the reasons for the exclusion seem to be a pretext, or in any case have no valid relevance. The common background of both cases is the assumption that the excluded individuals do not have the same legitimate interests as do other people, or that their interests are hierarchically of less importance and thus do not merit the same degree of protection.

Level 3: the status of a specific, individual being

The third-worst, and arguably most widespread, form of exclusion in modern, democratic and liberal societies is one in which people are granted rights, and their status as beings with rights is recognised, but they are not regarded as concrete and specific – i.e. distinctive – others, with particular needs, interests and achievements. Instead, they are viewed solely as members of a social group, such as "the disabled".

The consequence for those affected is that they are deprived of their own genuine, subjective interests in inclusion. One likely effect of such forms of exclusion is that the persons targeted have fewer and qualitatively poorer opportunities to fulfil their needs and interests relating to inclusion, or else they have to make an enormous personal effort to realise their own needs and interests in the way that other people are able to do.

This form of exclusion has many facets. One way it can be expressed is through a lack of social esteem, such as when people are not supported and educated in a way that allows them to form and develop their own personal life plans and visions. For blind people, for example, it was the case for a very long time, at least in Central Europe, that they effectively had to choose between two occupations: They either had to become basket weavers or brush makers. So, instead of being able to consider their own vocational wishes, as others might do, these blind people were left with a narrow, predetermined choice, which moreover expressed the assumption that they had no specific, unique characteristics apart from the fact of their blindness. This kind of exclusion can also be observed in situations where the friendship of certain people (or entire groups of people) is less sought after, making it difficult for them to form and maintain close relationships on an equal footing and a reciprocal basis.

Unlike the first two forms of exclusion, which, respectively, disregard key aspects of humanness *per se* and of life in modern societies with developed legal systems, this form is more open-ended and, at least in a singularly experienced form, neither particularly negative nor exceptional. We might even say that it is paradigmatic and crucial for certain contexts that people are *not* seen as genuinely "other", with their own specific interests and characteristics, or are not treated in that way. Consider, for instance, all those areas of society that are necessarily characterised by a degree of anonymity: If I make a claim for basic minimum support from the state, for example, because I have become ill or unemployed, I can rightfully expect this claim to be assessed by officials who possess a certain impartiality, meaning that they will put aside their own personal sympathies as well as my idiosyncrasies, hobbies, specific interests and appearance. Such forms of generalised treatment or address can hardly be referred to as exclusion. However, this does not apply to the majority of our social experiences. And even in relatively anonymous and role-based interactions within society (for example, between a counter clerk and a customer), we would like to see an absence of stereotyping, and a friendly and approachable way of communicating rather than, for example, an expression of obvious disgust towards a body image that may deviate from the norm.

The reasons for this kind of exclusion, especially for people with disabilities, stem not least from stereotypes about disability or disabled people, as well as social assumptions about what "adequate" life plans might be for them, or what they can contribute to shared life within society. Such ideas include freedom-restricting and marginalising notions attached to a charity-oriented vision of how people with disabilities should be and live, and how they "are".

This form of exclusion – which as I noted probably accounts for the bulk of the real-life exclusion experienced by people with disabilities in modern, liberal and democratic societies – does not always have to be intentional or even conscious. It is often expressed in unconscious and unquestioned norms, behaviours, symbols and assumptions, which, in turn, reflect societal structures as well as categories of action and thought, and from there extend into the personal and interpersonal spheres, coalescing into a comprehensive experience of life. It is therefore a rather subtle form of exclusion, albeit one that causes suffering.

Interim conclusion

The first approach to exclusion, dealing with experiences and modes of human existence, has brought to light three hierarchical levels of exclusion: First, exclusion from the community of human beings as such; second, exclusion through the denial of basic needs and interests and, subsequently, the denial of rights to the protection and satisfaction of such needs and interests; and third, exclusion from the sphere of those whom we perceive as unique, distinctive individuals with their own desires and preferences.

Such an approach makes it possible to examine very fundamental forms of exclusion, some of which are associated with great cruelty, potentially even leading to people's death. Not least in view of recent historical events, this kind of understanding proves indispensable. The killing of the African American George Floyd, for example, was not only a barbaric racist act; his treatment was also a form of exclusion that white Americans do not experience, or at least not in a systematic way.

This first approach to inclusion, unlike the second approach, which I will discuss presently, is based – at least implicitly – on a theory of human suffering. But what constitutes suffering, and what are its causes?

Suffering can have various sources (Miller, 1999). These can first be biological or at least quasi-biological in nature.[14] We know, for example, that a lack of vitamin C leads to a serious malfunction in the human body, and that an interruption in the supply of oxygen for several minutes can result in severe brain damage or even death.

Second, shared societal norms govern the view of what can be considered a minimally dignified and worthwhile life (although of course these understandings change over time and are subject to cultural contingencies). According to these norms, needs can be defined as referring to things that protect people from falling below a certain minimum standard of life within a society. Suffering is thus considered to exist when a person cannot live in accordance with these shared social norms. Such norms are not necessarily of a purely material nature. Poverty and suffering in this regard are thus not simply about a lack of material goods, but also about a lack of participation in, and suffering through, socially accepted and shared ways of life that go far beyond the material.

And third, the specific goals and interests that are unique to each individual can become a source of deprivation and thus cause suffering, at least when this occurs systematically and over a long period of time. Suffering is measured here by the question of whether and how one's own personality, interests and plans can be expressed at all, or to what extent it is possible for them to be formed and lived out.

It is therefore the case that suffering is always gauged, albeit often implicitly, against the basis of human needs, whether these are of a general human nature, group-specific or individual and personal. Following Amartya Sen's (1999) proposal, needs can be regarded as a set of functions that each person expects to be able to perform.

We believe, for example, that every individual should be able to read and write, move their body, have a job, get married, have a family and so on. This does not imply that every person *must* be active across the whole possible range of functions. For example, someone may decide not to marry or start a family; yet, they do not necessarily suffer hardship as a result. What matters is that the individual has the capacity and the opportunity to engage in a given function, *not* whether they actually do, or wish to.

In this understanding, it is not only the functions that we need to survive that are important, but also those that help us to live with dignity, navigate the public sphere without shame and lead a life characterised by freedom of choice. The question now arises, however, of whether such an approach, oriented as it is towards general functions, might not lack sensitivity towards individual differences, as well as individual interests and needs, of the kind addressed in the third form of exclusion.

Miller (1999) puts forward several arguments why this is not the case: First, it should be clear that each person's needs are different, even if we assess them in terms of the same functions. The specific educational resources that *I* need in order to learn to read may differ from those needed by others (for example, if they have dyslexia). Second, those functions that we call needs to represent only a small subset of the functions that someone may perform within a society. Therefore, it is primarily the needs that affect a minimum standard of living that are at issue. Above this minimum threshold, it is assumed in liberal societies, people should be able to live as they wish. Third, again from a liberal point of view, people should not be forced to perform important functions in which they see no value.[15]

The limits of the first system

An approach of the kind I adopted in the first step is not sufficient in itself to render visible the enormous practical complexity involved in inclusive education or exclusion from it. For one thing, it would be inaccurate and also too bold to claim that exclusion from inclusive education is about not being recognised as a human being, or as a human being with full needs and rights. Such failure of recognition may indeed take place (as occurred with the children who were not allowed into the bathing facility and the girl who had to stop her schooling before the age of 20). But in many instances, that is not the rationale behind exclusion from mainstream schooling and placement in a special school. Rather, efforts to provide adequate schooling for children and young people with disabilities are often based on good, or at least plausible, motives.

170 Values that matter

For instance, as already discussed in Chapter 3, protection is an important motive underpinning special education: The aim is to protect children and young people from the often harsh consequences – which may even threaten their well-being and learning progress – of being educated with many other children in a mainstream class, namely by sending them to a smaller, more personally managed special school that is individually tailored to their needs.[16]

This leads us to the realisation that if we were to limit our full understanding of the normative meaning of exclusion to the examples mentioned above (exclusion from the bathing facility, or from schooling because no progress was expected), or if we were to interpret all examples of exclusion solely according to the first system presented here, our gaze would only fall on cases of overt, morally problematic discrimination. However, exclusion from inclusive education is in many cases much more subtle and it may certainly involve well-intentioned concerns (such as the protective considerations mentioned above), even if it has a damaging impact on the affected pupil or group of people. Moreover, exclusion very often takes place *within* educational settings, not in the form of exclusion from schooling itself. Structural access may well exist in this case, while exclusion occurs at other levels (for example, at the level of social integration). For these reasons, we need a second system that clarifies when, and above all why, even well-intentioned and partial exclusion can be morally problematic (under certain circumstances).

Such a system must go further than the first, and also enter morally difficult terrain. This is one reason why, from an analytical point of view, it is less selective than the first.

The second system of exclusion: inclusion viewed in the negative

The second systematic approach to exclusion in some ways follows the structure of the dialectical counterpart of exclusion, namely inclusion, but interprets it negatively. A negative perspective of this kind is adopted, for example, by Judith Shklar, who addresses the issue of justice through that of injustice, or, as already mentioned, by Avishai Margalit, who studies dignity by examining humiliation and the forms in which it is manifested. We can also take such an approach towards inclusion and exclusion. Instead of asking which values are protected and fostered in the context of inclusion, and indeed constitute its ethical-normative content, we can ask which non-values are actually expressed through exclusion.

However, we are faced with the difficulty that, although the various elements of inclusion and exclusion can be distinguished analytically, it makes little sense to analyse the ethical-normative meaning of inclusion and exclusion separately according to the respective elements. If, for example, we assume that exclusion is associated with a certain form of social inequality, then this inequality may not only show itself in the lack of access to structures, but also (or perhaps above all) in diminished participation, deficient social relations and damage to people's sense of their own inner life and their psychologically perceived belonging.

Indeed, we can assume that it is precisely this interaction of the various elements of exclusion that makes the phenomenon so tragic.

Exclusion therefore does not usually take the form of inevitable, unilateral, automatic mechanisms. Rather, the various aspects exist in complex interrelationships, so that while minor instances of exclusion do not generally have a broad negative impact on human well-being and are not problematic on grounds of justice, we can nevertheless assume that some systematic risks of exclusion represent clusters of exclusionary elements, which also particularly affect certain groups within society. Just as black people in the United States are much more likely to be victims of police violence than are white people, disabled people also face specific risks of exclusion in certain respects. A study by Wiebke Kuklys (2005), for example, provides a convincing demonstration that disability leads to a significantly higher risk of living in materially disadvantaged circumstances for those affected, as well as their families. Specifically, it shows that people with disabilities would need on average 40% more resources to attain the same standard of living as non-disabled people. As they often do not have these additional resources at their disposal, however, they are also more affected by material poverty than are people without disabilities.

Marginalisation and exclusion do not necessarily mean that fundamental needs – such as for basic material goods or shelter – are not met. Rather, they often consist in the vague feeling of being "superfluous" and other aspects that cannot be translated into a logic of distribution, as is possible in the case of material goods. Therefore, we can also agree with Young (1990b, 55) when she remarks:

Most of our society's productive and recognised activities take place in contexts of organised social cooperation, and social structures and processes that close persons out of participation in such social cooperation are unjust. Thus while marginalisation definitely entails serious issues of distributive justice, it also involves the deprivation of cultural, practical and institutionalised conditions for exercising capacities in a context of recognition and interaction.

The costs of exclusion are not only borne by the individuals affected. In other words, it is not only they themselves who are exposed to the consequences of exclusion, discrimination, marginalisation or other forms of social disadvantage: "The true cost of segregation is the stigmatisation and alienation of those people who would otherwise have been able and willing to take a fuller part", writes Gary Thomas (1997, 104). The alienation and stigmatisation he refers to are thus not only directed at specific individuals or social groups. They also have negative effects on society as a whole, by showing everyone that there are certain people or groups who do not belong, who do not have a valuable place in society (Wolff, 2017, 166).

In essence, it is not only individual ethics that are at issue here, but also two specifically social-ethical problems (Barry, 2002): First, exclusion and marginalisation hinder the opportunities of whole groups within society and prevent their experiences from being taken into account. This is also accompanied by impoverishment of the range of social perspectives considered, even though their incorporation would actually be essential and helpful for the solution of complex social problems. And second, societal solidarity and thus overall societal cohesion – in other words, the common good – is also damaged.

The material side of exclusion is reflected in the refusal of access to structures or the lack of opportunities to participate in certain contexts. Exclusion can be very complex in this respect, and it always takes place in a dynamic relationship between people's inner and outer worlds, i.e. in relation to external conditions (societal structures and opportunities for participation), interpersonal negotiation processes (social integration) and internal, mental processing (personal belonging).

In addition to the material side, we must also consider the epistemological side of exclusion. This has only recently been recognised as an independent form of injustice in the literature. In her much-discussed book *Epistemic Injustice* (2007), the British philosopher Miranda Fricker introduced the concept of epistemic injustice to analyse situations in which actors are restricted in their status as subjects of knowledge. The epistemic form of exclusion must not be confused with the material form, or reduced to it. And of course, it is often the case that, while material injustice clearly exists, it is not incorporated in collective knowledge and social considerations. As Fricker (2007, 149ff), for instance, shows with the example of sexual harassment in the workplace, women affected by it *before* the concept of sexual harassment was introduced in the 1970s had to face the additional epistemic obstacle that their lived experience was difficult to articulate as (a socially recognised form of) injustice. This was partly because any attempt at articulation could be dismissed as hysteria or over-sensitivity by the largely male workforce. A similar phenomenon can be observed with respect to disability. People with disabilities often experience excessive and unwanted pity, open rejection or disgust, as well as forms of paternalistic attention. It is not least through the media, the political struggle for self-determination, and literary accounts of life and experience that such epistemic dimensions of injustice have been, and can be, substantially perceived and understood.[17]

Fricker has two types of cases in mind with her concept of epistemic injustice: "testimonial injustice" and "hermeneutical injustice". Both types play a key role in exclusion. What Fricker identifies as testimonial injustice occurs when the mainstream society harbours an identity prejudice against a specific group and attributes "a deflated level of credibility" to members of that group (ibid., 158). The result is a targeted, if perhaps unconscious, downgrading of confidence in the statements and claims of people from this group. This form of injustice is harmful and insidious, not least because it reflects an indiscriminate reaction to a member of a group, but does not at all take into account the individual circumstances of the person concerned (Scully, 2018, 108). We have already seen this phenomenon in the first system of exclusion, where it was referred to as the third form of exclusion. Now we can see this form of exclusion not only in its material dimensions, but also interpret and assess it in terms of its genuinely epistemological effects. When it comes to the topic of disability, cases of testimonial injustice fill many books and accounts of personal experience. It is well-documented in the school context, for example, that pupils with disabilities are asymmetrically devalued in their ability to contribute and participate, even when other persons involved, such as teachers, believe themselves to be unaffected by stereotypes (Haslanger, 2014b).[18]

Hermeneutical injustice, as a second form of epistemic injustice, is expressed when significant aspects of the social experiences of the members of certain groups cannot be adequately articulated, or can only be articulated in a distorted way, or perhaps not at all, because of the hermeneutical resources available to them. Therefore, this form of injustice is more fundamental than the first, and it points both to the individual *and* to social consequences of marginalisation and discrimination against people's needs and interests.[19]

The existence of collective epistemological resources is of fundamental importance both for establishing a social epistemology and for purposes of social coexistence. Here, too, there is a social-ethical significance that transcends the dimension of individual ethics. To understand the world in the first place, it is necessary to have pre-generated concepts, vocabulary, narratives and so on. The resources required to this end are internalised early in life, but they originate externally in shared community knowledge, which to some extent reflects the collected perspectives of various groups. If this knowledge is depleted, i.e. because the perspectives of certain groups and individuals are not included in collective knowledge and the collective view of social conditions, or they are not included systematically, then this entails an impoverishment that is not merely individual, but also collective and social.

It is not just that the world, in a sense, fails to recognise or share the worldview or experiences of a particular group of people, thus pursuing a kind of imperial epistemology. Epistemic exclusion can also arise, as previously mentioned, when subjects can only articulate their own experiences with difficulty, or not at all. And such exclusion can even result when experiences are only available in a vague or opaque way to the very subjects who experience them, or these subjects are unable to recognise their experiences as such in the first place (Celikates, 2017, 58).[20] In other words, the problem in such cases is not simply a lack of language to express one's own experiences. Rather, the individual, psychological experience may itself be damaged. In relation to disability – and especially cognitive impairment – there is empirical and experiential evidence suggesting that it is precisely this dimension, the access to one's own experience, that is often obstructed. One indication of this is that disabled people often content themselves with living situations characterised by a high degree of dependence and by a lack of resources, as well as other conditions of deprivation (Albrecht & Devlieger, 1999; Silván-Ferrero et al., 2020; Werner, 2015). A possible explanation is to interpret this acceptance of problematic experiences of exclusion as a form of learned helplessness, which is to assume that a person's psychological experience of their own life situation – and not just its narration – has become damaged (Basil, 1992; Valås, 2001).

Like material resources, epistemic resources are also very unequally distributed in society. The disparities of social and material power result in hierarchies of social position. This aspect plays an important role in the types of experiences that individuals are likely to have, the knowledge and meaning they can derive from those experiences, and consequently the epistemic resources they possess. Social and material power also confers epistemic authority. Only some individuals have the clout and authority to establish and enforce epistemic practices as legitimate. This means that certain people can, for example, set the criteria for the credibility of experiences or organise the ways in which knowledge is fed into public discourse or policy debates. They are believed and their experiences receive predominant consideration in the discourse. The content of a community's epistemic resources thereby tends to reinforce and cement pre-existing social and political contours as well as influential understandings about the world. In this way, privileged groups have a disproportionate influence on the resources available to all members of society, while socially marginalised groups are effectively excluded from contributing their experience and knowledge to the collective enterprise (Scully, 2018, 109). And this has consequences not only for the people concerned, but for society as a whole, as I have already emphasised. Indeed, it might be argued that, even if individual members of society do not notice or subjectively do not suffer from this phenomenon, society itself is harmed because its epistemic resources have the potential to be richer and more detailed than they actually are. For example, there may be damage to the capacity for empathy and consequently to the knowledge that would really be needed for innovative projects, because inadequate awareness of the circumstances affecting other people or groups means that projects are not planned in a way that benefits everyone equally.[21]

The assumption behind these ideas is that society depends on collective epistemic resources to achieve comprehensive knowledge of problematic situations and potential solutions. If there are gaps (because, for example, certain groups are not consulted at all, or are only dealt with in a paternalistic manner), these resources become impoverished. And because the existing knowledge resources are distorted, oriented as they are towards the powerful groups in society, the foundations of material resources also become structurally skewed. But what is the best way to understand this situation? One proposal found in Sally Haslanger's work is to consider structures as phenomena arising from looping effects. Haslanger (2014a, 389f.) speaks of looping effects because ideological schemata – which she regards as intersubjectively shared patterns of perception, thought and behaviour – also manifest social meanings in material forms. In the example of schools, these can range from assessment systems and curricula to the aforementioned design of school buildings and classrooms. Haslanger also refers to these material manifestations as resources, considering that actors orient their actions around them and rely on them: Ideological schemata thus manifest themselves in resources that are structured in a certain way, which then, in turn, confirm, solidify and reproduce the ideological schemata – a loop in the course of which structures are formed and consolidated. Hegemony, according to Haslanger (ibid., 391), colonises not only consciousness but also the world – and mediates consciousness via the world in a feedback loop.[22]

This dynamic looping process results in social structures that appear quasi-natural, and therefore practically unalterable, so that the influence of epistemological factors remains invisible. Haslanger (2012, 467) writes:

> This loopiness can obscure the social dimension of social structures. When ideology is uncontested and hegemonic, it is insufficiently conscious to be aware of its own effects. So the causal impact of hegemonic schemas on resources is typically invisible. Because the 'trigger' for a schema is external – in the world – we attend to this, and social structures come to seem inevitable, natural, 'given': Although all ongoing social organizations incorporate contest and struggle over the constitution of their world, most aspects of social structure are taken for granted [...]. Social actors accept a good part of their social worlds as necessary, and often as natural, as perhaps they must do to function at all in those worlds.

This can be observed in a range of areas extending beyond the topic of disability. For example, binary gender perceptions lead to the creation of social spaces that are designed to accommodate them: There are toilets for men and toilets for women, but rarely for those who do not feel they belong to either gender, such as trans people. This is not only a problem for the individuals who cannot recognise themselves in this binary view; it is also a societal problem, insofar as the associated, problematic binary gender schemata are continually renewed and consolidated.

The two systems of exclusion viewed in conjunction

If we now combine the two approaches to exclusion, a complex picture emerges:

Exclusion has negative consequences for individuals, which can range from disregard for their very humanness, to disregard for general and group-related needs and interests (for example, conversing in sign language or being able to learn the skills necessary to do so), to the inability or unwillingness to see certain people as genuinely "other", i.e. as individuals with their own needs and interests. And it also has a social aspect, in the impact that it exerts on communities or society as a whole by directly or indirectly impairing social cohesion. Exclusion is further manifested in the extent and manner in which structural access is barred (i.e. external, effectively alterable barriers are not removed); access to important goods and participation is denied (often these correspond to a supplementary, disability-related need, but they may also be general goods to which everyone is entitled) and social integration is lacking, or a psychological sense of belonging cannot be experienced, or only inadequately. Exclusion does not only have a material dimension, which, as already mentioned, can be observed in concrete structural access, in participation in goods, in social integration and in personal belonging. It also has an epistemic dimension, which is often even more essential, laid like a thin blanket over what we are able to perceive as the material dimension of exclusion.

The powerlessness associated with various forms of exclusion is particularly evident in politics and the media as forums of public perception in which marginalised, excluded people either do not appear at all or are made a topic of discussion, or in which they can participate with significantly less influence than other groups. Often the reasons for this are structural in nature, and not the result of individual decisions or actions. And because exclusionary structures are frequently hidden, even while being tightly woven into our social world, they are also very challenging to eliminate, as Iris Marion Young (1990b, 41) observes:

In this extended structural sense, oppression refers to the vast and deep injustices some groups suffer as a consequence of often unconscious assumptions and reactions of well-meaning people in ordinary interactions, media and cultural stereotypes, and structural features of bureaucratic hierarchies and market mechanisms – in short, the normal processes of everyday life. We cannot eliminate this structural oppression by getting rid of the rulers or making some new laws, because oppressions are systematically reproduced in major economic, political and cultural institutions.

The elimination of such oppression can only be achieved through comprehensive social and cultural change. And the topic of how such change might take place will be dealt with in Chapter 8.

In the following, I would like to turn to the dialectical counterpart of exclusion, namely inclusion. It must be emphasised, first, that inclusion processes are not simply exclusion processes in reverse. We therefore cannot draw conclusions about inclusion directly from exclusion, or vice versa. Second, and related to this, it can be assumed that the positive demand for inclusion goes further than the largely negative demand for non-exclusion, non-discrimination or non-segregation. Frequently (although not always), it is sufficient for purposes of the latter demand that certain actions be refrained from, but that is not the case for the former. The demand for inclusion instead leads to more far-reaching and positive calls for structural access, participation, social integration and the social foundations of individually perceived belonging. So, what constitutes the specific, ethical-normative content of inclusion understood in a positive, holistic way?

Step 2: the ethical-normative significance of inclusion

Building on basic assumptions and the background of human well-being and justice, as well as the two systems of exclusion, we can now enquire into the ethical-normative value of inclusion understood in a positive way, based on well-being and justice. In this context, as I have noted, the meaning of inclusion lies not simply in the avoidance of exclusion, discrimination or other forms of marginalisation and social disadvantage, but also in positive contributions. The issue of the value of inclusive education is treated in the literature primarily as a systemic question, i.e. as a decision between special and mainstream schooling. However, it will become clear in the following that this is too simplistic an equation. Temporary or even longer-lasting spatial separation or special schooling may well be compatible with the goal and value of inclusion. What is important is not so much the location of schooling, but the values that are expressed through inclusion or exclusion. The joint schooling of children with and without disabilities in the same space can also be exclusionary if, for example, it is characterised by disregard or a lack of freedom.

We must be careful in general not to limit the concept and ethical-normative meaning of inclusive education solely to structures and access to educational resources. As a reminder, in Chapter 4, I proposed that we should understand inclusion as a comprehensive, holistic concept that encompasses four elements, namely structural access, participation in goods, social integration and subjective feelings of belonging. All of these elements are distinct, which means that they cannot be mutually offset, nor can individual elements be dispensed with (at least not if we assume that a person is to be included in a holistic way). In concrete terms, for example, structural participation cannot be replaced by subjective belonging, or vice versa. Nor is it the case that one automatically leads to the other. A person who is structurally part of a mainstream school is not necessarily also an important and respected member of the school community. One prescriptive consequence of the distinct nature of the individual elements is that people cannot simply be made to feel contented with their social relations and forms of participation without changes being made to structures that are ultimately discriminatory. And the reverse is also true: Even when structures are maximally inclusive, this does not mean that they are able to strengthen subjective belonging or make it possible in the first place. Both aspects – and, strictly speaking, all four – are so distinct that they cannot replace one another, even as they stand in a complex, interdependent relationship.

For the ethical-normative evaluation of inclusion, this means that we should not make the mistake of determining the ethical-normative content of inclusion based on the content of each individual element in isolation. But we must also avoid the trap of thinking that mere affirmative allusions to certain values – such as human dignity, equality, justice or human rights – are sufficient to complete the task of justification, or to clarify the interpretation of individual values and their relation to inclusion. Because, for one thing, more is not more: Inclusion does not become ever more important as additional values are associated with it. And second, the links that inclusion undoubtedly has to other values are not always free of tension; on the contrary,

for example, as will later be discussed in more detail, inclusion has an important relationship to freedom. Especially for the psychological sense of belonging, it is crucial that inclusion – even if it is perhaps not chosen voluntarily – can be affirmed and found to be positive. But there is also a great deal of tension between freedom and inclusion: First, inclusion implies something like interconnectedness (on various levels, of course), and this contrasts with the value of freedom in that inclusion is not so much about the importance of people's independence, but about their *inter*dependence and integration in a larger whole. Second, it is certainly the case that we often cannot choose contexts of inclusion, and we have relatively little say in the processes they involve. For instance, we are born into a family, and are part of it, without asking for this. School is another example: Pupils cannot choose whether they want to go to school or not, as school attendance is compulsory, at least in primary education. And meanwhile, because of the role relationships in school (and the special rights and duties of teachers that go with them), pupils have relatively little influence – starting with the goals and content of learning, and ending with the questions of how and when they wish to learn.

Equality and hierarchy

All aspects of inclusion are therefore of equal value and stand in a close, relational balance. This is particularly evident when we consider possible modes of inclusion in which one aspect is absent, for example, when structural access is ensured but no substantive participation is enabled through it. This problem has been addressed many times, not least in the capability approach developed by Amartya Sen and Martha Nussbaum, emphasising that freedom must be substantive and not consist merely of formal access rights.

However, even if the various elements of inclusion are of equal value and cannot be mutually offset, a certain hierarchy is inherent in them. Structural access and participation are of priority because, taken together, they represent the societal building blocks of inclusion. For this reason, it makes sense that structural access and the removal of external, structural and societal barriers as well as the provision of resources (for example, to compensate for personal disadvantages) are given so much weight in the literature on inclusive education. For it is only when children and young people have structural access to a mainstream school that they have the opportunity, in the first place, to participate in the educational goods offered there, and to maintain certain social relationships (for example, with children and young people without disabilities).[23]

"Hierarchical" in this sense means that some elements are a prerequisite for others; it does not imply any judgement about their importance for holistic inclusion. It does not signify that structural access and participation in goods automatically lead to social integration and psychological belonging, nor that the latter are unimportant. On the contrary, it might be argued that psychological well-being with and in inclusion contexts is an especially crucial, but sadly neglected, aspect of inclusion. Indeed, a number of values closely related to inclusion are of special importance precisely because of their contribution to, and significance for, the elements of social inclusion and personal belonging.

In my remarks on exclusion, I noted that exclusion can be morally problematic not only on grounds of individual ethics – i.e. because of what it means for individuals – but also for communities and societies. This social-ethical viewpoint brings two aspects to light: First, exclusion is bad when it leads to an impoverishment of social perspectives within a society, and second, it is harmful when it results in damage to solidarity, social cohesion or the common good.

The same is true for inclusion. In addition to its importance for the richness of social perspectives within society, it also gains social-ethical significance through the fact that it can strengthen social cohesion and the common good. But what do we mean by the common good, and to what extent is the social-ethical impact of inclusion related to individual capacities to contribute to this common good?

Civic spirit and the common good

Humans are vulnerable beings who are doubly dependent on community: On the one hand, they need to be protected from encroachment by the state, and on the other hand, they need community alliances to boost their morale. The community is thus constitutive for the individual insofar as personal identity can only be developed in a dialogical way. The education of children to become community members is therefore always both an end and a means in the formation of communal bonds.

Civic spirit and the common good (in German: *Gemeinsinn* and *Gemeinwohl*) are interrelated concepts. In abstract terms, the common good represents a normative point of orientation for social action, while civic spirit refers to the willingness of those acting socially to truly align themselves with this normative ideal and to realise its aspiration of social commitment in their behaviour and action (Münkler & Fischer, 2002, 9). In relation to the social-ethical significance of inclusion, this means that inclusion in the sense of a social good is the normative goal that guides the actions of persons involved (e.g. pupils and teachers).

The concept of the common good can be understood in two ways (Sedmak, 2010, 159): On the one hand, it can be viewed instrumentally, i.e. as the sum of all those values that are a prerequisite for the members of a community to realise their values. On the other hand, the concept of the common good can also express a societal aim that orients the socially harmonised endeavours of individuals, families, groups and institutions. The focus is on what people have in common, not on what divides them. So, the emphasis here should not be on overcoming exclusion, but on creating inclusion.

Individual civic spirit, meanwhile, is the prerequisite for realising the common good. Only in this way can we ensure that there is any orientation at all towards the ideal of the societal common good. However, civic spirit (and thus also the common good) represents a very fragile social-moral resource within society, because the state, at least where it is liberal and secularised, cannot guarantee, enforce or reproduce alignment with this ideal by political or legal means without imposing it through ideological control or other dictatorial measures (Böckenförde, 1976). Nonetheless, a state with a liberal constitution can and must be able to influence the social and political framework conditions and shape them in a way that increases the possibility of reproducing the social-moral resources on which a liberal society is based. To this extent, even a liberal state cannot avoid this responsibility, with which it is generally concerned in school education, as a place where the rules of peaceful coexistence are negotiated and practised.

The dynamic and complex relationship between the values that underpin inclusion

One aspect, as previously noted, characterises all of the values with which inclusion is associated: They all have a reciprocal and dynamic relationship with inclusion. This means that they are both a prerequisite for inclusion and a consequence and expression of inclusion.

The proposal presented here occupies the narrow middle ground between over-complexity and over-simplicity. For this purpose, we can make use of the concept of inclusion developed in Chapter 4, which is to be fleshed out in normative terms in the following. In this discussion, I proceed from a further basic assumption, which is embedded in what I have called the background, i.e. the assumption that good forms of inclusion, which are significant from both a societal and an individual perspective, must be measured against the background of human well-being and justice. This basic assumption goes back to remarks in Chapter 4, where I discussed, among other things, Tönnies' distinction between community and society and Parsons' more complex, but ultimately similar, concept of pattern variables. The tendency, at least, seems to be that structural access and forms of participation in resources are formed and shaped more strongly by society than is the case with social integration and individually perceived belonging. The latter two elements tend to develop in closer, more concrete social associations, which often take the form of communities. For these reasons, the values associated with inclusion also take on varying focal points. Values that are closely interrelated with inclusion are freedom, equality and recognition. In the following, we will examine their relationship to the concept of inclusion.

Equality

In relational terms, equality is an ideal that governs certain types of interpersonal relationships, but it is also one that extends to the framework conditions for creating a society in which equal rights prevail. Both understandings of equality play an important role in calls for inclusion. While structural and resource-related aspects predominantly relate to societal framework conditions, the demand for social integration is underpinned by a vision of interpersonal relationships characterised by equality.

We already touched on the importance of equality for inclusion in our discussion of exclusion. One important aspect of exclusion, after all, is that people experience unequal treatment. This is most pronounced in a fundamental form of exclusion where people are treated like animals or are even killed. But the two other forms of exclusion in our first system also have close links to equality and inequality, respectively. In the second form of exclusion, this manifests in the failure to recognise people's human needs, which means that they are not regarded as equals. And in the third form, it is expressed as an unwillingness or inability to see other persons as human beings with their own characteristics, interests and plans.

A view of another person solely as a different and unequal being is based on five assumptions that are, for the most part, unthinkingly accepted, as the American legal scholar Martha Minow (1990) has observed: First, we often assume that differences are intrinsic rather than relational. The reasons for the otherness of persons, we suppose, lie in their selves, not in the relationships we have with them or the circumstances in which they find themselves. Thus, for example, in a medical, individualised approach to disability, we assume that children with disabilities are only disabled because they suffer from an impairment. Second, we adopt an undisclosed frame of reference, a normality, which, in turn, determines who is normal and who is not, who has important interests and who does not. In many cases, it is not the frame of reference itself that is problematic, but the fact that it is not made explicit and, in particular, that it promotes the interests of some persons over others. Moreover, it often means that those who do not conform to the norm do not have the power or opportunities to challenge the norm themselves. Third, we treat the individuals responsible for making judgements (for example, by giving diagnoses, as in the case of school psychologists or doctors) as people without a personal perspective, that is, as objective and neutral observers who, in a sense, hold a "view from nowhere" (Nagel, 1986). Fourth, and related to this, we assume that the perspectives of those being observed or assessed are either irrelevant or are already taken into account through the perspectives of others (e.g. those of psychologists or doctors). This is the case, for example, if it is assumed that the personal experience of an individual with autism is not pertinent because all relevant aspects are already revealed from the standpoint of the professional making the diagnosis. Fifth, it is assumed that the existing social and economic regimes are natural and neutral. When jobs and living conditions are regarded as natural rather than socially fashioned, they are considered to be inevitable and not very malleable.

Equality is expressed in a positive sense when we appear as societal equals, that is, as beings and persons with the same entitlements as other citizens. This implies, among other things, that we have the right, just like others, to live a dignified life characterised by the basic requirements of human well-being. To this end, it is undoubtedly important to be integrated into the basic structures of society (i.e. school, families, work relationships and the political system). And participation in goods is also essential, not least because they are the building blocks for allowing substantial life opportunities to develop out of the formal opportunities that result from involvement in structures.

But if equality is further understood as an ideal that governs genuine interpersonal relationships as well as people's relationships to themselves, and thus also the important interpersonal and personal aspects of inclusion, then we find ourselves confronted with the question of what actually constitutes such relationships of equality. Samuel Scheffler (2015, 25) describes egalitarian relationships as follows:

> In a relationship that is conducted on a footing of equality, each person accepts that the other person's equally important interests – understood broadly to include the person's needs, values and preferences – should play an equally significant role in influencing decisions made within the context of the relationship. Moreover, each person has a normally effective disposition to treat the other's interests accordingly. If you and I have an egalitarian relationship, then I have a standing disposition to treat your strong interests as playing just as significant a role as mine in constraining our decisions and influencing what we will do. And you have a reciprocal disposition with regard to my interests. In addition, both of us normally act on these dispositions. This means that each of our equally important interests constrains our joint decisions to the same extent.

Equality can thus be described, in a careful approximation, as a social value referring to the desire or demand to be treated as an equal in a moral sense.[24] The basic postulate of moral equality is that each person has a moral entitlement to be treated with the same respect and regard as all others. This refers to an equivalence of value, not descriptive equality. Specifically, it means that, *despite* descriptive differences, all people are to be considered and treated as moral equals in certain relevant respects, and should essentially be granted identical rights and obligations. The principle therefore does not mean that all persons should receive equal treatment, but that they are to be treated as equals. This equality does not imply a claim to an equal share of goods or resources, but rather a claim to be treated with the same respect and consideration as everyone else. This ethical and political-democratic principle of moral equality is founded on an assumption of the equal dignity of all persons (Gosepath, 2004).

However, "treatment as an equal" or even "equal respect and regard" are open to interpretation, and may thus be realised and manifested in many different ways (Feinberg, 1973, 93). The same applies to another understanding of equality, usually founded on moral equality, which is often referred to as "luck egalitarianism". This approach proceeds from the assumption that the equal moral status of people, i.e. their equality of dignity, is an argument for all people being entitled to an equal share of relevant goods. Luck egalitarianism relates the proposition of equal moral dignity (i.e. moral equality) to questions of distributive justice. Depending on the standard on which distribution is based, the demands might be equality of resources, of well-being, of opportunities or of capabilities. The idea is that they should be accessible to all on grounds of justice.[25]

Proponents of luck egalitarianism thus assume, first, that the most just mode of distribution is equal distribution. Second, and more importantly for the present context, approaches based on luck egalitarianism also make certain assumptions about individuals' responsibility for their own lives as well as their autonomy. In these approaches, unequal distribution is morally acceptable if the causes of inequality lie in the self-determined and self-responsible decisions of people, and not in factors outside their control. Thus, luck egalitarians distinguish between responsible decisions, or "option luck", and unhappiness based on chance circumstances, called "brute luck". Compensation is due in the latter case, but not in the former.

Although this perspective or basic assumption may seem convincing at first, it is problematic for at least two reasons: First, it makes fraught assumptions about what people themselves are responsible for and what they are not. Is a person who is unable to work in full or in part due to depression, for example, responsible for their own condition? And does this mean that they have a lesser entitlement to inclusion as a result? And what applies to a person who becomes paraplegic after a skydiving accident? Is this person, on the basis of a one-time decision that was perhaps made in high spirits, to be denied all assistance beyond the bare minimum on the grounds that their situation is self-imposed, i.e. are they legitimately exposed to the danger of societal exclusion? And second, for people who are in need through no fault of their own, it sends signals that are problematic because they are pejorative and paternalistic, as Elizabeth Anderson (1999, 305) observes, considering disability as an example with a slightly polemical undertone, in a fictional letter to those affected:

To the disabled: Your defective native endowments or current disabilities, alas, make your life less worth living than the lives of normal people. To compensate for this misfortune, we, the able ones, will give you extra resources, enough to make the worth of living your life good enough that at least *one* person out there thinks it is comparable to someone else's life.

Inclusion, in other words, only benefits disabled people for paternalistic reasons, in this interpretation. A third, general problem of equality understood in purely distributive terms is that paternalistic, pejorative and stigmatising relationships, especially relationships of dominance and dependency, but also problematic societal structures that make such relationships possible in the first place, are not illuminated or criticised. Societal causes of exclusion are thus not taken into account.

Relational and democratic equality

To avoid reducing or limiting equality to basic moral equality, or even to distribution issues, we need to address those fundamental problems that were described above as persistent challenges, in particular the problematic relationships and structures that are accompanied by severe inequality. A theory of equality that fills this gap can be called "relational" or "democratic" egalitarianism. Relational or democratic theories of equality are advocated, for example, by Elizabeth Anderson (1999), Jonathan Wolff (1998) and Samuel Scheffler (2015, 2010).

According to Scheffler (2015, 31), equality in these approaches is

> [...] ultimately a form of practice rather than a normative pattern of distribution. An egalitarian relationship is one in which the parties have certain attitudes, motives, and dispositions with respect to one another. Among other things, they satisfy a fundamental deliberative constraint when making decisions that fall within the scope of their relationship. And the point is not that these attitudes, motives, and dispositions must be distributed equally between the parties. Admittedly, the relationship will not have an egalitarian character if one of the parties exhibits the relevant attitudes and dispositions and the other does not. The attitudes and dispositions must hold reciprocally. But neither will the relationship have an egalitarian character if the parties possess those attitudes and dispositions to an equal but low degree.

The relationship must therefore be equal on both sides, and both parties must put the ideal of equality into practice to a substantial degree.

This egalitarian view could also be expressed, however, as a principle of distribution, according to which the aim would be to distribute the status of people equally, i.e. to grant all people the same structural access opportunities. So, does relational equality ultimately converge with equality as a principle of distribution, after all? Not according to Scheffler (ibid., 41f.). In his view, the differences between a distributive and a relational view of equality go much deeper. For one thing, equality from the relational perspective is a complex ideal whose plainly egalitarian aspects cannot be viewed independently of links to other values such as reciprocity and respect. Thus, for purposes of inclusion, equality does not only concern intersubjective, structural and participatory aspects. This presents a subtle but significant contrast to the distributive conception of equality, according to which the ethical-normative content of equality is simply to be found in the idea of equal distribution, while other aspects such as resources or status only gain relevance because they help to determine the things to which the idea of equal distribution should be applied. Such a perspective, unlike the relational view, treats equality as a normatively autonomous value.

The distributive view second regards equality as a value that can *by itself* generate a supposedly definitive principle of distribution. Considered in this light, equality is not only an independent value, but a self-sufficient one. By contrast, equality understood in relational terms does not in itself contain a fully established principle for governing the distribution of resources. Rather, decisions about distribution must be made in conjunction with other values.

A relational or democratic approach regards equality as a property of interactions and relationships, and thus as a good that can only be constituted on a shared basis. Accordingly, relational egalitarianism calls for relationships based on parity, in a positive sense, and for the transcendence of social status hierarchies and asymmetrical relationships of dependence and dominance, in a negative sense. This understanding of equality thus extends the aspirations of inclusion into the realm of social integration and, to some extent, psychological belonging (especially as far as its social foundations are concerned). This approach is not about achieving complete equality in social positions. In fact, we legitimately accept inequality in at least two respects: First, a society must be politically organised for orderly and prosperous coexistence, and this implies, among other things, hierarchically graded roles with corresponding forms of authority, which inevitably entail certain inequalities of power, influence, prestige and income. And second, complex, modern societies in which cooperation must be organised based on the division of labour also require a sufficient differentiation of roles and functions in order to operate effectively. These roles and functions differ not only in terms of their performance requirements, but also potentially in terms of the remuneration and societal power attached to them. Both reasons make it plausible to consider inequalities in social position as somewhat necessary or unavoidable for purposes of ensuring an efficient social order, at least in modern societies, benefitting not only those in privileged positions, but also to some extent the worse-off members of society.

But in our societal reality, relations of dominance, concentrations of social power and status inequalities are not limited to the above scope. Indeed, problematic forms of inequality permeate societies quite thoroughly, and social disadvantages and forms of marginalisation often accumulate and mutually reinforce each other. This applies in particular to the risk situation created by disability.

Risks of inequality in the case of disability

Wolff and de-Shalit (2007, p. 70) has distinguished three forms of risk of morally relevant social inequality associated with disability, based on a capability analysis. First, there are risks that certain functions will deteriorate. In the case of disabilities, this might result from worsening illness or complications following injury, for example. Second, there are risks that endanger further functions due to injury and practical life impairments. For instance, people with disabilities risk poverty, losing their homes or failing to complete education because of their impairments. Third, according to Wolff and de-Shalit, there are risks that arise precisely *because* a person seeks to protect another function. This might be a person with a severe facial disfigurement who, in order to avoid being laughed at, does not leave the house and as a result suffers from great loneliness.

The latter two forms of deprivation are particularly relevant to the question of equality, because – unlike the first example, which applies predominantly on a physical level – they stem from relational causes that are often also genuinely social.

At this point, we can see not only how the demand for equality, understood relationally and democratically, is important for inclusion, in the sense of persons not being dominated (not least by harmful master narratives) and being able to live in relationships characterised by equality, but we can also see the importance of freedom as a form of equal opportunity that enables people to escape such risks. But what do we mean by freedom, as it applies to inclusion?

Freedom

In a classic formulation, most notably popularised in an essay by Isaiah Berlin (1969), a distinction is made between negative and positive freedom. Hobbes, and more recently Robert Nozick (1974), are two representatives of such an understanding of freedom. In this view, a person is free if and insofar as no constraints emanating from other people or institutions impede that person's actions. With relation to inclusion, this would mean: I am free when I can participate in societal structures unhindered by coercion from other people or institutions, allowing me to stand for election as a politician, for example, or meaning that I, as a child, am not prevented from attending the mainstream school in my neighbourhood. What is important in this understanding of freedom is that it does not refer to natural constraints: We would not say that someone is unfree because they are unable to perform a ten-metre jump. And in this understanding, a person who does not meet school performance requirements due to cognitive impairments and therefore has to attend a special school is also not unfree. In the negative understanding of freedom, however, someone whose freedom of expression is restricted by state censorship, who is held as a slave by a master, or who is fundamentally prevented from being able to take advantage of school education or is excluded for invalid reasons not related to the core domain of schooling, would indeed be considered unfree.

By contrast, positive freedom emphasises the individual capacity for self-determination, whether this is understood in a Kantian sense as "autonomy" or, following a more recent interpretation by Harry Frankfurt (1971), as "self-realisation". Individuals are thus free in a positive sense if they enjoy both the internal and external conditions that allow them to experience active, substantial freedom.

The positive approach to freedom is not merely an alternative to the negative approach. Rather, it also seeks to address the core flaw of the negative approach, that of ignoring more complex conditions of freedom and assuming that freedom consists solely in the existence of external conditions. In particular, the capability approach developed and advocated by Amartya Sen and Martha Nussbaum has contributed substantially in recent years to a new debate on freedom that addresses this lacuna. According to the proponents of positive freedom, a person is free not only if they are not prevented from participating in a given context, but also if they have the necessary resources (meaning both internal resources and external, environmental resources) to enable their participation. The capability approach, for example, emphasises that freedom must fulfil both internal and external conditions in order to be considered substantial. In Sen's (1999) view, freedom in this sense encompasses both procedures that enable freedom of action and decision-making as well as real opportunities in terms of achieving outcomes. Positive freedom thus has a procedural aspect *and* an opportunity or outcome aspect.[26]

Axel Honneth (2014) brings a third form of freedom into play, namely social freedom. He believes that even positive freedom (which he calls reflexive freedom, because it refers to people's internal self-reference) remains cut off from "objective" conditions, i.e. the reality that individuals owe their freedom to other subjects with whom they share the context of a common "ethical life". The assumption of social freedom is therefore that people can only be considered truly free if, under the right institutional conditions, they perceive each other as necessary for the realisation of their own reflexive goals, that is, if they recognise each other's claims. In this understanding, freedom is thus interpreted in social terms, not purely on an individual basis as in the perspective of positive freedom (ibid., 61). Following Hegel, to whom this concept of social freedom can be traced back, it refers to the relational attainment of "being with oneself in the other". Hegel writes: "But the freedom of mind [*Geist*] is not merely an independence of the Other won outside the other, but won within the Other; it attains actuality not by fleeing from the Other but by overcoming it" (Hegel, 2007, § 382, 16). In this context, inclusion does not refer to the freedom of individuals – whether determined externally or complex in nature – but is something generated socially.

Of course, all forms of freedom hold significance in the framework of inclusion. The necessity of negative (legal) freedom stems from the safeguards it places on the fundamental rights and duties required for basic subjective freedoms as well as the basic structural conditions of human inclusion, such as the protection of life and property. This has already been addressed by Marshall (1950). Meanwhile, through positive freedom, people can realise and live out their own ideas of communal and societal inclusion. However, the possession of negative and positive freedom alone is not enough to achieve or safeguard freedom in a full sense. Their limits lie particularly in the abstraction of both concepts from the dense context of institutionalised relations of recognition in which social freedom is realised and protected. In a way, they are thus also abstracted from the social core of inclusion itself.

If we accept Hegel's conception of social freedom (as advocated in his *Elements of the Philosophy of Right* (Hegel, 2004)), we find that it has close links to recognition. Freedom can namely be understood as "being with oneself in the other". This means that we are free in relationships, such as friendship and love, precisely because we do *not* see the other person as a restriction on our freedom but, on the contrary, as a precondition for it. Freedom is thus based on reciprocal recognition both of the other as a person with similar needs and of the other as a source of sought-after recognition. Honneth (2014, 44) writes: "The striving for freedom no longer forms an element of merely subjective experience as soon as we encounter other subjects whose aims complement our own". And a little later: "In the first instance, therefore, 'mutual recognition' merely refers to the reciprocal experience of seeing ourselves confirmed in the desires and aims of the other, because the other's existence represents a condition for fulfilling our own desires and aims" (ibid., 44f.). As soon as the parties involved recognise the need to achieve their respective goals and also perceive them in the other, reflexive freedom becomes intersubjective and thus constitutes social freedom.

This view of social freedom as a "need for completion" through other individuals seems compelling when we think of friendship and love, and thus of communal forms of inclusion. If we follow Honneth's reconstruction of modern practices of friendship and love, then we find that they enable us to experience our own will as something whose articulation or expression is also desired by a concrete other, who is therefore not in opposition to it. A friendship of this kind is devoid of instrumental considerations, according to Honneth (ibid., 141). And that is why "the normative rules of friendship ensure today that two individuals complete each other within the framework of friendship by bearing trustworthy witness to the existential decisions of the other and by providing advice" (ibid., 150).

Social freedom in modern societies

But how can we imagine social freedom in larger societal contexts, i.e. in relationships that are not characterised by friendship or love between concrete others, people who are close to each other, but rather by anonymity, and certainly to some extent by instrumental considerations? What form does freedom then take, and what significance does it have? Roughly speaking, we might say that social freedom, at least in a thin form, results or must result from the societal division of labour, to ensure that gains result from cooperation. We might also say that the existence of social freedom is conditional on societal cooperation.

Social freedom in the societal sense is also republican freedom (Pettit, 1997, 2001), which means that it encompasses the active and democratic participation of all citizens in decisions of importance to society, as well as solidarity with the polity and thus, in a sense, the inclusion of all citizens within the polity. Freedom can thus be seen as a good that is intrinsically social and relational in nature, arising from the existence and active promotion of the right kinds of institutions and relationships, which may potentially be shaped by intersubjectivity and concreteness. The societal division of labour, as envisioned by Durkheim in particular, also gives rise to solidarity, albeit not of a mechanical kind, but of a more distanced, organic kind. This form of solidarity is fostered not by personal contact, but by an awareness of the contribution of all people to the polity.

Two problem areas related to disability

Inclusion thus requires – and conversely expresses – social freedom above all, not merely negative and positive or reflexive freedom However, two problem areas cannot be ignored. The first of these highlights a systematic difficulty in the debate on social freedom, specifically the question of the extent to which the discourse of social freedom is able to identify the deeper structural causes of unfreedom, such as in cases where someone does not participate in the epistemic resources of a society at all, or at least not in an equitable way. This question acquires vital importance especially in the context of disability and its lack of representation in society (as expressed not least through books and teaching materials) and the lack of political power for disabled people and their advocates (such as parents and other relatives). If it is only the perceptual and operational resources of societal majorities that are considered and perpetuated, then it is likely that minorities such as people with disabilities will not participate in societal cooperation to the same extent, or that their disadvantage will be reflected in their marginalisation at precisely this juncture.

The second problem is that the debate about the contours of freedom in general, especially in the context of social freedom, raises the question of what happens to individuals who are unilaterally and completely dependent on the social cooperation of others, such as children and many elderly people, but also and not least people with disabilities. These include, in particular, people with severe cognitive impairments who are exposed to the risk of total and systematic dependency, and thus potentially also to violence and abuse.

To imagine an organic solidarity that also encompasses individuals who are not, no longer, or not yet effectively part of societal cooperation is to highlight the need for a debate within society on the importance of caring relationships as well as the recognition of human vulnerability (Kittay, 1999; Nussbaum, 2001; Tronto, 2013). Here, we must combine the idea of freedom with the idea of care for others. If we understand social freedom in the Hegelian sense as a form of "being with oneself in the other", then, as I have already noted, the relationship to others is the prerequisite for all of our freedom. In this view, freedom is thus based on mutual recognition, both the recognition of the other as a being similar to me and as the source of my own recognition. And this leads us to recognition itself, as the third value constitutive for inclusion.

Recognition

Inclusion stands in a dynamic, reciprocal relationship to recognition, just as it does to equality and freedom. That is, we assume without a doubt that everyone who is included is also recognised in a certain manner, and vice versa. The value of recognition thus points in a specific way to the goodness of inclusion, and the same is true in reverse: It can be expected that persons who are included in a good way are also recognised in a positive way. But this assertion must already be qualified in an important respect, for not every form of recognition is positive and valuable. If a person is recognised as something or someone they do not wish to be, this form of recognition does not contribute to human well-being. We might even say that the opposite is the case.[27]

The system behind the concept of recognition

But what exactly do we mean when we speak of recognition as a value? We are all familiar with the phenomenon and the importance of recognition (or the experience of disregard) in our own lives: We want to be loved as unique, special individuals by our family and friends; we want our presence in a room to be noticed and acknowledged; we want our achievements and efforts to be valued and our rights to be respected and recognised rather than trampled on. With reference to Iris Marion Young (2000), who uses the concept of inclusion prominently in her work, we are also reminded that the demand for recognition is a very important one in the context of inclusion in democratic frameworks. Democracy is characterised, among other things, by the fact that all citizens in a society have a say, and therefore minority groups are also empowered to give expression to their existence, their needs and their rights.

If we examine the systemic aspect of the concept of recognition, it becomes clear that it is interpreted and used in a very heterogeneous way – in contrast to everyday usage – that is by no means limited to its relationship to democracy. This plurality of meanings can be celebrated as a source of enrichment, but it can also be viewed critically (Margalit, 2001). One reason for diverse interpretations is certainly the fact that the German word *Anerkennung* has no direct equivalent in the English "recognition".[28]

Generally speaking, the English term "recognition" has three usages (Ikäheimo, 2014, 8f.; Margalit, 2001, 128): First, it means something like identification, in the recognition of objects, for instance (e.g. "The mountain on the horizon is Mount Everest"). Used in this way, recognition need not refer to people, but may apply to any kind of object. Second, recognition can be understood in the sense of "accepting" or "conceding". As Margalit (2001) notes, this variant refers primarily to the acknowledgement of error. But this usage of recognition also covers values, norms, principles, rules, reasons, responsibilities, obligations, etc. (Ikäheimo, 2014, 9). And third, finally, there is recognition in the normative sense, which applies only to persons. This is the usage of recognition that will concern us in the following.

We can further clarify the heterogeneous ways in which the normative concept of recognition is used if we consider four key qualifications that must be applied for the topic of inclusion, as introduced into the debate by Heikki Ikäheimo (2014).[29] First, it is important to understand whether the recognition of persons is responsive or constitutive; that is, whether recognition is somehow a response to a situation that demands recognition (which may be for a variety of reasons), or whether it serves to generate or constitute something, such as subjective identity. The two aspects are not mutually exclusive, but they have differing emphases. It makes a difference whether we think of recognition as being essential to individual self-development and the formation of subjective identity, or as something that is expressed through the protection of a person's rights. The importance of the element of inclusion for personal belonging, for example, cannot be adequately understood only in the responsive sense. After all, to feel a sense of belonging is not only a reaction, for example, to love or social esteem. Rather, the full moral significance of recognition is revealed through its constitutive contribution to personal belonging and individual experience of the self. Recognition of a constitutive kind thus demonstrates that it is only through forms of positive recognition that a sense of personal belonging can be established and felt, especially as such belonging is also conditional on individuals having a positive relationship to themselves, or at least one that is not seriously damaged. Because identity can only be developed and affirmed in a dialogic manner, it is clear that recognition is necessary in a constitutive way for a positive relationship to the self and a sense of personal belonging. And also when understood in a non-psychological sense oriented around status, the constitutive mode of recognition highlights a key point in the inclusion debate, namely the demand for the "recognition of difference", the scope of which is not limited to interpersonal relationships, but extends to calls for rights and thus a certain deontic status.

Ikäheimo (2014) second distinguishes between vertical and horizontal recognition. Vertical recognition can flow in both directions. In a descending direction, it refers to the recognition of citizens by the state in the sense that the state guarantees and safeguards the rights of citizens. This is precisely what does not occur, for example, in the second form of exclusion described, in which people are regarded as beings with needs that are fundamentally different from others' needs. So, if a bathing facility systematically turns away groups of children with disabilities, or a disabled girl no longer has access to schooling on the grounds that her education will not result in any learning progress, these are examples of disregard in a vertical direction. The state or institutions may disregard citizens or other members of society in certain fundamental ways by excluding them from important goods and structures.

In the vertical upward direction, citizens for their part recognise the state and its institutions as legitimate. For our topic here, vertical downward recognition plays a particularly important role. To have rights and be able to take on roles (as an expression of structural involvement) is also to enjoy vertical recognition by the state or society. If society, or the state as an actor in society, is of the view that education for all children and young people should take place inclusively in a mainstream school, then it also conveys recognition in a vertical downward direction. But the vertically ascending form of recognition has a certain significance for inclusion, as well, albeit rather indirectly. This is because the state depends on the recognition of its educational goals by citizens, the representatives of the state (such as teachers, school headmasters and education officials) and the people targeted by such efforts (including children and their parents). If any of these goals or educational ideals is no longer supported in a given arena, this can have far-reaching consequences for the relationship between the state and its citizens. This is significant because the ideal of inclusion – just like the contrasting idea that children with disabilities should be educated separately – must have societal and institutional support in order to become and remain effective.

Meanwhile, horizontal recognition, unlike vertical recognition, is something that genuinely takes place between individuals, not between the state or institutions and individuals, even if it may be mediated through the latter aspect, as in the case of access to inclusive education. Institutional or institutionally mediated (horizontal) recognition specifically refers to the recognition of a subject as the holder of institutional roles that come with certain deontic capacities such as rights and duties. The great importance of this form of recognition is reflected not least in the existence of human rights conventions. Because the status of being regarded as a being with rights, although experienced intersubjectively, is institutionally mediated, i.e. attributed, it therefore also retroactively shapes the relationship between the state and individuals (vertical recognition in both directions).

Purely intersubjective recognition, however, does not involve any internal or conceptual relationship to the institutional roles of the recognised person, and relates to this person solely as the bearer of a certain psychological disposition. Precisely because of this, however, it also has more psychological depth and far greater psychological significance than vertical or institutionally mediated recognition. The purely intersubjective form of recognition is primarily something that has to do with attitudes and related mental states and processes. In Hegel's view, such intersubjective recognition mediates the intentionality or the subjective perspectives of subjects in their dealings with each other, so that the recognising party assumes the perspective of the recognised party to some extent, and thus sees the world partly from that position.

Ikäheimo notes (2014), third, the importance of realising that recognition does not refer to attitudes that are pure, disconnected or atomistic. Attitudes of recognition are always part of a more complex set of attitudes that one person has towards another, and these, in turn, are part of an even wider set that encompasses the attitudes of both parties towards each other. This two-sided structure is furthermore part of an overarching context of all those attitudes adopted towards third persons, oneself and the world in a broader sense. And this world in general contains structures and institutionally moulded opportunities for participation.

An attitudinal complex thus involves many psychological phenomena, not only attitudes themselves, but also emotions and sensations. A relationship between persons does not consist solely of psychological and subjective aspects. Indeed, the category of "concrete interpersonal relationships" also includes all the "objective" elements that can be meaningfully regarded as essential or important for a relationship between persons (ibid., 13). If we relate this aspect to the topic of inclusion, it becomes clear once again that even recognition relating to the intersubjective and psychological components of inclusion (i.e. social integration and psychological feelings of belonging) is not a purely psychological and intersubjective phenomenon, but one that encompasses more than the attitudes of individuals. Rather, structural and goods-related aspects are always involved here as well. They form the framework, so to speak, for the way in which relationships – both with oneself and with others – can be lived out.

Dimensions of recognition

We can distinguish various levels or dimensions of recognition in terms of content. Because the German philosopher Axel Honneth has certainly undertaken the most ambitious work in this area, his theory of recognition will now also be discussed, supplemented by Ikäheimo's (2014) helpful qualifications, mentioned earlier.

Honneth is part of the tradition of critical theory developed by the "Frankfurt School" (whose representatives range from Max Horkheimer to Theodor Adorno to Jürgen Habermas), and in this context seeks to describe and understand the content of social struggles. Honneth himself perceives this moral content in the struggle for recognition. In his view, struggles for recognition are struggles for inclusion, and vice versa. But according to Honneth's thesis, mutual recognition is also the basis of identity development in humans. In his view, the experience of recognition in its various forms is essential for the successful establishment and maintenance of subjectivity and equitable social relations, and it thus also serves as a background and guide for critical social theory.

In his most important work, Honneth (1995) distinguishes three dimensions of recognition: First, the (axiological) dimension of love; second, the (deontological) dimension of respect and third, the (contributive) dimension of esteem or positive evaluation. Drawing on Hegel, but also on psychoanalytic and psychological theories (especially George Herbert Mead's symbolic interactionism), Honneth posits the existence of three basic dimensions of personal relations-to-self that are fundamental to the development of individual identity, namely self-confidence, self-respect and self-esteem. All three are formed and maintained dialogically through the corresponding forms of recognition – love, respect and social esteem. Moreover, in modern, liberal, bourgeois-capitalist societies, the three dimensions of recognition are institutionalised as norms or moral expectations and are constitutive for the relevant spheres of social life: The family and close personal relationships for love,[30] law and rights for respect, and work for the dimension of social esteem. This means that the various dimensions of recognition range from psychological to intersubjective to societal contexts.

The axiological dimension of love is the most fundamental dimension in terms of developmental psychology, and certainly the most important from an ontogenetic perspective during the early period of life. Because young humans are immature not only physically, but also psychologically and cognitively (although, as we have seen in Tomasello's work, endowed with great potential for intentionality as the basis for empathy and cooperation), they require continuous care from those close to them (ideally parents), which translates into experiences of being cared for.

Just as the axiological dimension of love strengthens self-confidence, the experience of being respected, as a second form of intersubjective recognition, also supports another form of individuals' relation-to-self, namely self-respect. Honneth's discussion of respect highlights the close connection that it has to institutionalised, legal justice. Rights, according to Honneth (1995), drawing on Joel Feinberg (1970), enable people to move through life with their heads held high and to interact with others on an equal footing. In the concrete reconstruction of rights, Honneth follows, among others, T.H. Marshall's theory of the three-stage genesis of modern rights (civil rights, political rights, social rights).

He shares Marshall's view that each new level of rights also expresses a new form of inclusion, allowing an increasing number of citizens to enjoy equal status as full members of society.

While love, according to Honneth, relates to objects as vulnerable, concrete beings, and respect relates to them in a general way as moral beings with equal rights, recognition in the sense of social esteem (or solidarity, as Honneth also calls it), as the third form of recognition, relates to human beings as the bearers of certain qualities and abilities.

According to Ikäheimo (2014, 147), not all possible human abilities and characteristics can be considered or regarded as objects of esteem. Rather, what counts are those abilities or qualities that others see as making a valuable contribution to their lives or to some aspect of life they consider valuable (i.e. of societal importance). Honneth's theory, however, largely fails to clarify the exact nature of "esteem". And it is this very dimension that requires elucidation, as it proves both pivotal and problematic in the context of schooling (consider, for example, the evaluation of academic performance) and in its specific relevance for people with disabilities (think here of limited, norm-oriented esteem in the form of "despite his disability, X does outstanding things"). So, what does it mean, from the viewpoint of recognition theory, that someone is esteemed for an activity that benefits others or the common good? And must esteem always be understood instrumentally, as implied in the view that it means recognising someone for their contribution to the welfare of others? In other words, can esteem also exist in non-instrumental form?

Recognition is mostly discussed in the mode of equivalent reciprocity, where it seems to function as a pattern of give-and-return, thus turning into a scarce resource and an object of struggle. But Ricoeur (2005), another important recognition theorist, in particular argues that recognition can also be seen as something that is given to the other without any expectation of reciprocity. Indeed, in his view, it is precisely this moral dimension of esteem that distinguishes it from an economic logic. Ikäheimo (2014, 150) refers to this form of esteem as gratitude, for only acts that are disinterested, and thus non-instrumental, deserve gratitude. Therefore, gratitude is a good example of non-instrumental, or even selfless, forms of esteem.

Questions of how narrow or broad our standards of recognition are, and what merits social esteem (or perhaps gratitude), have a great deal to do, among other things, with the extent to which human diversity is recognised, and the ways in which this occurs (Baker, 2015, 70):

> [...] the inequality of our esteem for others depends on the breadth and generosity of our own evaluative standards. A society in which people have a broad, expansive and generous appreciation of diversity obviously presents fewer obstacles to relationships of equal esteem than one in which people have narrower views. Quite a lot of the movement towards greater equality of esteem in our own times has been based on a greater acceptance, appreciation and,

indeed, celebration of diversity. This is not simply the toleration of people of whom we deeply disapprove, but a widespread social revaluation of people who used to be disapproved of and are now socially accepted. These revaluations have mostly resulted from on-going struggles for recognition related to a wide range of social factors including gender, disability, ethnicity, age, sexual orientation, social class, migration, and religions. To present these changes of status simply as cases of basic respect would be to neglect the very important processes of revaluation that have made them possible.

These crucial societal milestones in terms of gaining recognition for many forms of human diversity are thus not synonymous with tolerance. They do not imply the rejection of an existing way of life – as is actually the case with tolerance – but the positive affirmation of it. And they do not stop at an attitudinal, i.e. a linguistic or intellectual, level, but result in practical changes – epistemological as well as material – within society.

If we understand humans as being genuinely cooperative by nature (corresponding to the empirical description of human nature in Tomasello's research, but also reaching back theoretically to Hegel and Marx), then the existence of societal cooperation is dependent on shared goals and reciprocal contribution. In modern societies, however, it is precisely the essential regard for that which is commonly considered good and important that is fragile, having become the subject of societal disputes and struggles. And this fragility has an impact not least on people's experiences of inclusion in our society. For, if it is increasingly unclear what esteem can be considered to mean, and if narrower and more elitist understandings of the grounds for social esteem become prevalent, ever more people will be left with the sense of ending up on the losing side in the struggle for recognition.[31]

Vulnerability and care

The importance of the axiological dimension of love as well as the contributive dimension of social esteem can, in particular, highlight the complex relationship between vulnerability and care, referring simply to our dependence on other people and our ways of dealing with such dependence. This topic has already come up in our discussion of freedom and its preconditions. But what do we mean by vulnerability?

Philip Pettit (2001) proposes a two-level normative model of vulnerability that is very illuminating for the context of inclusion.[32] Specifically, he distinguishes between fundamental vulnerability and problematic vulnerability. The first of these represents an anthropological category. Fundamental vulnerability is a shared, irreducible fact of human life that arises from our interdependence. Vulnerability in this sense is therefore a structural aspect of human existence that can neither be completely eliminated nor excluded from interpersonal relationships (Honneth, 1995; Nussbaum, 2006; Tronto, 2013).

For our examination of inclusion, this means first that these fundamental forms of involvement, but also of human vulnerability, deserve our fullest attention. Looking back, we can see that the forms of exclusion in the first system we discussed also make us aware of the ways in which people can be violated in anthropological terms: First, in their humanness in general (which includes being treated as an animal or a thing), second, in their human needs (also encompassing social needs for belonging and integration), and third, in their specific uniqueness and distinctiveness.[33]

However, there is a tendency (apparent not only in care ethics) to reduce vulnerability to this anthropological constant. It is forgotten in this context that some people are actually more vulnerable than others. Therefore, as Pettit argues, it is also important to consider the second form of vulnerability, namely the problematic vulnerability that arises through relations of power and dominance. Unlike the first form, this second form of vulnerability describes the long-term and subjective effects of a relationship in which the dominated person is deprived of autonomy by being denied the kind of recognition that equality and respect would call for. Domination can generate vulnerabilities that manifest as feelings of powerlessness and fear, and ultimately a lack of self-esteem on the part of the dominated.

We have already seen that people with disabilities are particularly vulnerable in this respect. As Wolff (2009c) explains, the risks of disability are not only that damage and functional impairments will worsen, but also that these primary and perhaps even easily treatable or manageable impairments will encroach on other functions of life, or that in the attempt to safeguard certain functions, other, tertiary functions will, in turn, be jeopardised.

Vulnerability in its problematic dimension, as an expression of relations of dominance, is also a moral problem from the perspective of freedom and equality. For domination is a relational expression of inequality, which at the same time closes off spaces of freedom. Relations of dominance both exacerbate the basic vulnerability of human beings and also inhibit their autonomy (Garrau & Laborde, 2015, 56).

It is therefore not surprising that calls for inclusion are linked to calls for more democracy or a different form of democracy (Young, 2000). The idea of an inclusive, discursive, participatory democracy, in which every participant feels compelled to find solutions that are equitable for the needs and interests of all, is based on suppressing the raw power of the majority over a minority. Such an understanding of democracy has close ties to values such as recognition, care and solidarity. For it is only in a context where people respect each other and care about each other's needs and interests that we can hope to establish a respectful, caring dialogue that underpins genuinely collaborative decision-making, rather than merely preventing the overt exercise of power by some over others (Baker, 2015, 82).

This idea of democracy is shared by both John Dewey (1937) and Philip Pettit (1997), despite all the specific differences in their theories. For Dewey, in particular, inclusion is a fundamental condition for democracy, but also an expression of it, in the sense of people being able to participate in the formation of political opinions and decisions, namely in a way that is not limited to the political sphere, narrowly defined, but that permeates all aspects of life in society. Schools in particular are of great importance in this respect. The exact reasons for this will be addressed in the following, with a look at the specific value of inclusion within schooling.

Step 3: inclusion and education

The negative side: exclusion in the school context

Even when applied concretely to the context of schooling, the ethical-normative meaning of inclusion is easier to see against the backdrop of its dialectical counterpart, exclusion. We can therefore first consider which problematic forms of exclusion must be avoided in school education, or rather, what exclusion means in the context of school in the first place.

If we apply our two-part system, the following picture emerges:

In the first system, exclusion from school is bad when children or young people are not recognised as human beings, their needs and interests are not valued equally to those of others, or they are not recognised in their own unique needs and interests. Based on this system, we can identify a number of ways in which children and young people may be exposed to morally problematic forms of exclusion in the school context. The first and most important is, of course, the complete denial of opportunities to participate in school education. Such a general exclusion from schooling can be regarded without exaggeration as a major violation of human rights, given the great importance of school education for life in modern societies. This kind of exclusion not only deprives individuals of important life prospects, but also has enormous social and societal consequences. First, exclusion from education affects not only children and young people (who learn through this exclusion that they are ineducable), but also their families, wider communities (for example, whole village communities) and society as a whole, which later has citizens who did not receive even minimal education and who will therefore always be dependent on state support. Second, the exclusion of individuals or social groups from schooling also has societal implications, signalling that certain members of society are less deserving of respect and dignity than others.

Of course, scholastic exclusion in this first system should not be interpreted as being bad if the specific, subjective interests of children are not (constantly) taken into account. After all, school is also largely about building skills and competences that are considered important for society (such as reading, writing and arithmetic). These may coincide with children's individual interests, but very often they do not, or only to some extent. On the contrary, many children enjoy going to school because that is where they see their friends, not because they acquire certain functional skills or knowledge there. However, we also do not have to understand needs and interests in this exclusively subjective interpretation. Rather, as I have already noted, subjective interests can also be traced back to objective human needs on a more abstract level. It is thus not the specific interests of a particular child that are deprived through scholastic exclusion, but the underlying objective structures of needs that concern human life in general or life in a given society. But what does this mean in concrete terms?

It means that children can be deprived both through exclusion *from* school, which robs them of opportunities to acquire and enjoy education and forms of capital, and they can be deprived *in* school, for example, when they are structurally and physically part of the school and their class, but are not considered a full member of those contexts. Concretely, this can mean that no one plays with these children on the playground, or that they always sit on the side lines in school, perhaps surrounded by professionals who look after them, but not by peers (who always seek other partners in group work), even as they are largely ignored by the teacher. The deprivation here concerns the human needs for social integration and psychological well-being as well as the need to be considered a valuable and valued part of a human cooperative group.

Both the material and the epistemic sides of exclusion are already expressed in this first system. First, by being excluded from and in school education, children and young people are denied structures and opportunities for participation that other people generally enjoy and that are important for human life and life in modern societies. Social structures determine opportunities (Dahrendorf, 1986). This applies to schools as well as to other social structures (from friendships to nation states). So, if structures are largely exclusionary, it is very likely that people's life prospects will also be diminished. Second, exclusion from education reinforces structural prejudices and stigmatisation by barring certain people from society's epistemic resources, and also by depriving society of access to the epistemic resources of these people and groups.

The negative effects of exclusion run vertically and horizontally in both directions: They undoubtedly harm individual children and young people, but they also damage the social and epistemic fabric of groups and societies, with an impact that is both epistemic and material. Here, we can see how the epistemic dimension of exclusion reveals, or points back to, its moral element. Indeed, when people are excluded from the structures and resources of society – for example, from the organisations and institutions of schooling and the goods of education they produce – their discrimination is reinforced and they themselves remain in structurally powerless positions (as spectators, so to speak, of their own life *and* of societal life). Material exclusion from the cultural attainments of education as well as the cultural, social and symbolic goods – namely qualifications – acquired at school is also associated with major epistemic exclusion. And material exclusion on various levels – including at the level of social interactions with peers – is further accompanied by an impoverishment of knowledge, specifically knowledge about "normal" life, both for those who are excluded from school education *and* for those who are able to participate in such contexts.

The assumption that exclusion in and from education does not only affect the children and young people directly concerned, but also the social fabric of the class community, the wider community and society as a whole, is of course also the basis for assuming that school promotes a number of important capacities oriented around civic spirit and the common good. These are the abilities and dispositions that must be acquired as a matter of key importance for social coexistence, namely the ability (1) to accept and use rational arguments, (2) to correct oneself, (3) to make judgements in context, especially when it comes to morally relevant issues, and (4) to take seriously and recognise the points of view, needs and hardships of others (Reichenbach, 2010). Not all of these abilities are directly threatened by the exclusion of specific children and young people. For example, it would be absurd to claim that it is not possible to learn the capacity for rational argumentation or self-correction without all children in a given cohort being part of the same mainstream class. But it is certainly plausible to assume that the ability to judge things in context and to take the needs and hardships of others seriously is at least impoverished, if not damaged, when some persons are consistently, or even only partially, excluded from this dialogue and from the learning of such skills in the context of a school for all. The epistemic exclusion of a group of children and young people has the consequence that these abilities can only be learned and experienced to a limited extent by those who remain.

This point is expressed even more strongly by the second system, which addresses these material and epistemological aspects in greater depth than the first. In material terms, exclusion from and in school is not only about individuals being prevented from participating in or gaining access to basic structures and goods that are important for human life, or even for survival. Rather, it is also about the possibility that exclusion can lead to a (perhaps vague) feeling of being superfluous or alienated. This aspect thus primarily concerns the ability and opportunity to experience psychologically perceived social belonging.

In epistemological terms, the second system demonstrates the significance of both testimonial and hermeneutical injustice. The importance of epistemic injustice is evident in a variety of contexts, from school assignment procedures to school life in and out of the classroom. It becomes apparent, for example, when children and young people with disabilities and their parents or guardians are not allowed to be present at school assessment, evaluation or diagnostic discussions, or they are ignored and their statements are given less weight; when their assessments are interpreted and translated in a distorted way by other people; when disabled children or young people are not asked for their views and opinions or are not addressed by teachers during lessons; when they are not provided with tools and opportunities to actively participate or when no one plays with them on the playground, to name just a few examples.

In the professional context of teaching, such forms of disregard or pathological recognition can manifest in three different ways (Niemi, 2015): First, as professional indifference, for example, through the use of stereotypes about disabled children and young people (even if they are positive, such as "people with Down syndrome are always in a good mood and laugh a lot"); second, as professional disesteem, when children and young people are looked down upon, or when others do not value their efforts or believe in their future; and third, through professional disrespect, which manifests itself, for example, in paternalistic attitudes. The latter problem is particularly common among well-meaning educators, including those who are so convinced of the value of inclusion and inclusive education that they assume – perhaps contrary to the explicitly expressed needs of children with disabilities or their relatives – that inclusion is only genuine if it takes place alongside non-disabled people, or if they themselves always claim to know what the right form of inclusion should be (i.e. in mainstream schools). However, this attitude in fact reflects not only a lack of recognition, but also a lack of choice for people with disabilities, because, as Osgood (2005b) notes, a right to inclusive education does not imply an obligation to claim this right. Rather, she writes (ibid, 199f.):

> It becomes a matter of *choice*, with decisions regarding the choice vested in those who would choose to exercise it. Yet the difficulty with this scenario is twofold: What if the school were also required to support extensive public alternative segregated settings for those who wished (e.g., classes for the totally deaf); and what if individual or groups of children decide they don't wish to participate in the regular class for reasons other than the school's inability to address their disability, or choose to transfer from a 'failing' school […]? Would nondisabled children have a right to segregated settings, removed from 'undesirable' classmates?

Recognition must therefore always be linked to freedom and equality as further values of inclusion.

This also suggests that it is not so much physical placement that accounts for exclusion in school; in other words, it is not the fact that a child or young person is educated in a special school instead of a mainstream school that is problematic on moral grounds, at least not *per se*. Rather, we have to understand physical placement as an expression of structural involvement. But this assertion is, in turn, subject to certain qualifications. We here need to draw on the discussion of human well-being at the outset of this chapter, which can help us better comprehend the role of structural involvement (i.e. physical placement in a mainstream or special school). Two considerations are important at this point:

First, people care about their (and others') well-being for instrumental reasons on the one hand, and for intrinsic reasons on the other. This means that they are dependent both on the cooperation of their fellow human beings and on their own involvement in cooperative societal contexts. To be able to participate in the goods thereby produced (such as education), they need to be given substantial opportunities (such as resources). Belonging (including structural belonging) is crucial because people are social beings, and find their intrinsic value in this sociality. People recognise that this belonging is not only an inherent need of theirs, but that it also extends to all other people who are equal to them in this profoundly human respect. For instrumental (and also positional) reasons in particular, education in a mainstream school is of great importance, because the place where education happens is empirically decisive for further opportunities in education and the labour market, both in terms of qualifications and of the networks that are thereby established (Almalky, 2020; Powell & Pfahl, 2019; Wagner, Newman & Javitz, 2016). It can therefore be argued that there are a number of instrumental reasons relating to human well-being in favour of educating children inclusively in a mainstream school. There is less conceptual and empirical clarity when it comes to the intrinsic importance of well-being and its relevance for inclusive education. Here, we must instead observe the conditional relationship between the place where education happens and the degree of inclusion and well-being that can be achieved through it. In concrete terms, it appears that the location itself is not as important as the quality of the goods (specifically, education) and relationships that can be formed in this context. Ultimately, the quality of education must be measured against these criteria.

Second, people are not only concerned about their current happiness, but also about their future happiness. In the case of children, the vision of future well-being is still developing, but parents and teachers adopt this perspective on children's behalf. While they acknowledge that a number of activities at school are arduous and strenuous for pupils, they consider these efforts to be justified because they are important for the pupils' later well-being as adults. And this perspective towards future well-being and the well-being of others also justifies the struggle for inclusive education that families wage for their children with disabilities. They are aware, as we have seen, of the great positional and instrumental importance of education for life in modern societies. However, the prospect of later happiness may be so overshadowed by current unhappiness and suffering – including of a psychological nature – that there is a high probability of future well-being also being compromised. In such cases, the relevance of well-being that can be attained in the future through mainstream education is qualified, and well-being in the moment takes on a much higher significance.

For the question of the importance of structural involvement, it now follows that we have to distinguish between aspects that are systematically closed to pupils because of special education and those that are contingent on the place of structural involvement, and thus have to do with the quality of inclusion that is present in a particular context. This, in turn, means, in relation to education, that we have to consider the specific type and quality of education that can be achieved in a given context. This implies a range of considerations, for school must be viewed as a site where social, cultural and symbolic capital is acquired, but also as a place where social relationships and psychological belonging are experienced. And at this point, we again need to reflect on the value basis of inclusion – in short, on equality, freedom and recognition.

As far as the aspect of structural exclusion in the education sector is concerned, the data available is relatively clear. In Germany, to take one example, three-quarters of pupils in special education leave school without any qualifications. Graduates of a special school have hardly any chances of a successful transition into vocational training or the labour market. Many still struggle with the stigma of being abnormal years later (Pfahl, 2011). And even if both pupils educated in mainstream schools and those in special schools have access to the education system, i.e. they are not completely excluded from education, it is still the case that in Germany, for instance, four-fifths of special education pupils leave school without the most basic certificate, the *Hauptschulabschluss* (Powell, 2009, 165). The same certainly applies to other countries. Moreover, these pupils suffer from a negatively reinforcing cycle of cumulative disadvantage later in life. They represent the growing societal category of the "working poor" and are much more dependent on state social support than are other people. With regard to social integration and psychological well-being in mainstream classrooms, the data is somewhat more contradictory. There are studies which show that children with disabilities often suffer more and are less accepted in mainstream classrooms than are other children, while different studies find no negative effects, or even record positive effects (Nakken & Pijl, 2002; Pijl, Frostad & Flem, 2008; Wendelborg & Tøssebro, 2011). Pupils in special schools are also often exposed to a limited, less rigorous curriculum that includes lower expectations, in turn, leading to reduced academic and post-secondary opportunities. Pupils in special schools furthermore have less contact with non-disabled peers. Special education classes often serve as a "dumping ground" for pupils that are considered problem cases, instead of providing a supportive and caring environment for those who really need such assistance in the framework of a special school (Duhaney & Salend, 2000).

When it comes to securing individual life opportunities, in particular, we see that special education has a disastrous effect on certain people, especially in terms of stigmatisation and discrimination that can have a lingering impact. Indeed, this is the first reason for advocating inclusive education: The importance of education is too great, and the potential consequences for individuals too severe, for us to recklessly send pupils (especially without consulting them) to special educational institutions that segregate and stigmatise them, and therefore, in the long run, can end up having the opposite effect of their original protective purpose. To demand mainstream schooling for all is thus a postulate of justice that relates to the significance of education – above all instrumental and positional – in an empirically informed way.

The positive side: inclusive education

With reference to the securing of life opportunities, freedom of choice and recognition, we have seen both the positive contours of inclusive education as well as the difficult questions that arise. What can we learn from this discussion for a positive understanding of the value of inclusive education? Two things to begin with: First, good inclusive education avoids problematic modes of exclusion, discrimination, marginalisation and stigmatisation at various levels. Second, good inclusive education seeks to anchor inclusion instrumentally in its processes as a form of participation, involvement and engagement, even as it also pursues the objective of inclusion in a way that pertains to, and beyond, the sphere of education.

To recognise the possibilities of keeping in mind both aspects – processes as well as objectives – it is necessary, first of all, to recall the discussion of the specific characteristics and functions of modern school education from the previous chapter. And second, we need to make transparent some further ethical-normative ideas that concern the normative content of school education, i.e. the aims and values of education itself. Robin Barrow (2000, 305) discusses this point in a critical commentary on John Wilson:

To determine what would be included in the idea of inclusion in this case, we should need to argue about and establish not just moral values, but more specifically educational values; for the questions of who should be included or excluded in relation to various different aspects of schooling, and on what grounds, can only be answered by understanding what the criteria of educational success, achievement, quality and so forth are. Similarly, by extension, a variety of empirical claims relevant to arguments about inclusion (e.g. "inclusive classes provide better education") can only be properly researched if we are clear about both what counts as "inclusive" and what counts as "better" or good education.

As with inclusion, there is a vast and centuries-old debate about the values and goals of education, which is important, of course, but also leads too far from our focus here. For our purposes, we can draw on the contribution of Harry Brighouse (2009), who distinguishes between two types of educational goals: "aims goals" and "distributive goals". The latter encompass considerations of how resources are distributed and who can participate where, and in what way. But aims goals, according to Brighouse, represent the true goals of education, in the sense that they form the ideals of what it means to be an educated person, and identify the values that underlie those ideals. For Brighouse, aims goals are not monistic, i.e. they do not consist of a single value (e.g. autonomy), but of several. In his view, the aims goals of education encompass the following values: Personal flourishing, autonomy, the ability to contribute to social and economic life, democratic competence and the capacity to cooperate, on the one hand in an instrumental sense, in order to make a contribution to the societal order, but on the other hand for the sake of the value itself, as an expression of cooperation with others as equals.[34]

If we look back over the value relationships we have been discussing in this work, as well as fundamental considerations of the social and cooperative content of inclusion and its embedding in and significance for human well-being, then we see the high degree of overlap between the aims goals of education and the values associated with inclusion – namely, those of equality, freedom and recognition. The focus of relational and democratic equality is closely related, in particular, to two aims goals: That of teaching pupils democratic capabilities and that of achieving cooperation among equals. Here, Dewey's concept of a reflexive and experimental democracy acts as a kind of bracket for these two aims goals. Indeed, Dewey's remarks make it clear why we need a rich, diverse and vibrant society in which people see each other as equal partners for co-operation in order to have a good, thriving democracy. Dewey's vision of the close connection between inclusion, education and democracy also points to the need for a more holistic view of education and the contribution of schooling to broader social inclusion. For Dewey, democracy is a form of lived practice, not mere theory, and indeed a practice that is important not only in an instrumental way, but as an expression of humanity itself. It is for precisely these reasons that Dewey places so much importance on interaction, communication and cooperation. Inclusion is structured by a constellation of practices, experiences and habits, and not only by educational and social-policy decisions, individual attitudes or institutional conditions. Inclusion is thus a continuous process of negotiation about, and critical engagement with, the conditions of our social life and coexistence. Following Dewey, inclusive education must be about creating and strengthening community *within* the school. Moreover, values must be formed at school in a way that carries these ideas out into the world. To this end, the institutional organisation of education through schools must be directed at forming the conditions for such growth. One of these conditions is that a school must be a democratic community, in the sense that it respects, enables and encourages the active co-determination and participation of all involved.

Here, it is worth clarifying once again what we mean by an "atmosphere of inclusion". First, an atmosphere of inclusion supports and enables love or friendship and regard (from an axiological perspective), respect (from a deontic perspective) and social esteem (from a contributive perspective). Of course, this is not possible to a full extent at school, as the differences between the family and the school context are too fundamental and crucial. Pupils and teachers must be protected from too much encroachment on their integrity and personhood in school; they also cannot be expected to exhibit affection in the form of love and friendship. Pedagogical care, while important, has its limits. Second, despite the extensive institutional "forced inclusion" involved in school, it is necessary to create islands, moments and methods that offer opportunities for voluntary co-determination and consultation, thus enabling children to affirm their inclusion (and that of all others in the class). More specifically, this is an atmosphere in which each individual child can be appreciated as a special human being, whose needs are taken into consideration and who is treated with dignity and respect. It is an environment in which children can experience themselves as self-determining beings, and in which empathy and participation are encouraged and given scope for expression as combined capabilities.

This is achieved indirectly through the creation of a sense of belonging and mutual solidarity, which is a collective task (not only to be accomplished by teachers). But it is also achieved directly when teaching activities use and promote opportunities for social co-determination and the learning of empathy and care. That is not a task that would fall under any specific school subject, and it would make little sense to create such a subject. Rather, this is an interdisciplinary project that must be continually refreshed in the classroom, and one that also finds expression outside of obviously relevant contexts like "class councils" (for example, it is also at stake when teachers ask about children's emotions after the holidays). But this atmosphere should not be viewed in isolation from academic teaching. Empirical research has shown that teachers play a key role in this context, although they cannot be considered solely responsible for the success or failure of inclusion. For example, empirical studies by Anne Jordan and her colleagues (Jordan, Lindsay & Stanovich, 1997; Jordan, Schwartz & McGhie-Richmond, 2009) found that teachers' ideas about disability, and the degree to which they felt responsible for children with disabilities under their care, were crucial both for the social inclusion of these children and for their learning success. Teachers who primarily viewed disability as an impairment and an unalterable fate appeared to be less willing to engage with disabled pupils. Consequently, these children were more poorly regarded by their classmates and also had significantly worse learning outcomes. Teachers therefore function in some ways as the mediators of academic and social learning, and as role models for how other people – in this case, children – are to be treated. Educators who believe in the potential of each child, in their moral equality and uniqueness, have a good foundation for creating an atmosphere of inclusion in the classroom.

The importance of equality and recognition is revealed at this ultimately concrete and communal level, with reference to an atmosphere of inclusion that needs to be embraced both throughout the entire school and in individual classrooms. However, the significance of inclusive education is not limited to this scope; it also has a crucial societal value and function, in terms of both its goal orientation and its process orientation. Education can first be seen as the "main public investment that can foster both economic and civic cohesion" (Giddens, 2000, 73). Second, education is a civil right because it is a prerequisite and guarantor for a democracy and a society of enlightened citizens (Dahrendorf, 1965). Education is a precondition as well as a dimension of full social and political participation. The status of individual pupils who experience inclusion also serves to express their powers of co-determination over their own lives and personal situations.[35] Beyond that, there are also epistemic reasons with moral significance in favour of inclusive education for all children. First, diversity *per se* has epistemic value because it broadens and pluralises the perspectives on problems and solutions (Robertson, 2013). And second, the importance of diversity in school takes on moral value in that both pupils and teachers benefit from interacting with pupils who possess a range of abilities and differing traits.

The success of inclusive education cannot be measured solely through institutional contexts *per se*, but rather primarily through the forms of recognition they express and the freedoms they make available to people. The latter aspect is not so much a matter of current freedoms – we have already seen that the organisational structure of schools clearly limits the options for pupils' participation and co-determination. Pupils have no say in whether they are educated in the first place, and to a large extent they cannot determine what they learn, or when. We must therefore always keep in mind that educational situations are characterised by structural asymmetry, which can be addressed, but not eliminated (Ricken, 2006).

The specific challenge that schools pose for the inclusion of children is thus that, while schools are structurally committed to "institutional forced inclusion", they should at the same time provide an arena in which voluntary inclusion based on affinity can be learned and practised. Here, we see the difficulty of encouraging the affirmation of, and participation in, inclusion in the face of strong constraints and external determination, which is particularly not conducive to intersubjective, communal forms of inclusion. How can this be done, and through what means? In other words, how can we create an atmosphere of inclusion that fosters recognition and freedom when the context itself at least partially conflicts with that aim? This brings up another dilemma of inclusion, which Clemens Sedmak (2010) calls the "identity dilemma". Social integration is constitutive for human identity, which is, after all, formed through bonds that are also emotionally shaped. And these emotional ties are linked to familiarity, which primarily arises from small-scale contexts, characterised by concreteness and particularity (ibid., 157). The dilemma stems from the fact that, on the one hand, small groups in which trust is built up – such as school classes – are essential for establishing the necessary degree of familiarity in the first place. But on the other hand, inclusion is intended to transcend local, particular identity processes; it is meant to play out on the societal level. School fulfils a crucial role in that context.

At this point, we have identified two dilemmas: The first has to do with the conflict between freedom and coercion that is deeply embedded in educational processes, while the second stems from the inherent tension between the communal and societal perspectives on the value of inclusive education. Neither dilemma can be resolved, but approaches must be found for dealing with them. One way of addressing the double tension is to broaden the question of inclusion, moving away from a purely individual level of enquiry to a social one, so that inclusive education is understood in terms of how it contributes to the promotion of civic spirit and the common good.

The promotion of civic spirit and the common good in schools

Numerous authors have proposed ideas on how a group can be given space to develop as an educational community without running the risk of becoming totalitarian or exclusionary. Such reflections can be found, for example, in Karl Mannheim's concept of a "space of experience" (in German: *Erfahrungsraum*) (Mannheim, 1980), but also in Dewey's coupling of "habit" and "experience" (Dewey, 1916). Both Dewey and Mannheim focus on the coexistence of people in social units, from which a common web of meaning and forms of action can emerge through a shared mode of life and resulting experiences. This scenario, in turn, calls for practices of cooperation and communication that have to be learned and applied.

By participating in the life of a community, Dewey maintains, individuals adopt the habits that have been established in that community, or as he puts it: "Through habits formed in intercourse with the world, we also in-habit the world. It becomes a home and the home is part of our every experience" (Dewey, 2008a, 109). But this is not to be understood as a mere reproduction of social dispositions. In the reflexive mode of learning through experience, habits are acquired in a dialectic of confirmation and renewal. Dewey describes this as a "mixture of a museum and a laboratory" (Dewey, 2008b, 142).

To promote the common good in schools ultimately means creating a framework that establishes a value-based common ground, one that extends beyond individual, particular contexts. Martha Nussbaum, for example, in her observations on the educational role of schools, argues for the ability to think in universal terms and to use categories that encompass the whole of humanity as the first and most important goal of education (Nussbaum, 2011). Harry Brighouse also identifies the acquisition of democratic competences and the ability to cooperate as two key "aims goals" of education. The capacity for cooperation is significant not only because it is instrumentally important in a networked world that ultimately depends on the cooperation of all, but also because it is intrinsically valuable, namely as an expression of the equality of all people.

However, those who believe that such aims can only be achieved if all people are friends with each other are putting too much pressure on the idea of an educational community, not to mention civic spirit and an orientation around the common good. Such a scenario would overtax people's human, moral capacities. And beyond that, it is also likely that any idea of inclusive education featuring a strong orientation towards communality in the form of friendship would founder all the more because it would pre-emptively subject the good of friendship – which must develop and flourish voluntarily – to a doctrine of societal and pedagogical obligation.

Rather, in many cases, it is enough simply to be decent, to put it casually. And this virtue of decency should not be underestimated in the context of inclusive education. Decency implies the possibility of tactfully keeping distance and sometimes avoiding one another (Fumet, 2000, 104). Admittedly, the display of decency, rather than affirmative recognition, is not what we aspire to as a goal of inclusive education, or what we would primarily wish to embed in our processes or instil in pupils. To strive for more is certainly noble and important; indeed, it should be part of the educational vision of teachers and the school as an organisation, expressed in a lived ethos of inclusion. However, limits to such enactment of inclusion are apparent on grounds of justice and also for pragmatic reasons, suggesting that inclusive visions need to be grounded in a more realistic perspective. For one thing, as I have noted, it places too much strain on role bearers (both pupils and teachers) if the obligatory expectation is that they should be deeply attached to and friendly with everyone. One purpose of the role-based relationships in school is to protect both teachers and pupils – in temporal and above all emotional terms – from having their whole persons absorbed by the context. Second, it is neither possible from a justice perspective nor pragmatically feasible to have deep and close personal relationships with all individuals in a class. Indeed, we can even assume that a compulsory framework imposed on grounds of justice might destroy such relationships, including friendships among peers, rather than allowing them to flourish.

Conclusion

We have seen that the value-based pedagogical concept of inclusion is linked to political and ethical values such as equality, freedom and recognition, with which it stands in a dynamic, reciprocal relationship. Not all of these values can be realised in their pure form, of course, and they are affected by systemic limitations and dilemma structures in certain aspects.

First of all, we can observe that hierarchies and relations of dominance cannot be completely avoided in schools, and the idea that relationships should be based on parity also needs to be qualified in at least two important ways in the school context: In compulsory education, first, a certain relationship of dominance inevitably applies, namely that of the state over its emergent citizens. And second, school relationships between teachers and pupils are always characterised by a power imbalance between the two groups due to their differing roles. Teachers have a deontic position that pupils do not, accompanied by certain rights and duties that pupils are not entitled to or expected to have.[36]

Second, an inclusive school can of course instil new ways of handling diversity and heterogeneity, among other things through the moral values and norms of shared life that it imparts. It does this by demonstrating both that such heterogeneity exists and that differing models of life can be dealt with successfully, in a way that transforms difference into equality. At the same time, schools naturally also create difference via their structures and organisational processes. Through various forms of selection (from the discussion of or failure to discuss certain problems, to the awarding of marks, to praise and reprimands in the classroom), this creation of difference has an impact on the micro-level of school instruction. These double, dilemmatic aspects cannot be resolved through concepts such as "egalitarian difference" (Prengel, 2001) or "participation parity" (Fraser, 2000), as these antinomies of equality and difference are deeply embedded in educational processes and practices (Berlak & Berlak, 1981; Norwich, 2013).[37]

Third, there is also a tension between compulsion and the aspiration of freedom or autonomy. We have seen that school is a coercive institution for many reasons, of the kind that already inspired Kant (1900) to ask: How shall I cultivate freedom under conditions of compulsion? The dilemma is that, on the one hand, educational activity itself is not free of constraints; it takes place within the framework of social rules and norms. On the other hand, it is of course the intention of educational activity and an important goal of education overall to enable young people to make responsible use of freedom and to achieve autonomy (which, in turn, is linked to certain social constraints). This is part of the core of pedagogical practice. But in the goal of empowering pupils to be autonomous, there is a danger of seeing them as deficient and unfinished beings. This results in strong asymmetries and a power imbalance on top of the existing organisational power structure. And this tension has major implications for inclusive education in that the possibility (not the certainty!) of having even structural access to an inclusive school is a very important point, and one that takes priority in the hierarchy. This, in turn, means that it is necessary to have a voice in decisions, both about access to the place of schooling itself and, above all, about the resources that are necessary for substantial and successful participation in the context of schooling. This co-determining voice is an expression of equality, in terms of the general entitlement to be an equal member of society, and thus to have rights to educational goods and systems that are ordinarily open to all. The goods that are acquired and formed in school are, as we have seen, not only cultural capital, but also social and symbolic capital. Having a say about the place of education and the necessary educational resources is not only an expression of equality, but also of freedom: First of all, of negative freedom, in that persons are not forced to attend a special school if they do not want to; but of course second, and above all, an expression of positive freedom in that individuals receive the resources that allow them to lead a life of their own choosing. And third, this necessary co-determination implies a degree of vertical recognition of the state towards its fledgling citizens, which expresses itself in respect and thus becomes a source of self-respect for the individual.

We have also seen, however, that the value of inclusion and therefore of inclusive education is not limited to what it provides, and means, for individuals. It has further become clear that inclusion and inclusive education must not be restricted to structural access to education and participation in the goods of education, but must encompass aspects of social integration and psychologically perceived belonging, as well.

This double holism of the concept of inclusion means two things for the discussion of the normative content of inclusive education: First, the aspects of equality, freedom and recognition extend into the interpersonal and psychological spheres and do not remain only at the level of structures and resources. This shows that (a) equality is also experienced on an interpersonal level, as an expression of social esteem, care and specific consideration in the face of disability-related limitations; (b) freedom in inclusive education is granted on a reciprocal basis, which, in turn, means that freedom is, in a deeper sense, social and relational in nature; and (c) recognition has a constitutive function, insofar as inclusion both contributes to subjective well-being and is important for the individual, dialogically shaped identity development of children and young people.

Second, the view of inclusion as a social good implies that inclusive education is established through dialogue and collaboration. This is particularly evident at the interpersonal level, but it extends to the structures of inclusive schools, which are necessarily formed in a vertical feedback process involving various stakeholders (education policy-makers, teachers, parents, pupils, etc.). If, for example, in the context of the link between inclusive education and equality, it is argued that this equality refers to relational, democratic equality and thus to "relationships of equals", then this idea quite simply implies a social view of inclusion. Inclusive, i.e. relational, democratic equality is not something that can be achieved by individuals in isolation: It must be created collectively and anchored in processes dialogically. This again illustrates the great importance of the school ethos for the implementation of inclusion in schooling. And social freedom and recognition, as an expression of inclusive relationships, also highlight this aspect of the social praxis of inclusion. From this point of view, fewer individuals are included. Inclusion should instead be seen as expressive of social relations and processes.

This brings us to the real question we have been heading towards for a long time: How can we truly recognise whether inclusion is successfully implemented and practised in schools?

At this point, we have to backtrack a little. The idea that we have, on the one hand, a basket containing principles of inclusion, and on the other hand a basket of various concrete situations to which the principles can be applied, is tempting but short-sighted. This is because applied ethics, which ultimately encompasses the question of the ethical-normative content of inclusive education, differs in key respects from other disciplines (O'Neill, 2009, 220):

Applied ethics clearly differs from the truth-oriented enquiries of the natural sciences. More surprisingly it also differs from most of the supposedly non-naturalistic work to be found in the humanities and in so-called "qualitative" social enquiry. The natural sciences seek to explain natural events and their causes. Work in the humanities and qualitative social enquiry aims primarily at description (above all at thick description), at an understanding of meaning or (as it is often rather oddly put) of meanings, but eschews normative claims.

Unlike the natural sciences in particular, applied ethics is prescriptive, i.e. it arrives at certain "should" conclusions on normative grounds. Normative theories are based on the assumption that aspects of the world should be altered to comply with certain principles, not vice versa (Brownlee, 2009, 231).

The application of ethical-normative principles is not concerned with specific situations, but with types of situations (Sedmak, 2013). In concrete terms, it is not a matter of assessing the case of a specific child or school class, but about the kinds of situations involved, for example, shared work on a topic in a classroom, design of therapy situations, admission and assessment interviews, the structural and spatial layout of school buildings, etc. The challenge in such typology is that attention must be paid to concrete details even while an abstract perspective is maintained. If we follow Onora O'Neill (2009), however, the point when dealing with questions of applied ethics is not to find a balance between principles and concrete situations, but between various principles themselves. So, the question cannot be: How can we apply the principles of equality, freedom and recognition, as values of inclusion and inclusive education, to a specific case? Rather, the question must be: What courses of action and strategies emerge when we weigh the various principles involved? What does a particular case express, or what weighting should it have? This, in turn, raises the question: How can we establish rules to guide our actions?[38] Specifically, how can we transform schools so that they become more inclusive? The next and final chapter will deal with these very questions.

Notes

1 There are of course many cases of people living with impairments that do not have a significant impact on their opportunities for inclusion in present-day societies. However, in my view, that only applies for a relatively privileged minority among people with disabilities. All others have to live with disadvantages and obstacles, resulting in the very life experiences that necessitate a struggle for inclusion.
2 Despite the benefits that such an approach brings to the topic of inclusion and inclusive education, it is still a desideratum in relevant debates (Kronauer, 2010, 2015). In philosophy, by contrast, this kind of perspective is used in a number of theories (Fricker, 2007; Margalit, 1996; Sen, 1992, 2000; Shklar, 1990; Young, 1990a). Avishai Margalit, for example, describes his decision to explore the aspect of humiliation rather than dignity as follows:

> I believe that it is not justice that brings us into normative politics, but injustice. Not equality, but inequality. Not freedom, but despotism, and more to the point – not recognition and respect, but rejection and humiliation. There is, on my account, more urgency to dealing with humiliation than to dealing with recognition and respect. Moreover, it is much clearer what counts as humiliation, namely treating humans as non-humans – e.g. as animals, as instruments, as mere statistics, as sub-humans – than what counts as respecting them.
> (Margalit, 2001, 127)

The assumption behind a negative approach is that it will ultimately lead to better, more intuitively comprehensible answers concerning the struggle for inclusion (Shklar, 1990, 16).
3 See here some recent and well-known examples, in addition to Rawls, of course: Cohen (1989), Walzer (1983), Dworkin (2000), Sen (2009) and Nussbaum (2006).
4 This can be illustrated with a negative example: Inclusion in a prison or in a dictatorship like that of North Korea can also be referred to as inclusion. But neither of these forms of inclusion interest us here, especially not from a justice perspective. For no one would demand that there must be a general right to inclusion in dictatorships or prisons.
5 Nussbaum (2006, 163f.) writes specifically:

> Unlike Rawls, […] I view such a consensus as fully available internationally across lines of tradition and religion. […] Thus it is part of what justifies the conception: that it can over time be justified to people who hold different comprehensive conceptions of the good life. Justification thus involves an idea of accountability to all, or at least to the major conceptions of value. Acceptability is relevant to justification both for the reasons of stability – a conception that is acceptable to all can be stable over time – and for reasons of respect. […] Requiring accountability as a condition of justification builds in the idea that the theory of the good is not independent of human agreement, but can be justified as the right political conception of the good only in relation to the possibility of such an agreement (for good reasons, not just as a mere *modus vivendi*).

6 The social relationships formed at school, in particular friendships with peers, are also clearly important for well-being in the school context.
7 In general, we can distinguish between "push" and "pull" factors of exclusion. Push factors are those that cause society or communities to exclude people, while pull factors are those that lead individuals or groups to exclude themselves. Very often, pull factors are a reaction to or an anticipation of push factors.
8 Consider, for example, the worldwide ban on child labour, which is not always enforced.
9 Here, we touch on the difficult tension between subjectively perceived importance and urgency and the moral claims that result (or rather, often do *not* result) from this. For no one would claim that there is a right to be a member of the Zurich Canary Breeders' Association, for instance. Rather, each association has the right to choose its own members. The same also applies to a whole range of human affiliations, including friendships. No one can force me into a friendship, nor do I myself have the right to enter into a specific friendship. Rights reach their limits especially when it comes to free will and communal forms of inclusion. But we can observe that certain people are exposed to multiple and recurrent forms of communal exclusion that have a lasting and negative impact on their well-being. For these and other reasons, some philosophers call for rights to be established in this sphere, or at least for certain phases of life, such as childhood (Brownlee, 2013, 2016, 2020; Liao, 2015; Nussbaum, 2013). It does not seem absurd to claim that children have a right to the love of their parents and to inclusion in the form of social integration and physical subsistence.
10 To give one example, the head of the Buchenwald concentration camp, Karl Koch, is said to have trained his St Bernard mix to chase and maul prisoners on the command "Man, get that dog!". The gruesomeness of this exclamation lies not only in the physical torture that awaited the prisoners should they be bitten to death by the dog, but also in the linguistic exclusion inherent in the command itself. And this double form of exclusion is so fundamental that it can justifiably be doubted whether people who are subjected to it are really viewed as human beings in a basic way before they are cast out of the human realm, as Margalit claims.
11 Historically, people with cognitive impairments have often been considered close to the animal world, for example, through claims about their "ape-like" appearance (Carlson, 2009). Such assumptions are not limited to theoretical observations, but have far-reaching practical consequences, as Wolfensberger (1972), for example, points out in his classic work on normalisation. Thus, for example, the character of mentally disabled people, which was assumed to be "subhuman" and "animal-like", led to the belief that they were not sensitive to heat or cold. That assumption was, in turn, used to deprive them of warmth from heating systems in winter.
12 Certain organisations work to raise public awareness of such cases, including the European Disability Forum, Handicap International, UNHCR and UNICEF.
13 Both cases can be found on the homepage of the Inclusion Handicap umbrella organisation, at www.inclusion-handicap.ch.
14 We must be careful, however, not to overstretch the biological model by assuming that all kinds of needs have an incontrovertible biological basis. This is an error that may be identified in Maslow's model of needs, for example.
15 Precisely in this respect, there is also a moral difference between someone starving because of a food shortage and someone undergoing a voluntary fast, for instance.
16 This does not mean, of course, that these motives are appropriate in every case, or that we should give them too much weight. But the truth is that they exist, and the protection of people in general is a legitimate moral motive.
17 The literature of people with autism is particularly striking in this regard. Featuring figures such as Temple Grandin and Daniel Tammet, among others, not to mention films like *Rain Man* and *Hors Normes*, this literature has significantly contributed to a better and deeper understanding of the situation of people with autism.

Values that matter **213**

18 Here, we should again acknowledge the many years of research carried out by Anne Jordan and her team. Since 1992, Jordan has been developing a research programme called Supporting Effective Teaching (SET) (Jordan, Kircaali-Iftar & Diamond, 1993; Jordan, Lindsay & Stanovich, 1997; Jordan, Schwartz & McGhie-Richmond, 2009; Jordan & Stanovich, 2001; Stanovich, 1998), which is of great interest in this context. The results of the team's studies show a striking correlation between teachers' beliefs about inclusion and disability, their sense of responsibility for teaching pupils with special needs and the overall quality of their teaching practices. In particular, these studies show that teachers who feel responsible for their pupils with special needs also have epistemological beliefs about the nature of disability that reflect a social-interactive model of disability rather than a medical-individual model.

19 The social consequence is that a significant portion of human experience does not become part of the collective hermeneutic resources due to structurally conditioned prejudices. Collective hermeneutic resources in schools include textbooks, for example, and particularly the materials used to learn reading and history.

20 It may sound paradoxical to speak of experiences that have not been experienced. What this means is that, while these experiences have happened in reality, they are not ontologically recorded as such in the individual's subjective store of experience.

21 This is particularly evident in the architectural planning of school buildings. There are legendary examples where architects seem to have forgotten for whom a building was actually intended, and thus have installed adult toilets, for instance, that could only be used by the kindergarten children with the help of stairs. And then there are the well-known cases of recent school buildings where the planners neglected to provide barrier-free access for children in wheelchairs or designed ramps so steep that they could not possibly be negotiated by such children.

22 This view does not, however, explain why certain loops solidify globally into structures (such as the economic order of capitalism), while others do not, or do so only partially or under certain historical conditions (such as communism as a governance structure).

23 This does not tell us anything about the quality of these relationships or the personal sense of belonging, but it does illustrate that structural access (and to some extent participation in goods) plays something of a gate-keeping role, which is not the case for the other two aspects, i.e. social integration and personal belonging.

24 According to Gosepath (2004), this postulate of moral equality represents the "egalitarian plateau" of all current moral theories in the Western tradition. Even if this must often be understood more as an intellectual consensus and a declaration of intent, no one today would dare to justify an action on the basis of the moral inequality of people. An internal contradiction would immediately arise in that case. And the second possibility, of simply contesting moral equality as such, would likely lead to exclusion from the moral community.

25 Cf. the "equality of what" debate, in particular the influential contributions of Sen (1979), Dworkin (1981a, b) and Cohen (1989). G. A. Cohen (1989, 906), for example, presents a view of equality as a question of distributive justice when he writes: "I take for granted that there is something that justice requires people to have equal amounts of, not no matter what, but to whatever extent is allowed by values that compete with distributive equality". If this view of egalitarian justice is adopted, then the main issue is to identify its "currency", i.e. the objects by which equality is gauged.

26 It is unclear, however, whether this approach should be situated strictly in a positive paradigm or should be understood as signalling a transition to the subsequent, third understanding of freedom to be discussed.

27 Our first system of exclusion focused precisely on cases of this kind. And in Chapter 3, we examined how people with disabilities in particular have been systematically excluded, both in theory and in practice, from many areas of societal life, including school education, over many centuries.

28 This is significant insofar as the concept of recognition historically derives from German-language literature (especially works by Johann Gottlieb Fichte and Georg Wilhelm Friedrich Hegel) and is still largely native to or rooted in the German-speaking world, as evidenced by the translation of major works of modern recognition literature, e.g. by Axel Honneth, Rainer Forst and Heikki Ikäheimo. Although the last of these authors has been teaching in Australia for years, he first published his book on recognition in German.
29 Ikäheimo advocates a highly nuanced system of recognition, which would, however, go too far for our purposes. I here present the distinctions that I consider crucial for the topic of inclusion.
30 Love is thus understood here in a broad sense and includes all close interpersonal relationships characterised by associated feelings (friendship, love, care, trust, etc.). Honneth, in one of his articles (2000, 235f., author's translation), describes the aspect of love in somewhat more detail, as an act encompassing all "acts [...] that, like unconditional care or understanding forgiveness, make it clear that they are done solely for the sake of the individual well-being of a concrete other".
31 We are clearly dealing with partly contradictory tendencies here. While some people have seen a rapid evolution of recognition in the form of esteem for their way of life – LGTBQI people come to mind here – others have lost out badly or still cannot see any evolution. The former certainly include people with a strongly religious lifestyle, the latter not least people with disabilities.
32 It can be described in a general way as follows:

> Vulnerability results from a situation in which an agent is both *dependent on* and *exposed to* another agent. To be vulnerable is to be exposed to the power of someone we depend on – physically, affectively, socially or economically. In this respect, vulnerability supposes the existence of a relationship of dependency between agents who have the power to act on one another, and potentially, to harm one another.
>
> (Garrau & Laborde, 2015, 52)

33 The latter aspect can also be considered an anthropological constant of human life. The interest in personal expression and self-realisation that is reflected in this sense can be seen not least in the wall paintings of very early humans, as well as their production of toys and objects of art, representing an aspect of humanness that has persisted across history and all cultures. Any systematic violation of this component is therefore also problematic on grounds of justice.
34 The basis of arguments for preparing children for autonomous living and the labour market is that the relevant skills are extremely valuable for efforts to lead a good (flourishing) life. Well-being is therefore the prerequisite for the first two aims goals, and one of the responsibilities that falls to schools. And this responsibility, in turn, extends to the long-term well-being of pupils, not just their short-term happiness (Brighouse, 2009, 39).
35 Power also has an epistemic and a material side. It is, on the one hand, a distributive good within society, while on the other hand it represents a socio-cultural grid of interpretation and communication (Benhabib, 1992).
36 Teachers may, for example, reprimand or expel pupils for inappropriate behaviour, but pupils may not do the same. Teachers must also participate in professional development programmes, ensure that the curriculum and timetable are adhered to, and provide individual pupils with the learning materials appropriate to them. Pupils do not have these same responsibilities.
37 Considering that these constitute dilemmas and not problems, according to Norwich (2014b, c), they can be addressed, but they cannot be resolved. Nilholm (2006) also argues that a perspective specifically targeting these dilemmas needs to be developed in special and inclusive education, and that inclusion can only be achieved via an inclusive approach in decision-making and assessment processes.

38 The challenge here is twofold (Sedmak, 2013): First, we need to translate the vision of inclusion and the understanding of the values that constitute inclusion into a language of guiding ideas and principles. And second, we need to translate these guiding ideas and principles into questions. These questions will, in turn, function as indicators of how inclusion and inclusive education can be concretely implemented and enacted in practical situations and life contexts. The focus, especially from a justice perspective, should be on the institutional arrangements and framework conditions of schools, in particular structures and cultures.

8
CONCLUSION
The transformation of education

What guiding ideas and principles have emerged in our discussion? How can we translate them into sets of questions that can, in turn, serve as indicators of how well these ideas and principles are put into practice? And how can we generate and stabilise the relevant structures and cultures, but also the intersubjective and personal aspects of inclusion, which are often "softer" and more fragile? These are some of the questions that have arisen in the course of this book.

Debates surrounding inclusive education often leave the impression that two things in particular are missing for the implementation of a truly inclusive school system: On the one hand, there is a deficit in terms of political will and individual attitudes, for example, on the part of teachers or school administrators, and, on the other hand, there is a shortage of individualised learning and teaching approaches, of material, suitable didactics and methodologies, and appropriate teaching and support staff.

However, this book should have made it clear that we need to do far more than address these issues alone if we are to implement inclusion in a holistic sense. There are several reasons for this. First, the belief that it is enough to adopt these measures, and *only* these measures, is based on the assumption that they ultimately address the substance of inclusion or inclusive education, namely, structural access, sufficient resources that are adapted to individuals' personal situations, and instructions provided by teachers who have the "right" attitudes. But as demonstrated in the fourth and sixth chapters, this is a very limited conception of inclusion that moreover reflects a problematic allocation of responsibility for the implementation of inclusive education. Important aspects of inclusion and inclusive education also encompass issues of social integration (and recognition in groups) as well as personally perceived belonging. Unlike structures and resources, which – once established and maintained – are relatively stable and

DOI: 10.4324/9781003221326-8

accessible to individuals, the interpersonal and personal aspects of inclusion have to be continuously regenerated in a processual way. They are fragile and fleeting.

Because all aspects of inclusion – structural access, participation in resources, social integration and psychologically perceived belonging – are necessary elements, we cannot avoid addressing them in their entirety.[1]

The shift towards inclusion

What changes must occur in order to make schooling inclusive in the "full" or "substantive" sense? And how, and at what levels, must this transformation take place?

First, we need to change our dichotomous idea of inclusion. Instead of viewing inclusive education as an "all or nothing" concept, as it usually appears in public discussions, inclusion should be regarded as a gradual phenomenon. People may be included in many ways and contexts, with varying forms of recognition, and may enjoy a range of freedoms in and through these modes of inclusion. The equality expressed in inclusion also takes a different form depending on whether we think of it in the sense of equal rights (for political citizens, for example) or in the sense of a situation of interpersonal care between teachers and pupils. The aim is not to view these values in a static or absolute way, but to weigh them and consider how they fit into and apply to concrete life situations. Inclusion is therefore a complex and ceaseless work in progress. The bad news in this context is that inclusion can always fail, for it remains forever fragile, and will never be fully achieved. It cannot be secured once and for all institutionally, nor maintained solely on an interpersonal basis, as it is too dynamic and multifaceted. All of its aspects are interdependent and mutually reinforcing, and can therefore also have a negative or damaging effect on each other.

Second, change must happen at various levels and must not be regarded as a bureaucratic and structural act that – once completed – will automatically set all the others in motion. This means that inclusive processes do not necessarily take place in a top-down manner, but very often emerge from the bottom-up, for example, through personal contact and friendships. Personal transformative experiences can also serve as precedents for broader social transformation (Yacek, 2020). Freire (1993), for example, argues that a kind of "conversion" or "rebirth", a liberation from deeply internalised values and ideals, is necessary for large-scale social change to occur.

According to Yacek (2020), personal transformation is characterised by four features: First, it signifies a meaningful change in a person; second, this transformation is irreversible, such that the person is permanently altered; third, in a phenomenological sense, the change represents a rupture, a discontinuity; and fourth, it takes place quickly – even a moment can suffice in many cases. It is admittedly difficult to imagine that there can be many such moments of "awakening" in the context of inclusive education. The education system is far too unwieldy, and organisationally and structurally geared towards differentiation and exclusion, for the transformation of individuals to have much effect. We should also be careful not to place too much emphasis on individual attitudes. Inclusive education must not only be anchored in individual attitudes and transformations, but also expressed in action – not least in organisational action and structures – and constantly reconstituted through processes.

It is undoubtedly the case, however, that the process of shaping meaning – from perceptions of disability, to the role of teachers themselves, to conceptions of the aims and functions of school education – is of crucial importance. Indeed, by incorporating the core values of inclusion into our consciousness and internalising them, we do not only create meaning, or change the meaning we assign to inclusion and inclusive education; we also change our epistemology when we start thinking differently about disability and the importance of schooling children together with their peers (Kegan, 2009). The aim of the transformative approach is then also, according to Fitch (2002, 471f.):

> [...] to redress misrecognition, stigmatization and cultural oppression by transforming discourses and altering the underlying structures that generate them. It seeks to challenge, to blur, to reimagine, and to redescribe social structures, discourses, and binary distinctions (such as normal and abnormal, male and female, gay and straight, able and disabled, and special and regular). [...] The intent is not simply to affirm the worth of those currently outside the norm and dominant cultural group, but to reframe all social identities, to transform the norm itself.

In the words of the organisational theorists Bartunek and Moch (1987), a change or transformation in the direction of inclusive education calls for third-order changes, and thus also for triple-loop reflexive processes in the relevant organisations.[2] A third-order change involves recognising and potentially enabling the ability to alter the operational, entrenched social imaginaries in which organisational schemata reside. To change these established traditions, the aforementioned "triple-loop processes" are needed (Walsh, 2004, 307). These are processes that help individuals to identify and potentially change key values and behaviours that are by no means universally accepted. Triple-loop processes or the inauguration of a social imaginary create the kind of change that Bartunek and Moch (1987, 24) describe as "the opportunity to transcend schemata". Third-order changes are initiated in situations where a particular organisation or group determines that its organisational schemata are not suitable for a given task. This process involves development of the ability to recognise and change elements of operational, established social imaginaries that inform and preserve organisational schemata. In the case of third-order change, the capacity to recognise the system of cultural traditions that generates and sustains organisational schemata helps to create a social imaginary that can transform the entire epistemological system (Walsh, 2004, 307). This can be achieved through deliberately managed and implemented team and school development processes that continuously alternate between upper, middle and lower decision-making levels, i.e. between policy-makers, school administrators, and teachers and pupils. All participants must share the decisions and embrace the ethos of inclusion if transformation in the direction of inclusive education in a holistic sense is to become a reality.

But how likely is it that a system like the school can be transformed? Two factors seem to be important here. The first factor is the resilience of a system, i.e. the degree to which it is able to absorb disturbance without having to change itself. Resilience is very pronounced in schools, as can be observed merely from considering the historical development of the school system, which has changed only marginally in its basic outlines since the introduction of mass schooling. The other factor concerns the importance our society attaches to school education, especially with regard to school-leaving qualifications. School education universally enjoys the highest level of societal acceptance, although of course different groups within society take differing views of its role and design. Moreover, because the siblings and parents of today's school generation have already gone to school themselves, school education has become a "natural" stage in the educational process that is hardly questioned anymore (Vanderstraeten, 2004b, 61f.). The changes that can be witnessed here are correspondingly slow, while the conservative pressure is strong. The relationship between individual behaviour and structural injustices must also be kept in mind. It is true that individual ethical conduct and attitudes may mitigate a structural problem, but ultimately they do not change anything at the structural level. Structural problems primarily require collective rather than individual action.

This means that we are all called to reflect on our role in changing the substance of schooling and the epistemological basis of our knowledge and thinking about disability as well as the entitlement of disabled children and young people to be taught in an inclusive way. All of us (meaning the whole of society, not just educational practitioners such as teachers and school administrators) therefore need to revise our ideologies and work on transforming societal structures. This can only be achieved through a variety of processes, because ideologies such as those asserting that children with disabilities should be educated in special schools, or occupy a marginalised position within schools, are very powerful.

As Haslanger (2012) points out, ideologies are first embedded in the ideas and meanings that we use to classify social phenomena – for example, the grouping of people into separate races, castes and genders, or normative concepts such as "illegal immigrant" or "cripple". If we wish to combat or at least mitigate the effects of these ideologies, we must therefore be clear about the underlying social ideas and meanings, which may be implicit and unconscious. Often these prevailing ideas already carry racist and discriminatory connotations, such as the belief that black children and adolescents tend to be behaviourally deviant and lazy, or that disabled people cannot take on leadership roles due to physical frailty.

Second, these meanings pervasively shape the social practices and norms needed to coordinate action and produce important goods, even if they simultaneously reproduce oppression or have the potential to do so.[3] We should therefore be careful (especially in special education diagnoses) not to apply these categories too broadly and indiscriminately to all forms of disruptive behaviour, but should instead strive to become aware of what diagnoses reveal about structures and not only about people.

Third, while the meanings of categories provide orientation for our habits and practical abilities, they are implicit and therefore not readily subject to open, direct critique. It is therefore particularly hard to situate the starting point for critiques of inclusive education. Accordingly, we face the important challenge of making visible its true ideological and habitual foundations. For socially critical thought and action, this means, among other things, that a great deal of effort and public debate is needed to make critique open and transparent, a process that can currently be witnessed in the racism debates in the United States, for example.

Fourth, it is important to remember that a change in people's explicit beliefs does not necessarily cause their habits to shift, as explicit beliefs do not regulate habits. Although the modification of habits is far more strenuous and challenging, for that very reason it represents a crucial step in the fight against injustice. We should therefore be careful not to jump to the conclusion that a change of terminology (for example, from mongoloid to trisomy 21 or Down syndrome) will achieve very much for the real-life inclusion of the people concerned. The same is true for inclusion: Just because many interlocutors (especially in the German-language debate) routinely speak of inclusive education, while consigning exclusion, separation and integration to the historical past, this does not mean that inclusion necessarily exists where it is claimed to exist.

A fifth aspect to be noted is that the social coordination produced by ideological, perpetuated meanings has mental shaping effects. In other words, it brings people to understand themselves and others by shaping their cognitive and behavioural predispositions in accordance with cultural representations of who they are. It creates lived identities that align with the given ideology, as individuals take their place in the oppressive social system and possibly even identify with that place. This means, then, not only that the oppressors have internalised their mechanisms of oppression, but that the oppressed occupy the places assigned to them. Because oppression also affects the self-image of sufferers, we must respond with empathy and understanding to these self-identities, and gently transform them into new, self-determined ones. All this is not necessarily a consolation for those who would like to believe that there is a shortcut or highway to the implementation of inclusion and inclusive education. The path is long, difficult and rocky, but it is passable.

Closing remarks

The story mentioned at the very outset of this book, of the singer Rihanna associating the successful launch of her fashion brand Fenty with the values of diversity and inclusion, has been mirrored in global education policy for a number of years. Lifelong learning, diversity, equal opportunities, and – crucially! – inclusion, are the core values, for example, of the Education 2030 Agenda supported by UNESCO and based on the UN Sustainable Development Goals (UNESCO, 2015; United Nations, 2015). The idea of making education inclusive is thus gaining popularity all over the world. This process will not be completed for a long time, considering the reality that – according to Winzer and Mazurek (2010, 96)

> [...] change is not always neat and may require many detours; transformation is not an event but a slow, incremental, and multifaceted process that occurs in stages, with disruptions, contradictions, and tensions as natural occurrences. Through the lens of evolution, inclusion is not a decisive perspective but a growing reality as schools and systems provide evidence of the capacity for change.

Patience and persistence, then, are proving to be the essential virtues in the struggle to realise inclusion and inclusive education.

Notes

1. This is true even if structures and resources are situated upstream hierarchically insofar as they shape the possibilities for the forms of social integration and psychological belonging that are available or feasible in the first place.
2. Third-order changes are distinct from first- and second-order changes. In the case of first-order changes, the existing operational schemata are left intact or are deemed unproblematic, while questions are raised, for example, about potentially better or more efficient ways of dealing with problems. Such changes are often set in motion when existing processes prove inefficient (Bartunek & Moch, 1987, 487). The underlying core values are not examined or altered in this context (Walsh, 2004, 306). Second-order changes involve the deliberate alteration of existing schemata in a particular direction, and take place more generally within organisational schemata. This means that "a second order change seeks to change the schemata themselves ... [i.e.] one interpretative schema or set of schemata is 'phased out' as another is 'phased in'" (Bartunek & Moch, 1987, 486). Here, we see a shift in terms of the underlying mental constructs. This kind of change usually constitutes a reaction to the discovery that shared epistemic resources or organisational schemata are in some way inadequate in light of the goals of the organisation itself. Walsh explains that second-order changes result from single- and double-loop processes. A double-loop process occurs when individuals or groups are willing to change their values and thereby develop new strategies or ways of thinking, feeling or acting that genuinely improve their effectiveness (Walsh, 2004, 306).
3. This holds true for many of the criteria used to identify special educational needs, as in the case of ADHD and autism.

REFERENCES

Ahlberg, J., & Brighouse, H. (2014). Education: *Not* a Real Utopian Design. *Politics and Society, 42*(1), 51–72.
Ainscow, M. (2007). Taking an Inclusive Turn. *Journal of Reseach in Special Educational Needs, 7*(1), 3–7.
Ainscow, M., Booth, T., & Dyson, A. (2006). *Improving Schools, Developing Inclusion*. London: Routledge.
Ainscow, M., & Miles, S. (2008). Making Education for All Inclusive: Where Next? *Prospects, 38*(1), 15–34.
Albrecht, G. L., & Devlieger, P. J. (1999). The Disability Paradox: High Quality of Life against All Odds. *Social Science & Medicine, 48*(8), 977–988.
Allan, J. (2012). Inclusion: Patterns and Possibilities. *Zeitschrift für Inklusion*, (4). https://www.inklusion-online.net/index.php/inklusion-online/article/view/31
Allen, K. E., & Schwartz, I. S. (2001). *The Exceptional Child: Inclusion in Early Childhood Education*. Albany, NY: Delmar.
Almalky, H. A. (2020). Employment Outcomes for Individuals with Intellectual and Developmental Disabilities: A Literature Review. *Children and Youth Services Review, 109*, 104656.
Aly, G. (2013). *Die Belasteten: 'Euthanasie' 1939–1945 – eine Gesellschaftsgeschichte* [The Burdened: 'Euthanasia' 1939–1945 – a Social History]. Frankfurt a. M.: S. Fischer.
Anastasiou, D., & Kauffman, J. M. (2013). The Social Model of Disability: Dichotomy between Impairment and Disability. *The Journal of Medicine and Philosophy, 38*(4), 441–459.
Anderson, E. (1999). What Is the Point of Equality? *Ethics, 109*(1), 287–337.
Anderson, E. (2010). *The Imperative of Integration*. Princeton, NJ: Princeton University Press.
Archer, M. S. (1981). Fields of Specialization: Educational Systems. *International Social Science Journal, 33*(2), 261–284.
Arendt, H. (1958). *Die Krise in der Erziehung* [The Crisis in Education]. Bremen: Angelsachen-Verlag.
Artiles, A. J., & Dyson, A. (2005). Inclusive Education in the Globalization Age. In D. Mitchell (Ed.), *Contextualizing Inclusive Education: Evaluating Old and New International Perspectives* (pp. 37–62). London: Routledge.

Artiles, A. J., Harris-Murri, N., & Rostenberg, D. (2006). Inclusion as Social Justice: Critical Notes on Discourses, Assumptions, and the Road Ahead. *Theory into Practice, 45*(3), 260–268.

Artiles, A. J., & Kozleski, E. B. (2016). Inclusive Education's Promises and Trajectories: Critical Notes about Future Research on a Venerable Idea. *Education Policy Analysis Archives, 24*(43), 1–25.

Artiles, A. J., Kozleski, E. B., Dorn, S., & Christensen, C. (2006). Chapter 3: Learning in Inclusive Education Research: Re-mediating Theory and Methods with a Transformative Agenda. *Review of Research in Education, 30*(1), 65–108.

Baker, D., & LeTendre, G. K. (2005). *National Differences, Global Similarities: World Culture and the Future of Schooling.* Stanford, CA: Stanford University Press.

Baker, J. (2015). Conceptions and Dimensions of Social Equality. In C. Fourie, F. Schuppert & I. Wallimann-Helmer (Eds.), *Social Equality: On What It Means to Be Equal* (pp. 65–86). Oxford: Oxford University Press.

Ballard, K. (2019). Inclusion, Paradigms, Power and Participation. In C. Clark, A. Dyson & A. Millard (Eds.), *Towards Inclusive Schools?* (pp. 1–14). Abingdon: Routledge.

Barnes, E. (2016). *The Minority Body.* Oxford: Oxford University Press.

Barrow, R. (2000). 'Include Me Out': A Response to John Wilson. *European Journal of Special Needs Education, 15*(3), 305–307.

Barrow, R. (2001). Inclusion vs Fairness. *Journal of Moral Education, 30*(3), 235–242.

Barry, B. (2002). Social Exclusion, Social Isolation, and the Distribution of Income. In J. Hills, J. LeGrand & D. Pichaud (Eds.), *Understanding Social Exclusion* (pp. 13–29). Oxford: Oxford University Press.

Barton, L. (1997). Inclusive Education: Romantic, Subversive or Realistic. *International Journal of Inclusive Education, 1*(3), 31–242.

Barton, L. (1999). Market Ideologies, Education and the Challenge. In H. Daniels & P. Garner (Eds.), *World Yearbook of Education: Inclusive Education* (pp. 54–62). London: Kogan Page.

Bartunek, J. M., & Koch, M. K. (1987). First-Order, Second-Order, and Third-Order Change and Organization Development Interventions: A Cognitive Approach. *The Journal of Applied Behavioral Science, 23*(4), 483–500.

Basil, C. (1992). Social Interaction and Learned Helplessness in Severely Disabled Children. *Augmentative and Alternative Communication, 8*(3), 188–199.

Benhabib, S. (1992). *Situating the Self: Gender, Community and Postmodernism in Contemporary Ethics.* New York: Polity Press.

Berger, P. A., & Luckmann, Th. (1971). *The Social Construction of Reality.* Harmondsworth: Penguin.

Berlak, A., & Berlak, H. (1981). *Dilemmas of Schooling: Teaching and Social Change.* New York: Methuen.

Berlin, I. (1969). Two Concepts of Liberty. In I. Berlin (Ed.), *Liberty* (pp. 166–217). Oxford: Oxford University Press.

Biesta, G. (2012). Philosophy of Education for the Public Good: Five Challenges and an Agenda. *Educational Philosophy and Theory, 44*(6), 581–593.

Biklen, D. (1985). *Achieving the Complete School: Strategies to Effective Mainstreaming.* New York: Teachers College Press.

Biklen, D. (1987). The Culture of Policy: Disability Images and Their Analogues in Public Policy. *Policy Studies Journal, 15*(3), 515–535.

Biklen, D., & Bogdan, R. C. (1985). *Achieving the Complete School: Strategies for Effective Mainstreaming.* New York: Teachers College Press.

Blatt, B., & Kaplan, F. (1966). *Christmas in Purgatory: A Photographic Essay.* Boston, MA: Allyn and Bacon.

Blümner, H. (2019). The Power of Style, Sex and 76 Million Followers. *Der Spiegel, October 25, 2019.*

Böckenförde, E.-W. (1976). *State, Society, Freedom. Studies on State Theory and the Constitutional Law.* Frankfurt a. M.: Suhrkamp.

Boissevain, J. (1975). *Friends of Friends. Networks, Manipulators, and Coalitions.* New York: St. Martin's Press.

Booth, T. (1995). Mapping Inclusion and Exclusion: Concepts for All? In C. Clark, A. Dyson & A. Millard (Eds.), *Towards Inclusive Schools?* (pp. 96–108). London: David Fulton.

Booth, T., & Ainscow, M. (2002). *The Index for Inclusion.* Bristol: Centre for Studies in Inclusive Education.

Bourdieu, P. (1984). *Distinction: A Social Critique of the Judgement of Taste* (R. Nice, Trans.). Cambridge, MA: Harvard University Press.

Bourdieu, P. (1986). The Forms of Capital. In J. G. Richardson (Ed.), *Handbook of Theory and Research for the Sociology of Education* (pp. 241–258). New York: Greenwood Press.

Bourdieu, P., & Passeron, J.-C. (1990). *Reproduction in Education, Society and Culture* (2nd ed.). New York: Sage.

Bourdieu, P., & Wacquant, L. J. D. (1992). *An Invitation to Reflexive Sociology.* Chicago, IL: University of Chicago Press.

Bourdieu, P., & Wacquant, L. J. D. (1999). *The Weight of the World: Social Suffering in Contemporary Society.* Cambridge, MA: Polity Press.

Boydston, J. A. (2008). *John Dewey: Volume 11: 1935–1937.* Carbondale: Southern Illinois University Press.

Bratman, M. E. (2014). *Shared Agency – A Planning Theory of Acting Together.* New York: Oxford University Press.

Brighouse, H. (2008). Education for a Flourishing Life. *Yearbook of the National Society for the Study of Education, 107*(1), 58–71.

Brighouse, H. (2009). Moral and Political Aims of Education. In H. Siegel (Ed.), *The Oxford Handbook of Philosophy of Education* (pp. 35–51). Oxford: Oxford University Press.

Brighouse, H. (2015). Nonideal Theorizing in Education. *Educational Theory, 65*(2), 215–231.

Brownlee, K. (2009). Normative Principles and Practical Ethics: A Response to O'Neill. *Journal of Applied Philosophy, 26*(3), 231–237.

Brownlee, K. (2013). A Human Right Against Social Deprivation. *Philosophical quarterly, 63*(251), 199–222.

Brownlee, K. (2016). The Lonely Heart Breaks: On the Right to Be a Social Contributor. *Aristotelian Society Supplementary, xc,* 27–48.

Brownlee, K. (2020). *Being Sure of Each Other: An Essay on Social Rights and Freedoms.* Oxford: Oxford University Press.

Brzinsky-Fay, C., & Solga, H. (2016). Compressed, Postponed, or Disadvantaged? School-to-work-transition Patterns and Early Occupational Attainment in West Germany. *Research in Social Stratification and Mobility, 46,* 21–36.

Bude, H., & Lantermann, E.-D. (2006). Soziale Exklusion und Exklusionsempfinden [Social Exclusion and Perceptions of Exclusion]. *Kölner Zeitschrift für Soziologie und Sozialpsychologie, 58*(2), 233–252.

Burbules, N. C. (2018). Philosophy of Education. In P. Smeyers (Ed.), *International Handbook of Philosophy of Education* (pp. 1417–1427). Cham: Springer.

References

Campbell, J. M. (2006). Changing Children's Attitudes Toward Autism: A Process of Persuasive Communication. *Journal of Developmental and Physical Disabilities, 18*, 251–272.

Capella, E., Hughes, D. L., & McCormick, M. P. (2017). The Hidden Role of Teachers: Child and Classroom Predictors of Change in Interracial Friendships. *The Journal of Early Adolescence, 37*(8), 1093–1124.

Carey, A. C. (2009). *On the Margins of Citizenship: Intellectual Disability and Civil Rights in Twentieth Century America*. Philadelphia, PA: Temple University Press.

Carlson, L. (2009). Philosophers of Intellectual Disability: A Taxonomy. *Metaphilosophy, 40*(3–4), 552–566.

Castel, R. (1996). Work and Usefulness to the World. *International Labour Review, 135*(6), 615–622.

Castel, R. (1999). *Les métamorphoses de la question sociale. Une chronique du salariat* [The Metamorphosis of the Social Question: A Chronicle of Wage]. Paris: Gallimard.

Castel, R. (2002). *From Manual Workers to Wage Laborers: Transformation of the Social Question*. New Brunswick: Transaction.

Celikates, R. (2017). Epistemische Ungerechtigkeit, Loopingeffekte und Ideologiekritik. Eine sozialphilosophische Perspektive [Epistemic Injustice, Looping Effects and Ideological Criticism. A Socio-Philosophical Perspective]. *WestEnd - Neue Zeitschrift für Sozialforschung* (2), 53–72.

Chang, L. (2003). Variable Effects of Children's Aggression, Social Withdrawal, and Prosocial Leadership as Functions of Teacher Beliefs and Behaviors. *Child Development, 74*(2), 535–548.

Chang, L. (2004). The Role of Classroom Norms in Contextualizing the Relations of Children's Social Behaviors to Peer Acceptance. *Developmental Psychology, 40*(5), 691–702.

Cohen, G. A. (1989). On the Currency of Egalitarian Justice. *Ethics, 99*(4), 906–944.

Crockett, J. B. (2001). Epilogue: The Contemporary Crucible: Putting Scientific Evidence to the Test in the Context of Schools. *Behavioral Disorders, 27*(1), 69–73.

Crowson, R. L., & Boyd, W. L. (1996). The Politics of Education, the New Institutionalism, and Reinvented Schooling: Some Concluding Observations. In R. L. Crowson, W. L. Boyd & H. B. Mawhinney (Eds.), *The Politics of Education and the New Institutionalism: Reinventing the American School* (pp. 203–214). Washington, DC: Falmer.

Cummings, C., Dyson, A., & Millward, A. (2003). Participation and Democracy: What's Inclusion Got to Do With It? In J. Allan (Ed.), *Inclusion, Participation and Democracy: What Is the Purpose?* (pp. 49–65). Dordrecht: Kluwer.

Dahrendorf, R. (1965). *Bildung ist Bürgerrecht: Plädoyer für eine aktive Bildungspolitik* [Education Is Civil Right. Pleading for an Active Edcuation Policy]. Hamburg: Nannen.

Dahrendorf, R. (1986). *Lebenschancen. Anläufe zur sozialen und politischen Theorie* [Opportunities in Life. Approaches to Social and Political Theory]. Frankfurt a. M.: Suhrkamp.

Dalin, P. (1998). *School Development: Theories and Strategies*. London: Continuum.

Danforth, S. (2006). From Epistemology to Democracy. *Remedial and Special Education, 27*(6), 337–345.

Danforth, S. (2015). Under the Mentorship of John Dewey. Democratic Lessons for Inclusive Education. *Foundations of Inclusive Education Research (International Perspectives on Inclusive Education), 6*, 133–148.

Danforth, S., & Jones, P. (2015). From Special Education to Integration to Genuine Inclusion. *Foundations of Inclusive Education, 6*, 1–21.

Davis, L. J. (1997). Universalizing Marginality: How Europe Became Deaf in the Eighteenth Century. In L. J. Davis (Ed.), *The Disability Studies Reader* (pp. 110–127). New York: Routledge.

De Beco, G. (2014). The Right to Inclusive Education According to Article 24 of the UN Convention on the Rights of Persons with Disabilities: Background, Requirements and (Remaining) Questions. *Netherlands Quarterly of Human Rights, 32*(3), 263–287.

De Waal, F. (2009). *The Age of Empathy: Nature's Lessons for a Kinder Society.* New York: Harmony Books.

Dewey, J. (1927). The Public and Its Problems. In J. A. Boydston (Ed.), *Later Works, Vol. 2.* Carbondale: Southern Illinois University Press.

Dewey, J. (1937). Democracy Is Radical. In J. A. Boydston (Ed.), *John Dewey: The Later Works 11.* Carbondale: Southern Illinois University Press.

Dewey, J. (1966): *The Child and the Curriculum and The School and Society* (8th ed.). Chicago, IL: The University of Chicago Press.

Dewey, J. (2004 [1916]). *Democracy and Education: An Introduction to the Philosophy of Education.* Dehli: Aakar Books.

Dewey, J. (2008a). Art as Experience. In J. A. Boydston (Ed.), *The Later Works of John Dewey, 1925–1953, Vol. 10.* Carbondale: Southern Illinois University Press.

Dewey, J. (2008b). Construction and Critisism. In J. A. Boydston (Ed.), *The Later Works of John Dewey, 1925–1953, Vol. 5.* Carbondale: Southern Illinois University Press.

Dijkers, M. (2006). It Takes Two to Do the Twist, Two to Tango, But the Tango Requires Interaction Between Partners: Comment on Van de Ven et al. *Disability and Society, 21*(1), 93–96.

Donati, P., & Archer, M. S. (2015). *The Relational Subject.* Cambridge: Cambridge University Press.

Down, J. L. (1995 (1866)). Observations on an Ethnic Classification of Idiots. *Mental Retardation, 33*(1), 54–56.

Doyle, W. (1986). Classroom Organization and Management. In M. C. Wittrock (Ed.), *Handbook of Research on Teaching* (pp. 392–431). New York: Macmillan.

Dreeben, R. (2002 (1968)). *On What Is Learned in School.* New York: Percheron Press.

Duhaney, L. G., & Salend, S. (2000). Parental Perceptions of Inclusive Educational Placements. *Remedial and Special Education, 21*, 124–126.

Dunn, L. M. (1968). Special Education for the Mildly Retarded: Is Much of It Justifiable? *Exceptional Children, 35*(1), 5–22.

Durkheim, E. (1984). *The Division of Labor in Society* (G. Simpson, Trans.). London: Macmillan.

Dworkin, R. (1981a). What Is Equality? Part 1: Equality of Welfare. *Philosophy and Public Affairs, 10*(3), 85–246.

Dworkin, R. (1981b). What Is Equality? Part 2: Equality of Resources. *Philosophy and Public Affairs, 10*(4), 283–345.

Dworkin, R. (2000). *Sovereign Virtue - The Theory and Practice of Equality.* Cambridge, MA: Harvard University Press.

Dyson, A. (1999). Inclusion and Inclusions: Theories and Discourses in Inclusive Education. In H. Daniels & P. Garner (Eds.), *World Yearbook of Education 1999: Inclusive Education* (pp. 36–53). London: Kogan.

Earl, D. (2011). 'A Group of Parents Came Together': Parent Advocacy Groups for Children with Intellectual Disabilities in Post-World War II Australia. *Health and History, 13*(2), 84–103.

Enzensberger, H. M. (1988). *Mittelmass und Wahn. Gesammelte Zerstreuungen* [Mediocrity and Delusion. Collected Diversions]. Frankfurt a. M.: Suhrkamp.

European Agency for Special Needs and Inclusive Education (2014). *Five Key Messages for Inclusive Education. Putting Theory into Practice.* Odense: European Agency for Special Needs and Inclusive Education.

Feinberg, J. (1970). The Nature and Value of Rights. *Journal of Value Inquiry, 4,* 243–257.
Feinberg, J. (1973). *Social Philosophy, Foundations of Philosophy Series.* Upper Saddle River, NJ: Prentice Hall.
Fend, H. (1980). *Theorie der Schule* [Theory of School]. München: Urban & Schwarzenberg.
Fend, H. (2006). *Neue Theorie der Schule. Einführung in das Verstehen von Bildungssystemen* [New Theory of School. Introduction to Understanding Educational Systems]. Wiesbaden: VS Verlag für Sozialwissenschaften.
Feuser, G. (2002). *Von der Integration zur Inclusion – 'Allgemeine (integrative) Pädagogik' und Fragen der Lehrerbildung* [From Integration to Inclusion – 'General (Integrative) Pedagogy' and Teacher Education Issues]. Baden: Vortrag an der pädagogischen Akademie des Bundes, Niederösterreich anlässlich der 6. allgemeinpädagogischen Tagung [Lecture at the Federal Pedagogical Academy, Lower Austria, on the occasion of the 6th General Pedagogical Conference].
Fitch, E. F. (2002). Disablity and Inclusion: Form Labeling Deviance to Social Valuing. *Educational Theory, 52*(4), 463–477.
Florian, L. (1998). An Examination of the Practical Problems Associated with the Implementation of Inclusive Education Policies. *Support for Learning, 13*(3), 105–108.
Florian, L. (2007). Reimagining Special Education. In L. Florian (Ed.), *The SAGE Handbook of Special Education* (pp. 8–21). London: SAGE Publications Ltd.
Florian, L. (2014). What Counts as Evidence of Inclusive Education? *European Journal of Special Needs Education, 29*(3), 286–294.
Florian, L. (2019). On the Necessary Co-Existence of Special and Inclusive Education. *International Journal of Inclusive Education, 23*(7–8), 691–704.
Foot, P. (1958). Moral Arguments. *Mind, 67*(268), 502–513.
Foucault, M. (1972). *Madness and Civilization: A History of Insanity in the Age of Reason.* New York: Pantheon Books.
Frankfurt, H. (1971). Freedom of the Will and the Concept of a Person. *Journal of Philosophy, 68*(1), 5–20.
Fraser, N. (2000). Rethinking Recognition. *New Left Review, 3,* 107–120.
Frederickson, N. (2010a). Bullying or Befriending? Children's Responses to Classmates with Special Needs. *British Journal of Inclusive Education, 37*(1), 4–12.
Frederickson, N., Simmonds, E., Evans, L., & Soulsby, S. (2007). Assessing the Social and Affective Outcomes of Inclusion. *British Journal of Special Education, 34*(2), 105–115.
Freire, P. (1993). *Pedagogy of the Oppressed.* Translated by M. B. Ramos. London: Penguin Books.
French, S. (1993). Disability, Impairment or Something in Between. In S. Swain, V. Finkelstein, S. French & M. Oliver (Eds.), *Disabling Barriers, Enabling Environments* (pp. 17–25). London: Sage.
Fricker, M. (2007). *Epistemic Justice: Power and the Ethics of Knowing.* Oxford: Oxford University Press.
Fumet, Y. (2000). Can Civility Be Taught? *Revue française de pédagogie, 132* (juillet-août-septembre), 101–113.
Gajewski, A. (2017). Conceptualizing Professional Ethics in Inclusive Education. In A. Gajewski (Ed.), *Ethics, Equity, and Inclusive Education* (pp. 1–21). Bingley: Emerald Publishing.
Garrau, M., & Laborde, C. (2015). Relational Equality, Non-Domination, and Vulnerability. In C. Fourie, F. Schuppert & I. Wallimann-Helmer (Eds.), *Social Equality: On What It Means to Be Equal* (pp. 45–64). Oxford: Oxford University Press.
Gartner, A., & Lipsky, D. (1987). Beyond Special Education: Toward a Quality System for All Students. *Harvard Educational Review, 57*(4), 367–369.

References

Giddens, A. (2000). *The Third Way and its Critics.* Cambridge Cambridge University Press.

Gilbert, M. (2014). *Joint Commitment: How we Make the Social World.* New York: Oxford University Press.

Goffman, E. (1968). *Asylums: Essays on the Social Situation of Mental Patients and Other Inmates.* Chicago, IL: Aldine.

Goffman, E. (1983). The Interaction Order. *American Sociological Review, 48*(1), 1–17.

Goodin, R. E. (1996). Inclusion and Exclusion. *European Journal of Sociology, 37*(2), 343–371.

Goodlad, J. I. (1984). *A Place Called School. Prospects for the Future.* New York: McGraw-Hill.

Göransson, K., & Nilholm, C. (2014). Conceptual Diversities and Empirical Shortcomings – A Critical Analysis of Research on Inclusive Education. *European Journal of Special Needs Education, 29*(3), 265–280.

Gosepath, S. (2004). *Gleiche Gerechtigkeit. Grundlagen eines liberalen Egalitarismus* [Equal Justice. Foundations of a Liberal Egalitarianism]. Frankfurt a. M.: Suhrkamp.

Groce, N. E. (1985). *Everybody Here Spoke Sign Language: Hereditary Deafness on Martha's Vineyard.* Cambridge, MA: Cambridge University Press.

Guralnick, M. J., Connor, R. T., Hammond, M., Gottmann, J. M., & Kinnish, K. (1995). Immediate Effects of Mainstreamed Settings on the Social Interactions and Social Integration of Preschool Children. *American Journal on Mental Retardation, 100*(4), 359–377.

Hare, R. M. (1952). *The Language of Morals.* Oxford: Oxford University Press.

Haslanger, S. (2012). *Resisting Reality: Social Construction and Social Critique.* Oxford Oxford University Press.

Haslanger, S. (2014a). The Normal, the Natural and the Good: Generics and Ideology. *Politica & Società, 3*(3), 365–392.

Haslanger, S. (2014b). Studying While Black: Trust, Disrespect and Opportunity. *Du Bois Review, 11*(1), 109–136.

Hegarty, S. (2001). Inclusive Education. A Case to Answer. *Journal of Moral Education, 30*(3), 243–249.

Hegel, G. W. (2004 [1820]). *Die Philosophie des Rechts. Vorlesung von 1821/22* [The Philosophy of Right. Lecture from 1821/1822]. Frankfurt a. M.: Suhrkamp.

Hegel, G. W. (2007 [1821]). *Philosophy of Mind (translated by M. Inwood).* Oxford Oxford University Press.

Hehir, Th. (2002). Eliminating Ableism in Education. *Harvard Educational Review, 72*(1), 1–32.

Hendrickx, M. M. H. G., Mainhard, T., Oudman, S., Boor-Klip, H. J., & Brekelmans, M. (2017). Teacher Behavior and Peer Liking and Disliking. The Teacher as a Social Referent for Peer Status. *Journal of Educational Psychology, 109*(4), 546–558.

Herzog, W. (2009). Schule und Schulklasse als soziale Systeme [School and School Class as Social Systems]. In W. Herzog (Ed.), *Schule und Schulklasse als soziale Systeme* [School and School Class as Social Systems] (pp. 155–194). Wiesbaden: VS Verlag für Sozialwissenschaften.

Hinz, A. (2002). Von der Integration zur Inklusion – terminologisches Spiel oder konzeptuelle Weiterentwicklung? [From Integration to Inclusion – Terminology Game or Conceptual Evolution?]. *Zeitschrift für Heilpädagogik, 53*(9), 354–361.

Hinz, A. (2006). Inklusion [Inclusion]. In G. Antor & U. Bleidick (Eds.), *Heil- und Sonderpädagogik. Handlexikon der Behindertenpädagogik. Schlüsselbegriffe aus Theorie und Praxis* [Therapeutic and Special Education. Special Education Reference Guide. Key Terms in Theory and Practice] (pp. 97–99). Stuttgart: Kohlhammer.

Honneth, A. (1995). *The Struggle for Recognition: Moral Grammar of Social Conflicts*. Cambridge: Polity Press.

Honneth, A. (1998). Democracy as Reflexive Cooperation. John Dewey and the Theory of Democracy Today. *Political Theory, 26*(6), 763–783.

Honneth, A. (2000). Liebe und Moral. Zum moralischen Gehalt affektiver Bindungen [Love and Morality. On the Moral Content of Emotional Ties]. In A. Honneth (Ed.), *Das Andere der Gerechtigkeit* [Disrespect. The Normative Foundations of Critical Theory] (pp. 216–236). Frankfurt a. M.: Suhrkamp.

Honneth, A. (2014). *Freedom's Right: The Social Foundations of Democratic Life*. Cambridge: Polity Press.

Honneth, A. (2016). Education and the Democratic Public Sphere. A Neglected Chapter of Political Philosophy. In O. Lysaker & J. Jakobsen (Eds.), *Recognition and Freedom: Axel Honneth's Political Thought* (pp. 17–32). Leiden: Brill.

Horkheimer, M., & Adorno, T. (1973). *Aspects of Sociology*. Boston, MA: Beacon.

Hughes, B., & Paterson, K. (1997). The Social Model of Disability and the Disappearing Body: Towards a Sociology of Impairment. *Disability and Society, 12*(3), 324–340.

Hughes, J. N., Cavell, T. A., & Wilson, V. (2001). Further Support for the Developmental Significance of the Quality of the Teacher-Student Relationship. *Journal of School Psychology, 39*(4), 289–301.

Ikäheimo, H. (2014). *Anerkennung* [Recognition]. Berlin: De Gruyter.

Itard, J. M. G. (1994). *Victor de l'Aveyron* [Victor of Aveyron]. Paris: Editions Alla.

Jackson, P. W. (1986). *The Practice of Teaching*. New York: Teachers College Press.

Jackson, P. W. (1990). *Life in Classrooms*. New York: Holt, Rinehart and Winston.

Jaeggi, R. (2005). *Entfremdung: Zur Aktualität eines sozialphilosophischen Problems* [Alienation]. Frankfurt a. M.: Campus.

Jaggar, A. (2015). Ideal and Nonideal Reasoning in Educational Theory. *Educational Theory, 65*(2), 111–126.

Jaggar, A., & Tobin, T. W. (2013). Situating Moral Justification: Rethinking the Mission of Moral Epistemology. *Metaphilosophy, 44*(4), 383–408.

Jordan, A., Kircaali-Iftar, G & Diamond, C. T. (1993). Who has a Problem, the Student or the Teacher? Differences in Teachers' Beliefs About Their Work with At-Risk and Integrated Exceptional Students. *International Journal of Disability, Development and Education, 40*(1), 45–62.

Jordan, A., Lindsay, L., & Stanovich, P. J. (1997). Classroom Teachers' Instructioanl Interactions with Students Who Are Exceptional, At-risk and Typically Achieving. *Remedial and Special Education, 18*(2), 82–93.

Jordan, A., Schwartz, E., & McGhie-Richmond, D. (2009). Preparing Teachers for Inclusive Classrooms. *Teaching and Teacher Education, 25*, 535–542.

Jordan, A., & Stanovich, P. J. (2001). Patterns of Teacher-Student Interaction in Inclusive Elementary Classrooms and Correlates with Student Self-Concept. *International Journal of Disability, Development and Education, 48*(1), 33–52.

Jörke, D. (2003). *Demokratie als Erfahrung. John Dewey und die politische Philosophie der Gegenwart*. [Democracy as Experience. John Dewey and Contemporary Political Philosophy] Wiesbaden: Westdeutscher Verlag.

Jurt, J. (2012). Bourdieus Kapital-Theorie [Bourdieu's Theory of Capital]. In M. Bergmann, S. Hupka-Brunner, T. Meyer & R. Samuel (Eds.), *Bildung – Arbeit – Erwachsenwerden* [Education – Work – Maturing] (pp. 21–41). Springer: Wiesbaden.

Kant, I. (1900 (1803)). *Kant on Education* [Über Pädagogik]. Translated by Annette Churton. Boston, MA: D. C. Heath & Co., Publishers.

Kastl, J. M. (2010). *Einführung in die Soziologie der Behinderung* [Introduction to the Sociology of Disability]. Wiesbaden: VS Verlag für Sozialwissenschaften.

Kastl, J. M. (2014). *Fünf Thesen zum Inklusionsdiskurs* [Five Theses on the Inclusion Discourse]. Stuttgart: Diakonisches Wert Württemberg.

Kastl, J. M. (2016). Inklusion und Demokratie. Beeinträchtigung, Behinderung, Benachteiligung im sozialen Rechtsstaat [Inclusion and Democracy. Impairment, Disability, Disadvantage in the Social Constitutional State]. In: Tübingen: Vortrag bei der Tagung 'Integration – Inklusion. Querschnittaufgaben im Widerstreit?' 40. Tübinger Sozialpädagogiktag, 25.11.2016 [Tübingen: Lecture at the Conference 'Integration – Inclusion. Cross-sectional Functions in Conflict?' 40th Tübingen Social Pedagogy Day, 25.11.2016], Neue Aula, University of Tübingen.

Kastl, J. M. (2017). *Einführung in die Soziologie der Behinderung* (2., völlig überabeitete und erweiterte Auflage ed.) [Introduction to the Sociology of Disability (2nd, completely revised and expanded ed.)]. Wiesbaden: Springer.

Kastl, J. M. (2018). Inklusion. In H.-U. Otto, H. Ziegler, H. Thiersch & R. Treptow (Eds.), *Handbuch Soziale Arbeit* (6., überarbeitete Auflage ed.) [Handbook of Social Work (6th, revised ed.)]. München: Reinhardt.

Kauffman, J. M. (1976). Nineteenth Century Views of Children's Behavior Disorders: Historical Contributions and Continuing Issues. *The Journal of Special Education, 10*(4), 335–349.

Kauffman, J. M., & Badar, J. (2014). Instruction, Not Inclusion, Should Be the Central Issue in Special Education: An Alternative View from the USA. *Journal of International Special Needs Education, 17*(1), 13–20.

Kavale, K. A., & Mostert, M. P. (2003). River of Ideology, Islands of Evidence. *Expetionality, 11*(4), 191–208.

Kegan, R. (2009). What ‚Form' Transforms? A Constructive-Developmental Approach to Transformative Learning. In K. Illeris (Ed.), *Contemporary Theories of Learning* (pp. 35–52). London: Routledge.

Kerzner Lipsky, D., & Gartner, A. (1996). Equity Requires Inclusion: The Future for All Students with Disabilities. In C. Christensen & F. Rizvi (Eds.), *Disability and the Dilemmas of Education and Justice* (pp. 145–155). Buckingham: Open University Press.

Kirchin, S. (2013a). Introduction: Thick and Thin Concepts. In S. Kirchin (Ed.), *Thick Concepts* (pp. 1–19). Oxford: Oxford University Press.

Kirchin, S. (Ed.) (2013b). *Thick Concepts*. Oxford: Oxford University Press.

Kittay, E. F. (1999). *Love's Labor: Essays in Women, Equality and Dependency*. New York: Routledge.

Koster, M., Pijl, S. J., Nakken, H., & Van Houten, E. (2010). Social Participation of Students with Special Needs in Regular Primary Education in the Netherlands. *International Journal of Disability, Development and Education, 57*(1), 59–75.

Kronauer, M. (2010). *Exklusion - Die Gefährdung des Sozialen im hoch entwickelten Kapitalismus* (2., aktualisierte und erweiterte Auflage ed.) [Exclusion – The Endangerment of the Social Sphere in Highly Developed Capitalism (2nd, updated and expanded ed.)]. Frankfurt a. M.: Campus.

Kronauer, M. (2015). Wer Inklusion möchte, darf über Exklusion nicht schweigen. Plädoyer für eine Erweiterung der Debatte [Those Who Want Inclusion Cannot Remain Silent About Exclusion. Plea for a Broadening of the Debate]. *Jahrbuch für Pädadgogik, 2015*(1), 147–158.

Kuklys, W. (2005). *Amartya Sen's Capability Approach: Theoretical Insights and Empirical Application*. Berlin: Springer.

232 References

Langer, A. (2019). Keiner hat sich getraut, das zu hinterfragen [No One Dared to Question It]. *Der Spiegel*, https://www.spiegel.de/panorama/justiz/luebeck-urteil-gegen-maike-b-keiner-hat-sich-getraut-das-zu-hinterfragen-a-1296158.html.

Lazerson, M. (1983). The Origins of Special Education. In J. G. Chambers & W. T. Hartman (Eds.), *Special Education Policies: Their History, Implementation and Finance* (pp. 3–47). Philadelphia, PA: Temple University Press.

Levinson, M. (2012). *No Citizen Left Behind*. Cambridge, MA: Harvard University Press.

Liao, M. S. (2015). *The Right To Be Loved*. Oxford: Oxford University Press.

Liesen, C. (2006). *Gleichheit als ethisch-normatives Problem der Sonderpädagogik – dargestellt am Beispiel "Integration"*. [Equality as an Ethical-Normative Problem in Special Education – Illustrated through the Example of "Integration"] Bad Heilbrunn: Klinkhardt.

Lindemann Nelson, H. (2001). Knowledge, Authority and Identity: A Prolegomenon to an Epistemology of the Clinic. *Theoretical Medicine, 22*, 107–122.

Lockwood, D. (1964). Social integration and System Integration. In G. K. Zollschan & W. Hirsch (Eds.), *Social Change. Explorations, Diagnoses and Conjectures* (pp. 370–383). New York: Wiley.

Lortie, D. C. (1975). *The Schoolteacher*. Chicago, IL: University of Chicago Press.

Luhmann, N. (1977a). Arbeitsteilung und Moral: Durkheims Theorie [Division of Labour and Morality: Durkheim's Theory]. In E. Durkheim (Ed.), *Über die Teilung der sozialen Arbeit* [On the Division of Social Work] (pp. 17–35). Frankfurt a. M.: Suhrkamp.

Luhmann, N. (1977b). Differentiation of Society. *The Canadian Journal of Sociology / Cahiers canadiens de sociologie, 2*(1), 29–53.

Luhmann, N. (1980). *Gesellschaftsstruktur und Semantik. Studien zur Wissenssoziologie der modernen Gesellschaft* [Social Structure and Semantics. Studies in the Sociology of Knowledge in Modern Society]. Frankfurt a. M.: Suhrkamp.

Luhmann, N. (1995). *Gesellschaftssturktur und Semantik. Studien zur Wissenssoziologie der modernen Gesellschaft. Band 4* [Social Structure and Semantics. Studies in the Sociology of Knowledge in Modern Society. Volume 4]. Frankfurt a. M.: Suhrkamp.

Luhmann, N. (1997). *Die Gesellschaft der Gesellschaft* [Theory of Society]. Frankfurt a. M.: Suhrkamp.

Luhmann, N. (2002). *Das Erziehungssystem der Gesellschaft* [Society's Education System]. Frankfurt a. M.: Suhrkamp.

Luhmann, N. (2013). *Theory of Society (Volume 2)* (R. Barrett, Trans.). Stanford, CA: Stanford University Press.

Luhmann, N., & Schorr, K. E. (1982). *Zwischen Technologie und Selbstreferenz. Fragen an die Pädagogik* [Between Technology and Self-Reference. Questions Adressing Pedagogy]. Frankfurt a. M.: Suhrkamp.

Luhmann, N., & Schorr, K. E. (1988). *Reflexionsprobleme im Erziehungssystem* [Problems in Reflecting Educational Systems]. Frankfurt a. M.: Suhrkamp.

Mackert, J. (2004). Die Theorie sozialer Schließung [The Theory of Social Closure]. In J. Mackert (Ed.), *Die Theorie sozialer Schließung : Tradition, Analysen, Perspektiven* [The Theory of Social Closure: Tradition, Analyses, Perspectives] (pp. 9–24). Wiesbaden: Springer.

Margalit, A. (1996). *The Decent Society*. Cambridge, MA: Harvard University Press.

Margalit, A. (2001). Recognition: Recognizing the Brother and the Other. *Aristotelian Society Supplementary Volume, 75*(1), 127–139.

Markman, A. B., & Stilwell, C. H. (2001). Role-Governed Categories. *Journal of Experimental and Theoretical Artificial Intelligence, 13*(4), 329–358.

Marshall, T. H. (1950). *Citizenship and Social Class and Other Essays.* Cambridge: Cambridge University Press.
McAuliffe, M. D., Hubbard, J. A., & Romano, L. J. (2009). The Role of Teacher Cognition and Behavior in Children's Peer Relations. *Journal of Abnormal Child Psychology, 37*(5), 665–677.
Mead, G. H. (1934). *Mind, Self, and Society.* Chicago, IL: University of Chicago Press.
Mikami, A. Y., Swaim Griggs, M., Reuland, M. M., & Gregory, A. (2012). Teacher Practices as Predictors of Children's Classroom Social Preference. *Journal of School Psychology, 50*(1), 95–111.
Miles, S., & Singal, N. (2010). The Education for All and Inclusive Education Debate: Conflict, Contradiction or Opportunity? *International Journal of Inclusive Education, 14*(1), 1–15.
Miller, D. (1999). *Principles of Social Justice.* Cambridge, MA: Harvard University Press.
Mills, C. W. (2005). "Ideal Theory" as Ideology. *Sociology, 20*(3), 165–184.
Minow, M. (1990). *Making All the Difference – Inclusion, Exclusion, and American Law.* Ithaca, NY: Cornell University Press.
Mitchell, D., & Snyder, S. (2003). The Eugenic Atlantic: Race, Disability, and the Making of an International Eugenic Science, 1800–1945. *Disability & Society, 18*(7), 843–864.
Mitchell, D. E. (1995). Institutional Theory and the Social Structure of Education. *Journal of Education Policy, 10*(5), 167–188.
Münkler, H., & Fischer, K. (2002). Einleitung. Rhetoriken des Gemeinwohls und Probleme des Gemeinsinns [Introduction. Rhetorics of Common Good and Problems of Community Spirit]. In H. Münkler & K. Fischer (Eds.), *Gemeinwohl und Gemeinsinn: Rhetoriken und Perspektiven sozial-moralischer Orientierung* [Common Good and Community Spirit: Rhetorics and Perspectives of Socio-Moral Orientation] (pp. 9–17). Berlin: Akademie Verlag.
Nagel, Th. (1986). *The View from Nowhere.* Oxford: Oxford University Press.
Nakken, H., & Pijl, S. J. (2002). Getting Along with Classmates in Regular Schools. A Review of the Effects of Integration on the Development of Social Relationships. *International Journal of Inclusive Education, 6*(1), 47–61.
National Center for Education Statistics. (2020). *Students with Disabilities.* Washington, DC: National Center for Education Statistics.
Niemi, I. P. (2015). The Professional Form of Recognition in Social Work. *Studies in Social and Political Thought, 25,* 174–190.
Nilholm, C. (2006). Special Education, Inclusion and Democracy. *European Journal of Special Needs Education, 21*(4), 431–445.
Nilholm, C., & Göransson, K. (2017). What Is Meant by Inclusion? An Analysis of European and North American Journal Articles with High Impact. *European Journal of Special Needs Education, 32*(3), 437–451.
Norwich, B. (2008). *Dilemmas of Difference, Inclusion and Disability.* London: Routledge.
Norwich, B. (2013). *Addressing Tensions and Dilemmas in Inclusive Education: Working with Uncertainty.* London: Routledge.
Norwich, B. (2014a). Recognising Value Tensions that Underlie Problems in Inclusive Education. *Cambridge Journal of Education, 44*(4), 495–510.
Norwich, B. (2014b). How Does the Capability Approach Address Current Issues in Special Educational Needs, Disability and Inclusive Education Field? *Journal of Research in Special Educational Needs, 14*(1), 16–21.
Norwich, B. (2014c). Recognising Value Tensions that Underlie Problems in Inclusive Education. *Cambridge Journal of Education, 44*(4), 495–510.

Nowicki, E. A. (2003). A Meta-Analysis of the Social Competence of Children with Learning Disabilities Compared to Classmates of Low and Average to High Achievement. *Learning Disability Quarterly, 26*(3), 171–188.

Nowicki, E. A., & Sandieson, R. (2002). A Meta-Analysis of School-Age Children's Attitudes Towards Persons with Physical or Intellectual Disabilities. *International Journal of Disability, Development and Education, 49*(3), 243–265.

Nozick, R. (1974). *Anarchy, State and Utopia*. Oxford: Blackwell.

Nussbaum, M. C. (2000). *Women and Human Development: The Capabilities Approach*. Cambridge, MA: Cambridge University Press.

Nussbaum, M. C. (2001). Disabled Lives: Who Cares? *New York Review of Books, 48*(1), 34

Nussbaum, M. C. (2006). *Frontiers of Justice: Disability, Nationality, Species Membership*. Cambridge, MA: Harvard University Press.

Nussbaum, M. C. (2011). *Creating Capabilities: The Human Development Approach*. Cambridge, MA: Belknap Press.

Nussbaum, M. C. (2013). *Political Emotions: Why Love Matters for Justice*. Cambridge, MA: The Belknap Press of Harvard University Press.

O'Neill, O. (1996). *Towards Justice and Virtue: A Constructive Account of Practical Reasoning*. Cambridge: Cambridge University Press.

O'Neill, O. (2009). Applied Ethics: Naturalism, Normativity and Public Policy. *Journal of Applied Philosophy, 26*(3), 219–230.

O'Neill, O. (2018). *From Principles to Practice: Normativity and Judgment in Ethics and Politics*. Cambridge: Cambridge University Press.

Ochs, E., Kremer-Sadlik, T., Solomon, O., & Sirota, K. G. (2001). Inclusion as Social Practice: Views of Children with Autism. *Social Development, 10*, 399–419.

Osgood, R. L. (2005). *History of Inclusion in the United States*. Washington, DC: Gallaudet University Press.

Parker, W. C. (2005). Teaching Against Idiocy. *Phi Delta Kappa, 86*(5), 344–351.

Parsons, T. (1959). The School Class as a Social System. Some of Its Functions in the American Society. *Harvard Educational Review, 29*(4), 297–318.

Parsons, T. (1960). Pattern Variables Revisited: A Response to Robert Dubin. *American Sociological Review, 25*(4), 467–483.

Parsons, T. (1967). *Sociological Theory and Modern Society*. New York: The Free Press.

Parsons, T. (1968). Durkheim, Emile. In D. L. Sills (Ed.), *International Encyclopedia of the Social Sciences, Vol. 4* (pp. 311–320). New York: Macmillan.

Parsons, T. (1969). Full Citizenship for the Negro American? In T. Parsons (Ed.), *Politics and Social Structure* (pp. 252–291). New York: The Free Press.

Parsons, T. (1970). Equality and Inequality in Modern Society, or Social Stratification Revisited. *Sociological Inquiry, 40*(2), 13–72.

Parsons, T. (1971). *The System of Modern Societies*. Englewood Cliffs, NJ: Prentice-Hall.

Parsons, T. (2007). *American Society: A Theory of the Societal Community*. Boulder, CO: Paradigm.

Peetsma, T., Vergeer, M., Roeleveld, J., & Karsten, S. (2001). Inclusion in Education: Comparing Pupils' Development in Special and Regular Education. *Educational Review, 53*(2), 125–135.

Pettit, P. (1997). *Republicanism: A Theory of Freedom and Government*. Oxford: Claredon Press.

Pettit, P. (2001). *A Theory of Freedom: From the Psychology to the Politics of Agency*. Oxford: Oxford University Press.

Pfahl, L. (2011). *Techniken der Behinderung. Der deutsche Lernbehinderungsdiskurs, die Sonderschule und ihre Auswirkungen auf Bildungsbiografien* [Techniques of Disability. The

German Discourse on Learning Disabilities, Special Needs Schools and Their Impacts on Educational Biographies]. Bielefeld: transcript.
Pijl, S. J., Frostad, P., & Flem, A. (2008). The Social Position of Pupils with Special Needs in Regular Schools. *Scandinavian Journal of Disability Research, 52*(4), 387–405.
Plato. (2000). *The Republic*. Cambridge: Cambridge University Press.
Powell, J. (2009). To Segregate or to Separate? Special Education Expansion and Divergence in the United States and Germany. *Comparative Education Review, 53*(2), 161–187.
Powell, J., & Pfahl, L. (2019). Disability and Inequality in Educational Opportunities from a Life Course Perspective. In R. Becker (Ed.), *Research Handbook on the Sociology of Education*, (pp. 383–406). Cheltenham: Edward Elgar Publishing Limited.
Powell, J. J. W., Edelstein, B., & Blanck, J. M. (2016). Awareness-raising, Legitimation or Backlash? Effects of the UN Convention on the Rights of Persons with Disabilities on Education Systems in Germany. *Globalisation, Societies and Education, 14*(2), 227–250. doi:10.1080/14767724.2014.982076
Prager, J. (1981). Moral Integration and Political Inclusion: A Comparison of Durkheim's and Weber's Theories of Democracy. *Social Forces, 59*(4), 918–950.
Prengel, A. (2001). Egalitäre Differenz in der Bildung [Egalitarian Difference in Education]. In H. Lutz & N. Wenning (Eds.), *Unterschiedlich verschieden. Differenz in der Erziehungswissenschaft* [Differently Diverse. Difference in Educational Science] (pp. 93–107). Opladen: Leske + Budrich.
Pring, R. (2007). Reclaiming Philosophy for Educational Research. *Educational Review, 59*(3), 315–330.
Pring, R. (2007a). *John Dewey: A Philosopher of Education for Our Time?* London: Continuum.
Pring, R. (2007b). Reclaiming Philosophy for Educational Research. *Educational Review, 59*(3), 315–330.
Proctor, R. N. (1988). *Racial Hygiene: Medicine Under the Nazis*. Cambridge, MA: Harvard University Press.
Putnam, H. (1992). *Realism with a Human Face*. Cambridge, MA: Harvard University Press.
Putnam, H. (2002). *The Collapse of the Fact-Value Dichotomy*. Cambridge, MA: Harvard University Press.
Qvortrup, A., & Qvortrup, L. (2018). Inclusion: Dimensions of Inclusion in Education. *International Journal of Inclusive Education, 22*(7), 803–817.
Rawls, J. (1971). *A Theory of Justice*. Oxford: Oxford University Press.
Rawls, J. (1996). *Political Liberalism*. New York: Columbia University Press.
Raz, J. (1986). *The Morality of Freedom*. Oxford: Claredon Press.
Reichenbach, H. (1968). *The Rise of Scientific Philosophy*. Berkeley and Los Angeles: University of California Press.
Reichenbach, R. (2010). *In Commercio of Thoughts… "Civility, Common Sense and Moral Development and Education*. Basel, January 15th, 2010.
Reindal, S. M. (2008). A Social Relational Model of Disability: A Theoretical Framework for Special Needs Edcuation. *European Journal of Special Needs Education, 23*(2), 135–146.
Reindal, S. M. (2016). Discussing Inclusive Education: An Inquiry Into Different Interpretations and a Search for Ethical Aspects of Inclusion Using the Capabilities Approach. *European Journal of Special Needs Education, 31*(1), 1–12.
Reynolds, M. C., Wang, M. C., & Walberg, H. J. (1987). The Necessary Restructuring of Special and Regular Education. *Exceptional Children, 53*(5), 391–398.
Richardson, J. G. (1999). *Common, Delinquent, and Special: The Institutional Shape of Special Education*. New York: Falmer.

Richardson, J. G., & Powell, J. J. W. (2011). *Comparing Special Education: Origins to Contemporary Paradoxes*. Stanford, CA: Stanford University Press.

Ricken, N. (2006). Education and Recognition. Notes on the Constitution of the Educational Problem. *Vierteljahresschrift für wissenschaftliche Pädagogik, 82*(2), 215–230.

Ricoeur, P. (2005). *The Course of Recognition*. Cambridge, MA: Harvard University Press.

Rizvi, F., & Lingard, B. (1996). Disability, Education and the Discourses of Justice. In C. Christensen & F. Rizvi (Eds.), *Disability and the Dilemmas of Education and Justice* (pp. 9–26). Buckingham: Open University Press.

Roberts, D. (2013). Thick Concepts. *Philosophy Compass, 8*(8), 677–688.

Robertson, E. (2013). The Epistemic Value of Diversity. *Journal of Philosophy of Education, 47*(2), 299–310.

Robeyns, I. (2005). The Capability Approach: A Theoretical Survey. *Journal of Human Development, 6*(1), 93–114.

Robeyns, I. (2008). Ideal Theory in Theory and Practice. *Social Theory and Practice, 34*(3), 341–362.

Rödder, A. (2017). *21.0: Eine Kurze Geschichte der Gegenwart* [A Brief History of the Present Age]. München: C.H. Beck.

Rotzoll, M., Fuch, P., Richter, P., & Hohendorf, G. (2010). Die nationalsozialistische 'Euthanasieaktion T4' [The National Socialist 'T4 Euthanasia Campaign']. *Der Nervenarzt, 81*(11), 1326–1332.

Sayer, A. (2011). *Why Things Matter to People – Social Science, Values and Ethical Life*. Cambridge, MA: Cambridge University Press.

Scheffler, S. (2010). *Equality & Tradition: Questions of Value in Moral and Political Theory*. Oxford: Oxford University Press.

Scheffler, S. (2015). The Practice of Equality. In C. Fourie, F. Schuppert & I. Wallimann-Helmer (Eds.), *Social Equality: On What It Means to Be Equal* (pp. 21–44). Oxford: Oxford University Press.

Schmid, H. B. (2005). *Wir-Intentionalität: Kritik des ontologischen Individualismus und Rekonstruktion der Gemeinschaft* [We-Intentionality: A Critique of Ontological Individualism and a Reconstruction of Community]. Freiburg: Karl Alber.

Schramme, T. (2003). *Psychische Krankheit aus philosophischer Sicht* [Mental Illness from a Philosophical Point of View]. Frankfurt a. M.: Psychosozial-Verlag.

Schuelka, M. J., Johnstone, C. J., Thomas, G., & Artiles, A. J. (2019a). Introduction: Scholarship for Diversity and Education in Education in the 21st Century. In M. J. Schuelka, C. J. Johnstone, G. Thomas & A. J. Artiles (Eds.), *The SAGE Handbook of Inclusion and Diversity in Education* (pp. xxxi–xiii). London: SAGE.

Schuelka, M. J., Johnstone, C. J., Thomas, G., & Artiles, A. J. (Eds.). (2019b). *The SAGE Handbook of Inclusion and Diversity in Education*. London: SAGE.

Scully, J. L. (2008). *Disability Bioethics – Moral Bodies, Moral Difference*. Plymouth: Rowman & Littlefield Publishers.

Scully, J. L. (2018). From „She Would Say That, Wouldn't She?" to „Does She Take Sugar?" Epistemic Injustice and Disability. *International Journal of Feminist Approaches to Bioethics, 11*(1), 106–124.

Searle, J. R. (2005). What Is an Institution? *Journal of Institutional Economics, 1*, 1–22.

Searle, J. R. (2010). *Making the Social World: The Structure of Human Civilization*. New York: Oxford University Press.

Sedmak, C. (2010). Inklusion und Exklusion in Europa [Inclusion and Exclusion in Europe]. In E. Klaus, C. Sedmak, R. Drüeke & G. Schweiger (Eds.), *Identität und*

Inklusion im europäischen Sozialraum [Identity and Inclusion in European Social Environment] (pp. 147–164). Wiesbaden: VS Verlag für Sozialwissenschaften.
Sedmak, C. (2013). Zu ‚Enactment' und Inkulturation des Fähigkeitenansatzes [About Enactment and Inculturation of the Capability Approach]. In G. Graf, E. Kapferer & C. Sedmak (Eds.), *Der Capability Approach und seine Anwendung. Fähigkeiten von Kindern und Jugendlichen erkennen und fördern* [The Capability Approach and It's Application. Recognising and Promoting Children's Capabilities] (pp. 13–22). Wiesbaden: Springer VS.
Seeman, M. V. (2006). What Happened After T4?: Starvation of Psychiatric Patients in Nazi Germany. *International Journal of Mental Health, 35*(4), 5–10.
Sen, A. (1979). Equality of What? The Tanner Lecture on Human Values (May 22nd, 1979), Stanford University.
Sen, A. (1990). Justice: Means versus Freedoms. *Philosophy and Public Affairs, 19*(2), 111–121.
Sen, A. (1992). *Inequality Reexamined*. Oxford: Oxford University Press.
Sen, A. (1999). *Development as Freedom*. Oxford: Oxford University Press.
Sen, A. (2000). *Social Exclusion: Concept, Application, and Scrutiny*. Manila: Asian Development Bank.
Sen, A. (2006). What Do We Want from a Theory of Justice. *Journal of Philosophy, 103*(5), 215–238.
Sen, A. (2009). *The Idea of Justice*. London: Allen Lane.
Shakespeare, T. (1996). Disability, Identity and Difference. In C. Barnes & G. Mercer (Eds.), *Exploring the Divide* (pp. 94–113). Leeds: The Disability Press.
Shakespeare, T. (2014). *Disability Rights and Wrongs* (2nd ed.). London: Routledge.
Shakespeare, T., & Watson, N. (2001). The Social Model of Disability: An Outdated Ideology? In S. N. Barnartt & B. M. Altman (Eds.), *Exploring Theories and Expanding Methodologies: Where We Are and Where We Need to Go* (pp. 9–28). Bingley: Emerald.
Shklar, J. (1990). *The Faces of Injustice*. New Haven, CT: Yale University Press.
Silván-Ferrero, P., Recio, P., Molero, F., & Nouvilas-Pallejà, E. (2020). Psychological Quality of Life in People with Physical Disability. The Effect of Internalized Stigma, Collective Action and Resilience. *International journal of environmental research and public health, 17*(5), 1802.
Simeonsson, R. J., Leonardi, M., Lollar, D., Bjorck-Akesson, E., Hollenweger, J., & Martinuzzi, A. (2003). Applying the International Classification of Functioning, Disability and Health (ICF) to Measure Childhood Disability. *Disability and rehabilitation, 25*(11–12), 602–610.
Simmel, G. (1908). *Soziologie: Untersuchungen über die Formen der Vergesellschaftung* [Sociology: Studies on the Forms of Socialisation]. München/Leipzig: Duncker & Humblot.
Simmel, G. ([1908] 2009). *Sociology: Inquiries Into the Construction of Social Forms*. Leiden: Brill.
Siperstein, G. N., Leffert, J. S., & Wenz-Gross, M. (1997). The Quality of Friendships Between Children with and without Learning Problems. *Americal Journal on Mental Retardation, 102*(2), 111–125.
Siperstein, G. N., Norins, J., & Mohler, A. (2006). Social Acceptance and Attitude Change. Fifty Years of Research. In J. W. Jacobson & J. A. Mulick (Eds.), *Handbook of Intellectual and Developmental Disabilities* (pp. 133–154). New York: Kluewer/Plenum.
Siperstein, G. N., Parker, R. C., Bardon Norins, J., & Widaman, K. F. (2007). A National Study of Youth Attitudes Toward the Inclusion of Students with Intellectual Disabilities. *Exceptional Children, 73*(4), 435–455.

Skrtic, T. M. (1995). *Disability and Democracy: Reconstructing (Special) Education for Postmodernity*. New York: Teachers College Press.

Slee, R. (1997). Inclusion or Assimilation? Sociological Explorations of the Foundations of Theories of Special Education. *The Journal of Educational Foundations, 11*(1), 55–71.

Slee, R. (2001). 'Inclusion in Practice': Does practice make perfect? *Educational Review, 53*(2), 113–123.

Slee, R. (2001a). 'Inclusion in Practice': Does Practice Make Perfect? *Educational Review, 53*(2), 113–123.

Slee, R. (2001b). Social Justice and the Changing Directions in Educational Research: The Case of Inclusive Education. *International Journal of Inclusive Education, 5*(2–3), 167–177.

Slee, R., & Weiner, G. (2001). Education Reform and Reconstruction as a Challenge to Research Genres: Reconsidering School Effectiveness Research and Inclusive Schooling. *School Effectiveness and School Improvement, 12* (1), 83–98.

Smith, C. (2010). *What Is a Person?* Chicago, IL: Chicago University Press.

Snyder, S. L., & Mitchell, D. T. (2006). *Cultural Locations of Disability*. Chicago, IL: University of Chicago Press.

Solga, H. (2015). Impact of Limited Education on Employment Prospects in Advanced Economies. In R. A. Scott & S. M. Kosslyn (Eds.)*: Emerging Trends in the Social and Behavioral Sciences: An Interdisciplinary, Searchable, and Linkable Resource*, https://doi.org/10.1002/9781118900772.etrds0176

Stainback, S., & Stainback, W. (1988). Educating Students with Severe Disabilities. *Teaching Exceptional Children, 21*(1), 16–19.

Stainback, W., & Stainback, S. (1984). A Rationale for the Merger of Special and Regular Education. *Exceptional Children, 51*(2), 102–111.

Stainback, W., & Stainback, S. (1990). *Support Networks for Inclusive Education: Interdepended Integrated Education*. Baltimore, MD: Brookes.

Stanovich, P. J. (1998). Canadian Teachers' and Principals' Beliefs about Inclusive Education as Predictors of Effective Teaching in Heterogeneous Classrooms. *The Elementary School Journal, 98*(3), 221–238.

Stentiford, L., & Koutsouris, G. (2020). What Are Inclusive Pedagogies in Higher Education? A Systematic Scoping Review. *Studies in Higher Education*.

Stichweh, R. (2016). *Inklusion und Exklusion: Studien zur Gesellschaftstheorie* [Inclusion and Exclusion: Studies in Social Theory]. Bielefeld: transcript.

Sunderland, N., Catalano, T., & Kendall, E. (2009). Missing Discourses: Concepts of Joy and Happiness in Disability. *Disability and Society, 24*(6), 703–714.

Taylor, C. (1985). *Human Agency and Language*. Cambridge, MA: Cambridge University Press.

Terzi, L. (2007). A Capability Perspective on Impairment, Disability, and Special Needs. In R. Curren (Ed.), *Philosophy of Education – An Anthology* (pp. 298–313). Malden, MA: Blackwell.

Thies, K. M. (1999). Identifying the Educational Implications of Chronic Illness in School Children. *Journal of School Health, 69*(10), 392–397.

Thomas, C. (1999). *Female Forms: Experiencing and Understanding Disability*. Buckingham: Open University Press.

Thomas, G. (1997). Inclusive Schools for an Inclusive Society. *British Journal of Special Education, 24*(3), 103–107.

Tomasello, M. (2004). Learning Trough Others. *Daedalus, 133*(1), 51–58.

Tomasello, M. (2008). How Are Humans Unique. *The New York Times*, May 25th, 2008.

Tomasello, M. (2009). *Why We Cooperate*. Cambridge, MA: MIT Press.

Tomasello, M. (2019a). *Becoming Human: A Theory of Ontogeny*. Cambridge, MA: Harvard University Press.
Tomasello, M. (2019b). The Role of Roles in Uniquely Human Cognition and Sociality. *Journal for the Theory of Social Behaviour, 2019*, 1–18.
Tomlinson, S. (1996). Conflicts and Dilemmas for Professionals in Special Education. In C. Christensen & F. Rizvi (Eds.), *Disability and the Dilemmas of Education and Justice* (pp. 175–186). Buckingham: Open University Press.
Tönnies, F. (2001). *Community and Civil Society* (J. Harris Ed.). Cambridge: Cambridge University Press.
Tronto, J. C. (2013). *Caring Democracy: Markets, Equality, and Justice*. New York: New York University Press.
UNESCO (1994). *The Salamanca Statement and Framework for Action on Special Needs Education*. Salamanca: UNESCO.
UNESCO (2015). *Education 2030: Towards Inclusive and Equitable Quality Education and Lifelong Learning for All*. Incheon: UNESCO.
UNESCO (2020). *2020 Global Education Monitoring Report*. Paris: UNESCO.
United Nations (1948). *Universal Declaration of Human Rights*. Geneva: United Nations.
United Nations (1989). *Convention on the Rights of the Child*. Geneva: United Nations.
United Nations (1990). *World Declaration on Education for All*. Geneva: United Nations.
United Nations (1993). *Standard Rules on Equalization of Opportunities for Persons with Disabilities*. Geneva: United Nations.
United Nations (2006). *Convention on the Rights of Persons with Disabilities*. Geneva: United Nations.
United Nations (2015). *Transforming Our World: The 2030 Agenda for Sustainable Development*. New York: United Nations.
Valås, H. (2001). Learned Helplessness and Psychological Adjustment II: Effects of Learning Disabilities and Low Achievement. *Scandinavian Journal of Educational Research, 45*(2), 101–114.
Valentini, L. (2012). Ideal vs. Non-Ideal Theory. A Conceptual Map. *Philosophy Compass, 7*(9), 654–664.
Valentini, L. (2021). The Natural Duty of Justice in Non-Ideal Circumstances: On the Moral Demands of Institution Building and Reform. *European Journal of Political Theory, 20*(1), 45–66.
Vanderstraeten, R. (2004a). Interaktion und Organisation im Erziehungssystem [Interaction and Organisation in the Educational System]. In W. Böttcher & E. Terhart (Eds.), *Organisationstheorie in pädagogischen Feldern. Analyse und Gestaltung* [Organisational Theory in Paedagogical Fields. Analysis and Structuring] (pp. 54–68). Wiesbaden: VS Verlag für Sozialwissenschaften.
Vanderstraeten, R. (2004b). The Social Differentiation of the Educational System. *Sociology, 38*(2), 255–272.
Vanderstraeten, R. (2006). The Historical Triangulation of Education, Politics and Economy. *Sociology, 40*(1), 125–142.
Vislie, L. (2003). From Integration to Inclusion: Focusing Global Trends and Changes in the Western European Societies. *European Journal of Special Needs Education, 18*(1), 17–35.
Višňovský, E., & Zolcer, S. (2016). Dewey's Participatory Educational Democracy. *Educational Theory, 66*(1–2), 55–71.
Vlachou, A. (2004). Education and Inclusive Policy-Making. Implications for Research and Practice. *International Journal of Inclusive Education, 8*(1), 3–21.

Waddington, E. M., & Reed, P. (2017). Comparison of the Effects of Mainstream and Special School on National Curriculum Outcomes in Children with Autism Spectrum Disorder: An Archive-Based Analysis. *Journal of Research in Special Educational Needs, 17*(2), 132–142.

Wade, D. (2006). Why *Physical* Medicine, *Physical* Disability and *Physical* Rehabilitation? We Should Abandon Cartesian Dualism. *Clinical Rehabilitation, 20*(3), 185–190.

Wagner, M. M., Newman, L. A., & Javitz, H. S. (2016). The Benefits of High School Career and Technical Education (CTE) for Youth With Learning Disabilities. *Journal of Learning Disabilities, 49*(6), 658–670.

Wahlström, N., & Sundberg, D. (2018). Discursive Institutionalism: Towards a Framework for Analysing the Relation Between Policy and Curriculum. *Journal of Education Policy, 33*(1), 163–183.

Waitoller, F. R., & Thorius, K. K. (2015). Playing Hopscotch in Inclusive Education Reform: Examining Promises and Limitations of Policy and Practice in the US. *Support for Learning, 30*(1), 23–41.

Wakefield, J. C. (1992). The Concept of Mental Disorder: On the Boundary between Biological Facts and Social Values. *American Psychologist, 47*(373–388).

Waks, L. J., & English, A. R. (2017). *John Dewey's Democracy and Education. A Centennial Handbook.* Cambridge: Cambridge University Press.

Walsh, K. (2004). Interpreting the Impact of Culture on Structure. The Role of Change Processes. *The Journal of Applied Behavioral Science, 40*(3), 302–322.

Walzer, M. (1983). *Spheres of Justice.* New York: Basic Books.

Weber, M. (1978). *Economy and Society: An Outline of Interpretative Sociology.* Berkeley: University of California Press.

Wendelborg, Ch., & Tøssebro, J. (2011). Educational Arrangements and Social Participation with Peers Amongst Children with Disabilities in Regular Schools. *International Journal of Inclusive Education, 15*(5), 497–512.

Wentzel, K. R. (1998). Social Relationships and Motivation in Middle School: The Role of Parents, Teachers, and Peers. *Journal of Educational Psychology, 90*(2), 202–209.

Werner, Sh. (2015). Public Stigma and the Perception of Rights: Differences Between Intellectual and Physical Disabilities. *Research in Developmental Disabilities, 38*, 262–271.

White, K. J., & Jones, K. (2000). Effects of Teacher Feedback on the Reputations and Peer Perceptions of Children with Behavior Problems. *Journal of Experimental Child Psychology, 76*(4), 302–326.

White, K. J., Sherman, M. D., & Jones, K. (1996). Children's Perceptions of Behavior Problem Peers: Effects of Teacher Feedback and Peer-Reputed Status. *Journal of School Psychology, 34*(1), 53–72.

Williams, B. (1985). *Ethics and the Limits of Philosophy.* Cambridge, MA: Harvard University Press.

Wilson, J. (1999). Some Conceptual Difficulties about 'Inclusion'. *Support for Learning, 14*(3), 110–112.

Wilson, J. (2000). Doing Justice to Inclusion. *European Journal of Special Needs Education, 15*(3), 297–304.

Wilson, T., & Ryg, M. (2015). Becoming Autonomous: Nonideal Theory and Educational Autonomy. *Educational Theory, 65*(2), 127–150.

Winzer, M. A. (1986). Early Development in Special Education: Some Aspects of Enlightenment Thought. *Remedial and Special Education, 5*(7), 42–49.

Winzer, M. A. (1993). *The History of Special Education: From Isolation to Integration.* Washington, DC: Gallaudet University Press.

Winzer, M. A. (2006). Confronting Difference: An Excursion Through the History of Special Education. In L. Florian (Ed.), *The SAGE Handbook of Special Education* (pp. 22–33). Thousand Oaks, CA: SAGE
Winzer, M. A. (2009). *From Integration to Inclusion – A History of Special Education in the 20th Century*. Washington, DC: Gallaudet University Press.
Winzer, M. A., & Mazurek, K. (2010). Including Students with Special Needs: Implications for Social Justice. In J. Zajda (Ed.), *Globalization, Education and Social Justice* (pp. 87–101). Dordrecht: Springer Netherlands.
Wittgenstein, L. (1998). *Culture and Value*. Oxford: Blackwell Publishers.
Wolfensberger, W. (1972). *Principles of Normalization in Human Services*. Toronto, ON: National Institute on Mental Retardation.
Wolff, J. (1998). Fairness, Respect and the Egalitarian Ethos. *Philosophy and Public Affairs*, 27(2), 97–122.
Wolff, J. (2002). Addressing Disadvantage and the Human Good. *Journal of Applied Philosophy*, 19(3), 207–218.
Wolff, J. (2009). Cognitive Disability in a Society of Equals. *Metaphilosophy*, 40(3–4), 402–415.
Wolff, J. (2009a). Disability, Status Enhancement, Personal Enhancement and Resource Allocation. *Economics and Philosophy*, 25, 46–68.
Wolff, J. (2009b). Disability among Equals. In K. Brownlee & A. Cureton (Eds.), *Disability and Disadvantage* (pp. 112–137). Oxford: Oxford University Press.
Wolff, J. (2017). Forms of Differential Social Inclusion. *Social Philosophy and Policy*, 34(1), 164–185.
Wolff, J. (2019). *Ethics and Public Policy: A Philosophical Inquiry* (2nd ed.). London: Routledge.
Wolff, J., & de-Shalit, A. (2007). *Disadvantage*. Oxford: Oxford University Press.
World Health Organization, & World Bank. (2011). *World Report on Disability*. Geneva: World Health Organization and World Bank.
Wright, E. O. (2010). *Envisioning Real Utopias*. London: Verso.
Yacek, D. W. (2020). Should Education be Transformative? *Journal of Moral Education*, 49(2), 257–274.
Young, I. M. (1990). The Ideal of Community and the Politics of Difference. In L. J. Nicholson (Ed.), *Feminism/Postmodernism* (pp. 300–323). London: Routledge.
Young, I. M. (1990a). *Justice and the Politics of Difference*. Princeton, NJ: Princeton University Press.
Young, I. M. (2000). *Inclusion and Democracy*. Oxford: Oxford University Press.

INDEX

aims goals 203–204, 207; distributive goals 203; non ideal approaches 18

barriers 6–7, 108–118, 122–125, 129–131
basic needs 166
belonging 89–91
Bourdieu, Pierre 81
bullying 131

capability approach 83
capital 81
change 217–218; third-order change 218; triple-loop processes 218
Christmas in Purgatory 165
civic spirit 179, 199, 206–207
classroom 131–151, 199, 202, 205
common good 68, 172, 179, 194, 199, 206–207
communication 92, 144–149, 204
compulsory education 14, 35–36, 45
conflicts 143, 147
conversion factors 121
cooperation 133, 143–148, 160–161, 170–171, 188–189, 200–207
COVID–19 pandemic 73, 150
Cureton, Adam 90, 95
curricula 118, 129–133, 142–145

de l'Epée, Charles Michel 33
democracy 144–149, 157, 190, 196, 204–205
Dewey, John 25–27, 144–149
digitalisation 98, 143
dilemma of difference 44

disability 2–3, 32–38, 43, 105–126, 172–175, 183, 185, 188, 205, 218–219
discrimination 126, 148, 158, 161–162, 198–202
diversity 35, 43, 45–47, 81, 106–109
Dreeben, Robert 130–141
Durkheim, Emile 64–67, 69–70, 72–73, 91

educational goals 191, 203
Education for All 2, 5
empathy 143, 157, 174, 193, 204, 220
epistemic injustice 171–173, 199; hermeneutical injustice 172; testimonial injustice 171
epistemic resources 174–175
epistemology 173, 218
equality 178, 180–185
exclusion 44, 132

family 129–130, 136–138
Fend, Helmut 130, 141–142
freedom 186–189; negative 186; positive 186; social 186–189
Fricker, Miranda 172
functions of schools 141–149; allocation 142; enculturation 142; inclusion 142–143; integration and legitimation 142; qualification 142

globalisation 98, 143
growth 144–146, 148, 204

Hanselmann, Heinrich 38–39
happiness 121, 160, 201

Haslanger, Sally 174–175, 219
heterogeneity 45, 54, 108, 117–118, 144, 150
hidden curriculum 131, 161
history of disability 31–40; antiquity 32; Enlightenment 32–34; Middle Ages 32; National Socialism 38–39
human rights 2, 11, 14, 31, 38, 47, 57–58, 77, 108, 157, 177, 192, 197
humiliation 137, 165, 170

identity politics 107–108, 117
ideologies 219
Ikäheimo, Heikki 190
inclusion: definitions of inclusion 50–51; description vs. evaluation 53–55
independence 24, 139, 162, 178
Itard, Jean-Marc Gaspard 34

justice 158–161, 180

Kastl, Jörg Michael 58, 60, 75, 79

labelling 110–112, 123
limits of inclusion 28, 136
looping effects 174–175
luck egalitarianism 182
Luhmann, Niklas 64, 74–76

Marshall, Thomas H. 74–75, 77, 187, 193–194
mass schooling 37–38, 45, 219
migration 15, 143, 150, 195
models of disability 105–121; 'barrier' model 112; 'deconstruction' model 109; social-relational model 119–121
multicultural societies 143

national education 37
Nussbaum, Martha 83, 159, 178, 186, 207

ontogenesis 91–95
oppression 14–16, 110, 117–120, 176, 220

Parsons, Talcott 66, 74–75
participation 81–84
pedagogical care 204
performance 132, 138–142
pluralisation 143–144
powerlessness 163, 176, 196
professional disesteem 200

Rawls, John 22, 62, 158–159
recognition 189–193; esteem 193–195; horizontal 191–192; love 193; respect 157; vertical 191
Reindal, Solveig M. 119–120
relationships 59–61, 65–67, 69–70, 72
resilience 219
resources 79–81
rights 77
roles 77–79

Salamanca Statement and Framework for Action on Special Needs Education 2, 10–11
Scully, Jackie Leach 122–124, 172–174
Séguin, Édouard 34
shaming 165
Simmel, Georg 63, 70, 72–73
slavery 13–16, 165
social construct 8, 109–111
social integration 84–89
societal interconnectedness 143
special education 28–44; critique 28, 32; dual motive 34–36; history of 31–40; situation today 43–44
specificity 75, 138–139
stereotypes 164, 167, 173, 176, 199
stigmatization 54, 76, 110, 113, 123, 126, 131, 156, 161, 171, 198, 202–203
structural involvement 60, 62, 75–81, 83
structure of modern education 130–135
suffering 121, 159, 165, 168–169

teachers 40, 118–119, 126, 131–137, 140–141, 151, 178, 191, 199, 205, 216, 219
theory of school 130
thick concepts 55–57
Tomasello, Michael 91–95, 193, 195
Tönnies, Ferdinand 63–70
transformation 145–146, 163, 216–219

United Nations Convention on the Rights of Persons with Disabilities 1–2, 17, 23, 55, 58, 77–78

vulnerability 195–197

Weber, Max 63, 69–73, 87–88, 130
Williams, Bernard 55

Young, Iris Marion 156–157, 171, 176, 190

Printed in the United States
by Baker & Taylor Publisher Services